Mel

The Story of Melvin Nation, a Cowboy and Cattleman of Western Nebraska

MONI HOURT

©2023 Moni Hourt. All Rights Reserved.

All rights reserved. No part of this book may be used or reproduced by any means, graphic, electronic or mechanical, including photocopying, recording, taping or by any information storage retrieval system without the written permission of the publisher, except in the case of brief quotations embodied in critical articles and reviews.

www.MelvinNation.com

Hardcover ISBN 978-1-945505-07-2
Paperback ISBN 978-1-945505-08-9
Kindle ISBN 978-1-945505-09-6

All rights reserved. No part of this book may be used or reproduced by any means, graphic, electronic or mechanical, including photocopying, recording, taping or by any information storage retrieval system without the written permission of the publisher, except in the case of brief quotations embodied in critical articles and reviews.

Library of Congress Cataloging Number and data on file with the publisher.
Production by Concierge Marketing Inc.
Printed in the United States of America
10 9 8 7 6 5 4 3

DEDICATION

This book is dedicated to my Dad who entrusted me to write his story, and to Joe who never doubted for one minute that I could.

CONTENTS

Acknowledgments vii
Photographs ix
Foreword by Con Marshall xi
Prologue xiii
The Boy Who Loved Horses 1
Two Different Backgrounds 7
Life on Spud Ridge 29
Behind a Whistle 37
Building a Life on the Prairie 49
School Days—the not so, "Dear Old Golden Rule Days" 57
My Friend Midgey 63
Doing It My Way 67
The War Years 77
Damn Rebel 87
The Hoover Ranch 109
Warbonnet 117
The Cycle of Ranch Life 127
John 143
Hired Men and Cantankerous Beasts 147
Cows Rule 157
Supporting Characters 163
Horse Sense 169
No Looking Back 181
A New Decade 187

The Beauty and the Beasts 197
Something New Every Day 205
The Dawning of a New Era 215
Celebrations 221
Moving On 233
The Home Place 237
Hat Creek: the Return 277
Cowboys and Cattlemen 309
Until You Can't 315
Epilogue 343
Bibliography 347

Appendix 1 375
Appendix 2 377
Appendix 3 379
Appendix 4 381
Appendix 5 383
Appendix 6 385

About the Author 401

ACKNOWLEDGMENTS

I'd like to thank my family who encouraged me over the years and listened to my stories. I'd also like to thank Bob Reichenberg, who with his "tough" editing and endless fact verification requirements, demanded that I become a better writer. He was willing to edit this book in its beginning stages. I'd also like to thank Con Marshall, who edited the final copy and was adamant that it needed printed. And of course I'd like to thank everyone who put up with my hundreds of questions and interviews, shared their stories and pictures, read through the book, and made comments and edits. I may have typed the contents, but you made this possible.

PHOTOGRAPHS

All photographs are from the Nation/Hourt photo collection. Many of the older black and white photos were taken by Thelma Nation, Velma Rising, or Verna Callaham. The Hoover collection pictures were given to Moni Hourt by Ridge Hoover Chlanda. All other photographs and images are attributed to their creator. Most of the other photos were taken by Moni Hourt.

FOREWORD
BY CON MARSHALL

MONI HOURT WRITES HER FATHER'S STORY

Moni Hourt's book about her father, Melvin Nation, is a masterpiece. Anyone who has lived on a ranch or even visited one will appreciate the book. Perhaps it should be required reading for anyone who thinks they'd like to be a cowboy/rancher. It's filled with easy-to-read, lively, and interesting stories. Not much glamour is involved. It's about a nitty-gritty, hard-working way of life. It tells about both good days and bad days, good years and bad years, and neither is exaggerated nor diminished. When her father gave his approval to write his life story, he admonished her not to include any nonsense—although he used a different term.

In particular, it also tells about a daughter's admiration and love for her father. She spent the first 18 or so years of her life watching, following, and helping him while he did what cowboys and ranchers (in this case they were the one and the same) do while caring for the cattle they are entrusted to manage. No doubt about it they were close.

And, as Moni passed into adulthood, she never lived far from her parents. She was continually in touch with their way of life and activities. She knows of what she wrote. No one had to explain to her what or why something was happening when she described that incident. She'd been there and done that.

This book isn't only about the daily activities of the Mel and Thelma Nation. It's more far-reaching. It's filled with northwest Nebraska history and numerous other personalities are introduced. This is another reason it is special. The author has done painstaking research to verify the developments and explains them in depth. It's also filled with interesting tidbits and contains hundreds of clear and concise footnotes to help the readers fully absorb what they have read.

There's another reason that guarantees this is a tremendous book. It was written by someone who because of her creativity and boundless energy has excelled in everything she's done. She earned two Peter Kiewit Foundation Teacher Achievement Awards, has been the Northwest Nebraska Region's Wal-Mart Teacher of the Year, the National Rural Education Association's Teacher of the Year and guided dozens of students in their development of programs and projects that were high award winners at local, state and national History Day competitions. Chadron State College is proud to have presented her with its Distinguished Alumni Award.

Moni Hourt has always been a high-achiever, and this book adds to that legacy.

PROLOGUE

We held a family celebration in November 2008 to commemorate the fact that Mom's cancer seemed to be in remission, Shari Packard took a family picture. We were all there, all smiling, all thankfully celebrating. However, within two years, Dad, Mom, and Sis were all gone—proving that time and life are both very fleeting.

When Dad was in the hospital in 2009, he told me I could write a story about him, but that it could not include any "bullshit." I had already written several short stories about him, and he had apparently approved of them—anyway he didn't tell me that I couldn't print them. I wrote the beginning of his life story and read the first few pages to him when he was in the hospital. He didn't tell me it was full of BS so I was encouraged, but time slipped away. I didn't get any more written. Then as Dad would say, "Life happened."

In the summer of 2014, I panicked. The book wasn't done. I promised him I would write it, but suddenly I didn't know if I would ever get it completed. I wasn't able to get the project restarted until the fall of 2015. Every night after he finished work, my husband, Joe, came into my office, and we discussed the day's progress. He made suggestions, and I took notes. One evening when I was worried about getting everything completed around the house, he quietly reminded me that the book was much more important than the laundry. I kept writing.

My biggest concern was the BS factor, so the entire book is as factually written as possible. It contains footnote verification and quotation sources. Most of the book's contents were gleaned from the dozens of hours of taped interviews that I did with Dad over a period of nearly 20 years. Other information came from NETV interviews recorded in 2006-2007. I used information from Dad's tally books and interviewed friends and family members. I verified many dates and events in *The Harrison Sun* and other local newspapers. And yes, I drew from my memory and from my journals. Some people may dispute the facts, the memories, or even the interpretation, but frankly I don't care. I promised my Dad a book without BS. It doesn't matter if anyone ever reads it, or if someone argues about the placement of a verb, or the provability of an anecdote or a memory.

I kept my promise.

THE BOY WHO LOVED HORSES

"All my life, if something was buggin' me, I could get on a horse and ride up to the top of a big tall hill and watch the sun come up. It just soothed me. Getting on a horse was my therapy—it really was." Melvin Nation

Melvin Nation, age about 12, with one of his horses.

The big gelding popped into view above the horizon—he and his rider silhouetted against the treeless prairie. The tow-headed boy was watching. He wriggled out of the confines of the chicken-wire yard fence and crawled under the bottom plank of the corral. He stood waiting just inside the gate, not so far in that he'd get yelled at for going into the corral, but close enough to see the back gate when his big brother reached down and opened it. The older boy didn't even acknowledge him. He just pulled his horse to a stop, stepped out of the saddle, snagged his tow-headed brother from the ground, and tossed him into the high-cantle seat. The gelding danced and stomped at the end of the reins making several circles before Elvin Nation plucked his horn-clutching sibling from the tall rawhide wrapped horn.

Elvin Nation before he left for the Army.

"I don't suppose old Rowdy was serious about dumping me," Melvin Nation said smiling. "He was just playing. I probably did quite a lot of squalling, but it didn't scare me too much. All I ever wanted to do was ride a horse. I've been lucky that I've spent most of my life doing just that."

Born in 1930 at the beginning of the Great Depression, Melvin grew up in a time of few luxuries, but he said he didn't really notice. "I guess we were poor. By today's standards we were, but no one around us had much. We never went hungry."

By the time, Melvin was born automobiles bounced along city streets, but in rural Nebraska, horses were still the main mode of transportation. Few people bothered to buy even the dependable Model T in the region where roads were still glorified cow trails. The nearest railroad station located in the town of Glen, a tiny community featuring less than a dozen homes, was 10 miles northeast of the section where the Nation family lived. Bigger towns like Crawford,[1] to the northeast, and Harrison,[2] to the northwest, were at least 20 miles away. Neither town was easily accessible even by a team and wagon. Cars in the region seldom ventured out of the city limits and were a rarity on county roads.

"I don't think we had a decent car until Dad bought a 1936 Plymouth. Even then we didn't use it very often. We pulled it around with a team more than we drove it," Melvin said his bright blue eyes twinkling at the memory. "We rode a jillion miles a-horseback and did all of our work with a team. It was just our way of life. My Dad was a good teamster and drove a team everywhere. I understood he was a good horseman in his younger days, but he didn't ride much after I was born."

---

[1] According to the Nebraska Blue Book, Crawford's population in 1930 was 1703.
[2] According to the Nebraska Blue Book, Harrison's population in 1930 was 480.

Earl Nation and Nick Nichols about 1907.

As a young man, Melvin's father, Earl, used his riding skills as a cowboy on round-up crews in the Osage-Upton, Wyoming country.[3] For several months in 1907 and 1908, he and friend, Nick Nichols, worked for cow outfits on the Wyoming Plains. When Nick died from the grippe,[4] Earl headed home. He was homesick and anxious to renew his friendship with the "young lady I left behind."[5]

Halfway through Nebraska, Earl's horse, a two-year-old colt, "played out." He unsaddled the horse and bedded down for the night. The moonlight dodged between rolling clouds. Howls of wolves echoed off the nearby hills, and the cold seeped through Earl's worn clothing. The next morning, tired and harried,[6] he rode to a ranch house. The woman on the homestead provided breakfast; her husband traded Earl a fresh horse. The next day he rode back into Nebraska. He hayed for Dave Hamaker[7] that summer. He seldom left Nebraska again.[8]

---

[3] The wagon boss for one of the trips was the grandfather of Jim Lemmon. Fifty years later, Jim became one of Melvin's best friends.
[4] Modern medical journals identify "grippe" as a case of severe influenza.
[5] Earl Nation. Taped interview with Fred Hamaker. Earl Nation home, Crawford, NE, October 1957.
[6] Robison, Anita Nation, Personal interview with Moni Hourt, 1999. Hourt home, Sioux County, NE. Anita said her Dad told her he was scared "to death" all night long. He worried that the wolves would rush his camp and kill his horse.
[7] Dave Hamaker, Iva Hamaker's uncle, and Earl developed a friendship before Earl left for Wyoming. That friendship would last the rest of their lives.
[8] Nation, Merlin. Personal interview with Moni Hourt, 1996. Hat Creek Ranch, Sioux County, NE.

Earl Nation.

Iva Hamaker, the woman Earl returned to Nebraska to eventually marry, had many attributes that he appreciated. Among them was the fact that she had grown up riding a horse and could handle a team as well as most men.

"I don't remember seeing her do it, but the older kids said Mama would tuck her dress into a pair of Dad's coveralls and help in the fields. They said she piled them onto a little wagon and pulled them around with Bluebell, a horse her Uncle Dave had given her," Melvin Nation said. "I can remember helping her hook up the team so she could go somewhere. She never really did drive a car much. It was just too foreign to her."

Earl Nation with a pair of the family's milk cows.

Eva Nation Gray, one of the family's older children, verified that her mother was more than "good with a horse." "One night, the boys went after the milk cows, but they couldn't get them in. There was a storm coming: those old black clouds rolling and boiling up over the prairie. Those cows were precious to all of us; we sure couldn't leave them out at night. They had to be milked. Mother climbed on a horse, and boy, did she bring them in. I can still remember her whistling and hollering, slapping at those cows with her reins. Her hair had come loose and was blowing in the wind. Her glasses were a little twisted on her face, but she just kept shoving, until the cows bounced through the gate. Then, she climbed down, pinned her hair up, threw the reins to the boys, and went to the house. The boys didn't say much, but they were sure embarrassed," Eva Nation Gray chuckled when she remembered her brothers' discomfort.[9]

Iva and Earl Nation with Melvin and Mildred. Taken at the RSQ Hamaker farm during the Hamaker family reunion in 1933

Although horses were always part of her life, Iva didn't want her youngest son to have anything to do with the "dirty animals." When Melvin was born, she told her husband, in a rare act of defiance, that he'd "raised" her other six children. She said she was going to teach Melvin to be a bit quieter and gentler than the rest of her rambunctious crew.

"Mama tried to make me a girl," Melvin said with a grin. "She tried to teach me to play the piano and I could play it—a little—chopsticks. She tried to keep me away from the corrals and the horses. That didn't work at all. I guess I was just too much boy right from the beginning."

Family folklore involving the white sailor suit gives his words credence. Melvin's Aunt Bertha, Iva's sister, gave him a starched white sailor suit with "short pants." The combined efforts of his aunt and his mother, finally resulted in Melvin's incarceration in the crisp white ensemble. Their pride in his "dandified" appearance was short-lived. As soon as the women slackened their grips on the red-faced piece of struggling rebellion, he bolted down the stairs of the huge barn-shaped house, scattering bits and pieces of his new outfit behind him.

"I don't think it would have hurt me to have tried to be a little bit more like Mama wanted me to be, but it just wasn't in me. The piano-playing was the extent of my "gentlifying."

---

[9] Gray, Eva Nation. Personal interview with Moni Hourt, 1998. Gray home, Chadron, NE.

Nation was about four when he further proved that he probably wasn't ever going to join the ranks of the civilized gentry. Riding bareback,[10] he had headed out into the pasture to gather the cows. On the return trip, the horse decided to outrun the "cow herd." He entered the yard at a "dead run."

"I could hear my Dad calling 'Hang on boy.'" Smiling, Melvin shook his head at the memory. "I was hangin' on for dear life, but I was also sliding steadily up toward the horse's ears. He slid to a stop right in front of the cistern where Dad was standing and flung me over his shoulder. When the dirt cleared, I was standing on the cistern, holding the lead rope that was tangled around my hand. It was probably the only graceful landing I ever made off a wild horse. I can remember my Dad saying, 'Good landing, Boy.'"

Reportedly, Iva Nation, watching from the front gate, looked as if she wanted to whip someone. But, she stopped trying to mold her youngest son into her ideal of the "perfect boy."

Melvin Nation, the Home Place house in the background, rides one of the colts that he loved to train.

---

[10] Melvin rode bareback until he was nearly 10. Several area newspaper stories in the years before Melvin's birth reported that young men, including several boys were thrown from horses and dragged to death. A new story dated April 24, 1930 in the Harrison *Sun*, reported that Peter Swanson an early homesteader in the area who lived in the Glen region, was killed in that manner two weeks after Melvin's birth. Earl refused to let his younger children use a saddle telling them it was just too dangerous.

TWO DIFFERENT BACKGROUNDS

Historical Data

(Warning: This chapter contains a large amount of historical data about Crawford, Belmont, Chadron State Normal School, and the Belmont Tunnel. Reading may plunge an unsuspecting reader into a history-coma.) :)

"I don't think my Mom's family ever thought my Dad was good enough for her, but I don't think she ever regretted marrying him. She never complained that I heard of."

Melvin Nation

Back: Carl. Front: RSQ, Iva, Frank Alice, Paul, Ray. (Not pictured) Bertha. Daniel (Tot) died when he was 11.

Iva Hamaker and Earl Nation came from two totally different backgrounds both reflecting the "melting pot" that has always represented America. Iva's family history states that Johann Adam Hammacher's[11] family came to the United States from Deutschland[12] (the German lands) in 1740. They settled with the Quakers near Hershey, PA.[13]

Proof of the family's footprint in early Pennsylvania was confirmed in 2002. In the process of constructing a new facility on their Pennsylvania land, Hershey Chocolate Plant workers unearthed a family graveyard. The burial site contained headstones of early Hammacher family members. On July 26, 2003, seventy-five Hammacher descendants, including Iva's niece, Naomi Galey, joined the company's staff to officially dedicate the site. Although a plaque at the site lists the family surname as Hamaker , the name on the recovered stones was spelled "Hammacher."[14]

Iva Hamaker's father RSQ[15] Hamaker,[16] never lived in Pennsylvania. He was born in 1858 in Andrews County, Missouri. A year after the 12-year-old moved with his family to Kansas, his father, Daniel, died. Alma (Harris) Hamaker gathered her children, loaded them into a wagon, and moved to Marshal County, IA. It was there that RSQ spent his childhood, and where in 1879, he married Alice (Haworth).[17]

On Alice's wedding day, Alma Harris gave her daughter a copy of a poem her mother, Sally Harris, had composed in 1857. The poem verified Sally's belief that a woman must be committed to her marriage. (Appendix 1)

The couple spent six years operating a farm in Iowa, then moved to Abilene, Kansas. Alice Hamaker told her granddaughter, Pauline, that drought devastated their Kansas crops. The family milked cows and raised turkeys, selling their produce to local residents, but even that

---

[11] The family name was changed to Hammacher when they arrived in the United States. It was changed to Hamaker sometime after they left Pennsylvania.

[12] Oral Nation family history stated that Iva Hamaker's family was Dutch. (Apparently the misunderstanding was based on the mispronunciation of the word Deutschland, meaning Germany.) Members of the family said the fact that the family all had blond hair and blue eyes, as did many people from the Netherlands, proved their assumption. DNA testing does show a strong Scandinavian influence, but a stronger German influence..

[13] According to family oral history the Hammachers (original German spelling) came to America with William Penn. The family actually arrived in Pennsylvania in about 1740, many years after Penn's original group established their community in 1682 and 22 years after Penn's death.

[14] Hershey Derry Township Historical Society. "Hammacher Burial Ground." Available at: http://www.hersheyhistory.org/hamaker.html

[15] RSQ Hamaker's name was RSQ. In the letter to the Land Office, Hamaker said "The initials did not stand for any name." He was often known as "Quie."

[16] Son of Daniel W and Alma (Harris) Hamaker

[17] Alice Berthena Haworth, daughter of William Cox Haworth and Sarah Emeline (Pierce) Haworth was born into a Quaker community in Winchester, Indiana in 1861.

steady income couldn't pay the bills. In 1887, Alice sold her last turkeys for $50. The family headed for Nebraska where the future looked brighter.[18]

> "It was a beautiful fall day in October, 1888, when my husband, his brother Dave, myself and our three sons, Carl, Ray and Daniel (Tot) left Kansas for Nebraska where the future looked brighter and more prosperous." Alice Hamaker wrote in a letter that was given to her granddaughter, Pauline.[19] "Drought had taken our crops and all we had were sixteen head of cattle. My husband and Dave rode horseback and drove the cattle. I drove the covered wagon loaded with our household goods, supplies for the journey, and a plow. Carl was only five-years-old, but he helped sometimes with the cattle. It was tiresome and tedious going most of the time. We never made more than fifteen miles a day, usually nine, and once only three. We could have made better time but for the cattle which got footsore, and the calves got tired. We had our own milk and butter but other supplies were bought along the way wherever they could be obtained. When we ran out of bread we stopped at a ranch house and baked on their stove. We traveled through a stretch of land called Death Hollow.[20] It was about 18 miles long, and there was not a living thing

Alice Haworth about 1878.

---

[18] Alice Hamaker. Excerpt in *Crawford, Nebraska 1886-1961*, pg. 78. Full document published in *Belmont Memories*. 2013, pg. 34-34.

[19] Alice Hamaker document written in 1934, given to Pauline Hamaker. Located in Aline Dyer scrapbook and shared with Moni Hourt in 1998. Part of this document was printed in the book, *Crawford, Nebraska 1886-1961*, 78. The whole document was printed in *Belmont Memories*. 2013, pg. 34-34.

[20] Extensive research did not reveal the exact location of Death Hollows. It was probably a location on the Smoky Hills Trail which was later incorporated into the Butterfield Overland Trail that crossed Logan County, Kansas. *The Rocky Mountain News* on 7 May 1859 said that "many emigrants were enticed by charlatans to travel the route, but the emigrants found very little road, very little food, and very little water along the trail." Although there is no proof that Alice and RSQ traveled the route thirty years later, it was a logical route through the Sand Hills and into the Belmont area. Although the trail wasn't as dangerous as it was 30 years before, it still traversed some desolate country. The name and reputation of the area probably lingered. A family of German emigrants was killed here, possibly by Cheyenne warriors. Some information about the trail can be located in the book, *Trails of the Smoky Hill* by Wayne C Lee. Other information can be located at the website: www.kshs.org. "The Pikes Peak Gold Rush and the Smoky Hill Route" by Calvin W Gower.

in those eighteen miles except grass, and it was tall, tough, and coarse. No people, rabbits, birds, deer, antelope, or any other kind of an animal lived there. We even had to take our own fuel with us for our fires at night because there was not even any wood. One day we saw a few cedar chips that someone had left. I got out and picked them up so we would have something to start our next fire, as we were nearly out of fuel. That same afternoon I gathered some of the tall, coarse grass and twisted it so we could use it for fuel also.

Soon after we left Death Hollow, we came to a small settlement. We stopped there for a few days to rest ourselves and our weary footsore cattle. While were there, we stayed at the home of the Ravens. I baked bread for us and helped Mrs. Ravens cook and bake her bread. The people in this settlement had no milk or butter. We needed supplies and the people there were willing to give us the supplies we needed in exchange for milk and butter. Most of the people who lived on the ranches and in the few settlements were pleasant and very hospitable, however, this was not always true. One cold, stormy and very windy night we came to a rancher's home in the Sand Hills. We stopped and my husband went to the house and asked the old man, whose name was Nenzell,[21] if we could stop for the night and use his stove on which to get our supper. The old man was very disagreeable and cranky.

"No! You cannot come in and use our stove. We don't even want you to stop! Go on!"

That was the answer he gave my husband. My husband said, "Do you want us to start a fire out there tonight with this wind blowing like it is? There would be great danger of setting a terrible prairie fire, no matter how careful we are, and we must have a fire to keep us warm and cook our supper."

"Go on! Don't stop!" was the old man's only answer.

My husband came back to the wagon and said to me, "Go on up to the house with the children and get supper."

I went to the house, went in, and prepared our supper on their stove. The old man did not say a word. The wife and two daughters of fourteen and eighteen were slightly more pleasant and hospitable than the old man. The two daughters, who had just come in from herding sheep, were just eating their supper of bread and beans.

---

[21] A town located in the Sandhills was established in 1885 by George Nenzel. Members of the community were known for their hospitality. It's difficult to know if there was a connection.

The next morning after staying all night in their house, we prepared to again be on our way. The weather was nice again. Before we left my husband bought some hay from Mr. Nenzell for our cattle. Also he bought a plow and a corn planter.

One of the difficulties we encountered was fording the rivers. At one river, the Calamus, we had trouble due to quicksand. We searched for some time before we could find a suitable crossing; then we could take only a few cattle across at one place and had to find another place for some more to cross. We had to change the crossing places because it was more dangerous to cross when the sand was riled up. If we took the whole herd across at once, those going across last would not have been able to get across. This was the only river that we had much trouble crossing.

Most of our journey was made without encountering many great hardships or disasters. It was tiring to both men and beast and a very long journey. The weather was good most of the time. There were a few cold days and a little snow but not enough to hinder our progress very much.

On the 10th day of December 1888, we reached our journey's end—Deadman, Sioux County,[22] Nebraska. Our cousins and my mother-in-law saw us coming off in the distance and they came to meet us. We were happy to be with our relatives once more and happy to reach the end of our journey—our new Nebraska home.[23]

A deed recorded in 1898, gave Alice Hamaker possession of 160 acres of located south of North Belmont Road. Records from the Department of the Interior, United States Land Office in Alliance, show that Nebraska officials threatened to scuttle his application.[24]

"In your original and final papers in the matter of your homestead, your name is given as RSQ Hamaker. The Commissioner required you to furnish an affidavit within sixty days showing at least one Christian name in full." [25]

Apparently RSQ was able to verify his identity as a man without a "Christian name" because he was granted his homestead near Belmont, NE. The homestead lay the tree-covered

---

[22] The family homesteaded in Dawes County was a few miles from the Sioux County line.
[23] Alice Hamaker. This article was reprinted in the book, *Crawford, Nebraska 1886-1961*, 78.
[24] Hamaker family. *Belmont Memories*. "RSQ and Alice Hamaker."
[25] Hamaker family. *Belmont Memories*, 16.

RSQ Hamaker and his brother, Dave, were good friends throughout their lives.

canyons a few miles southeast of the Fort Robinson military post[26] and the newly established town of Crawford.[27]

In a letter dated November 31, 1889,[28] almost a year after they had arrived in Nebraska, RSQ Hamaker told his father-in-law that he wasn't sure he'd be staying in the state, but he was reasonably sure he wouldn't go back to Iowa to live in a Democratic State. He went on to say a neighbor was returning to Missouri in February. The man sold his claim for $125, but had declared that "the improvements on the claim cost more than that." The letter went on to say that he had taken a contract to cut wood for the Poast (Presumably Fort Robinson), but lamented the fact that he was only making about a dollar a day, $2 per "coard." On a more positive tone he said that Davy had a good job at "the Poast" and that Crawford was growing fast.

"…Property is worth about three times as much as it was a year ago. The town is full of teames especily on Saturday. Busness men are bussy. I don't see how it is there is nothing to sell but wood. Chickens is worth $1.25 to $1.50 per doz. Hogs $4.00. Dressed fat cattle 2 cts on foot.

Corn is 50 cts per 100 lbs., it has been 90 cts per 100 lbs till yesterday; Oats 75 cts; wheat 60 cts per bushel; the best we get 30 lbs of good flour per bushel for our wheat. I have been siling flour for $2.80 per 100 that is the way I am going to sell my wheat I thing. This place is better for wheat than any other crops unless it is flx. I want to put in some of boath next year if we Stay."[29]

The letter went on to discuss a possible land deal but RSQ admitted that he didn't want to rent anything. He also said he would not take any of the "Government Land" because if he couldn't prove up on it he didn't think the work that went into a claim was worth it.

---

[26] Fort Robinson was established in 1874 and was a major military post by the time the Hamakers arrived.
[27] Crawford, Nebraska was incorporated as a town in 1886.
[28] Letter, RSQ Hamaker to William Cox Haworth, November 31, 1889. Aline Dyer collection.
[29] Letter, RSQ Hamaker to William Cox Haworth, November 31, 1889. Aline Dyer collection.

"I don't think it is worth anything till people is settling it up. There have been thousands of acres taken on the table land sence we came here. It is from 150 to 500 feet to watter and ruff and sandy. They raised nothing this year but the grass is much better for stock out there but again no watter…School commenced last Monday. I don't Know how long it is to be but 3 months at least. We live about ¾ mile from School house. The teacher boards with us. Her and Carl has gone horseback riding. Now Carl road a Coalt he thinks he can ride anything and he can get as much go out of a horse as anyone. He is not sadisfide unless they are on the run. He is the handiest little Boy with a team or horses I ever saw. Well I will stop for this time and will ask you to write soon and tell us how you are making it. Yours as Ever."[30]

The house Alice and RSQ built near Belmont, NE is in 2022 owned by their great-great grandson, Paul (Bud).

Despite his trepidation, RSQ Hamaker did not leave Nebraska. Hard work eventually produced a successful ranching and farming operation, and the original homestead was expanded. In 1910-1911, he and Alice built a beautiful two story house that included four bedrooms upstairs, a formal living room, a dining room with a large bay windows, and a kitchen featuring a "Home Comfort" wood-burning stove. A 4-pillared porch graced the front of the house. RSQ became an area livestock buyer,[31] or what was known as a commission man. The livestock he purchased: cattle, sheep, and hogs, were loaded onto train cars at Belmont or Crawford to be transported to Omaha, the major livestock market in Nebraska. Buyers examined the livestock

---

[30] Ibid.
[31] RSQ frequently boarded the train and accompanied a customer's livestock to market. When he returned he received a commission on the sale of his customer's livestock. There were no contracts signed on these business deals; they were secured with a handshake and a man's word. Today cattle buyers either bid on livestock directly or fill verbal orders from customers. Again, trust is an important component in the process.

brought to the Union Stockyards[32] and placed their bids. The seller could either accept the bid or make a counter offer.

In a 1909 letter, Frank LeRoy Hall, the president of the First National Bank of Crawford, officially introduced RSQ Hamaker to prospective clients.

> "We have known Mr. R.S.Q. Hamaker, whose signature appears below for the past twenty years. We have always found him to be strictly honest, a man whose word is as good as a bond,[33] and who always tries to do clean honest business. We consider his worth at $35,000 above all debts. We will honor his checks on this bank to the amount of $2000, two thousand dollars, and any courtesy you may show him will be appreciated."[34]

A few months later, First National Bank cashier, CA Minick drafted a similar letter, but this one dealt with Hamaker's role as a farm producer.

> "I wish to say that in 10 years of dealing with Mr. Hamaker. I have always found him a gentleman and a man of his word. He is a large farmer on the highest land we have in this country and has grown over 3000 bushels of dry land potatoes which he expects to ship to southern Nebraska and into Kansas and offer for sale."[35]

RSQ's personal stationery emphasized his pride in his potato operation. Below the letterhead, "Evergreen Stock Farm—R.S.Q. Hamaker and Sons," a framed banner proclaimed, "Potato Growing A Specialty." A second version of his stationery declared: "Cattle and Horses—Bought and Sold on Commission."

One page of stationery in his granddaughter's scrap book[36] recorded the results of a local horse sale. The animals ranged in price from $25 for a yearling mare, to $85 for a well-broke 8-year-old gelding. RSQ purchased the top seller of the day, a five-year-old bay stallion for $160.[37] The same tally sheet indicated that calves were averaging $25 a piece.[38]

---

[32] The Union Stockyards of Omaha, Nebraska were founded in 1883. By 1890 they were ranked third in the nation for livestock sales. In 1947, they were second to the Chicago Union Stock Yards, the nation's largest livestock market and meat packing industry. They became the largest center in 1955 and held onto the title until 1971. The 116-year old business closed in 1999.
[33] Melvin Nation, RSQ's grandson, based his life's philosophy on the same concept: A man's word must be as good as his bond.
[34] Letter, LeRoy Hall introducing RSQ Hamaker. Aline Dyer collection.
[35] Letter, CA Minick, letter of support. Aline Dyer collection.
[36] Aline Dyer collection. Aline was the daughter of RSQ's son, Paul.
[37] US Inflation Rate 1900-2016. http://www.in2013dollars.com/1900-dollars-in-2016?amount=160. Taking into consideration the average year's inflation rate of 2.88 percent, a $160 horse in 1900 would be worth approximately $4,300 in 2016.
[38] Letters and reports written by RSQ Hamaker. Aline Dyer scrapbook. Copied by Moni Hourt, 1999.

RSQ's success was not been a solitary achievement. While he traveled the rails buying and selling livestock, Alice managed the homestead. Her letters were full of information about the farm, neighborhood news, and at times gossip. Other letters[39] reflected her unease at being alone with her children.

> "Dear husband,
>
> We went to town yesterday, hoping to find you, but Lou Thornton said he saw you get on a train going east. I knew you were headed to Omaha.[40] We are having the nastiest weather—cold well; I guess so, and rain. We have had more rain since you left than at any time this summer. Monday morning when I got up, the yard looked like a lake."[41]

The letter went on say that Carl hauled two loads of wood and put up a heating stove. She said she needed to get some window lights and was very glad that he'd sent her a check via the First National Bank. She also reported that the flour mill, *Rolls Mill*, was struck by lightning and burned to the ground, that a neighbor was killed when the house he was moving fell off its blocks and crushed him, and that another neighbor left her husband and ran away with an "operator."

"School commenced Tuesday." She added in conclusion. "The teacher is quite a nice looking man. Mrs. Gillett says he looks quite 'Profeserfied.'"

The first few lines of an October 1, 1900 letter fussed that Carl had yet to return from the sale in Crawford, and that the "air was carrying every sound" which made her nervous.

> "It's so still you can here every word. People are driving cattle home, and I can hear people talking in the distance. I'm sure I just heard Carl yelling a minute ago, well because I herd him call someone a (son of a bitch). Actually this has been such a nice day. Mrs. Lemons was here with her babies. She is going to get a dinner set if she sells 80 pounds of baking powder. She will make it. She already had half enuf and has only been out a day and a half.
>
> Roosevelt is going to make a speech in Crawford Wednesday. Bertha says Teddies[42] (Appendix 2) going to speak and she is going down to sing for him. Carl just came

---

[39] Letter, Alice Hamaker to her husband, RSQ. Located in Aline Dyer's scrapbook. Copied by Moni Hourt, 1999.
[40] Established in 1883 the Union Stockyards in Omaha became the nation's largest livestock market. Thousands of head of livestock was bought and sold by commission men like RSQ Hamaker.
[41] Alice Hamaker letter to RSQ Hamaker, September 1900. Aline Dyer collection. Copied by Moni Hourt in 1999.
[42] Theodore Roosevelt traveled through Nebraska in 1900 as the vice presidential candidate. His journey helped propel presidential candidate William McKinley past Nebraskan William Jennings Bryan into the White House. Roosevelt became president upon McKinley's assassination in September 1901.

home; he was helping Sime Wright drive cows. Sime bought 28 head of cows at the sale. They averaged $25 a head. Yesterday I was up early at 5 o'clock to get Carl breakfast. He said he would be down to Harris's by 6 this morning, but it is so foggy one can barely see the barn.

(Later) Iva has to go to school early today to deliver milk. It will amount to $1.25 this week. She says she would rather deliver milk than churn butter to sell.[43]

As the first decade of the new century continued, RSQ expanded his role as a livestock commission man. Alice and the Hamaker children accepted their role as caretakers of their farm.

"Dear Husband,

This has been a fine day still and snowshiney. Pete says it is rather chilly on the wind mill tower. Carl went after the parts for the windmill this morning and helped put it back together. It was running by dinner time and pumped all afternoon, just as good as ever. Pierce is out of water. Carl and Pete are going to help him with his pump tomorrow."[44]

She went on to explain that she had not told him how many cattle there were because she didn't think either she or Carl had gotten an accurate count.

"I salted them yesterday morning and counted 92 head of calves and Carl rode the pasture yesterday and said that was all he had seen. Can you give us a description of each one of the DeWitte Cattle. We think there are three head of them gone, but don't any of us know them well enuf to know what they are. Carl branded 9 head of them. They never ought to have been turned loose without our brand. Yesterday I see the black cow lost her calf. I am afraid there will be others, but it wasn't the rye straw that did that, for they haven't had any. The cattle gaunted up in this last storm. There is one that is getting awful poor."[45]

Alice's letters provide great insight into the operation on the homestead and information about the surrounding community. She reported that the boys were planning on hunting coyotes. She wrote that Bertha was ill with a "bilious" attack— although the little girl had rallied enough to wash the dishes while Alice milked the cows, and "she seemed" to have energy

---

[43] Roosevelt also stopped in Crawford on April 25, 1904. "Remarks of President Roosevelt at Crawford, Nebraska, April 25, 1903," are located at the Theodore Roosevelt Center at Dickinson State College in North Dakota.
[44] Letter, Alice Hamaker to RSQ Hamaker, February 3, 1904. Aline Dyer collection.
[45] Letter, Alice Hamaker to RSQ Hamaker, February 3, 1904. Aline Dyer collection.

enough to play with her dolls. Alice also stated that a neighborhood family sold out and was moving to Idaho. "She asked me what you thought of Idaho. I can't think of anything good to tell her that you said of the country."

The letters also reassured her husband that she was keeping the home fires well lit.

> "Yes, I took the potatoes to Gooch, shortly after you left. I traded Gregory what Ray owed him in potatoes $7.50. Ray has had the grippe, but I think he is better. They had a party in town. I was invited but don't like to be out after night. Many were there, all the young folks in the neighborhood, our girls included."[46]

On February 5, Alice reported that the day was one of the finest days that anyone in the area had ever seen, but she was worried that the day was a "weather breeder." She said that it was too warm to keep a fire burning in the house, but wrote she had to keep it going in the cook stove because she rendered five gallons of lard that day. She also "ground three gallons of sausage" and baked bread. Alice reported the older children were looking forward to a party at neighbor, Guy Lemons' home. She later reported that they all had a splendid time.

A few days later, Alice informed her husband that she received another letter from him.

> "I got another letter from you. I wasn't looking for it, but it was welcome. I was afraid that you would be worrying about the windmill, but if you could see how smooth everything goes along you wouldn't worry so much. And don't worry about me. I ain't quite a fool. I'm just feeling fine and don't have very much to do. In fact, I'm having an easy time of it. I don't even have many to cook for right now. Paul got the manure hauled out of the calf barn. Things are just going good around here." [47]

Although grain and cattle were important products in the Belmont area, the main cash crop was potatoes. Belmont even featured a community potato cellar that could be used by area farmers who didn't have their own potato cellars. The farmers filled the labeled bins that lined the cellar with their potatoes and accessed them as needed. In the early fall, often for several weeks, everyone focused on getting the potatoes out of the ground and into the cellars.

As a testament to the harvest's importance, school classes were dismissed so that children of all ages could dig the potatoes out of the fields. Families packed lunches and walked the rows, tossing potatoes into sacks that they carried on their backs. Lakota Sioux and Cheyenne

---

[46] Ibid.
[47] Alice Hamaker letter to RSQ Hamaker, February, 1904. Aline Dyer Collection.

Indian families also helped with the harvest. The Hamakers hired the same Native families every year and according to Alice Porter[48] treated them well.

"Not everyone treated the Indian people fairly," Porter said. "There were a few guys that cheated them out of their wages or traded them whiskey for work. The Hamakers made sure they were paid a fair wage and took care of their families. They were kind people. They were well respected in the community."

Alice and RSQ Hamaker ready to take a motorcycle ride.

Although RSQ never officially retired, in Paul and Mabel,[49] moved their family from their Sioux County homestead to a house west of RSQ and Alice's two-story house. The extra help with the day-to-day operations of the farm/ranch gave the elder Hamakers more free time. They took train trips across the United States and drove their Model T on shorter journeys across the state. RSQ purchased a motorcycle, and drove it down the backroads, Alice perching behind him, a cap pulled over her white hair. During one trip to San Francisco, California, the couple explored the World's Fair of 115 and purchased an eight-piece set of hand carved furniture on display at The Japanese Pavilion, at the Panama-Pacific International Exposition. RSQ purchased the large ornate pieces of mahogany furniture for a whopping price of $1560,

---

[48] Alice Porter. Interview with Moni Hourt, 1999. Alice Porter home, Belmont, NE. Alice's family lived near Belmont. She was friends with Bertha and Iva Hamaker.
[49] RSQ and Alice's fourth son and wife, Mabel Claire (McHenry).

approximately $38,000 in the 2020 market. The furniture was displayed in the upstairs guest bedroom of the Hamaker's two-story home. [50]

Years later, Iva, the family's oldest daughter,[51] may have shared her family's pride in their "fancy" furniture[52] (Appendix 3) but at 18, she was prouder of her family's accomplishments as respected farmers and livestock owners. She was also determined to make her own mark in life and set her sights on a "teacher's degree."

"I was about Bertha's age. We were great friends, but I was very impressed with Ivy,[53]" Alice Porter said in a 1999 interview. "She excelled in all of her classes. Everyone expected her to become a teacher. She was even allowed to skip chores to study."

Iva attended District 39 Elementary/High School[54] in Belmont and graduated from the 10th grade in 1907. She enrolled at the Chadron Academy in Chadron, NE. in September of 1907.[55]

The Chadron Academy, an 11th and 12th grade high school that emphasized teacher training, began operations 19 years earlier than the opening of the 1907 school term. Ground-breaking ceremonies for the first Academy building occurred in 1888. According to a historical sketch in the 1907-1908 Chadron Academy Catalog, the Academy was established under the direction of Reverend Harmon Bross—Home Missionary Superintendent for Nebraska and the Rev. G.J. Powell, Home Missionary Superintendent for the Black Hills and Northeastern Wyoming.

> "Under the direction of these two pioneer missionaries and educators, the Northwestern Association of the Congregational Churches of Nebraska secured

---

[50] Paul Hamaker died in 1971; Mabel in 1980. The furniture was sold to the Pioneer Village on June 13, 1979 for a price of $1,000. Harold Warp who founded Pioneer Village in 1953, signed the receipt for the transaction made with RSQ's granddaughter, Aline Dyer. Information about the sale and the furniture is available at the Pioneer Village. Historian Monica Miller verified the transaction in December of 2020. In 1999, Moni Hourt visited the Minden museum and took pictures of the furniture display.

[51] In addition to the three children Carl, (1880); Ray, (1882); and Daniel/Tot (1887) who came to Nebraska with their parents, four other children Iva, (1889); Paul, (1892); Frank, (1894); and Bertha (1896); were born after the family arrived in Belmont. Tot died when he was 11. Ray and Frank died within a few weeks of each other during the flu epidemic of 1918, Ray in November and Frank in December. Alice died in 1937. Her obituary says the couple had nine children, two of whom died in infancy. RSQ Hamaker's 1932 obituary says the couple had seven children and does not mention the infants who died.

[52] Letter from Iva Nation to her sister Bertha, 1938. In the letter Iva is concerned over the distribution of the furniture.

[53] Many friends and area acquaintances called Iva Hamaker, "Ivy."

[54] School rosters published in the *Belmont Memories* show that Carl, Ray, and Iva Nation were enrolled at District 39 in 1897. Seven-year-old Iva was listed as Ivy that year. In later years, the school roster identified her as Iva. In 1899 and 1900 five Hamakers, Carl, Ray, Iva, Paul and Frank were enrolled in the school.

[55] Newspapers articles dated in November 1907 and March and April of 1908 reported that Iva Hamaker was attending the Chadron Academy. The November 1907 issue said Iva was home for Thanksgiving. The 1907 February issue reported that Iva had returned to school from a visit in Iowa. An April 17, 1908 note in the *Chadron Record* said that Iva visited classes that day.

possession of a tract of land at Chadron,[56] and early in the year 1888, ground was broken and the foundation laid for the first building." [57]

Since the school building was not finished when the first semester opened in 1889, classes were held in the "old public-school building." Enrollment was small, and church leaders considered suspending the program due to lack of funding. A permanent building was finally completed in time for the 1892 school year, but it was destroyed by fire on November 6, 1892. Funds were raised to complete a new building. By 1899, attendance had increased "materially." According to the historical sketch, "The future of the new enterprise seemed secure."[58]

> Purpose: The Chadron Academy, is the only Christian Institution within a radius of several hundred miles. Within this vast territory, in small towns and on lonely ranches thousands of young men and women are growing to manhood and women hood with little opportunity to attend school or church or feel the refining influences of the older sections of the country. The public schools are being steadily improved, but they do not and cannot meet the need. The purpose of the Chadron Academy is to offer to all these young people a home where Christian influences will predominate, where the truths of Christianity will be taught: where the physical and mental training will receive adequate attention."[59]

"In the early 1890s, Chadron newspapers often carried advertisements concerning the Academy and its features." Con Marshall wrote in his history of Chadron State College. "One of them called it, 'The only School of Higher Education in Northwest Nebraska.' Subheadings said, 'A Full Corps of Teachers' and 'Spring Term Begins April 1.'"

> "Thorough preparation for any College or Scientific School. Certificate admits to any College or University in the State. Beautiful grounds, building and furniture new. Home comforts and Christian influences. The Normal Course is attracting many who are preparing to teach. Special attention given to Normal students in Spring term. The Business Course offers the advantages of a commercial College.

---

[56] *Catalogue: Chadron Academy, 1907-1908.* Iva Hamaker Nation scrapbook. The catalogue listed Chadron as a town of about 2500 inhabitants located in the center of a great cattle region "comprising parts of three states: Nebraska, Wyoming, and South Dakota." The brochure said the main Academy Building was surrounded by a campus of eighty acres

[57] 1907-1908 "Historical Sketch," *Catalogue: Chadron Academy, 1907-1908.* Iva Hamaker Nation scrapbook.

[58] The Academy closed after the 1910 school term.

[59] *Catalogue: Chadron Academy, 1907-1908.* Iva Hamaker Nation scrapbook

Shorthand and typewriting taught. Superior opportunities for culture in music and art—no better in the state. Expense very low. Board starting at $2.50 a week. Total expenses for Spring term: $40. Many opportunities for self-support."[60]

The Academy catalog listed weekly tuition at $1, an 18-week semester: $15. Board for one week: $2.50. The semester fee of $8 was a considerable savings. Estimated book cost was $8 a year.[61]

Iva completed the 1907-1908 semester,[62] enrolled in education,[63] but there isn't any record that she attended classes during the 1908-1909 semester. She told her daughter Mildred that she "thought marrying Dad was better than goin' to school."

"Mom said she and Dad went to the same country school," Elvin Nation said in 1992.[64] "And of course they knew each other. Belmont was a pretty small community. But her Dad sure didn't want her marrying Earl Nation. They didn't think he was much more than white trash."

Melvin Nation agreed that his mother's family believed she had married beneath her 'station in life.' "They were pretty wealthy, and Mama was [at least in that day] a well-educated woman. Dad just growed up. His father, Henry T, must have been a dreamer and a wanderer. He came to this country in 1887 and homesteaded near Belmont, but I don't think anything worked real good for him."

John, the first Nation[65] to travel to the United States arrived as an Englishman's servant boy.[66] Two generations later, John's grandson, William, had acquired 1,799 acres of land in

---

[60] Con Marshall. *The Story of Chadron State College, 1911-1986*. South Dakota: Pine Hill Press, 1986.
[61] One hundred dollars in 1900 is equivalent to $2600 in 2015. Although Iva was an accomplished pianist there is no record that she paid the weekly fee of $10 to enroll in piano classes at the Academy. One year's tuition at the Academy, including board, was listed as $40--- equivalent to approximately $1300 in 2015 . The cost of tuition at Chadron State College in 2017 is listed at $4815. That does not include room and board.
[62] "Academy Notes." *Chadron Record*. January 17, 1908. This newspaper column featured Chadron Academy students. This "Note" includes the following statement: "Iva Hamaker has gone to Iowa for a visit, is expected back soon." On March 13, the "Notes" said that Iva had returned to school. An article in the November 29, 1907. "Belmont News" section of the *Crawford Tribune* says Iva is home for a short visit and is expected to stay until after Thanksgiving.
[63] *Catalogue: Chadron Academy 1907-1908*.
[64] Elvin Nation. Interview with Moni Hourt, 1992. Moni Hourt home, Crawford, NE.
[65] The last name, Nation, is often listed as Nations. It has been found listed both ways in the same generation, in the same family. Thelma Nation's research found that John Nations was listed as a servant boy in William Beakes' will written in 1711. No date has been listed for Christopher Nations' birth, but Thelma did discover that Christopher was married to Elizabeth Sharp, (not Swain as listed in many documents,) in Virginia. In 1790, the Christopher Nations family lived in Burke County, North Carolina. Isaac Nation, born 1786, married Margaret Tillman. Henry Nation, born 1814, married Mary Riddle. Henry Thomas Nation, born 1844-45 married Olivia Spotts. Their son Earl, born in 1888 was Melvin's father.
[66] William Beakes' will, written in 1711, lists a servant boy: John Nations.

Claiborne County, Tennessee. William's brother, Joseph found a unique way to finance his estate. When he died in 1804, his will left two liquor stills to his family and instructed them to make liquor for at least two years for the "benefit of the estate."[67]

During the War of 1812, William's son, Isaac Nation, fought in several battles including the Battle of New Orleans. After the war, members of the Nation family traveled to Tennessee, then to Ohio, and eventually to Missouri.

According to a 1958 story written by Frances Locker Nation,[68] during the Civil War, Henry Thomas, then just 16, joined the Union Army as a drummer boy. His brother, Jake also fought for the North, while his father, Henry Nation, fought for the Confederacy. After the war, the trio exchanged news of their survival, but after those messages, Frances said the men apparently never made any further contact.[69]

"There just isn't any proof that any of them served in the Civil War," Thelma Nation said in a 1998 interview.[70] "The family stories also said Henry Thomas was orphaned when he was a baby and was given to another family to raise. I found the census reports from Tennessee and discovered that story was false. Henry Thomas lived with his father, at least until he was 16. Family stories are easy to repeat, but not so easy to prove."

One family story took Thelma several months to untangle. According to the story, two of Henry Thomas's brothers traveled to Indian Territory Oklahoma after the Civil War and never saw their family again. Thelma could not find the brothers in Oklahoma, but located them in the South Dakota census records of 1870.

"I was sure the Indian Territory thing was just another story," Thelma said with chagrin. "Then I realized that in 1870, South Dakota was considered Indian Territory too. Making a mistake in genealogy is pretty easy."

Verifiable facts support the information that Henry Thomas Nation and his wife, Olivia Spotts,[71] emigrated from Missouri with their seven children[72] in 1887. The family shipped their household goods to Chadron, NE then using a team of mules, hauled the items on to a homestead four miles east of Belmont. In the next three years, as the couple struggled to establish a farm in the thin topsoil of their homestead, three more children[73] were born.

---

[67] Thelma Nation: genealogy research. Nation-Hourt library, Crawford, NE.
[68] Frances Locker Nation was the wife of Elvin Nation.
[69] Thelma Nation was never able to verify this information, partly due to the fact that many Civil War records were destroyed during the war.
[70] Thelma Nation. Interview with Moni Hourt, 1998, Hat Creek Ranch, Sioux County, NE.
[71] Olivia Frances Spotts (1870) was the daughter of Baylor Spotts and Margaret "Annie" Warford Spotts. She and Henry Thomas were married in 1870.
[72] William, known as Billy, born 1872; Anna Lou born 1874; John Clark, 1876; Grace Orien, 1878; Mary Irene, 1881; Edgar Madison, 1883; Susie, 1885.
[73] Earl Daniel, 1888; Jeff Davis, 1890; Jennie May, 1893.

Henry Thomas Nation family: Jim Boulden, Annie Nation Boulden, John, Grace, Willie Nation. Front: Edgar, Earl Daniel, Henry Thomas, Olivia Frances Spots, Jefferson Davis, Susan, Irene.

By the time Henry Thomas and his family arrived in Dawes County, hundreds of other homesteaders had already staked claims on the more desirable land in the region. According to historian Ephriam Dickson III[74] Dawes County was established in 1885. A short time later, two townships, located near the old Sidney-Deadwood Trail,[75] in the southwestern portion of the county were designated as the Evergreen Precinct. Between 1884 and 1896, nearly 250 individuals filed on land within this 72-square mile area, growing into a total population of about 600 people by 1890.

> "The Fremont, Elkhorn, and Missouri Valley Railroad better known as the Burlington and Missouri, constructed a line through the Evergreen Precinct in 1888-1889.

---

[74] Dickson, Ephriam D III. "Belmont a Brief History." *Belmont Memories,* 2015.
[75] The Sidney Deadwood trail between Sidney, NE and Deadwood South Dakota passed west of Belmont. It followed what is known now as Breakneck Road. Several stations, including White Clay Station were located on the trail. The trail saw heavy traffic between 1876 and 1880.

To negotiate the deep canyons of the Pine Ridge, railroad engineers determined that a tunnel would be necessary and soon established a construction camp nearby. By the summer of 1889, the rails had been laid as far as this temporary community, now known as Evergreen City, with passengers able to continue north by wagon to Crawford."[76]

"Evergreen City is lively now," wrote one resident. "Foreman Lyons has about 200 men employed at the tunnel, while the company has about 20 engineers and carpenters at work. The town site has been secured immediately as the south end of the cut that leads to the tunnel but [it] hasn't been platted yet.[77]

Belmont, Nebraska about 1900.

Evergreen City, surveyed in 1890, was renamed Belmont in honor of a Burlington Railroad official. At one point the town sported 28 buildings: a telephone office, lumberyard, grain elevator, saloon, machine shop, railroad depot, ice house, two general stores, a lumberyard, two churches, a brick school house, and about 100 residences within the "city" limits.

Henry Thomas Nation, became one of the many area residents who spent most of 1888 cutting logs on the nearby hillsides. Every other day, the logs were hauled to the railroad grade near Belmont. He and his older sons joined a 1200-man work force who earned between 15 and 20 cents an hour as they "hacked" the 698-foot tunnel through a sand/sedimentary rock canyon. The crew worked from opposite ends of the tunnel, opening an average of 3-feet a day,

---

[76] Dickson, Ephriam D III. "Belmont a Brief History." *Belmont Memories*, 2015
[77] Ibid.

Henry Thomas Nation was part of the crew that built the Belmont Tunnel north of Belmont.

6 feet on good days. At times, the rock walls were blasted with dynamite; other times the men chopped their way through the sandy shale. Men shoveled the massive piles of debris into farm wagons and straining teams hauled it away from the tunnel.

To keep the ceiling from collapsing on the workers, the tunnel framework, constructed from local timber, was erected behind the "digging crew."[78] Cement footings secured the timber framework. Guards posted on either end of the tunnel, day and night discouraged vandalism and also proved to local residents that the tunnel was indeed a valuable asset to the region.

"They had crews of men camped around. They all lived in tents. I think some of them were Chinese," Alice Porter said.[79] "I've always wondered how they kept enough food down there to feed them. My father-in-law[80] helped build the tunnel. He said sometimes, not often though, they used dynamite and once in a while everyone would have to run to safety. He said they used lanterns for light. I don't think the working conditions were very good, but they made the best of it."

Completed on August 25, 1889, the tunnel made it possible for passengers to travel by train from Alliance to Crawford and then into the Black Hills.[81]

---

[78] Alice Porter. Interview 1999 with Amy Fricke and Amelia Lux under the direction of Moni Hourt, Alice Porter home near Belmont, NE.
[79] Fricke and Lux created a video about the Belmont Tunnel. In the process they interviewed Alice Porter.
[80] David T Porter.
[81] Twice daily trains traveled through the tunnel until it was bypassed in 1982. The tunnel was considered so important during World War I and II that soldiers were assigned to protect it.

Tunnel Through Solid Rock near Crawford, Nebr.
—Pub. by H. W. Negus, Crawford, N

"Daylight is now shining through the Pine Ridge from end to end." *The Crawford Tribune* declared on August 25, 1889, in an article touting the state's only railroad tunnel. "The area will soon be teeming with settlers."

By the time Ray Hamaker was a young boy in the early 1920s, there were no guards in the tunnel and it quickly became a 'meeting place' for local kids. "We was always down there," Ray Hamaker said. "It's a wonder one of us didn't end up dead."[82]

When the tunnel was constructed, the crew carved rectangular notches at regular intervals along the tunnel's walls. The notches provided a safe haven for crew members who happened to get caught in the tunnel when a train was coming through. Area youngsters turned the notches into a "right of passage."

"The kids, mostly the boys thought that hiding in the holes when a train was going through the tunnel was a way to show their bravery," Hamaker said. "Sure—I hid in there—several times. That old steam engine belched a bunch of smoke, but it didn't scare me much."[83]

In November 1917, the tunnel collapsed on a train that originated in Texas. Carl Hamaker, Ray's father, told his son that he supposed the constant vibration in the old wood structure caused the collapse. Most of the geldings included in the trainload of horses headed for the remount station at Fort Robinson were killed. Carl Hamaker helped dig several of surviving geldings, all branded with a US, from the wreckage. He took one of the animals back to his farm. Ray said his Dad expected Fort personnel to collect the animals, but they never did. Ray finally broke the horse to ride. He became a permanent part of their horse herd.

"After the cave-in, they rebuilt the framework, drilled holes into it from the top and poured cement in there to reinforce the ceiling and the walls," Alice Porter said in 1999. "It took two

---

[82] Ray Hamaker. Interview with Amy Fricke, Amelia Lux, and Moni Hourt 1999, Ray Hamaker home, Glen, NE. He was the son of Carl Hamaker and the nephew of Iva Hamaker Nation. He lived near the tunnel.
[83] Ibid.

years and about 200 men to repair the damage, but it's still there. Think of that. That tunnel was built with a pick ax and hand labor, and it's still there. That is truly amazing."

"Most of those steam engines were coal fed. The 109 came in from the south," Hamaker said. "We could hear it chugging along for four or five miles before it got to Belmont. We'd climb up on the tunnel and use sticks to shove the coal off the coal train. Then we'd climb down and pick it up and take it home. We'd get a good supply of coal that way."

Hamaker added that the neighborhood kids, "lived on top of the tunnel." They rolled rocks onto the trains or even onto the tracks. "One time we were prying up a rock, and we hit wood. The older boys knew what it was. They dug the keg of moonshine up and took off with it. The Phelps boys had a 'still' around there. We always figured the keg was theirs, but those boys sure didn't give it back."

Two passenger trains traveled through the tunnel every day. Area residents could catch the train and travel south to Lincoln or north to Billings, Montana. The daily schedule also made excursions to Crawford and Alliance possible. There were times, according to Hamaker, that passengers reported the tunnel was haunted.

"I heard that a bunch of those boys hid in the tunnel and shined light[84] on their faces. Sure scared a bunch of those passengers. But I couldn't REALLY say that that happened," Hamaker chuckled.

Eventually railroad officials hired local residents including 17-year-old John Porter, Alice Porter's future husband to guard the tunnel. The young guards slept in a hut at the south end of the tunnel. It was their responsibility to keep people from "riding the rails," or sneaking into the tunnel.

"They were even allowed to carry guns," Alice laughed. "I don't think that would be allowed today.[85] Everyone wanted a job on the railroad back then. Farming was tough; the railroad offered a somewhat steady salary."

Although Henry Nation worked part-time for the railroad, and eventually served as a section foreman in Osage, Wyoming, in 1894, neither the railroad nor farming offered the future he and Olivia had envisioned. They sold their homestead to George Boulden, whose son, Jim, had married their daughter, Annie. Their wagon train consisting of six wagons, arrived in Lamar, Missouri July 10, 1894. The next morning, Olivia was spanking one of her children when she suffered from a stroke. She died instantly. Henry reloaded the wagons and headed back to Nebraska. On Christmas Day 1894, the Nation family arrived back in Belmont. They settled close to the homestead they'd recently vacated.

---

[84] The boys who could secure them carried lanterns into the tunnel. It was hard to keep their candles lit.
[85] During World War II, the Belmont Tunnel was considered so important to the war effort that military guards were posted 24 hours a day at both ends of the tunnel. The train was reportedly transporting ammunition from Igloo, South Dakota to sites in the east.

"Olivia must have been one tough woman. Dad said she had an old sow that kept eating its piglets, so she held it down and sewed its eyes shut. Dad never told me if the sow quit eating its young, but he used to story to prove how tough she was. The kids must have been as tough as she was, but it sure weren't easy for those poor little motherless kids," Melvin said. "My Dad didn't have much fetchin up.[86] He just growed up, a urchin in the hills. My granddad hired him out to herd cattle for Jim Tollman when he was just seven. I think all in all, he had about three months of formal schooling. He never made it past the third grade."

In a 1963 recorded interview,[87] Earl Nation said he "grew up tough." His family was hired to herd sheep on a homestead in southern Sioux County when he was about eight. When Earl's older brother, working for another homesteader, sickened with typhoid fever, friends brought him back to the homestead. The younger siblings took turns herding the sheep, often camping for weeks at a time, in the isolated prairie, 25 miles from their home. Those left at home nursed their brother back to health.

One winter morning, Earl said he and his brother were just 'rasslin.' "We knocked the stove over and set the house on fire," Earl said.[88] "Good thing we had some water. We got it out."

Earl admitted the children weren't paying attention the day Earl and Susie, mounted barefoot on a "renege horse" ran "right over" their little brother. "The sharp edge of the horse's hoof cut his toe clean off.[89] We wrapped his foot up. I guess it healed. He wasn't bothered by it much."[90]

Henry Nation had a "down to earth" way of curing an injury. When Earl, while chopping wood, sliced the inside of his leg. Henry stopped the bleeding by packing dirt in the wound. The wound healed although, for the rest of his life, a long scar wriggled down the full length of Earl's leg.

Iva Hamaker's life was very quiet in comparison. Although she completed the chores on the farm and was considered a good horsewoman, on horseback and with a team, she also spent many Sundays visiting with friends. Fourth of July found the family in Crawford, Nebraska, watching the Army cadets from Fort Robinson put on their equestrian show. A picture taken when she was 18, captured the image of a sophisticated young woman, ready to take her place in the world. The path she chose a few months later, wasn't the one her parents had envisioned.[91]

---

[86] Earl was the third youngest of the family. The children included, Willie, (1872); Annie, (1874); John, (1876); Grace, (1878); Irene, (1881); Edgar, (1883); Susie, (1885); Earl, (1888); Dave, (1890); and Jennie, (1893).
[87] Earl Nation, Interview recorded by Fred Hamaker, 1963.
[88] Earl Nation. Taped Interview by Fred Hamaker. Crawford, NE. 1963. Merlin Nation gave a copy of interview to Moni Hourt in 1992.
[89] Ibid.
[90] Ibid
[91] Merlin Nation. Personal interview with Moni Hourt, 1992. Merlin Nation home, Everett, Washington.

LIFE ON SPUD RIDGE

"Some people thought that country was ole desolate country. I think Mama did, but she made it a home. That's what people did back then. They just growed where they was planted." Melvin Nation

Iva Hamaker

Earl Nation

On October 11, 1908, the day before Iva Hamaker's nineteenth birthday, she left her suitcase in a canyon a short distance from her home. "I just found that little suitcase in a little pile of trees, just sitting there. It had Iva Hamaker's name on it. She was running away as far as I could tell," Earl Nation's voice was full of smiles as he told the story in 1963.[92] "I just picked it up and found her going over the top of the hill 'on high'. I stopped and asked her if she wanted a ride."

---

[92] Earl Nation. Taped interview by Fred Hamaker, 1963.

The couple were married at noon at Carl and Helen Tollman's home. The Tollmans "stood up" for the younger couple then served them a dinner that included a chocolate cake frosted with seven-minute frosting that had been swirled into waves.[93]

'We took the 3 o'clock train for Newcastle and were there a couple of weeks,"[94] Iva Nation said on the day of their 55th wedding anniversary in 1963.[95] "They were all sneaking around trying to see if we were on that train, but they never found out. I wanted to get married, that's all."

*Iva Hamaker Nation hated to have her picture taken,
but in this candid photograph taken in 1963, she was caught smiling
as she shared a memory with husband of 55 years.
(Photo taken by 12-year-old Moni Nation.)*

For the first year of their married life, Earl and Iva worked for Fred Tollman and lived on his place not far from the Hamaker homestead. The couple's oldest son, Edwin was born in the Hamaker home in November 1909.[96]

---

[93] Iva Nation told her granddaughter, Moni that the cake look like it was covered with a cloud. Moni Nation diary April 22, 1961.
[94] The couple took the train to Marsland, then on to Newcastle, Wyoming, where they visited Earl's oldest sister and his father, Henry.
[95] Iva Nation. Taped interview by Fred Hamaker, 1963. Fifty-fifth wedding anniversary, Crawford, NE. Copy given to Moni Hourt by Merlin Nation, 1992.
[96] Family history said Edwin Nation was born in the upstairs bedroom of the big house that Iva's parents built the year before. However, some members of the Paul Hamaker family believe the new two-story house wasn't built until 1911.

"I had a little money gathered up when we got married," Earl said. "The summer of 1901, I worked the whole summer in the Black Hills,[97] cutting wood. I had $15 when I came back home. Dad bought me a yearling heifer, but she died of black leg. That same year Dad gathered up five head of cattle; by spring he only had two left. That's the way my Dad "made money" in the cow business. I wanted to do better." [98]

Carl Tollman bought Earl's cattle in the fall of 1908 for $10 a head. "They weighed 400 pounds. I managed to buy my brother's cows and calves for $25 a pair and his two-year-old calves for $16 each. I made a little money off the calves. Things were looking up."

In 1904, the Kinkaid Act, an addendum to the Homestead Act of 1862, allowed homesteaders to claim 640 acres of land, if they settled in one of 37 counties in northwestern Nebraska. According to an article written by Ruth V Zerbe[99] at 9 a.m. on April 28, 1904, the doors of the Sioux County Courthouse opened and County Clerk Pontius addressed the crowd that had been gathering on the streets of Harrison since midnight. He explained that individual tickets would be given to those in attendance to determine the order of homestead claims. HT Zerbe received Ticket #1 and filed on the county's first 640 homestead. Bessie Case received ticket #2. That day 164 filings were made for Sioux County land.

That first day, Charles Childers claimed Section 3, Township 29 North, Range 54, West of the 6th prime meridian. When he relinquished his homestead,[100] located west of Dave Hamaker's Sioux County[101] claim, Hamaker[102] told Earl and Iva that he'd "help them buy it." The cost:

---

[97] Belmont, NE was geologically part of an uplift area known as the "Foot of the Black Hills. It was about 100 miles from the forested Black Hills area of what is now South Dakota.

[98] Earl Nation. Taped interview by Jack Roberts. October, 1959. Accessed by Moni Hourt 1999.

[99] *Sioux County History-The First 100 Years.* 1986

[100] The Homestead Act of 1862 allowed anyone, men, women, citizens or non-citizens, who were over the age of 21 to claim 160 acres of land. (In 1904, in 37 counties in Nebraska, the homestead claim was expanded to 640 acres.) Once a claimant lived on the land for five years and made improvements on the land, equivalent to $1.25 an acre, they had "proved up" on the land and received title to the claim. Childers relinquished his homestead claim. Earl Nation filed at the Alliance, Nebraska land office. The original patent the 641.8-acre homestead was located on: Section 3, Township 29, North and Range 54. Accession No#: 409851, Document 08192. In 1914, five years after he and Iva had moved onto the land, records show that Nation paid the $8 filing fee and received the patent to the land. President Woodrow Wilson's signature is on the certificate, although it is doubtful, Wilson signed the certificate. (After 1833, patents were signed by a special secretary, not by the president.)

[101] On September 20, 1886, the boundaries of Sioux County were designated. The county consisted of all the territory in Nebraska that lay north of Cheyenne County. By 1883, the eastern part of the county had been divided into four counties: Rock, Brown, Keya Paha, and Sheridan. Two years later, the massive county was further divided into Sioux, Dawes, Box Butte, and Cherry County. The county contained four voting districts: War Bonnet, Bowen, White River, and Running Water. The first warranty deed filed in what was then Cheyenne County was that of Bartlett Richards who established the "Upper 33" Ranch on Niobrara County. When surveyors moved into the northern part of the county, they identified a piece of land in what was known as the Hat Creek Valley as "Coffee's Garden." Melvin spent the last years of his life on the land that became the Hat Creek Ranch.

[102] Dave Hamaker was RSQ's brother. He had worked at Fort Robinson, then used the money he earned to become a well-known homesteader and livestock operator.

$900, a little more than a dollar an acre. In 1909, the couple moved from the tree covered hills near Belmont to a windswept hillside, 17 miles west of the RSQ Hamaker's Dawes County homestead.

The 1916 Sioux County Nebraska Platt Book lists the Earl Nation (3) section. Later he and Iva used her inheritance to buy the Don H Gillette Section (4). From 1918 Sioux County Plat book

Although Mr. Childers never "proved up" on his claim, he had constructed a sod house. Located on the lip of a small canyon, it was accessed by a long winding dirt road that was often rendered impassable by snow and rain. The Nation family ignored the inconvenience and moved in. They arranged the $100 worth of furniture they purchased: a cot, a double bed, a table and four chairs, and a small armful of "tin ware." The roof leaked, but neighbors arrived to repair it. Walls that bulged from the weight of the sod roof, were reinforced.

Iva cooked on a small four-hole wood stove perched on curved legs that sunk unevenly into the dirt floor. She told her daughter-in-law that the uneven surface often threatened to spill the contents of her pots and pans until Earl "evened the stove up" by placing pieces of wood under each leg.[103] She said the oven created food that "came out pretty funny," but she

---

[103] Thelma Nation. Interview with Moni Hourt, 1999. Hat Creek Ranch, Sioux County, NE. Thelma said she really liked her mother-in-law and spent many hours discussing Iva's early life on the "home place."

*This drawing is representative of many Nebraska "soddies."
Drawing by Lula Callaham, second cousin of Thelma Callaham.)*

learned to make do. There was no running water, but there was an outhouse behind the sod house and within weeks, a neighbor, Frank Johnson, dug a well near the front door. The dugout was small, but when Henry Nation sickened in the fall of 1908, Iva suggested he live with them. He died in June of 1909.

In 1949, Iva told Verna Callaham[104] that she hated the "endless wind." She admitted that sometimes, she suffered "despair." Then she quickly added that she had a "fine" family and "that was all that really mattered."

"Mama told me they hadn't been living on the homestead very long when "Daddy" as she always called my Dad did something that disturbed her "terribly," Anita Nation Robison said in 1995. "Apparently he was shoeing a horse, and the horse kicked him. He was right outside the door and Mama hear him swear."

Iva burst into tears. She told her young husband that she never expected him to be such a "rough" man. He assured her that he would never cuss again. As far as his children knew he never did.[105]

"Nobody trotted after me, that's for sure," Iva said in 1963 with a note of defiance slipping into her voice. "And we made out. About a year after we moved out to the homestead, a young

---

[104] Verna Callaham. Interview with Moni Hourt, 2000. Hourt home, Sioux County, NE. Verna and her family lived about three miles from the Nation farm. She was injured in a tractor accident in the spring of 1949. Iva Nation spent many afternoons visiting and encouraging her new neighbor.
[105] Anita Nation Robison. Telephone interview, 1994, by Moni Hourt.

cyclone lifted the roof off the house and swept it away. I was sitting in the corner rocking the baby when Daddy got home later that night. The door was locked, but it didn't matter much: anyone could have gotten in. The neighbors came and helped us put the roof back on. We had awfully good neighbors."[106]

Within a few years, a new sod house was built across the canyon near the new windmill. Muslin lined the ceiling to keep dirt from falling into the food and onto the heads of the residents. The hewn wood floor was easier to sweep than the hard-packed dirt floor had been. A large woolen blanket separated the small bedroom from the main room. Tucked into the corner of the room, a shiny new stove, bigger and with a large oven, stood proudly next to a wooden kitchen table.[107] Merlin Nation said the "soddie" was warm in the winter, and the four-paned window glass, set deep into the recessed windows, provided a soft light.[108]

Despite the couple's determination to succeed, the early years of their marriage were haunted with hardships. The couple borrowed enough money from Iva's Uncle Dave to purchase a team of horses. A few weeks later, they were picking chokecherries beside a dry river bed. A storm swept through the table lands above the ravine where they had tethered their horses. An August 11, 1911 *Crawford Tribune* newspaper story reported that the couple lost their team during the deluge.

> Earl Nation lost a team of horses by drowning during the cloud burst on Saturday afternoon, south of Glen. He had placed the horses in a stable on the Fred Cogshell place and thought they were safe, but the stable was on low ground, near a gulch, and the water raised to a sufficient height to drown them.[109]

Years later Iva told Thelma Nation that she was in a small barn checking on the horses, when Earl noticed a wall of water coming down the draw. "I told her she better get out of there before she got her feet wet," Earl added to his wife's story. "I managed to pull the wagon across the canyon and went back for the horses. The water hit before I could get them both out. Unc's[110] little mare was swept down the canyon and drowned. The next day I went back and gathered up the harness. A couple months later, lightning killed the other horse. I went over to Unc's, and he set me up with more horses. It took me 10 years to pay off those dead horses."[111]

---

[106] Iva Nation. Recorded interview by Fred Hamaker, October 1963.
[107] Lucille Nation, wife of Merlin Nation. Personal interview with Moni Hourt, 1992. Everett, Washington. Lucille said Iva, smiling with pride, had told her young daughter-in-law about her new sod home,
[108] Merlin Nation. Personal interview by Moni Hourt, 1992. Everett, Washington
[109] "Home Happenings." *Crawford Tribune*, August 11, 1911.
[110] The Nation family referred to Dave Hamaker as "Unc."
[111] Earl Nation. Taped recording by Fred Hamaker, October 1963

The Nations narrow escape mirrored that of Mrs. George Zeller and a three-year-old child who were driving home from Mrs. Zeller's mother.

> …As the pair were crossing what is known as the Shipley Draw, south of Glen the force of water rushing through the draw upset their buggy, throwing the occupants into the water. They managed to scramble out of the buggy as it was swept down the stream. The team ran away and was caught by one of the neighbors…Mrs. Zellers and the child managed to get to Mr. Stiller's home and were taken to their own home. There was serious damage to the buggy. A hen and a brood of young chickens were also lost in the flood.[112]

Unexpected disaster lurked around many west Nebraska corners, but Iva Nation believed her family had evaded tragedy in December of 1916. In a letter to her mother who was wintering in California, she reported that her seven year old son, Edwin, was feeling better after a long, serious bout with the "grippe."[113] In a childish scrawl, the little boy reassured his grandmother that he was indeed better. A week later he died of complications of the disease.[114]

Eva, Clark, Merlin, Elvin, Front: Anita, Melvin, Earl, Iva, Mildred, Frances. There are no pictures of Edwin, but the family did have professional pictures taken on a fairly regular basis.

---

[112] "Narrow Escape from Drowning." *Crawford Tribune*, August 11, 1911.
[113] Some family members said Edwin died of the flu and pneumonia; others say he died of typhoid fever.
[114] Letter, Iva Hamaker to Alice Hamaker, 1916. Hamaker scrap book, Aline Hamaker Dyer collection.

A storm had hit the region and blocked the roads with snow. Iva wrapped Edwin's body in a blanket. Earl laid him in a shed near the sod house. Three days later the storms abated. Earl, Carl Hamaker, and Carl Randall loaded Edwin's body into a wagon and transported him to the Marsland cemetery about 15 miles east of the homestead. They took turns hacking a grave out of the frozen ground then laid the tiny body into a newly made casket and lowered it into the grave. Iva remained at the soddie, her two remaining children snuggled into her lap.

"I can't even imagine what that must have been like for my mother," sympathy sifted through Melvin's words. "She couldn't leave there. She couldn't say good-bye to her little boy. She couldn't go to her mother or even to Belle.[115] She just had to grieve, alone, out on that lonely ole hill."

---

[115] Belle Hamaker, Dave Hamaker's wife.

BEHIND A WHISTLE

"Some of my earliest memories are of my Mama whistling, mostly hymns, but sometimes a few old songs. She also used that whistle to get our attention. None of us ignored her whistle." Melvin Nation

Shortly before her death, Alice Hamaker hosted a family reunion at her home. Melvin and his younger sister, Mildred cling tightly to their mother's hand. They are flanked by their grandmother and their father. Others in the picture (left to right) Dave Hamaker, Bertha Siekert, Belle Hamaker, Lauren Haworth, Perla Kiefer, Pet Yost, Alice Hamaker, Iva Nation, Earl Nation, Paul Hamaker, Mabel Hamaker, Carol Mason.

RSQ Hamaker died in 1932; Alice in 1935. In 1938, Iva used her inheritance to purchase 641.68 acres, a full section of land[116] from Don Gillette's family. The Nations paid $2,650 for the section that bordered their original relinquishment. The purchase doubled the family's holdings, but didn't necessarily make life easier. Earl Nation said life would've "been harder by far" without Iva's Uncle Dave. "Unc was like a father to me. Don't know what we'd a done without him," Earl said in his interview with Dave's son, Fred Hamaker. "He did good by us."

Unfortunately for the young couple, Dave Hamaker's advice and counsel could not overcome the vagaries of homesteading the vast, open, unrelenting prairie. In a letter written March 11, 1912, to his son, Paul, RSQ Hamaker reported that a big blizzard was expected in the next 24 hours.

"It is getting to be something pretty bad here, has been no time cattle could "russle" for 2 months. Lots more snow out west than here and everything is thin. Carl[117] was down a few days ago. Said horses was in bad shape and cattle are about done, especially Earl's. No loss yet, but it must come spring soon. Our straw is just gone and there is no chance to get anything. Takes three days to get to Sioux County. Roads is drifted shut most everywhere."

"We have only 4 little lambs left out of 9; lost five. Our twin lambs died. We couldn't help it. Elvin hasn't caught any coyotes yet, but caught five dogs. We give the ewes straw and soy cubes—is hard but not as hard as oilcake. This sack is just too hard. The ewes don't like it," Iva Hamaker wrote to Clark Nation in 1935. "The cattle are pretty weak. We only have one bale of hay left."

In a letter a few weeks later, she looked forward, a technique that saved the sanity of many prairie dwellers. She stated that she had already planted a garden and that Earl had started farming, pulling a grain drill behind his disc and tractor. She thanked Clark for the "10 dollar bill," he sent the family. "If you boys could send me some [money] the first of April and then some the first of May, $50 would help. We bought $20 worth of feed in the last week. We haven't lost anything yet, just have high pockets."

"When we got to the homestead and for many years after that, we were in debt" Earl Nation said. "Unc told me to take care of my credit[118] above all else. That's something I always made sure I did. I, at least, paid the interest every time it was due and borrowed only when I had no choice." [119]

Community support helped lessen financial strain in most rural neighborhoods. Instead of hiring help, neighbors worked together to accomplish major tasks. In the fall of the year area residents brought their hogs to one location and butchered 8 or 10 in a single day. Since Earl

---

[116] Donald H Gillette received a patent for Section 4, Township 29 N, Range 54 W, 6th Prime Meridian, NE. in 1913. Accession 353370. Document 03124.
[117] Carl Hamaker lived near his brother-in-law, Earl Nation, and his uncle, Dave Hamaker.
[118] Dave Hamaker was a stock-holder in the Harrison State Bank as well as vice-president of the board.
[119] Earl Nation, October 1963---taped interview by Fred Hamaker.

Nation had a scalding vat[120] at his farm, the hog butchering was generally done there. Often a couple of 'beeves' would be butchered at the same time. During harvest season, the neighbors moved from field to field to complete the threshing. Ruth Hamaker Dyer described the event. [121]

Threshing machine crew, picture identified only as Sioux County threshing crew, 1912. Nation photo library.

"There was only one machine in the whole community. The owner started on his circuit and every neighbor traded work with enough other neighbors to assure himself a crew of 12 to 15 men. This took from two to four weeks for each farmer to pay back the threshing help. This began about the first of August and ran until sometime in September. I remember that Lauren Haworth owned the machine that served our community.[122]

The grain stood in the fields in shocks, unless the farmer happened to be on the last end of the run, and winter began creeping in too fast. Then the grain was hauled in and stacked in yellow igloos ready to be consumed by the machine. I remember my father's instructions for stacking. First we made a shock of bundles and built around and around it until it was as big as the base of the stack, with all the heads

---

[120] After a hog is slaughtered, it is dipped into a large vat filled with scalding hot water. The hair can then be easily scraped from the carcass.
[121] Ruth Hamaker Dyer, *Threshing*. Unpublished. Thelma Nation collection. The date the handwritten story was written and why is not clear. Thelma said Ruth, who was the daughter of Dave Hamaker, gave it to her, "when she was taking care of Mom." Ruth was Iva Nation's caregiver in 1967 when Iva lived in Chadron, NE.
[122] Ruth Hamaker Dyer, *Threshing*. Unpublished.

to the inside and the butts to the outside. We gradually built this stack in the same pattern until it was as high as they could toss the bundles. Always the heads to the inside and the stubble butts to the outside.

The "trap" wagon, loaded with stakes, horse powered sweeps, equalizing rods, sweep power braces, chains, oil, tools (which include 16 pound sledges) and awls the equipment came first. As they moved from farm to farm, this wagon's driver picked out the route across pasture and field which the outfit would follow, as there was seldom a road that would accommodate the heavy loads. Because of the weight of the machine which was more than two tons, and the power unit nearly as much, the trails they made lasted from year to year. The men took down the fences along the route and around the straw yard, making ready for the big red box-like machine, drawn by four horses pulled into place, ready for the setting. The setting of the straw carrier that looked like a great flat tail was unfolded and raised into position. The feeding platform was unhooked and dropped into place. The iron stakes were pounded into the ground to hold everything in place as the vibrations of the separation continued on, hour after hour.

Earl Nation was considered the best bundle wagon man on the outfit. He was usually the first man in with a load and by night had probably managed to get in one more load than any of the rest, or at his worst, be first in line for the new day with his wagon already loaded.

The men were not the only ones that were busy at threshing time. The women folk were busy, too. I can hear my mother say, "Now Dave, don't turn the chickens out 'til I catch some for dinner."

There were six to eight regulars who followed the machine then each farmer had to get extras to man the wagons, pitch the bundles and other jobs. This meant there would be from 12 to 15 men to feed and perhaps half as many to stay all night. The slept in the freshly threshed straw and were up at the bare glimmer of dawn, for there was much to be done, 10 to 15 teams to "wrangle" and harness, wagons and machinery to grease and breakfast to be eaten by sunrise at the latest. There were high stakes on a woman's reputation as a cook based on how she fed the threshers. One record that was set, which I don't not remember ever hearing was broken, was Fred Domey's 49 pancakes; he just couldn't hold the 50th one. Dinner was at noon and supper at sundown. Such food as we were expected to provide. A woman's reputation as a cook was based on how she fed the threshers. The stress was not on how it was served but WAS there enough and was it good?"[123]

Cooking for the threshing crew was just one of the many tasks Iva Nation performed on the farm. Regularly she tucked her dress into Earl's coveralls to do the "outside work": lambing ewes, feeding calves, or driving a team to the field. Although she didn't spend much time in the fields after Melvin was born, the older children said she could harness a team and guide them expertly to plant or harvest crops.

"Mama was a good hand with a team," Merlin Nation said. "She drove a team—both two-horse and four-horses many a mile. She could do it all. Mama was tough. The women out on that windblown ridge were either tough or they left."

Bluebell, a young mare that had been a wedding gift from Uncle Dave Hamaker, enhanced Iva's mobility. Early in their marriage, Earl built his young wife a small wagon that could be converted to a sled. She often saddled Bluebell, loaded her children into the sled/wagon and headed across the prairie to visit with Belle Hamaker or some of her other neighborhood friends. Merlin Nation said in the winter, his mother tucked a blanket around the sled riders and warned them to hang on. He said the excursions were "great fun."

Farming on the buffalo-grass covered plateau was generally not considered fun. It was difficult at best, but year after year, Earl hitched his team to a "four-bottom harrow" and dug furrows into acre-sized fields. The semi-arid landscape produced surprisingly strong crops of grains, but potatoes were the staple crop. The others were too susceptible to the caprices of the weather. Merlin Nation, Melvin's oldest brother, remembered watching one field of ripened grain disintegrate in less than an hour.

"We walked along the edge of the field. Dad tossed his Stetson out on the wheat. The stalk never even shivered. Dad told me that meant the field would yield good. He thought we'd cut it out the next day. About an hour later, the wind shifted. A hail storm boiled over the ridge. The hail beat that wheat into the ground and left the field looking like it had never been planted. It even beat Mama's cottonwoods into the ground. That was the day I started hating Nebraska."

"Many summer evenings, Dad would sit on the back steps watching storms that came over the ridge. He'd run his fingers back and forth along the arm of the rocking chair until grooves formed in the shape of his fingers. He'd sit there worryin' until the storm either passed us by or ran him inside," Melvin said. "I don't think anyone ever counted on the grain crops, but we generally had a good potato crop. We milked a whole herd of cows and sold the cream. We had chickens and turkeys. We survived. No one really thought about being rich or poor. We were in the same boat that our neighbors were."

---

[123] Dyer, Ruth Hamaker. *Threshing*. Unpublished document.

Thanksgiving gave the family a chance to celebrate their achievements—large and small. Melvin said he was about five the year he and his Dad were tasked with finding some fresh meat for dinner. He and his older sister had already carried a big pumpkin and a large bucket of potatoes in from the cellar. Fresh baked bread filled the house with its own very special aroma. Gooseberry pies, made from canned gooseberries, were waiting for their chance in the oven, but the family craved fresh meat after a long cold fall.

With his son bouncing along beside him, Earl headed for the canyons, an old ten-gauge shot gun cradled in the crook of his arm. He didn't have any shells that fit the gun, so he wrapped a twelve-gauge shell in paper so it wouldn't slip down into the barrel. The pair followed the jackrabbit tracks across the field and down into canyon. A few steps into the canyon, they spotted their prey. The long-eared rabbit was partially hidden by the snowy terrain, but Earl quietly inched closer and signaled for his son to wait while he took a shot. He aimed and fired. The old gun recoiled and barked into the stillness, knocking the man into the snow much to Melvin's delight. They'd killed the rabbit.

Many years later, when Melvin recalled the event, he said that rabbit killed with a twelve-gauge shell shot from a ten-gauge gun tasted better than any "boughten" turkey he'd ever eaten. "Dad let me give it to Mama. Really, I don't remember how it tasted; I just remember how proud I was when Mama brought it to the table."[124]

Potatoes were a staple on the family table, but they were also the family's main cash crop. In the fall, everyone helped pick potatoes, sort them for size, and pile them on large wagons for shipment to market. The dry-land crop seldom failed and brought good money at market. In the spring the potatoes were cut into quarters, an eye in each quarter, then they were planted in the fields for the next year's crop. It was hard back-breaking work, but Eva Nation Gray said there was a rivalry to see who could first pick to the end of their row first. By the time the younger children were born, Earl Nation was planting smaller crops of potatoes. Lakota Indians from Crawford were generally hired to complete the harvest, but Melvin and his younger sister, Mildred always helped prepare the seed potatoes for spring planting.

> Earl Nation, who lives northwest of town, just over in Sioux County, had the misfortune to lose his potato cellar, which burned down. There was considerable loss, among which was his automobile which had been driven into the cellar. They knew nothing about the fire until the next morning when they discovered that the cellar was completely distroyed.

Report of Merlin's car loss in the cellar fire. Crawford Tribune May 1, 1931.

"We climbed down into the big potato cellar where they kept the seed potatoes and cut them into pieces. We packed the pieces into gunny sacks for planting. We had a machine for planting

---

[124] A story about the "Jackrabbit Thanksgiving" was written by Moni Nation and published on the front page of the November 24, 1966 *Harrison Sun* newspaper.

the potatoes then. That made it easier," Mildred Nation Widel said.[125] "I can still remember the dark, earthy smell of that cellar and the taste of the sharp, crisp, red, Idaho potatoes. They were even good raw. After I was married I ate my first white potato. I never understood why anyone would eat those things. They didn't have any taste."[126]

In 1931, Merlin helped with the potato harvest then prepared to leave Nebraska for a job in Wyoming with his uncle, John Nation. Most of the potatoes had been sold; the rest were sorted for spring planting, leaving an empty area in the potato cellar. The night before his planned departure, Merlin parked his car inside the massive, mostly underground structure, to protect it from the cold. Apparently someone who knew the car was there tried to siphon the gasoline from the tank. The gas can ignited turning the cellar into an underground inferno. When the fire burned down the only clue identifying the culprit was a burnt glove and the charred gas can. A new cellar was built and potatoes were gathered from other growers for the next planting season. Merlin borrowed a friend's car and drove to Wyoming, but he said that he grieved for his automobile for most of his life.[127]

Merlin contended that his mother was so upset that he'd lost his car that she cried for hours. She knew that luxuries were hard to obtain.

"For years Mama only had two dresses," Melvin said. "One was a polka dotted thing that she wore to go to Meeting.[128] She thought it was cut too low, so she sewed a piece of black material in the front. She hated the dress, but Dad had bought it for her at Hartman's store in Marsland, so she wore it, probably for ten years. She made herself a dress out of flower sacks for every day. She'd wash it at night, then put it back on the next day. Mama pretty much deprived herself of everything so her kids would have what they needed."

Even as a child, Iva took pride in working hard. She continued the practice as a mother and wife. Melvin said he didn't remember seeing his mother shock grain, but his older siblings said she could shock as much grain as most men. He said he did see her milk cows, pick potatoes, and drive a four-horse hitch in the field, planting crops and even cultivating wheat and corn. However, Iva seemed to draw the line at driving machinery, including the family car.

On rare occasions, Iva, slowly and cautiously, drove the younger children to the bridge about a half mile from school. The children walked the rest of the three-mile trip. She also drove Melvin to Harrison so he could get his driver's license, or at least she drove once they reached the outskirts of town.

"She wasn't any more legal than I was," Melvin said, "I drove to Harrison, then she drove to the courthouse so I could take my test. I drove all the way home."

---

[125] Mildred Nation Widel, the youngest child of Earl and Iva Nation.
[126] Mildred Nation Widel. Personal Interviews by Moni Hourt, 1998, Hourt home, Crawford, NE.
[127] Nation, Merlin. Personal Interview by Moni Hourt, 1997, Merlin's home, Everett, Washington.
[128] The family called their church services "Meetings."

Nation said his father was a good man and a hard worker, but he didn't appreciate his mother like he should have. "There were times Mama never got to town for two or three years at a time. Dad would go, but Mama would stay home. Maybe she didn't want to go. She was very shy and not very comfortable around people, but I don't think Dad made it easy for her either. In later years, Dad really tried to take good care of Mama. But when we were growing up, everyone took her for granted. We'd all catch her crying sometimes. On the other hand, I don't think she was unhappy; she loved her kids. But she'd get lonesome for the pine trees and her family, and she didn't see much of either."

Betty Curtis Nation,[129] Clark Nation's wife, agreed that at times Iva's life was difficult. "Clark said once in a while the family would see Iva standing on the house balcony, crying quietly, looking east toward the Pine trees at Belmont. Earl and I respected each other, and we got along well, but he could have been kinder to Iva. She deserved that. I truly wish everyone could have had a mother-in-law like I had. She was the kindness, most unselfish, hard-working, women I ever knew. I truly loved her."

In the spring of 1949, Verna Callaham[130] and her family moved to a farm five miles from the Nation place. A few weeks later Verna was driving a tractor from one field to another when it flipped off the edge of a bridge and landed on top of her.[131] The 32-year-old was loaded in the undertaker's station wagon, the only vehicle capable of transporting a person with a broken back. When she was dismissed from the Crawford Hospital, Junior Houston, the undertaker, took her back to the farm. The doctor told her she'd never walk again. Every afternoon, Iva Nation drove her team to the Callaham farm house, to visit, help with the house work, or keep an eye on four-year-old Wilma.

"'Now dear, life is just what it is,'" Verna said Iva told her several times. "She kept telling me not to give up, that I could walk if I set my mind to it. One day when she came in the door to see me, I walked over to give her a hug. We were friends for the rest of her life."

Iva Nation often sang and whistled as she worked around the house. The songs, hymns or ditties she'd learned from her mother or grandmother, were passed on to her own children, but few lyrics or musical scores survived the passage of years.

"We never thought about writing them down," Mildred Nation Widel, said. "We were too busy growing up, and like most kids, we thought our mother would always be there."

Iva used flour and water glue to paste one of her favorite songs among the many clippings she glued into an old ledger. She also recorded the song, *Stay in Your Own Back Yard,* [132] a song

---

[129] Betty Curtis Nation. Personal Interview with Moni Hourt, 1999. Hourt home, Sioux County, NE.
[130] Verna's daughter, Thelma, eventually married Melvin Nation.
[131] *Crawford Tribune*. April 15, 1949 "Mrs. Elmer Callaham of Glen was admitted Wednesday, following an accident, when a tractor overturned with her. X-rays show a fractured pelvis….."
[132] Udall, Lyn/Kennett, Karl. "Stay in your own Back Yard," recorded by Dick Hyman and Arthur Pryor, 1899.

that certainly wouldn't be considered politically correct in the modern age, during her 55th wedding anniversary celebration.

At meal time, Iva's whistle became a utilitarian tool. She'd cup her hands together and whistle. Her children all remember that the whistle would carry across the farm, even reaching into the potato cellar.

"We knew better than to mess around," Elvin Nation said. "We'd all hustle to the house when Mom whistled."

Animals on the farm also responded to Iva's whistle: the cows would plod in for milking, the chickens would gather for their nightly grain, even the horses would trot out of the pasture and whinny at the gate waiting for her to stroke their soft muzzles, but the turkeys never seemed to care if they were fed or even survived. Shortly after Iva and Earl were married, Alice Hamaker gave her daughter a flock of chickens, geese, and turkeys. The chickens and geese flourished but Melvin said his mother never had much luck with her turkey flock.

"I think it was part our fault. We just couldn't let those old turkey hens alone. Turkeys are kinda flighty," Melvin said. "An old hen will set anywhere, and we'd always find their nests. We'd try to find out how many eggs she'd laid. The minute we'd start messing around, the old hen would leave her nest and often as not, never came back."

Disdain for the animals overpowered his guilt when he declared that "in truth" turkeys, weren't even smart enough to come out of the rain. "If we didn't get them into their pen, they'd just stand there with their heads up and drown, or they'd get chilled and die. Maybe it wasn't all our fault that they didn't do so good, but I guess we can take some of the blame."

Eggs produced by the turkeys, ducks, and geese were generally turned into quick, nutritious meals, but chicken eggs were important commodities that were often bartered and sold. Not all the eggs, however, found their way into egg cartons or into the isinglass[133] used to preserve them. Eggs made great ammunition.

Only a few of the chicken eggs became kid-propelled projectiles; the "half-rotten eggs" preferably large goose eggs were in more demand for the serious battles. Melvin said he and friend, Carroll Sample, launched a massive egg battle one afternoon, using any egg they could scrounge from the prairie. Then Melvin discovered the large goose egg—just itching to become a messy bomb.

"I warned him; I really did," Melvin laughed at the image that was still etched sharply in his memory. "I told him I had a "badwun." He took off and bailed over a bank. I let fly. He

---

[133] Isinglass was a gelatinous substance obtained from the swim bladders in fish. Dried then packaged and sold in small "tins," the isinglass had numerous uses. Before refrigeration was readily available, people often preserved eggs by pushing them into buckets or crocks that had been filled with the gelatinous solution that had been liquefied by adding it to water and heating it. Once cooled the isinglass became a white jelly substance that could preserve eggs up to six months. It was also used to clarify beer and wine.

wasn't fast enough. I can still see that egg smacking him in the back of the head. It exploded, shell flying, half-growed yolk and stringy white stuff runned down the back of his head and chunkied down his collar. I about died laughing."

The pair also liked to "suck" eggs, although they chose the fresh eggs for that endeavor. "One day he got started ahead of me. I got a glimpse of that slimy stuff slobbering across his lips," Melvin grimaced at the 70-year-old image. "That was the end of my egg sucking days. I always cooked mine after that."

Even the "funnest" activities were set aside at chore time. The family milked 10-12 cows, then sold the separated cream, sometimes by taking it to Glen to the train or to Crawford to one of the two creameries in town. If they weren't planning on a trip to town, they took the cream to the mail box and waited for the mailman, Oakley Edgell, to come by.

Mailmen in the region performed many more tasks than the US postal service decreed and often, as they made their long-lonely rounds, developed their own unique personalities. Opal Hanley,[134] who lived about 10 miles from the Nations, said their mailman helped rid the country of rattlesnakes— one snake at a time. She said the mailman really didn't hate rattlesnakes; he simply liked rattlesnake meat. He carried a forked stick and a gunny sack with him on his mail run. When he encountered a snake, he pinned it to the ground and popped it into the sack. That night he dined on "snake steak."

Edgell wasn't known for his snake catching prowess, but he was willing to haul cream-filled cream cans to Glen, the nearest post office. The next mail day, he returned the empty can, the cream money rattling inside. The income generated from the milk cows helped balance farming's inconsistent income. No one was "allowed" to shirk their milking duties. However, Anita Nation said her brother, Elvin, and her sister, Frances, were champion "milking time ditchers."

"They'd come down with 'cow diarrhea,'" Anita said.[135] "They'd go to the outhouse, and stay there as long as they could. The rest of us would be furious, but we never tattled on one another. That was our unspoken rule, but, oh, we wanted to tell on them."

Nation said his sister, Mildred, was also a "cow diarrhea" champion. He took revenge by spraying her with milk when she did come back to finish the chores.

None of the siblings remember exactly what actions led to the "boarding" incident, but those involved remembered the results.

"I'd pushed Nita's buttons just one time too many," Melvin said laughing at the memory. "She nailed me with a two-by-four. I fell on the ground, kicking and twitching, then I just quit breathing."

---

[134] Opal Hanley. Interview with Moni Hourt, 1993. Pink Schoolhouse. Opal and her family lived about 10 miles south of the Nation ranch. She said the mailman who loved snakes served the community for many years, often delivering the mail from a horse-drawn wagon.

[135] Anita Nation Robison. Recorded telephone interview by Moni Hourt, 2001.

"Nita fell on her knees beside him. She begged him to get up and swore that she'd never get mad at him again," Mildred grinned.

"I just couldn't hold my breath any longer. I started laughing. She about killed me." Melvin finished the story.

"I knew you were faking," Anita countered her younger siblings' story with a snort, then joined their laughter. Far into their 70s, when the Nation children gathered, there was laughter and eventually all of them would remember "Mama's reading."

"Mama would turn the wick up on the lamp and read to us," Melvin remembered. "She'd read magazine stories or pieces from the newspaper or lots of time a passage from the Bible. She didn't just say the words; she made them come alive. I think Dad enjoyed her reading almost more than we kids did."

Earl Nation was, according to his youngest son, totally self-educated. He was good at mental arithmetic, but Melvin said he doubted if his Dad had ever completely read a newspaper story. "In later years he read the Bible, but I think he'd heard Mama read it so many times that he had it memorized. What he did have though was toughness, what he always called 'intestinal fortitude'. My Dad wasn't much of one to give up."

Being financially viable took a great deal of "intestinal fortitude." Dave Hamaker told Earl that financial responsibility required "clean credit." Earl practiced the skill throughout his lifetime. When Ronald Smith wrestled his gasoline truck up the tangled roads to the Nation farm about once a month, he said he didn't worry about getting paid. There were no fuel or gas tanks on the farm, just jugs and buckets. Smith said Earl bought 15 gallons of gas or 10 to 15 gallons of tractor fuel at a time. He paid for it with cash from the "cream check" or from selling a hog. On rare occasion Earl would buy a "couple of barrels full" if he could afford it. Smith said he'd run the gas into five gallon cans then pour it into the barrels.[136]

"By the time I came along things were easier for my folks,[137]" Melvin said. "When I look back on it I realize they did pretty good. They raised a whole houseful of kids on two sections of land. None of us ever went hungry. That was a lot better than some could say."

---

[136] Ronald Smith. Interview with Moni Hourt, 1997, Smith home, Crawford, NE.
[137] Melvin was the second youngest of eight siblings, Edwin, Merlin, Clark, Elvin, Eva, Frances, Anita, Melvin, and Mildred.

In 1951, Earl and Iva Nation posed with their children and grandchildren for a family picture. Back: John Gray; Frances and Jack Roberts; Eva Gray; Lucille and Merlin Nation; Frances and Elvin Nation; Gordon, Betty, and Clark Nation; Thelma and Melvin Nation: Anita Nation; Mildred Nation; Middle: Joanne (Clark); Joyce (Merlin); David (Clark); Milton, Clark; Sheryl Lee. (a cousin) Front Row: Sheryl's sister, (a cousin); Louella Gray (Eva): Melody and Linda Nation (Elvin): Terrill Gray (Eva): Milton and Joyce Nation (Clark).

BUILDING A LIFE ON THE PRAIRIE

"My folks were tough. They had to be to survive, but that's the way all those old settlers were. If you weakened, you were done for." Melvin Nation

For the first nine years of their married life, the family lived in the sod house. In the spring of 1918, they constructed a new two-story wooden home shaped basically like the barn. A "house kit" one of many styles available, (Appendix 4) was ordered from the Montgomery Ward[138] catalog. Local carpenter, Clarence Jeanette, jig-sawed the pieces together. The new house perched atop a windswept hill, overlooked miles of flat grassland crisscrossed by shallow canyons.

The kit for the new house, finished in 1919, had a price tag of approximately $2000.

---

[138] Montgomery Ward, often called Montgomery Wards, or even Monkey Wards, provided goods of all types to consumers across the United States through catalog sales. The company was started in 1872 by Aaron Montgomery Ward, a traveling dry-goods salesman. He created a general merchandise mail-order catalog and promised satisfaction or "your money back." One of his main customers were the country's farmers and ranchers. The company closed in 2001 after 128 years in business.

With the help of several neighbors, Earl drilled a well, approximately 400-feet deep, to produce water for the farm. A windmill erected west of the house pumped a steady stream of water during some parts of the year, but the older children said they generally hauled water for both the stock and house use in the summer months. By the time Melvin was born another well had been drilled and a cement cistern was constructed around the well. It still dried up in the hot summer months, but not as regularly. Most of the time, water in the building provided cold drinks on a hot day and kept milk and cream cool until it could be taken to market.

"We never had an icebox in my life." Melvin Nation said. "We had a well-house where we kept everything cold. When I was in the 9th grade, about '45 or '46, we put in the new cistern. I did all the digging—or at least it felt like I did."

The cistern served as an icebox and a cold water dispenser. This picture taken about three years after the cistern was finished made a great backdrop for a three-generation picture. Earl and Iva Nation, Melvin Nation, and Melvin's baby son, Gary.

"The cistern was still full of water when I was small," Robbin Nation Oldaker[139] said. "They had a long-handled cup hanging in the well house. That water was so cold it hurt your teeth. I don't know why they quit using it. It was a wonderful place to go when we went down to visit Frances and Elvin."

Earl Nation planted the trees he'd brought from the Niobrara River inside the yard fence he built around the house. Iva watered the trees religiously, using her dish water and even the water left from her washing machine, but most never reached a height to shade the house effectively.

---

[139] Robbin was born in 1954, the second daughter of Melvin and Thelma Nation.

"They made it a good home. When Daddy built the new house, he piped water into it. Mama could pump water right into the bright and shiny white tin sink. It had a rubber drainboard, but Mama always wiped the dishes. She thought it was a great luxury, but she certainly enjoyed it. Eventually we even had an indoor toilet,"[140] Eva Nation Gray remembered with pride.[141]

The second floor included three bedrooms, two walk-in closets, and a dormer window. The main floor plan featured a kitchen, living room, bedroom, and later a bathroom. Large windows filled the main rooms with light. [142]A basement, poured with native gravel, stored canned goods: fruits, vegetables, and meat. Carbide lights and telephone service added modern touches. Within a few years, Earl Nation constructed a wind charger and installed one of the first electric light plants in the area.

For many years, Iva washed clothes on a wash board and later with a hand cranked Maytag. Earl added a gas motor to the Maytag, but it still didn't work very well. When the house was wired for 32-volt electricity, Earl bought his wife a new "washing machine," a modern Maytag from Midwest Hardware in Crawford.[143] Iva told him with mock seriousness that she didn't know what she'd do with all her spare time. Life was much easier.

From the time, Belle Hamaker, Dave's new wife, arrived on the Ridge in 1911, life became a little less worrisome for everyone, or at least a little less fearful. The Nation homestead was the first stop the new couple made after they arrived from Belle's home country of Canada. A registered nurse, Belle proved to be a valuable asset in the community. She prepared poultices[144] for chest colds, stitched hundreds of wounds, and served as a midwife to the local women, including Iva. She spent many hours at the Nation house, sometimes in an official capacity, but mostly as a valued visitor.[145]

"Belle was mostly our "Aunt Belle," Elvin Nation said, "but she sewed us up more than a couple of times, and of course, she delivered half of us kids."

Belle was in attendance when Eva, Elvin, Frances, and Anita were born. Elvin Nation was five when his sister Anita made her first appearance. He remembered clearly that the day

---

[140] Melvin Nation. Personal Interview, 2003. The bathroom and running water were added in 1944 according to Melvin Nation.
[141] Eva Nation Gray. Personal interview by Moni Hourt, 1997, Gray home, Chadron, NE.
[142] The windows' single-paned glass sections were covered with thick plastic in the winter to block the cold and the wind.
[143] "Spud Items." *Harrison Sun*. February 3, 1928. In this section of the "Spud Items" it was reported that "The Midwest Hardware Maytag salesman placed a new machine in the Earl Nation home on Thursday."
[144] Poultices are soft, moist materials, often made of flour or plant material like herbs, that are applied to the body to relieve soreness and inflammation. Thelma Nation remembered poultices of wool cloth soaked in camphor, *Vicks Vapor Rub*, created in 1894 and renamed *Vick's Magic Croup Salve* in 1905. She said she was allergic to wool, so the whole mess always "itched terribly," but they alleviated her cough.
[145] Hannah Belle's daughter, Ruth Hamaker Dyer, became a nurse, as did her granddaughter-in-law, Ruth Geiser Hamaker, and her great-granddaughters, Tessa, Tonya, and Tracy Hamaker.

was extremely cold and his aunt Belle's breath looked like smoke when she told him there was going to be a new baby in the house. He said he was very confused about the baby's whereabouts.

"There was a big door between the large main sections of the house. That way one part could be closed off when it was really cold outside. The house had a large wood burning stove, so even when the wind blew it wasn't too cold," Eva Nation Gray said. "I can remember Aunt Belle coming across the wooden floor the day Nita was born and opening the doors to the living room to tell us kids we had a new sister. Mama hadn't made one sound, so we hadn't even known what was going on."[146]

"Belle opened the doors and Mama said, 'Now don't be scared now. Come in and see your new baby sister.' I sure did. I really wanted to see that baby," Elvin Nation said. "Our friends were there and their son hid under a chair. Not me. I wanted to get acquainted right away."[147]

Melvin said his childhood, like those of his siblings, was filled with great memories, and good friends, but he also admitted he often felt like an outcast in his community. He attributed his feeling of alienation to the religion his parents adopted in 1915. That summer, John Doak and Will Wilkie literally walked their belief of a gospel based on a strict interpretation of the *New Testament of the King James Bible* into the Spud Ridge community.

"One of the greatest things that happened to us was when the "Truth" came to our house. We accepted its message for our home and for our lives," Earl Nation said.[148] "It opened our eyes and let us know what we were living for."

The religion was established by William Irvine in 1897-99 in Ireland.[149] Doak's Brother, Hugh, brought the religion to Nebraska from Canada in 1907. Wilkie's brother, Frank, became a major force in spreading the religion throughout other sections of the Midwest. Often known as "The Truth" or the "Black Stockings" it does not have an official name even in the 21st century. Believers still hold their services, called "Meetings" in local homes or in vacant schoolrooms. When "workers" were visiting the community they conducted the service, otherwise the services were conducted by those in attendance. Members of the congregation followed strict tenets, including a dress code that demanded short hair and high-buttoned, long-sleeved, shirts for the men. Women were expected to dress modestly, and most female members still wear dresses and stockings. Their uncut hair is worn in a bun or "French roll." Those practicing the religion follow a strict interpretation of the Bible. They do not dance or listen to the radio or television and do not celebrate any organized holidays.

---

[146] Belle Hamaker's services, as both a nurse and a midwife were greatly appreciated especially by the women in the area.
[147] Elvin Nation. Personal interview by Moni Hourt, 1997, Elvin Nation home, Everett, Washington.
[148] Earl Nation. Personal interview by Jack Roberts, October, 1959.
[149] Telling the Truth.info. First Missions–America. "The Gospel Comes to Nebraska, 1907." February 26, 2011.

Iva said many times that she hated to have her picture taken, but she agreed to several family photography sessions including this one in about 1940 shortly before Elvin left for the service. Pictured: (back) Betty and Clark Nation, Elvin Nation, Eva, Anita, Merlin and his wife, Lucille, Frances. (front) Mildred, Joanne, Milton, and Dave. Joanne and Dave are the children of Clark and Betty; Milton is the son of Lucille and Merlin. Melvin is on the far right in the front.

Children are expected to adhere to the rules without question. The Workers who direct most activities, do not accept donations or salaries and depend on their congregation to supply their needs.[150]

"Few people in our area belonged to the religion. Mama was often ridiculed because she wore dark socks and pinned her hair up," Melvin said. "But I'll tell you this much, My Mother and Dad lived that religion. It wasn't just a Sunday deal with them. They joined the religion because they believed what these men said. We were expected to follow their lead. It was a tough ole' road for me to follow."

Since it was the Religion's concept that no one knew the exact day Christ was born, the Workers preached that it was wrong to celebrate the "fictitious event." Melvin found the Religion's renunciation of Christmas particularly irritating.

---

[150] Ibid.

"I think they were a little narrow minded about Christmas," Melvin said with a shake of his head. "No one knows when Jesus was born, but December 25 was as good a day as any to celebrate the fact that he was born. Rejecting Christmas put us at odds with about everyone."

Mildred Nation Widel[151] said she convinced her parents to erect a Christmas tree in their living room one year. She even "played an angel" in one of the school plays, but she said neither event "felt right." She did, however, present Christmas programs during her tenure as a rural school teacher.

"Most of the other kids handled it better than I did. But I packed a chip on my shoulder for years, because of the way people treated us over the religion," Melvin admitted. "My family was clannish. We spent Sundays together. We celebrated the New Year and Thanksgiving with big get-togethers. We cared for each other; we really did, and I loved my family. But I have few good memories about school or the kids in our community, or even the community, as far as that goes. And most of that was because of the religion."

Frances Nation Roberts, six years older than Melvin also struggled to accept the religion and rebelled against the requirements. During their walk to school, she regularly ducked under the bridge a short distance from school. She discarded her stockings, unpinned her hair, and applied a splash of makeup and lipstick. She reversed the procedures on the way home.[152]

Other members of the family embraced the religion. After their marriage, Mildred and her husband, Raymond Widel, constructed a large conference center on their Missouri farm. Many believers from across the country, as many as 600 at a time, attended the bi-yearly gatherings at the Widel farm. Anita, Eva, and Merlin and part of their families also followed the religion throughout their lifetimes.

"If we were at Granddad's house on Wednesday night or Sunday, we attended Meeting, but no one ever shoved it down our throats," Melody Nation[153] said. "I don't remember much about it, except that the girls[154] sang at the top of their lungs—and they sang really, really, bad."

---

[151] Ibid.
[152] Frances Nation Roberts. Personal Interview with Moni Hourt, 1996, Roberts' home, Crawford, NE. Neither Elvin, Clark, Melvin, or Frances ever joined the religion. The other four siblings became dedicated members and stayed that way their entire lives.
[153] Melody Nation. Interview with Moni Hourt in 2005, Hourt home, Crawford, NE. Born in 1947, she was the second daughter of Elvin and Frances Nation.
[154] Anita and Eva always attended the Meetings at the Nation house. Sometimes Mildred was also in attendance.

Eva Gray, Frances Roberts, Mildred Widel, and Anita Robison. All the girls in the family practiced the Religion throughout their lives except Frances.

SCHOOL DAYS—THE NOT SO, "DEAR OLD GOLDEN RULE DAYS"

"There were three teachers that made school tolerable for me. They didn't make me feel like I was a dummy. But most of the time I hated school, or I thought I did anyway." Melvin Nation

District #51, later known as the Hillview School, was petitioned in November 1907, a year before the Nations arrived in the community. According to Sioux County Historical Society information, the school located on "Spud Ridge" southwest of Glen, Nebraska, occupied the east half of T29 R54, east of No. 53. (Township 29, Range 54, East of the 53rd meridian.)[155] A frame structure replaced the original sod school building. In 1934, the building which was three miles southeast of the Nation farm, was enlarged. It was moved to its current location three miles almost straight east of the Nation farm in the late 30s. The building was flanked by its requisite outhouses.

By the time Melvin enrolled as a student, a shed was built behind the schoolhouse to house the horses that transported the young scholars to their "house of learning." Melvin said the horses generally ate "post hay." Although a windmill was erected after the school was moved, in the early days of its

Taken when Melvin was about five, this picture was found inside Iva's scrap book

---

[155] According to a Nebraska geography website, http://geography.about.com/library, a township is both a square six miles long on each side as well as the method to locate the north-south (horizontal) row from the base line where the township lies. Ranges are rows of townships east or west of the meridian. Each 36 square-mile township is divided into 36 square-mile "sections." A section is made of 640 acres. Under the Land Ordinance of 1785, section 16 of each township was set aside for school purposes. Section 36 was also added as a school section in the western states.

existence, a well didn't exist on the school grounds. Teachers were expected to bring drinking water from their living quarters. At lunch time, water was poured into a wash basin. Students all shared the same water and the same towel. "You wanted to be one of the first to wash-up," Melvin said with a grin. "The water was pretty black by the time the last kid was done."

Melvin attended District 51, the Hillview school about three miles east of the Nation farm. He was a seventh grader in 1943 when this picture was taken. Photo: Courtesy Sioux County Museum

A column in The Harrison Sun *called* "Our Country School" several teachers discussed activities at District 51. Before Melvin started school in 1922, the roof blew off the building, "No one was hurt, but they were all pretty scared." In 1941, Mrs. Goldie Hamaker announced that there were 13 students in school including Melvin Nation and Vera Lanz in the sixth grade. She said they also have new world maps and that one of the students made a map of roads in the district. Another report said the student had given a reading demonstration to parents. In 1942, the report said Vera Lantz was riding her bike to school while Melvin and Mildred Nation rode their horses. Another article declared that Melvin Nation had won the arithmetic contest that day.[156] There is no proof, as Melvin claimed, that he tallied the largest words in the "bad English" box several weeks in a row. One of his teachers suggested that the words were used on purpose.

According to former teacher, Juanita Phipps,[157] school was too easy for Melvin. "He was bored and quite a rounder, because he just didn't have enough to do. He needed more to keep that sharp little mind of his busy. I gave him twice as much work as I did most of my students."

During the eight years that he attended District 51, Melvin said he liked and respected three teachers. Phipps was one of them. She brought books of many types to school for him to read and took the time to listen to what he had to say. His eighth grade teacher, Swede (Kathryn) Corbin also seemed to understand who he was. A Valentine Day card that she sent to him was pasted in his mother's scrapbook with the label, "To Melvin from his favorite teacher."

Helen Koenig, his fifth grade teacher also made the short-list of favorite teachers. She spent recesses and noon teaching him to construct kites from newspapers[158] and carefully honed willow twigs. Koenig often boarded with the Nation family. Many evenings were spent flying handmade kites or building other projects including suspension bridges. Melvin said Koenig was what was known today as a "hands on" type of teacher.

"I learned from Helen Koenig too. I was good in arithmetic and history and geography. I read everything I could get my hands one. *Call of the Wild* was one of my favorite books. I read it a dozen times. Every Friday, I'd read the *Weekly Reader* from one cover to the other. My big problem was that I was busy fighting everyone around me," Melvin said. "The one friend I had in school was Vera Lantz, although she did get me one of the worst beatings I ever had."

"I loved Melvin; I really did," Vera Lantz Leeling[159] said in a 1998 interview. "He had the most beautiful blue eyes. No one ever picked on me. Melvin wouldn't allow it; but—he wasn't above pulling a trick or two."

Vera's long braids hung down her back often trespassing on Melvin's desk located directly behind hers. He tugged the braids on a regular basis and even skewered them to the desktop with his jackknife. One afternoon, the then second-grader dipped Vera's errant braids into his inkwell. Unaware of her inked braid tips, Vera flipped her hair back over her shoulders scattering ink across her desktop. When the teacher realized the ink's source she jerked

---

[156] "Our Country School," *Harrison Sun*. Various dates: January, 1922, September 1932, September 1941, November 1942, March 1938, May 1937.
[157] Juanita Phipps. Personal telephone interview with Moni Hourt, 1997. Melvin said teachers often left the school during the year. He said Phipps would come in and teach when, "We'd run out of teachers that put up with us."
[158] Melvin said his favorite construction material was the Sunday funnies with their patterned cartoons.
[159] Vera was the daughter of Myrtle (Reynolds) Lantz and Edward (Blackie) Lantz. Melvin considered Blackie a top horseman in the region. Interview at Leeling home, Harrison, NE.

Melvin from his desk and dragged him down the basement stairs where she proceeded to whip him with a piece of stove wood. Winded she tossed the wood aside and headed back up the basement stairs. Melvin picked up the splintering piece of stove wood and flung it at her receding legs.

"I can still see the splinters catch in her nylons[160] and hang there dangling from the back of her leg," Melvin said. "She whirled and down the stairs she come. She slapped and kicked and stomped me. I thought she was going to kill me, but she didn't. Vera cried all afternoon. I didn't bawl at all."

Another teacher ordered Melvin to stay in his seat. He got up. "She came over the top of that seat and was boxing my ears. Two of the other older boys got in a fight—I know just to save my life. She got off me and went over there just slapping and beating on them. School, at least some of it, was quite a journey."

Several teachers at District 51 ordered "rebellious" students to the schoolroom corner. Melvin said the schoolroom's walls were covered in calcimine.[161] When he made his inevitable trips to the corner, he stood with his face against the wall and licked circles in the calcimine. "You could see how much I growed by the holes were in the wall. If you go to that building now and check out the northeast corner, I'll bet those holes would still be there."[162]

Children from one large area family filled eight seats in the school room. Melvin said all were exceptionally intelligent. During science class one morning, the teacher asked Melvin how many days were in a year. A fourth grader, he confidently answered, "365 days." The precocious family's first-grader piped up and said he hated to dispute Melvin's word, but there were actually 365 and a fourth-days in a year.

The oldest member of the "family intelligentsia" consistently bullied smaller students. Melvin, six years younger, became a frequent target. One afternoon Melvin said he was able to "get the trip" on the boy. "He fell on the ground. I jumped right in the middle of him and was slappin' his face from one side to the other. I was just a little guy, but I was mad and stubborn. I looked down. He had the most pitiful look on his face. I got up off of him and helped him get up. That was the end of the bullying."

---

[160] Silk stockings were available in the 1934 Sears Catalog. They came in two thicknesses, at a cost of .98 for a heavy service weight pair and .66 for the lighter. They were easily snagged which resulted in a "run" that snaked the full length of the leg. Stocking made of "nylon" were released for sale in 1939. They were sturdier, but still prone to "runs." Getting "a run" in a nylon generally negated its "sophistication" quality but the market was still very strong. On May 16, 1940, "Nylon Day," four million pair of nylons were sold in the United States for $1.50 a pair. When asked whether he'd ruined the teacher's nylon with his wood toss, Melvin always smiled and said, "I sure as hell hope I did."
[161] Calcimine was a white or tinted wash made of glue, whiting or zinc white. After it was mixed with water it was applied to plastered surfaces.
[162] By 2000, the northeast corner of the building was masked by a closet, but close examination, revealed a line of ragged holes marching up the wall behind the mops and brooms.

There wasn't much extra money, but Melvin said he never considered himself deprived. School lunches, packed in empty Karo Syrup cans, consisted of whatever was on hand. Favorites were biscuits with honey or leftover pancakes spread with butter and sugar. When the weather chilled, the children donned mittens that Iva constructed of worn quilts. The children seldom wore shoes in the summer time, but new shoes were purchased at the beginning of every school year.

Iva generally ordered the family's new shoes from the Montgomery Ward catalog. Two days before the start of his seventh grade year, Melvin rode down to the mail box. Sure enough, a long box leaned against the mailbox frame. Upon opening the box, he discovered a pair of black and white tennis shoes—size 13. He wore a 7.

"I thought it was the funniest thing I ever seen," Melvin said. "But poor Mama she just sat down and cried. I didn't have nothing to wear to school for the first few days until she could get a return on those shoes. I remember hiding my feet under the seat. It didn't hurt me to go to school without shoes. It just humiliated me, falsely so, but it did. I hadn't learned yet that most of the time, life was what you made it."

MY FRIEND MIDGEY

> "My sister, Mildred and I were good friends all of our lives. We had each other's backs long before anyone ever used that term. We were wild little heathens, but we stuck together."
>
> Melvin Nation

Although Vera Lantz was a great friend, Melvin's best friend in and out of the schoolroom, was his younger sister, Mildred, or Midgey.

"I had few friends outside of my sister, Mildred. She was a true friend. She was a bit fictitious, and conned anyone she wanted to, but she had a good personality and could really ride a horse. We played and fought together. She was as tough as I was. Almost every day we'd race our horses all the way to school, then we'd race them home again. We have been good friends all our lives," Melvin said in 2002.

Mildred[163] said her brother's antics often scared her to death. "We were headed home from school one afternoon right after Christmas. The teacher had thrown the Christmas tree into the ditch. Melvin convinced Jerry Witt to tie a rope on the tree and give him a ride. Well that tree flipped and flopped and Melvin, he just hung on. But the tree started bouncing up and down hitting Jerry's horse in the legs. The horse ran away kicking and bucking. Finally, Melvin rolled off the tree. Jerry hit the ground. The tree popped and hopped behind the horse

Melvin and Mildred about 1934.

---

[163] Mildred married Raymond Widel in 1953.

until it came loose. Melvin was all skinned up, but I don't remember Mama and Daddy asking us what happened. Maybe they were used to Melvin getting banged up."

The pair rode everywhere they went: generally bareback. Melvin said they rode like "Indians." When one of them got into trouble—both did—generally. Shared-trouble wasn't technically true after the incident of the "domiciled" goat, but trouble was still the result.

Years later, when the pair discussed the goat incident, they agreed that Melvin's temper may have caused it. On the other hand, John Peck had insulted Earl Nation—within earshot. Revenge was obviously necessary. The Nation children passed the Peck's house on the way to school. The day the Peck's car was not parked in his driveway, they took action. Mildred was appointed the get-away woman, or maybe more correctly, the horse-holding woman. Melvin dashed to the homestead, snagged the neighbor's goat and shoved him through the living room door. Then the pair departed in a cloud of dust—escaping undetected.

"The next morning I heard Mr. Peck screaming at my Dad saying that his brats put his goat in the house. I knew we were in trouble," Mildred Widel said. "Daddy yelled for us to come outside. Melvin didn't mention the insulting. He swore I wasn't involved, but Dad glared at both of us anyway. Mr. Peck stormed away muttering about disrespectful kids. Mama and I went with Melvin and spent all afternoon cleaning Mrs. P's house which was dirty even before the goat got in."[164]

Sometimes the pair's sense of outrage and vengeance originated closer to home. Melvin and Mildred raised rabbits. The baby rabbits created a great bunch of playmates. One night a cat sneaked into the cage and killed most of the babies.

"We probably left the damn door ajar, but that didn't matter. We went on a cat hunt," Melvin said. "We finally ketched this one old cat and tried to cut his head off. That was impossible. We wasn't big enough to hold him down and still swing the ax. So, I stuffed him in an old carbide can, dug me a hole down the bank, and buried him. I probably would have dug him up when I got over my mad, but my brother Elvin came along and heard the cat. He kicked my rear end and made me dig the cat up and turn him loose. It wasn't too long when a hawk came along and killed that ole cat. I didn't shed any tears. The damn Elvin called me "Cat Killer" after that, particularly if there was a young good-looking girl around."

The horse incident a few years later resulted in a reciprocal nickname that Melvin could throw back at his older brother. Shortly after he returned from World War II, Elvin decided to ride one of Melvin's young horses. Melvin didn't want anyone messing with his horses, but by the time he saw Elvin running the horse across the prairie, it was too late to mount a battle. The big brown horse had already launched his own fight. He "took his head" and dived over the hillside, slipping and sliding on the cow trails below. Elvin did his best to stay in the middle. Finally, he rode the horse up to where Melvin was working. He'd lost a spur and was

---

[164] Mildred Widel, interview with Moni Hourt, 1997, Hourt home.

decidedly irritated. He told Melvin to take his "damn horse." He said he wasn't gonna ride the idiot one step further.

Elvin left the horse in the pasture and walked home. For the rest of their childhood, Melvin who believed his brother ran a horse unnecessarily called his brother, "Horse Killer."

Even the daily trips to school created adventures. "Melvin's little Champ horse, an Arabian he was breaking to ride, was fast and ornery," Mildred remembered. "I rode Bud because he wasn't too ornery. Melvin's horse bucked him off that morning. His foot caught in the stirrup. Champ took off on a dead run. I can still see my brother's head hitting the ground. I whipped Bud up, and finally got even with him and grabbed those flopping reins. About the same time Melvin's foot popped out of the stirrup. I was terribly frightened that I had lost my dear brother, but I didn't."[165]

Mildred and Melvin and Anita in 1947.

Melvin and Mildred's activities were generally quieter than chasing cats and goats or conducting horse races or even producing nicknames. They gathered bones to create animals to populate their "bone farms." They gathered their mother's empty thread spools, and using

---

[165] Ibid

Melvin's one-bladed jackknife, whittled them into "tires," which were attached to match-stick axles. The match boxes created tractors that buzzed around the farms that featured bent-twig fences and discarded sickle auto-gates.

The pair rode nearly nine miles to the "Stiller Farm"[166] to gather pigeons that were transported back to the Nation farm and released. The children loved the sound of the cooing pigeons and celebrated their accomplishment. Their father wasn't so sure the pigeons and their frequent bathroom breaks were a great addition to the farmstead.[167]

"My brother was my friend, that's all." Mildred said in 2001. "He just was."

---

[166] Vaclav and Bozena Stiller came from Czechoslovakia to homestead in Nebraska. Their daughter Beatrice was married to Clyde Hizer, one of Melvin's close friends.
[167] Mildred Nation Widel. Personal Interview by Moni Hourt 2001. Hourt home, Sioux County, Nebraska.

DOING IT MY WAY

"I had quite a temper, and I'm sure I was a tough one to manage. My folks must've wanted to give up on me more than once, but they didn't. They also seemed to understand that I was better when I was horseback, so they just turned me loose."

Melvin Nation

Melvin, about 18.

Nothing, certainly not a touch of danger, deterred Melvin's horseback escapades. He said from the time he was little he'd slip away from the farm, climb on a horse, and head across the prairie. There were few trees in the region and fences, abundant across the area, were built with let-downs,[168] so women and subsequently young boys, could easily open them. Melvin had access to hundreds of acres. With a homestead located on nearly every section of land, there were also plenty of people to visit.

One of the few whippings he remembered came because of his meanderings. He was assigned—before the threshers arrived—to shock grain. However, a group of kids rode across the farm on their mission of selling *Cloverine Salve*.[169] They asked Melvin if he wanted to ride along. It was a great excuse to quit the field and the grain shocks. He didn't return to the farmstead until well after dark. When he rode into the corral, he could see his father's shadow sliding past the corner of the barn. He ignored the shadow, unsaddled his horse, and made sure it was fed and watered.

"When I came out the door, Dad grabbed me." Melvin remembered. "He had a strap in his hand. He went to whipping. He had me just by one arm, and he was catching me a little bit with that strap as I ran around him. We had us an old dog around there. We called him Jack. Old Jack jumped up in the middle of Dad's back."

Earl Nation whirled and knocked the dog off his back, but the dog took the rejection as an invitation to play and ran around the pair barking and sparring. That was the end of the whipping.

Melvin said the only whipping he ever received from his mother also came because he wanted to ride instead of do his chores. His mother sent him to the woodpile to get wood for the wood burning stove. He sneaked away to the barn. His mother was waiting when he returned. She finished her whipping.

One early morning ride ended at his Uncle Carl and Aunt Rose[170] Hamaker's homestead. Rose was happier than usual to see him. Someone had failed to close the gate to the milk cow pasture, and her milk cows had escaped into a large field. She asked her young nephew if he'd

---

[168] "Let downs" were constructed between posts centered on a fence line. Instead of staples being fastened solid to those fence posts, two staples were nailed side by side in the region where a single staple generally sufficed to hold the wire. A third staple was placed over the loose wire and stuck between the two staples to hold it in place. When someone wanted to let the fence down, they simply removed the single staples, pulled the wire free of the double staple brad and pushed the wires to the bottom of the fence. Then a rider or a car could step or drive over the fence. It was a great innovation in an area where fences often surrounded every section or even quarter-section of land.
[169] George Wilson developed a unique marketing system: recruiting children to sell *White Cloverine Brand Salve* door-to-door. The children actually didn't get any money for the sales; adults in charge of the program received the money. The children received points that could be traded for prizes. The prizes included yo-yos, dolls, baseball gloves, "Daisy" air rifles, "Radio Flyer" wagons, and bicycles. In 1967, the Federal Trade Commission decided that the company was exploiting the young salesmen and women.
[170] Rose was married to Iva's brother, Carl.

please gather her cows and bring them in to be milked. He readily complied, then helped her milk the cows.

"The milk was just running out of the cows. It took us quite a while to milk them. When we got done, she dug around and found a dime and gave it to me. I didn't want to take it, but she insisted. That was the first money I ever had," Melvin took the money home and placed it on a shelf in his parents' room. One day when he went to "check on it," it had disappeared.

The quarter he received from Press Wilson, a family friend who previously lived near the Nation homestead, effectively made it into the marketplace. Wilson established a business in Crawford in the early 1930s.

Fountain at the Crawford City Park. In 2015, shortly before his death,
Joe Hourt, restored the Crawford fountain that Melvin had eaten his lunch.
Photo: Crawford Historical Society

He was continually helping kids in his new community, but he was partial to the children from his former neighborhood. During one of Melvin's visit to his business, Wilson gave the little boy a quarter. Melvin walked to the local grocery store and after examining most of the goods on the shelves bought a large sack of "weenies"—a quarter's worth. He walked to the Crawford City Park and sat on the bench. While he ate the hot dogs he said he watched the water splashing against the sides of the fountain fascinated by the controlled motion of the cosseted water. He washed his lunch down with a drink from the fountain, then after a walk around the beautifully manicured park decided he'd sit down and eat a few more bites. By the time he met his Dad at the center of town, his hot dogs were gone.[171]

---

[171] Throughout his life Melvin loved "weenies" and often carried them with him in a cooler for a quick meal. Sometimes he was even known to stash them under his pickup seat.

Money was never easy to come by, but Melvin's folks did their best to make sure he had some spending money when he went to town. "We were all loaded up to go into town one morning, when Mom handed me an old fat hen," Melvin said. "I took her to the Fairmont Creamery and sold her for 25 cents. Then I went into the *Five and Dime Cents Store* and bought a little orange car with headlights on it. To my knowledge it was the only "boughten" toy I ever had. I'd play with that car by the hours."

The little yellow car with its bright, shining headlights was a fascinating addition to Melvin's fleet of homemade vehicles. It ranked even higher than the iron wagon his father brought home from a local farm sale. The little car certainly lasted a lot longer than the wagon. The day after Earl Nation brought the wagon home, Melvin's brother, Elvin "borrowed" it for a careening journey down a canyon's sloping side. When the wagon hit bottom, all four wheels popped loose, and one of the sides crumpled under the pressure. The car fared better and was a cherished possession for years. Eventually when he thought he'd outgrown it gave it to his oldest niece.

Even without spending money in his pocket, the trip to Crawford, 18 miles northeast of the farm, was always an "adventure." The road snaked down Cork Screw Canyon a rough and tumble path lined with pines and paralleled by steep canyons. The journey threaded through the Fort Robinson military base located between Glen, Nebraska, and Crawford.

Although Melvin never remembers watching a polo match at Fort Robinson, his older brother, Merlin, said he and some friends watched at least one. Bill Coffee and Marvin Rising participated in the matches at Fort Robinson.
Photo: Howard Dodd

The guard-lined highway was flanked by pens full of horses, sometimes as many as 3,000. Travelers often stopped just past the Fort to watch polo players practice their skills, or train for various military maneuvers. Between 1935 and 1939 the US Olympic equestrian team trained at the Fort. Five of the horses chosen for the 1940 Olympic team were from Fort Robinson. Unfortunately, the Olympic games in Tokyo were canceled in 1940.

During World War II, Cavalry troops filled the parade grounds as they prepared to ship out for war. On one occasion, Melvin remembered watching the gliders and small planes taking off and landing at the airfield west of the Fort. He said his father told him that one day the guards shoved everyone quickly through the Fort, but not before he heard canon explosions bouncing off the nearby butte as they practiced their shooting skills.

By the time he was 11 Melvin was making his own "town" money doing what he loved most—riding horses. "I never saw a boy as good with a horse as my brother, Edgar was," Earl Nation said in a 1959 interview.[172] "He could walk out and catch a horse when no one else could, and he could ride anything. Melvin was like that."

A member of the US Olympic Equestrian team practices for the 1940 Tokyo Olympics.
An exhibition at the Fort drew nearly 4000 spectators.
Photo: Howard Dodd

---

[172] From a personal taped interview with Fred Hamaker, 1959.

"If you couldn't ride a horse or use a team, you weren't gonna get much done," Melvin said. He added that he knew his Dad rode for a "big cow outfit" in Wyoming, even though he didn't ride much in later years. Merlin "could ride the hair off a horse," but Clark and Elvin never did ride much except out of necessity. However, according to his estimation, the men in his family were all better teamsters than he was.

"I never was good with a team." Melvin looked disgusted with the memory. "I drove horses a lot, but I could never get it into my thick head that I had to take hold of a horse's mouth and let them pull into it like you have to do to drive a team of horses. Put me on a team of horses, and I couldn't drive a straight row to fit my soul. I wanted to be a horseback."

Since Earl Nation insisted that his children ride bareback, Melvin mastered the skill. Mounting was accomplished by wedging a toe against the chestnut on a horse's leg, jumping and snatching the mane, and scrambling quickly onto a horses back. When he was seven, Melvin broke his first horse, a little brown mare his brother gave him. He admitted the mare's primary skill was chasing coyotes.

"That little ole mare loved to run those coyotes down. If the coyote went under the fence, she'd go over it. We'd be runnin' hard; she'd gather herself up and over it she'd go. One afternoon, she tripped and fell right on top of the coyote. She smashed him dead. She got to her feet and shook her head. She seemed a little confused that the coyote had quit running. I grabbed her mane and jumped on her back. Away we went to find another one. I called the little mare Midgey. She could give those coyotes a bad run if she had any room at all. She could scatter, but by the time I was 11, I outgrowed her. I sold her to Ed Franey for 25 dollars. That was a lot of money at the time."

He used the money from the first horse sale to buy his first pair of "Levis," and tossed the bib "overalls" that he always hated in the trash. A few months later his Dad gave him his first set of leather gloves. Early that morning the pair moved three carloads of cattle to the railhead at Glen, Nebraska. The crew that joined them bedded the cattle down at a farm on the outskirts of the village. The next morning, they trailed them to the livestock pens at the depot. A neighbor took his father on into Crawford to take care of business. When he returned Earl Nation handed his son a pair of leather gloves, size "8."

"Didn't say anything, just handed me the gloves. I never wore them," Melvin said. "I packed them around in my pocket until I lost one of them, then I set the other one up. I was proud of those gloves. I just didn't want to wear them out."

Once in a while, Earl Nation rode with his load of cattle from Glen to Omaha to the cattle sale and would generally bring back dry goods or even clothing on the return trip. During one trip he bought a bolt of material to make dresses for his family—all of the same pattern and design. The saddle he purchased in 1941 at a local farm sale was much more exclusive.

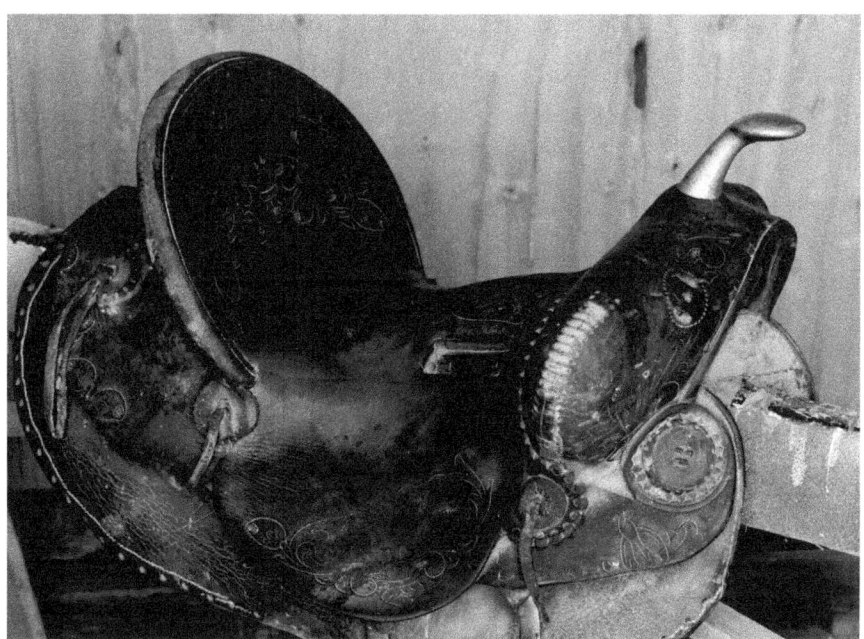

Although well-worn, Melvin's Coggshall saddle still features its distinctive Miles City Saddle Company stamp.

Earl paid $35 for the Coggshall saddle built by the Miles City Saddle Co. in Miles City, Montana. Melvin said it was worth every penny. "The saddle had big wide swells, a high cantle back, and a silver horn. When I was 14 years old, I didn't think there was anything in the world that could buck me off, not if I was sittin' in that saddle."

The saddle was seldom without a horse beneath it, but there were times that "saddling and deal making" took a detour. Shortly after selling the little brown mare, Melvin acquired another mare from his Uncle Paul Hamaker. He said the mare was a "snorty little thing." Earl Nation didn't think his son could ride her, so Melvin agreed to trade her to his brother, Clark, for a team of grey horses.

"Then that Clark slips around and he says, 'I'll give you a bicycle if you'll break that black mare to ride for me.' So I ended up breaking the mare anyway. Clark gave me a bicycle, then came back a year later and took it for his daughter, JoAnne. I ended up killing one of the grey team when he broke a leg," Melvin grinned. "Some of my horse deals worked better than others."

Horses were generally more reliable that their mechanical counterparts. Earl Nation bought a Plymouth in 1939. The car replaced the family's 1937 Whippet that Melvin said was generally pulled around with a team of white horses. But even the most modern vehicles didn't make much of an impression on the young man.

"There ain't much doubt that I pretty much always preferred a horse to an automobile. One morning brother Clark showed up with his; the trip that followed didn't impress me much."

After getting into a fight with his parents, Clark left Spud Ridge when Melvin was three years. "I remember seeing him ride away on a big white horse,[173] or I think I do. Later, it seemed like years, Dad finally found out where he was. We went out to visit him. Poor Mama got so sick going over the mountains, but she needed to see that Clark was still alive. We found him out in a hayfield on the farm where he was working in Greybull, Wyoming. I didn't remember very much more about Clark until my sister Frances got sick."

Ten-year-old Frances was not expected to survive her "broken appendix." Clark returned to Nebraska to see her. He was driving a Model A Ford when he pulled into the farm. He 'gathered up' his young brother and headed for the Alliance hospital to visit Frances.[174]

"He liked to have scared me to death. He drove like a maniac. I'd never been in many cars. I don't suppose he drove over 35 miles an hour. But it was awful fast for me. I don't remember much about visiting Frances, but I certainly remember that ride."[175]

Sometimes the dependability of the automobile was compromised by the driver. Early one morning Melvin drove his Dad to a farm sale at the Minnie Well's place. He was resplendent in a brand new pair of Kirkendall[176] boots that his Dad bought him a few days before at Schmidt's Dry Goods store in Crawford. He fully admits that he was also a little "full of myself."

---

[173] Actually Clark was gone about six months before Earl's brother, John let the family know that their second son was working for him. In a series of letters between Clark and his mother, she alluded to the fact that there had been an altercation between Clark and his father. In one letter, Iva told him that his father felt "very bad when he left. He cried most all night. We are so anxious that you be a good boy. Please take your Father's advice.......so that when I see you again, I won't be ashamed of you."

[174] A note in the gossip section of the *Crawford Tribune*, November 23, 1935, said the neighbors, Mr. and Mrs. Carl Randall and Mr. Britton had returned to their home after spending several days at the Earl Nation farm to help with the work while Mr. and Mrs Nation were in Alliance with their daughter. It also stated that the young lady was slowly recovering.

[175] It took Frances nearly a year to recover for appendicitis.

[176] Manufactured in Omaha, Nebraska by the Kirkendall Boot Company

It rained shortly before the pair left the sale, but they reached the T in the road about six miles from the Nation farm without incidence. Then they realized the road was washed out. Earl warned his young son that he was about to high-center the automobile.

Dad said, 'Boy, you better get out of the road, there's a place to turn out.' I say, "I can make it. And down the old road we go. We got along pretty good for a while, then I don't do so good and down in the washout I go."

Dad just got out and said, "Well, Boy, I guess we walk from here."

The pair headed up the road. The night was dark and the few stars peeking through the clouds didn't offer much illumination. They finally reached the Guy Yohe homestead, and Melvin suggested that they go into the farm and ask the owner to pull them out. His dad said they'd walk the rest of the way. "We finally got home. Those brand new pair of boots had worn blisters all the way through my heels. The next day we took a team of horses and pulled the car out of the mud. It was a good lesson."

Horses had neither headlights nor protection from the elements, but Melvin still preferred horses as his main mode of transportation. The one exception might have been the night he encountered a summer electrical storm. He spent several evenings that summer visiting the DeWitt sisters who lived on a farm about 10 miles west of the Nation farmstead. Melvin often ate supper with the family before heading back "across country." One evening he encountered what he called "one wild old electric storm."

"It was about 10 at night when I started home. It was pitch-dark and the air was saturated with electricity," he shivered at the memory. "There were balls of blue electricity running down the horse mane. It was a little spooky for a while."

During the night ride, electricity may not have seemed all that useful, but it became a convenient weapon in Melvin's encounter with a neighborhood bully. The man, a neighbor with a son Melvin's age, continually sought to exert his power over his much younger and smaller neighbor. During one incident, the man caught Melvin near a water tank and tried to force the boy's head under the water. Melvin wriggled free. He said he was reluctant to report the neighbor's animosity, because Earl and the neighbor were partners on a seed drill.[177] The drill partnership ended abruptly the afternoon that the neighbor told Melvin that his Dad, who'd been suffering from health issues, was "laying dead as a doornail" up in the field. Panicked Melvin ran to the field where he could indeed see his father lying in the shadow of the wagon, "just taking a rest."

"I told Dad what had happened. He quit the field and headed west. The next thing I knowed, the drill was at our place. He'd bought out the other guy's share. We never talked about it. Dad had just had enough."

---

[177] A seed drill is a mechanical device used for sowing seeds. The device selects quantities of seeds, then the drill positions the seeds in the soil, and covers them at a specific depth.

The animosity Melvin felt for the neighbor festered. That fall several neighbors met at Frank Harris's to dip cattle for parasites. A fire was built beneath the vat, then liquid pesticide was poured into the vat and heated to boiling. After it cooled, the cattle were prodded up a ramp and shoved into the "bath" which killed ticks, flies, mites, and lice. Melvin's job was to carry a telephone battery powered "hot shot," and encourage the reluctant cattle to jump into the vat.

"Old Bugger had been picking on my all day. I could see him up above me on the fence. He was using a pole to shove the cattle's heads under the surface. He was a big man. His pants hung down on his dirty old butt. His pants leg kept coming up above his shoe top. He looked like he was 10 feet tall. Then I hit him with that hotshot. He fell off that fence. I dropped the battery and ran like hell, but he caught me. I think the old bastard would have thrown me in the dipping vat[178] if Dad wouldn't have stepped in. Dad never had much to do with him after that."

---

[178] In 1928, Bob Jordan, who lived on the South Dakota, Nebraska border in northern Sioux County was helping prepare the dipping vat at the Mark Morteseen ranch. He slipped and fell into the vat that was full of boiling solution. He died a few days later of the burns he suffered. Whenever Melvin related the story of the dipping vat, he generally added the story about Bob Jordan and his death. (In later life, Melvin was good friends with Bob Jordan's great-nephew, Bob Jordan.)

THE WAR YEARS

"I grew up in a hurry when Elvin left for the War. I was 12 years old and my playing days were over. I became a man." Melvin Nation

Elvin spent most of his Army years on a ship in the Pacific.

Even the most toxic neighborhood battles were forgotten in 1942 when World War II erupted. Neighbors supported neighbors particularly when their "boys" were shipped off to war. Elvin Nation was one of the young men who left Sioux County to fight in the Pacific Theater.[179]

Fear hung over the homestead like an ugly, grey, dirt storm. In a July 1942 letter to his sister, Eva, 12-year-old Melvin told her he'd been praying. He said a church worker "Phillop," told him about some verses, John 36 and 37.

---

[179] During World War II, The Pacific Theater was the scene of primarily sea-borne warfare between the Allies and the Japanese. The intensive conflict reached to the far edges of the Pacific Ocean. The term European theater was characteristically used to identify the fighting that occurred across Europe against Germany. Several Sioux County boys fought in the Pacific theater, including Elvin and his first cousin, Bud Hamaker.

John 36: ³⁶ Believe in the light while you have the light, so that you may become children of light." ³⁷ On the last and greatest day of the festival, Jesus stood and said in a loud voice, "Let anyone who is thirsty come to me and drink.

"I'm enjoying those verses very much," he wrote to his sister. "I've enjoyed the verses that you mention too. Chapter 20 and 21 of Psalms. It has been hard to understand them, but I think I can do it. They make me think of Elvin."[180]

Earl and Iva's worry was palpable. Melvin said his folks lived from one mail day to the next. Luckily Elvin was a good correspondent, until the letters stopped for an agonizing 30 days. "They liked to go crazy. Elvin was in the thick of combat on one of those islands in the Pacific. When he finally wrote home, he told the folks he'd been sent to Sydney, Australia for R &R. That was a great day when that letter came."

Dear Mom Dad and all,

Well I feel pretty good this evening. My name was drawed for a furlough to Sydney, Australia. I'm going to write a check for $200 dollars on my account. O.K. I'll do it soon. There isn't no doubt that there's plenty to cover that much. It takes a lot of money in Australia for any fun. I've borrowed the money from some of the boys till I get where I can write a check. So long for this time. I've got to get ready to go. God bless you all. Your Loveing Son and Bud, Elvin[181]

"Most of the time, even when they got a letter, they didn't know where he was," Melvin said, "but they thought he was o.k. as long as that letter came. I think he wrote every week. Mama wrote back oftener than that. I think Daddy even wrote a few times. It was a hard time for my folks."

Elvin's letters never revealed the danger that he trudged through on a daily basis. One letter said he was sure glad a friend had sent him a couple of rolls of film. Another told his mother that he appreciated all the hard work that went into the candy she sent him, but admitted that even though she had packed it in popcorn, it often arrived in "pretty bad shape." He suggested that she might send cookies. Other letters poignantly reflected his longing to come home.

My Dear Dad Mom and All,

Surely am a happy soldier boy tonight. I got five letters from home. Boy, Boy what a treat. I'm very well. Couldn't feel any better if I had to. Glad to hear potatoes are

---

[180] The letter written to Eva Nation, Crawford, NE was sent to the care of James Soester for whom Eva was working as a "mother's helper."
[181] Elvin Nation, V mail from to his family. Dated August 25, 1944. Iva Nation scrapbook.

all out. Surely was surprised to hear I had that many cattle at home and thanks a million Dad. If I could come home tomorrow Dad and Mom, I would be more and glad to do my part in keeping the home going. I've been running around with my shirt off and have I ever got a sun burn, be o.k. in a few days. Was very glad to hear all is well. Please don't worry about me and keep well. Your loving Son and Brother, Elvin[182]

Elvin's absence propelled 12-year-old Melvin into instant manhood. From that point on he said he worked like a man, and his Dad treated him as one. Earl Nation made his young son a partner in his hog business, and paid him a small wage as well as a percentage of their hog market sales that averaged 29 cents a pound. Financially, the family's fortunes were improving. In 1942, Earl told his youngest son, that for the first time in their [Earl and Iva's] lives they didn't owe a dime to anyone.

"They'd been married for 34 years and were finally, totally out of debt." Melvin said. "Mama inherited enough money to buy another section of land when her dad died in 1932. They rented ground here and there. They accomplished a whole lot; they really did, and it wasn't easy. Those people that homesteaded this land, including my folks had to be tough."

The Nations and many others on the ridge acquired their land through the Homestead Act. Shortly after midnight on January 1, 1863, under the auspices of the newly signed Homestead Act,[183] Nebraskan Daniel Freeman filed the first homestead claim in the United States. In the ensuing years, over 270,000,000 public domain acres were claimed in the United States under the Act, 11 million in 1913 alone. Homesteaders filed 104,260 claims on 22,253,314 acres, forty-five percent of Nebraska's total land area, during the homestead era.[184] That number included acres claimed under the Kinkaid Act, an amendment to the Homestead Act, that went into effect in 1904 and expanded the 160-acre claim allotment to 640 acres in a specific 37- county area in western Nebraska.

In the late 1800s, a climate theory proposed by University of Nebraska professor Dr. Samuel Aughey proclaimed, "Rainfall follows the plow." Homesteaders flocked to the northern plains, but those hoping to turn the semi-arid prairie into productive croplands[185] soon discovered that turning the soil over did not increase the rainfall or produce bumper crops

---

[182] Elvin Nation, V mail from to his family. November 8, 1943. Iva Nation scrapbook.
[183] Todd Arlington, Homestead National Monument of American-Nebraska. The Homestead Act was officially signed into law on May 20, 1862 by President Abraham Lincoln to encourage western migration into the Midwest and Great Plains.
[184] Homesteaders claimed 32,050,480 acres of land in Montana, 35 percent of their total land area. Although homesteaders claimed more land in Montana than in Nebraska, they claimed 45 percent of Nebraska's total area.
[185] As seed stock, particularly wheat seed like "Turkey Red," fertilizer, and watering methods improved, the prairies were coaxed into farm production, but ranchers like Melvin always believed the prairie was "cattle country-plain and simple."

The drought of the 1890s further reinforced the idea that "Mother Nature," not politicians or climate theorists, was in charge. Many homesteads were simply abandoned.

"If the government would have been smart enough to give them old boys five sections,[186] most of them would have been successful," Melvin lamented. "As it was a lot of hearts were broken. I think the people who succeeded were the ones that had a little to start with or had someone to help them. Mama and Daddy bought a relinquishment claim. They went through the same damn hardships as those homesteaders, but Uncle Dave also helped them out. The people that survived have to be commended. I don't ever think I seen the day when I was tough enough."

Early Plat[187] books record homestead locations on every section in Sioux County; some owned entire sections, some just a quarter (160 acres). Melvin said many of the homesteaders struggled to feed themselves or their families. Although the Nations didn't have a great deal of surplus, Iva Nation regularly loaded potatoes, bread, or other "extras" and delivered them to several homesteaders in the area.

"There was one family that didn't have a damn thing. They had just one old sad horse to pull their wagon. He looked like he was on his last legs," Melvin looked far back in time still feeling the hopelessness the neighbors exuded. "We'd put what we could in a wagon and go over to their place. Kids would come out of every crack of their sod house. Then they'd smile. One day we went over there. They were gone. We never did hear what happened to them. I hoped they made it to Glen[188] and went back East."

In the spring of 1944, Melvin rode into Glen to take the Eighth Grade Exam at Glen High School.[189] Keal Rising, whose family lived on Glen's "main drag," intercepted Melvin as he generally did when he noticed "Nation" came to town. The ensuing horse race, between Keal on his trusty Shetland pony and Melvin on whatever "half-broke" horse he was riding that day, careened wildly down the county road that served as the village's Main Street.[190] When the race came to its "incredibly exciting" conclusion, the pair went to the Glen School and took their exams.

---

[186] A section of land consists of 640 acres.
[187] Plat books identify ranges, townships, and owners of specific pieces of land within sections. Most Plat books center around a single county. The Nation's land was recorded first in the 1918 Plat book of Sioux County. For information about Plat books in Nebraska go to http://nebraskaccess.nebraska.gov/MapsNebr.asp
[188] The nearest railhead was at Glen, Nebraska.
[189] Lifetime Glen, Nebraska resident Frances Kreman Olbricht said the Glen High School, which she attended, provided education through the 10th grade. Their teachers administrated the 8th grade exam to area rural school students.
[190] Keal Rising lived in Glen and challenged Melvin to a horse race every time the latter came to the community. Melvin always agreed to the race. Generally, his horse outran Keal's Shetland ponies, but winning wasn't the point anyway.

The Glen School House, near Glen, NE built in 1928 served as both a high school (to 10th grade) and elementary school. Melvin never attended the school, but his grandchildren, Buffy and Bryan Hourt were students there from 1982-1986. Moni Nation Hourt taught at the school from 1998-2006.

Glen, Nebraska in 1922.

"We always ended up at Keal's house whenever I showed up," Melvin grinned. "His Mom would fill us up with milk and cookies. We teased Doris[191] unmercifully. One afternoon she was ironing. Keal reached over and flipped her skirt up. I thought she was going to smash that iron alongside his head. He just laughed, ducked, and run. It's a wonder she didn't kill us."

A week after the examinations, Melvin donned a pair of bright orange "bibless" corduroy pants and a new four-peak creased hat that his dad had bought him at Clyde Hartman's dry goods store in Marsland.

"My sisters took me up to Harrison for graduation. Oh man, how it rained. We didn't get home that night. The Kreman Crossing[192] washed out. We stayed at Roy Randall's. I don't remember much about graduation, but I do know I never wore those orange pants again."

As the war wore on, Melvin became more involved in the farm. He took correspondence classes to complete his first two years of high school, but admitted he had too many things to do to concentrate on the class work. He and his father shingled the house. In the spring of 1944 they installed a septic tank and indoor plumbing. And there were always horses to ride. He tried to emulate the skill exhibited by the few "bona fide cowboys" in the area including neighbor, Blackie (Edward) Lantz.

Lantz, like many early bronc riders exhibited their skills in open pastures.
Photo: Hourt collection.

---

[191] Doris Rising Hamaker was Keal's only sister. He had three brothers.
[192] A bridge across the White River was known as Kreman crossing

"I idolized Blackie. He could ride anything with hair on it. I don't think he could teach a horse to drink, but he could sure do everything else and he could ride even the toughest ones. I thought he was one of the greatest men I ever knew."

By the time he was 15, Melvin conquered most of the tough horses he encountered. One horse "a good looking scamp," that came out of the Breakneck[193] country was the only "one man horse" he ever rode. "I often wondered what happened to that horse. I expect he ended up in a bucking string. He liked me but didn't like anyone else. He hated most men."

That summer, Melvin also broke a bay mare that he bought from his Uncle for five dollars. Carl said he didn't think Melvin could "hang his butt on that horse," but if he did he'd give him his money back. With Earl and Carl's help, the horse was finally trapped in a round corral and saddled with the Coggshall saddle.

Melvin spent his lifetime training horses.

"I got on that little son-of-a-gun. Dad opened the round corral gate and let her out into the canyon." Melvin's eyes filled with ornery glee. "We headed east. I'll bet we runned 15 miles before I got her turned around. By the time we got back to the corrals, she wasn't interested in bucking anymore, but Carl never did pay me the $5."

By the end of the summer Melvin tamed two truckloads of horses. Neighbors Ernest Pullen and Jack Corbett loaded the horses on their grain trucks and hauled them to the horse sale in

---

[193] Several ranchers in the Breakneck Rd region located southeast of Crawford, NE. raised horses. Many of them were sired by Fort Robinson stallions.

Lusk. The horses sold for $180, a tremendous amount of money for a 15-year-old kid. "I made a little money that day," Melvin said gazing back through time, "but more important, I runned into the greatest hand I'd ever seen—even better than Blackie."

The hand, Jess York lived north of Lance Creek, Wyoming. The day Melvin took his horses to Lusk, York was "messing" with a pen full of horses at the sale barn. Melvin said few of the animals were halter-broke.

"He'd just walk into a pen and throw a houlihan.[194] He'd get on and shoo him around a little bit. Someone would open the gate. They'd shove the horse into the alley and finally into the center ring. By that time, the horse did about anything Jess wanted him to do. Gawd, he was a hand. I knew him in later years, and he never weakened. He was a true cowboy. I watched him many times. I still think he was one of those greats."

On December 30, 1945, two months after the war ended on September 2, 1945, Elvin Nation landed in San Francisco. The next day his train pulled into Denver, Colorado where he mustered out of the Army. He spent New Year's Day in Crawford and returned to the ranch New Year's Day—1946.

"Merlin and I were grinding grain when he got back from Crawford." Melvin recalled. "It was quite a day for my mother and Dad. I guarantee it really was. But they had quite a time understanding Elvin when he got home. He was a lot like a wild animal turned loose. He went through hell over there. He couldn't settle down. He'd always tried to see everything with humor, but what he'd seen wasn't anything to laugh about."

Elvin saw action on many of the islands in the Pacific Theater. He watched a kamikaze plane dive toward his ship and explode in a hail of gunfire seconds before it plowed into the ship's main smokestack. He watched friends die at the hands of the Japanese army. Shortly after the end of the war, his ship moored off Luzon island in the Philippines. A few days later, his cousin, Bud Hamaker, was killed by sharks while swimming in the waters near the island.[195] Elvin returned to the farm, but resuming his quiet life on the Nebraska prairie was difficult.

In the fall of 1946, with Elvin back on the farm, Melvin was relegated back to "kid" status and enrolled in classes at Sioux County High School. His heart wasn't in his classes, and he no longer knew how to be a kid. In addition, he spent a great deal of time with his older brother as Elvin tried to unwind.

---

[194] A houlihan is a rope-flip that originates from a right or left side. The rope is not swung around a cowboy's head, but flipped quickly toward its target. The loop worked very well in a pen of "touchy" horses.

[195] A newspaper article in a July issue of the *Crawford Tribune* reported that "Mr. and Mrs. Paul Hamaker had received word that their son, Pvt, Paul (Bud) Hamaker, who was 19 years of age, was killed in action on Luzon, on June 3, 1945." It didn't reveal the details, that Bud was swimming off the island, while waiting to be shipped home. He suddenly disappeared below the water. Elvin, who was nearby, tried to find his cousin, but sharks drove him and the others back to shore.

Sioux County High School at Harrison, NE. Photo: Joe Hourt collection.

"I'm not gonna blame Elvin any, but we partied too much, drank too much whiskey. We put our folks through hell. I think it was easier for Dad to understand what was going on with Elvin than it was to understand me. We'd worked together for three years, but suddenly he didn't know who I was. He would say, 'Son, I'm never going to find a collar that will fit you, Boy.' And he never did. Nothing about Dad's operation suited me. I wasn't cut out to be a farmer. I could never understand why you'd take perfectly good grass, turn it over, and plant something else in it and expect it to grow. I left home the spring I was 16. In April I went with Merlin and Lucille when they moved to Washington. I'd made up my mind I'd never be a 'plow boy.'"

"Melvin drove a car out there for us," Lucille Nation said in a 1997 interview.[196] "We celebrated his 16th birthday while on the road. He was such a good kid. We'd have liked to have kept him, but eventually he decided to go home. He's been good for Nebraska, but then he would have been good for any place he settled."

The return trip to Washington nearly convinced Melvin that he needed to stay within the confines of the Cornhusker State—forever. Merlin and Lucille left him in a hotel in Seattle and returned to their home in Everett. He told them he'd be fine; he wouldn't miss the train the next day. That evening he was accosted by a stranger.

"Bout scared me to death. I'd never had to handle something like that guy. I think he liked to mess around with young boys. I locked myself in my room. I was waiting at the train depot way before the train pulled in the next morning. I was damn glad to be home."

---

[196] Lucille Nation. Personal interview with Moni Hourt, 1997, Nation home in Everett Washington.

DAMN REBEL

"I was wilder than a March Hare and didn't give a damn about much of anybody. It's a damn wonder I didn't end up dead. I think the thing that saved me was that I liked to work. I couldn't be a full-fledged drunk and work hard at the same time."
Melvin Nation

When Melvin returned to Nebraska he discovered there were a plethora of jobs waiting for anyone willing to put in a hard day's work. Crawford bricklayer , Ernie Tibbet, hired him to mix cement and stucco. Melvin said he helped Ernie stucco a lot of houses, but admitted he never "mixed a batch of mud" that suited the tough "old bastard."

A few years later, Melvin would revisit his "mud mixing" skills with better results. He and the minister of the Lutheran Church in Harrison. hauled 24 loads of bricks for the building and "mudded" them all in place. They worked well together and their wall building skills were admirable. Technically, however, their transport business was illegal. Neither the men nor the truck had a commercial license.

Clark, Melvin, Elvin, Merlin and Merlin's son, Milton.

"I was so full of me. I didn't think about anyone else. I did go home every chance I got though. And, if I didn't have a job, which wasn't very often, Dad would find me something to do."

In August of 1947, Earl and Iva took a trip through Wyoming, leaving their youngest son behind to manage the farm.

In a postcard postmarked August 28, Iva Nation told her son they were having a great time and were sure all was well at home. Although Iva was purported to discourage what she deemed Melvin's "wild-horse" side, the card featured a picture of a young man riding a bucking bull.

Shortly after his 17th birthday, Melvin decided to put some of his hard earned wages to work. A friend told him that he'd seen a 1941 Ford Business Coupe in a garage in Scottsbluff. The car, with its 85-horsepower engine could run 85 miles an hour in second gear and only had 6000 miles on it.

"The guy who bought it new was killed in World War II." Melvin said. "I felt bad about that, but I loved that car. I paid $1200 for it. There wasn't one thing wrong with it, not even a bar broke out of the grill. It was a pretty little black son-of-a-gun."

Melvin admitted he slid the car through the corners of Corkscrew Canyon on the way to town and often bounced it over the top of Chalk Hill outside of Fort Robinson. Then he slowed down to a fairly sedate pace as he traveled down the guard-lined road at Fort Robinson.

"Everybody was a little careful at Fort Robinson," Melvin said. "Up until 1948, it was still in control of the military. No one wanted to go up against those guys."

Fort Robinson military base about 1939. Photo by Frank Snook.

There wasn't any trepidation about going head to head with Crawfordite, Howard Jacobs, and his 44-Mercury convertible. Melvin said Jacobs, "thought his car was hotter than hell" and was determined to prove him wrong. Early one morning, the pair had "ourselves a race." Jacobs parked behind the wheel of the Mercury. Charley Quay and Melvin manned the Ford. The drivers headed their "steeds" down old Highway 2. Jacobs took the early lead spurting ahead as he hung onto the corners, "handing it to that son-of-a-gun."

"I was hanging on his bumper the whole way. I finally got enough extra stuff that I'm getting around him goin' into that curve," Melvin said. "The sun was just coming up. I'm hanging on that corner. I won't back off. You can't see one thing outside the road. There might have been someone else needing that road, but we didn't care. Finally, Howard lost his courage and let me get on around him. That old Ford ran like hell"

Cruising down Main Street generally including speeding through the Burlington Northern Railroad viaduct. There were two viaducts in Crawford, a pedestrian one on Elm street and the Chicago Burlington and Quincy viaduct that allowed traffic to travel below the train track above Main Street. The pedestrian viaduct on East Elm Street was constructed by April 1904 according to the *Crawford Bulletin*. The article decried the fact that "some persons appear to delight in placing scare-crows, obstructions or traps on the walk to annoy pedestrians during the night..." Although there was some discussion about closing the Elm Street viaduct in 1910, Crawford citizens objected because the walk way was the only convenient way for students who lived on the east side of the train track to walk to the Crawford schools that were located on the west side of the tract. Burlington finally agreed to improve the pedestrian viaduct when they constructed the Main Street vehicle viaduct in 1911.[197] It was completed in about 1913.[198] In 1944, lights were installed in the pedestrian walk way in 1944, but even then according to the June 9, 1944 issue of the *Crawford Tribune,* "holligans" removed or damaged the lights and insisted on "lying in wait" and scaring innocent individuals who needed the walk way to get to their homes.

"I don't think I ever walked through the little viaduct until after Mom and Dad bought the house on East Elm in about 1957," Melvin said. "But we used the viaduct on Main Street. It didn't drain very good and we'd hit it just as hard as we could to see just how far we could throw water without drowning out the motor."

---

[197] *Northwest Nebraska News*. This section of the "Twenty-Five Years Ago." column, originally dated June 11, 1911 says that city officials met with representatives of the Burlington railroad and reached an agreement "by which the Burlington will construct two viaducts on Main and Elm streets at their railroad crossings."

[198] "Twenty-Five Years Ago." *Crawford Tribune*. November 26, 1937. This article originally dated November 26, 1912 asked, "Wonder whether the main street viaduct will be completed before the winter is over." A "Twenty Years Ago." Column published September 8, 1933 in the *Crawford Tribune* says that work under the direction of JH Prieshoff is progressing rapidly

Viaduct Repair on Main Street in Crawford 1942. Photograph by Sam Schmidt

In 1916, eight cars broke loose from an east bound train and backed into a train just south of the Burlington's Elm Street viaduct. According the November 17, 1916 issue of the, all eight cars, heavily loaded "left the track and piled up in the ditch."

"When the train wrecked gasoline spilled down the street people ran out and filled buckets and cans with gas," Melvin said. "Dad wasn't in town at the time, but he heard about it. In about 1942,[199] about the time Elvin went to the Army, the viaduct started on fire. The fire department got it out, but it took them a while to repair everything.[200] By the time, I started driving around, it was in good shape. There was a walk way on either side, kids used to congregate there and drink a little beer. The rest of us just drove through it—most of the time as fast as we could."

---

[199] "Burlington Viaduct Damaged by Fire. "*Crawford Tribune*. November 20, 1942. This article from the Crawford Tribune said about $9,000 worth of damage was done to the viaduct that was fueled by the creosote on the bridge timbers.

[200] Photographs of the repair were taken by Sam Schmidt, a local photographer who lived in a small dugout under the train track, next to the Elm Street viaduct. He had one of the first CB radios in the region and set up a television in his front yard so his daughter Linda and her friends could watch the new medium. He was married to Betty Hamaker, Paul Hamaker's daughter, and RSQ Hamaker's granddaughter. The couple eventually divorced. Linda allowed his photographs to be copied and given to the Crawford Historical Museum.

Shortly after daybreak, Melvin and his friend Tuffy Bridge cruised under the viaduct and parked on Crawford's Main Street to drink a few beers and watch "other guys making fools of themselves." Officer Duckworth, the lone member of the Crawford police force, slid his ancient, "laboriously slow" police cruiser into a parking space beside them. He told the pair that a bunch of Chadron kids had been terrorizing the town. He'd stopped them several times that night. They promised to slow down, then zipped back down the street, "going like a bat out of hell."

Burlington train going over Main Street viaduct. Photo by Sam Schmidt

"We told him that was a damn shame and said if he needed our assistance we were there for him," Melvin said with a sardonic smile. "He jumped in our car and said, 'Catch those SOBs.'
"I didn't need to be asked twice. We were setting there with open bottles of beer, but we stuffed them between our legs and took off."

The cars headed south out of town and turned east toward Chadron. Melvin was doing about 85 miles an hour when he went into the corner southeast of Crawford. Duckworth quietly gulped that he wanted to catch the Chadron kids, but maybe "they didn't need to go so fast to get it done."

"My little old Ford was just flying right over the top of the hills. The other kids finally stopped and pulled over. We were big hero bastards. We helped Duckworth gather them up and took them back to city hall. One thing we did do though before we did any hero stuff, was dump the beer into the bar pit. That's the first and last time I was ever 'deputized.'"

City of Crawford, 1939. Photo by Frank Snook

Duckworth wasn't quite so accommodating late one winter night when he observed Melvin spinning circles in the middle of the icy street. The Ford's revolutions expanded exponentially in reaction to the increasingly slickened surface. The car flew into the curb blowing a tire in the process. Officer Duckworth gave Melvin a ticket that evening, but said he sure "hated to do it."

The consequences might have been a little more severe if the state patrolman would have caught up to the little black Ford as it was whipped through Crawford's back streets and alleys. Melvin finally ducked the car into a slot between some garbage bins behind the high school and escaped detection. The patrol car sped past. A few minutes later, Melvin slid back to the highway and quietly—but quickly—headed home.

"Melvin was a little like those wild horses he liked to ride, just on the verge of out of control. But he was such a likable, kind, boy that you couldn't be mad at him," Betty Curtis Nation[201] said. "He didn't really know it then, but we all knew he had a good soul."

"I don't think I was any wilder than anyone else running around about that time," Melvin said with irritation when asked if he could be considered unmanageable. "It was a little rougher back then. There was hardly a Saturday night when there wasn't at least a half dozen fights. Let's just say none of us had many 'inhibitions.'"

Late one summer evening, Melvin and another young man traded punches at a Saturday night dance in Andrews.[202] Melvin already sported a "bridge" on his upper gums, the result of

---

[201] Clark Nation's wife.
[202] Andrews, Nebraska was located between Glen and Harrison, about 20 miles from each town. At one time it had been a cattle shipping point on the railroad, but eventually it became known almost solely for its "dance hall" and its dances.

another fist fight. One blow sent his manufactured teeth hurtling to the ground. Melvin said he told his opponent he was done fighting. He had to find his teeth. The other boy helped him dig around in the weeds until they located the missing dentures. Melvin cleaned them off with a liberal douse of beer and put them back in. The fight was over. The dance went on.

Melvin and Gary in 1948.

In 1947, Melvin married Donna (Punky) Pliley. The couple's son Gary was born in January 1948. They were in the midst of a divorce when their second son, Michael, was born in April 1949. Donna's father, the manager of the Nash Finch Grocery Store and Warehouse in Crawford used his considerable influence and money in the community to gain custody of the boys. Melvin climbed into a car with Tuffy Bridge and Darrel Sample and headed west toward California.

"Let's just say I was fed up with life. I was madder than hell. And as I said, I had a big chip on my shoulder.[203] I'd made up my mind that I wasn't coming back—ever."

After a trip through Canada, the trio ended up in the San Diego, California, home of Darell's aunt and uncle, Mr. and Mrs. Kosinski.[204] The pair made the young Nebraskans welcome, although they demanded that the boys use proper table manners at their white "linened" table.

"The Kosinskis were great people. They were very wealthy. We were just laughing kids, basically a bunch of heathens. They taught me whatever dab of etiquette I have: how to handle a napkin and a fork, even how to hold a cup of tea with my pinky finger up—although, I've

---

[203] Melvin Nation. Personal interview with Moni Hourt. 2002.
[204] If Melvin ever knew the Kosinski's first names, he never used them. They were always called Mr. and Mrs. Kosinski. Author has tried to locate the Kosinskis but have failed. The name may have been spelled Kosiski or Kosicki. Melvin was never sure.

never used that skill much." he chuckled, his pinky finger held upward, parallel with his glass of sugar-laced ice tea. "Mr. Kosinski got me a job at Consolidated Aircraft as a timekeeper. He was a dentist, a kind man. But those people lived in constant fear that someone was going to get through their electrified fences and past their gates. They lived up there on Market Street, with the wealthy. They had everything you'd ever want, but I'll never forget how scared they were of life. One day I just decided it was time to go home. Those people were damn good to me though. I've never forgot them."[205]

On the night of December 31, 1948, Melvin was living part time at his folk's house, working for various neighbors. He went to town for New Year's Eve, planning on returning the next day. By mid-morning January 1, 1949, the storm that became known as the Blizzard of '49, raged across the treeless flats, making travel nearly impossible. It was a week before Melvin could catch a train to Glen, then ride a borrowed horse to the farmstead.

"The canyons were full of snow, but lots of country was blown free. You could ride quite always if you could keep to the ridges," he remembered. "Even then, it took me all day to get that 12 miles."

Snow piled to the top of telephone poles in some places. Photo Sam Schmidt

An open-mouth shed on the farm filled with snow, trapping Clark Nation's mustang mare and her stud colt. It was several days before Earl dug the horses out the shed, but they survived.

---

[205] Melvin Nation. Interview with Moni Hourt, 1998.

That spring Melvin bought the colt and named him Bill. He said the colt turned out to be one of the best horses he'd ever owned.[206]

Second Street in Crawford, in mid-January. Photo: Sam Schmidt

The horses on the Nation farm were lucky, three head of young horses were trapped in a neighbor's barn. It was nearly two weeks before they were extracted from their snow prison. Although they were able to lick the snow for water, they also ate the building's wood siding. All three died because the splinters damaged their intestines.

"The wind would go down long enough for you to get a few chores done, then it would start again." Melvin recalled many years later. "We'd shovel our way out to the windmill tanks and get water going, then the next day, we'd do it all over again. We were lucky, our cattle got into the canyons, and we didn't lose anything. The milk cows were up next to the barn. We could always get shoveled out enough to take care of them and the chickens. People around us weren't so lucky."[207]

It was later estimated that 100,000 cattle perished in the storm. Melvin said many of those cattle died from lack of water. "Cows

Melvin Nation admitted he was somewhat of a wild man as a young man.

---

[206] Although Bill suffered from sleeping sickness when he was about 10 and "crossfired like hell afterwards," the horse taught Melvin's three children how to ride.

[207] The exact number of cattle and other livestock lost during the blizzard has never been determined. The number is simply stated as "hundreds of thousands." In all 79 people were killed in the storm.

can't get enough moisture out of snow to survive. First thing in people's minds, was to get them something to eat, but lots of people didn't realize they needed to get them a drink of water. That's just as important to an old cow as food is."

Although thousands of bales of hay were dropped from airplanes to feed cattle and sheep, few realized the animals also needed water. Horses will lick snow for moisture. Cattle and sheep will not.

A Nation neighbor, Wayne Yohe[208] froze to death during the storm. That spring the Brott Place[209] he'd been renting came up for lease.

Melvin, sporting a full beard and unruly hair that spiked and swaggered around his shoulders, rode a wild, dancing-prancing, horse into the yard at the Yohe's farm sale. He immediately spotted the new renter's teenage daughters, Thelma and Velma, (Sis), "smatalecing" toward him.

"Thelma came sashaying up to me and asked me where I come from," Melvin said. "I told her from my mother. She acted like that embarrassed her, but I'm not sure it really did. As she and her sister walked away I heard her say she was going to marry me some day. I'm sure that got her the shocked looks she thought it would."

Thelma Callaham Nation told a slightly different version of the story. She agreed that Melvin was "sorta" a wild man. But she said one of their neighbors was trying to "match me up with her stupid son." She decided to shock the thought right out of the matchmaker's mind, so she pointed at Melvin and said she was "going to marry that man someday." The neighbor said that was impossible; he was already married. Thelma declared that she'd, "just get rid of the wife." Then she and her sister joined their cousin for another "prance" across the yard.

---

[208] Wayne, his wife, and daughter were headed for Cheyenne, Wyoming with a load of pigs when they were stranded. Yohe tried to walk for help and died in the blizzard. His family survived.
[209] The place was known as the Brott place because it had been originally owned by Fred Brott and his wife, Frances.

Whatever way it started, a few weeks later, Melvin was making the four-mile trip to the Brott Place to see Thelma who was home from the boarding high school in Harrisburg, Nebraska. Letters sufficed to keep the young couple in touch when she was finishing her sophomore high school classes at the Banner County High School. She was not excited about returning to Sioux County.

The oldest daughter of Verna and Elmer Callaham, Thelma spent most of her life on the farms that her father rented in the Harrisburg, NE area. From the time she was 11, she served as a hired

Thelma as a sophomore at Harrisburg High School.

girl, only returning to Harrisburg in the winter months to go to school. She fully admits being a little rebellious in her own right. And—she made it well known that she did not intend to move from the gentle treed valley in Banner County to the windblown hills of Sioux County.

"We were coming to check out the farm, when this man wallered up out of the bar pit and waved us down," Thelma recalled her first day in Sioux County. "He was wearing six shooters and clothes stained with deer blood. I begged my dad to turn around and go home to civilization. We didn't." Thelma always added that she hated that "damn place." Despite her dislike of the place, letters carefully preserved in Thelma's jewelry box[210] soon revealed a fast evolving relationship between Melvin and Thelma.

Many weekends Melvin made the nearly 200-mile round trip to Harrisburg to visit his future wife. He often picked her up, brought her back to Sioux County, then took her home on Sunday night. When Thelma's mother was badly injured in a tractor accident, [211]Thelma returned home. The following summer she went back to Banner County to work for Red McKillip.[212] Melvin "wore out a set of tires."

Thelma's family shortly before they moved to Sioux County. Thelma, Elmer, Wilma, Verna, Velma (Sis) (front) Norman, Pat. Sonny died in 1944.

---

[210] Melvin Nation letters to Thelma Callaham. Moni Hourt collection.
[211] Verna Callaham was injured on April 14, 1949, Melvin's 19th birthday.
[212] Thelma cleaned house, cooked meals, and babysat for the McKillip's children.

"That fall I went to Sioux County High School in Harrison. It wasn't long before I met a couple of other girls who didn't like the rules any better than I did," Thelma said with sauciness dripping across her syllables. "We drove the teachers batty.[213] I kept my school work up, but most weekends I went up to Hoovers with Melvin."

Buzz Hoover and his son, Buzzy[214] were building a stock contracting business at their newly purchased ranch on the Wyoming/Nebraska border. By the fall of 1949, most of the young men in the area were spending their spare time at the ranch. The young men congregating at the ranch helped build the arena and tested the Hoover's stock. On Sundays, jackpot rodeos gave the cowboys a chance to show their skills. At other times, the cowboys were tasked with encouraging the stock to buck. One trick: jerking a pulley-controlled, man-sized dummy from a young bucking bull's back after a three or four second "ride." The bull, free of his "opponent," bucked and cavorted from the arena, knowing that it could unseat anything. That confidence grew with each buck off. The cowboys, filled the "dummy" role for the young horses.

Cowboys in the region spent many weekends at the arena at the Hoover Ranch.

"We'd ride a horse for a couple seconds then bail out," Melvin said. "Some of those horses were rank from the word 'go.' They dumped the cowboys on their own. Some of them had to be encouraged to buck. If you'd of gone out and spurred the heck out of them for eight seconds, they'd have just stopped bucking. They're like everything else. They needed to succeed before they can get any confidence."

Bailing off bareback horses was relatively easy in the days when a bareback "riggin" was built with a soft handhold. The cowboy simply pulled his hand free; few ever "hung up" on a bareback horse.[215] Ditching a saddle bronc was even easier; a cowboy kicked his feet free and bailed off, hopefully landing on his feet.

---

[213] Thelma Nation. Interview with Moni Hourt 2004.
[214] Buzzy's name was actually Elzy A Hoover. His father's name was also Elzy A.
[215] Cowboys today ride bareback horses with a rigid "suitcase handle" riggin. They also heavily rosin their hands, so that they don't slip easily out of the riggin. Hang-ups on bareback horses are fairly common.

Pick up men were fairly uncommon at early rodeos, and seldom worked the small Hoover arena. Melvin said that was fine with him. Both times a pick up man moved in on his ride, a "wreck" followed. "One time I ended up with my head in a REA[216] pole; the other time the pickup man rode square over the top of me."

Weekends at the Hoover Ranch provided entertainment for most of the region. There were always a few men hanging around willing to ride the horses or simply have a good time. Townspeople from Lusk, Harrison, and even Crawford followed the meandering trail to the ranch and perched on the wooden bleachers to cheer for their favorite cowboy.

"It was just a fun place to go. Even during the week, guys showed up to help handle the livestock. We were always chasing the young Brahma bulls to dog[217] them," Melvin said with a little embarrassment. "We made them so damn wild that every time we rode into the pasture they headed for the rocks and hid."

An August 31, 1950, *Harrison Sun* advertisement featured action at "Hoover's Shady Grove Ranch," six miles West of Harrison. A $100 purse, equivalent to $1200 in 2022, was added to the saddle bronc, bareback, bull riding and calf roping events. Admission was $.75 but kids under five were free. Use of the picnic grounds and refreshment stands were encouraged. The bleachers at nearly every competition were filled.

Melvin became one of the part-time, paid members of the crew. He spent hours wrangling the dozens of horses that Hoover bought in search of good rodeo horses. Keal Rising often helped him sort the loads or separate the horses into different pastures. When the work was finished one afternoon, they decided to recruit one of the bucking horses as a bull dogging horse. Melvin sent Keal to get the horse out of the pasture, but Keal soon returned and said he just couldn't get her in by himself.

"She was a dirty bunch-quitten son-of-a-rip. But I told ole' Keal that we'd run her into the corner, and I'd catch her when she came out. When she went by, I just reach out and rope her. I was riding a no-good, two-dollar rascal. The minute that mare hit the end of the rope, he just stampeded. He run up on that mare. I looked down and both his front feet were over the rope. The rope was tied on hard and fast so I just got out."

Keal was some distance from the action when Melvin bailed. The horses, attached by the grass rope, headed in his direction. "Keal was out there in the middle on a horse that couldn't run fast enough to scatter his own manure," Melvin laughed. "The wild horses were closing in. One went one way; one went the other. He was whipping and riding trying to get away from their circle. They'd jerk each other down, then up they'd come again. They did that two or three times before they finally broke the rope. Finally, ole' Keal, he get out of the way. He was cussin' me with every breath he took."

---

[216] Rural Electric Association.
[217] Dogging or bulldogging is a common term for the rodeo sport of steer wrestling.

After the mare picked herself up, she headed for the corral. From that time on, all someone had to do was "let out a squall" and she'd head to the barn. She did make a good dogging horse. She'd had enough wild horse adventures.

Keal, Melvin, and another Hoover regular, Pat Drinkwalter, left the ranch one afternoon to catch a one-eyed bucking horse. "I told them to turn them horses down by the water gap and I'd ketch him," Melvin said. "The horses came down that fence and all turned toward the corrals except that one. I forgot he was blind on that side. He hit my horse and knocked us off the bank into the creek. My old horse flipped over the top of me and drove me down into that mud. I was riding a brand new saddle. I'd just bought it! I came out of that mud spluttering and spitting. It took me several hours to get the damn mud off that saddle. Those guys thought that was the funniest thing they ever seen. They thought they were pretty damn cute."

The horses on the ranch seldom cooperated. Many came from wild horse herds. Others were horses that farmers or ranchers in the area couldn't ride because of their penchant for bucking. Whatever the reason, when the horses arrived at the Hoover Ranch, they were hard to handle.

"The pair of us, Keal and I, tried to put the horses behind the chutes one afternoon," Melvin grinned. "They hit the gate and ducked back into the corral, just going a bat-out-of-hell. We rode toward them trying to turn them around. Like a couple of dummies, we hit head on and ended up in a heap, horses "faunching" and tromping, around and over us."

When they weren't working the stock, the cowboys found other ways to keep themselves entertained. They'd race to a post to see who could retrieve a dollar bill from the top of it. In the process, the riders tried to de-horse their opponents. Chasing antelope or coyotes provided hours of entertainment. Keal and Melvin fastened a saddle to a jeep hood. The idea was that one would drive while the other perched in the saddle and roped the antelope. They "figured" they could chase the animal down much faster in a jeep than on a horse. Luckily neither of them ever had "guts enough" to crawl into the saddle. They had to settle for occasionally roping an antelope off the back of a horse. Then, of course, the roper "hog-tied" the antelope, and threw it over the front of his dancing, bucking, horse and carried it to the corrals to show it off.

Rodeoing was a weekend, spare-time, extra-money, pursuit. Particularly in the winter months, Melvin held a full-time job on one of the neighboring ranches. In December of 1949, he "batched" on the Chuck Bourrett Ranch. Early one morning, he realized a small herd of cattle had crossed a narrow strip of frozen creek and couldn't seem to find their way back.

A skiff of snow had blown across what appeared to be a solid slab of ice. Melvin led his horse across the river. It held him. He gathered the cattle and shoved them across the ice bridge. They followed the horse's tracks back across the river. Melvin, who never believed a person should walk when he could ride, didn't think there was any sense in getting off the horse. When he was half-way across the river, the ice bridge collapsed.

"My old horse's front end went first, then he just turned a somersault with me underneath." Melvin said. "It was cold that day, freezing cold. That horse tromped and stomped me under that water for quite a while until he finally floundered out of there. I was still on top when it was all over. By the time I got to the ranch, I'd froze to the saddle. My clothes were covered with a layer of ice. I had a terrible time breaking my clothes off the saddle, but I was never really cold. That ice protected me from freezin' to death."

Throughout Thelma's junior year of high school, she and Melvin continued their courtship. They wrote dozens of letters. She told him about her days at school. He talked about horses, what was going on in the country, or simply told her how much he cared about her. She went with him to the Hoover Ranch on Sundays, or he took her to the Brott Place so she could visit her family. During the school week, Thelma boarded in town. She and a small group of girls enthusiastically enjoyed their year. She admitted they "raised a lot of hell, smoked a lot of cigarettes, and did a lot of giggling."

Thelma and Melvin on their wedding day.

The summer of 1950, she traveled to as many rodeos as she could with Melvin, but she also worked at a local ranch taking care of the house and the children. In the fall of 1950, she decided not to return to school. She took her senior high school classes through correspondence.

"School just didn't seem so important anymore," Thelma said in a statement that echoed the one Iva Hamaker made many years before. "I decided I wanted to get married. So I did."[218]

Melvin bought his bride a simple gold band[219] and presented it on their wedding day, December 2, 1950. His sisters Anita and Mildred served as attendants at the civil ceremony. Shortly after their marriage, the pair moved into a converted chicken house on a ranch west of Van Tassel, Wyoming. Thelma said the ranch owner was a "miserable bastard" who irregularly paid them their $150 a month wage. There was barely enough money to put food on the table.

"He raised sheep and promised me the money from every bum lamb I saved that winter," Thelma said. "He ended up cheating us out of that money too. I really hated that man."

That winter Melvin captured a tiny jackrabbit and brought it into the house for his new bride. It quickly adjusted to indoor living. The tiny animal spent most of his time following Thelma around the house. At night, it snuggled between the couple or jumped from one to the

---

[218] Thelma Callaham Nation. Personal interview by Moni Hourt, 1998.
[219] A year later Melvin saved enough money to buy his young wife a small diamond, wedding band set, but Thelma always wore the three rings together---when they weren't hanging on a nail in the cupboard. She worried about getting the rings dirty or damaged and often left them hanging in the cupboard. However, when the couple would go out, she dashed into the kitchen, often making Melvin stop the car so she could run back into the house to retrieve her rings.

Thelma and Melvin with his 1941 Ford Business Coupe.

other across the bed covers. It was hard to keep the rabbit off the cold cement floors, and he eventually caught a lupine's version of the flu and died. Thelma said Melvin was as upset over the rabbit's death as she was.

"We did everything to survive that year," Thelma remembered with a tinge of anger in her voice. "It was a good thing there were lots of antelope around. That's about all we ate. We literally pulled each other through the first year of our marriage."

Conditions at the ranch continued to deteriorate. Then the boss ordered a pregnant Thelma to clean his wife's house for a card party. Melvin told his boss that his wife could clean her own "damn house." Within an hour they left the ranch. The couple moved in with Melvin's parents while he stuccoed his boyhood home.[220] Later that month he started working for the Hoover Rodeo Company on a full-time basis.

The couple's oldest daughter Ramona, quickly nicknamed Moni, was born in June of 1951. The day after her birth, Nation "bucked out" a load of horses from the wild herds of the Red Desert. Only two of the 26 horses showed bucking horse skills.

"Those horses were wild little rats," Melvin said. "We'd throwed a bad party the night before. Those horses must've knowed that. I'd get on a horse, he'd run away, hit the fence, and I'd bail out. I'd go back to the chutes and get on another one. I was whipped at the end of the day, but I made it to the hospital to see Thelma."

---

[220] Melvin said his Dad gave him a $100 bill for stuccoing the house. That was more than their former boss had paid them for three months' work.

Melvin always said he was not a flashy bareback rider, but spectators said he was a tough one.

In a diary entry dated July 3, 1951, Thelma Nation wrote that Melvin did very well at the Crawford Rodeo the night before.

"He's cleaning up, she wrote. "He's placing in both the bull riding and the bareback riding. We went to the bar tonight and saw some guys we hadn't seen for a while. We had a good time."[221]

Melvin on a bull at Crawford.

---

[221] Thelma Callaham Nation. Diary 1951-52.

During one three-rodeo sweep the next month, Melvin won about a thousand dollars. Buzz Hoover senior, had been tightening the purse strings at the ranch which made it difficult for Junior to meet his obligations. Melvin's prize money was enough to pay the couple's grocery bill, pay the back payments on the Ford, and take a trip to Washington to visit Melvin's brother, Merlin.

When the couple returned to Nebraska in October of 1951, Melvin hired on at the Coffee Ranches north of Harrison, NE. Owned by John T Coffee and his son, Bill, the Hat Creek Ranch nestled in the Hat Creek Valley in northeastern Sioux County, near the abandoned town site of Bodarc.

Established in 1879, by CF Coffee,[222] Hat Creek was one of the first ranches developed in western Nebraska. Coffee and his crew planted hundreds of trees and diverted creek water to irrigate the grass and plants around the ranch buildings. In an 1883 map of the region, early day surveyors[223] listed the region as "Coffee's Garden." But, at that time, the Coffees actually owed very little of the ranch they had established. They built the foundation of their ranching legacy on public domain and ran cattle across an area that encompassed over 150 square miles. In 1882, the first homesteaders arrived in the region. CF Coffee, several members of his family, and hired men filed homestead claims[224] on their allowed 160 acres. Coffee also bought as many claims as he could from other homesteaders. The Homestead Laws, however, didn't favor ranching. They were geared to small farmers. In a country that took 12 acres to sustain one cow/calf pair for a year, 160 acres couldn't feed many cattle. At the turn of the century, CF Coffee, reportedly owned only 2000 acres of land, but he possessed nearly 20,000 cattle.[225] Although he retained his ranch, he also diversified. He sold much of his herd and went into the banking business.[226]

By 1951, the trees CF Coffee's crew planted at the ranch in 1879, huddled protectively around the cook house where the Nations were quartered and stretched like leafy soldiers

---

[222] CF Coffee was the father of John T Coffee and the grandfather of Bill Coffee. In 1871, he hired on as a drover on a Texas to Wyoming cattle drive organized by his brother-in-law, DH Snyder. The next year he was in charge of his own cattle drive. He established his first ranch in Wyoming, then moved cattle into the Hat Creek Valley in Nebraska in 1879, a year after the Lakota Indians who had historically inhabited the area were placed on the Pine Ridge reservation about 35 miles from Hat Creek.

[223] The surveyors map of the region is dated 1880 to 1883. A section is labeled Coffee's Garden. Another area is labeled Coffee Ranch. The map was registered on February 18, 1884

[224] The claims were filed near water sources. Running water in the Hat Creek valley was a precious commodity. The Coffees filed homesteads on most of the water sources.

[225] Bill Coffee. Taped interview by Moni Hourt—2000, Coffee home Harrison, NE.

[226] In 1895, Coffee traded 2000 cows with calves at side to Chadron banker, Bartlett Richards for the First National bank. Within the next 20 years, he owned several banks between Lusk, Wyoming, and Gordon, Nebraska.

Cowboys gather in front of a log bunkhouse at the Hat Creek Ranch. Photo: Coffee collection.

nearly two-miles from the ranch yard to the county road. In the ranch yard, CF Coffee's turn-of-the-century house,[227] barn, and bunk house stood as stately reminders of a respected ranching heritage.

On the couple's first day at the ranch, John T Coffee sauntered casually into the ranch house. Thelma said John obviously knew he had an 18-year-old ranch wife on board. He asked her if she needed help getting dinner on the table.

"He drained the potatoes for me, but left quite a bit of water in the bottom of the pot," Thelma always smiled when she recounted her first day on the ranch. "I mentioned it to him. He told me we could use it for gravy. Moni was bawling, so he told me he'd rock the baby. I thought he was going to rock her head right off. He was a good old guy. I liked John T.[228] He must have decided I could handle my job. After that day, he'd come in early once in a while to visit, but he never came in to help me again."

The couple liked the ranch tucked beside Hat Creek in the tree-studded valley and the work was challenging. More importantly, it was not "farming." Bill was in the process of developing a herd of Quarter Horses. The Coffees owned several hundred, Square Top[229] 3 branded, Hereford

---

[227] Coffee built the large two story house for his wife, Daisy, and his three children. They lived in Cheyenne, Wyoming until 1888 when a drought hit the region. Homesteaders were claiming much of the ranch land. According to Bill Coffee, his grandfather told his wife that he either sold the ranch or the house in Cheyenne. She moved to the ranch.

[228] Thelma Callaham Nation. Personal Interview by Moni Hourt 1997.

[229] The Square Top 3 brand was a herd brand used by CF Coffee to identify the cattle he brought down the Texas trail in 1873. The cattle on the ranch Coffee established in Wyoming were branded with the 010 brand. He branded the cattle in Nebraska with a Square-Top 3.

The home CF Coffee built for his wife, Daisy, in 1888 was demolished after Melvin and Thelma moved to the Hat Creek Ranch in 1951.
Photo: Coffee Collection

cattle. Ranches all over the United States purchased Coffee brood stock including the Parker Ranch in Hawaii.[230] The daily work revolved around both the cattle and the horses.

In 2002, Virginia Coffee was sorting pictures when she found this photograph of Melvin. It was labeled "Melvin Nation, winter 1952."

---

[230] Peg Coffee, John wife, purchased a 16 mm video cameras in 1930. Her miles of video tape show images of haying, branding, and working cattle on the Coffee Ranches. They also show Coffee cattle, suspended in slings, being loaded onto ships that were headed for the Parker Ranch in Hawaii. The Parker Ranch history does not specifically mention purchasing cattle from the Coffees but it does say cattle were purchased from western Nebraska.

That first winter, Melvin fed the cattle with a team of Jenny mules. When the hay stuck to the wagon Melvin simply "rared back" and pried the hay loose. In the process he splintered several wooden pitch fork handles.

Bill Coffee told Harrison merchant, Dick Herren, that Nation was a good man, then added with pseudo-sarcasm, "All he needs to feed a 1000 head of cows is a team of mules and an iron handled pitch fork."[231]

On their first Thanksgiving at the ranch, the couple ignored the foot of snow that blanketed the country and embarked on 80-mile round trip to Thelma's folks for Thanksgiving dinner. They packed their daughter in blankets in the back seat and fought their way across the

The couple's oldest daughter, Moni, spent most of her first year at the Coffee Hat Creek Ranch.

snow covered roads to the farm. There were few decent roads and even fewer four-wheel drive vehicles although Jeeps and Dodge Power Wagons were available in some parts of the country after World War II.[232] The couple wrestled through the deep snow in the roadway, then careened onto the pasture beyond. They tore the water pump out of their car and had to borrow Melvin's sister, Anita's car for their return trip. She reluctantly agreed. They ate lunch and left an hour later. It took them a whole day to go to a Sunday dinner. The baby reportedly weathered the journey quite well.

In June 1952, Melvin and Bill argued over the correct way to top off a stack of hay. From the top of the stack, Melvin javelined his pitch fork to the ground. It thudded between Bill's boots. Melvin leaped from the stack and proclaimed that his wife would fix the meal that noon, but by morning they would be gone. He returned to the Hoover Ranch.

"I'd decided I hated Bill Coffee worse than any man in the world. But really, I was just looking for an excuse to rodeo," Melvin said. "Buzzy had his operation up and running again.[233] He had a knack for building a good pen of rodeo stock. It always looked like he could really be successful 'this time.'"

---

[231] Dick Herren. Interview with Moni Hourt, 1988. Dick established a farm/ranch supply store in Harrison in 1946.
[232] Dodge Power Wagons were produced for military use during World War II. After the war, many were sold to farmers and ranchers across the country.
[233] According to an interview with Melvin Nation in 2000 and with Ridge Hoover Chlanda in 2017, Buzzy and his father were constantly fighting. When "Old Buzz" was mad, he quit funding the stock contracting business, forcing Buzzy to sell his stock. Buzzy restarted his business several times during his association with Melvin.

THE HOOVER RANCH

"Buzzy Hoover was the handiest guy I ever knew. He'd be walking along beside you. All at once his voice would change. You'd look over and his feet were dangling in front of your face. He was walking along on his hands. He had an eye for stock, and he knew how to run a rodeo. But his Dad controlled the money. He wouldn't let Buzzy grow up, so he didn't. His is a sad ole' story."
Melvin Nation

Sunday rodeos at the Hoover Ranch arena were popular events in the area.
Photo: Ridge Hoover Chlanda collection

Thelma's parents, Elmer and Verna Callaham, hired on with Hoover a short time after the Nations moved back to the ranch. Thelma left Moni with her mother and traveled with Melvin on his trips across the country. She was with him early one morning as they came over the 11,306-foot top of Berthoud Pass on Colorado's Continental Divide. That week, they made three trips from Harrison to Idaho Springs, Colorado. Melvin hadn't seen a bed for nearly 72 hours and was under the wheel for 24-straight hours. Suddenly Thelma realized that although her husband's eyes were open, he was asleep at the wheel.

"I let out a squawk, and he came to," Thelma said. "For a second or two things got a bit hairy. His hands clamped around that steering wheel. The drop-off at the end of the road was coming pretty fast. It was a long-ways off the top of those mountains. I was sure glad when he finally realized what was going on. I spent the next few hours pouring water over the top of his head to keep him awake."

Melvin hauled horses and bulls thousands of miles across the country.
Photo: Ridge Hoover Chlanda collection

Throughout that winter Hoover worked to improve his herd, and Melvin continued hauling bulls and horses into the ranch from different sections of the country. In the winter of 1952, while ferrying a load of bulls from the Smith outfit in South Dakota, he suddenly realized his bulls had broken the truck's center partition.

"I'd been driving most of the night. I stopped and had a cup of coffee with Neal Allen in Hot Springs, then headed back out. The sun was coming up. It was a beautiful morning, then I looked in the rear view mirror. There was a bull behind me. The next minute there was another one. It took me a minute before it dawned on me that those bulls hadn't been in front of me, so they must be getting' out of the truck. Four of them were out before I got stopped, ran back to the end of the truck, and jammed the tailgate shut. We never did find one of the bulls."

*Most of Hoover's bulls were Brahma, but a few were crossbreeds.
One was a Hereford. Bulls at feed trough at the ranch.
Photo: Ridge Hoover Chlanda collection*

Hoover had an affinity for his bulls. He even cared for them himself—if there weren't any men around. If one of the bulls was ridden, he'd be depressed for days. He certainly wasn't happy that one disappeared, but little was ever said on the subject.

"Buzzy had some of the 'ranks,'" Melvin said. "I rode Number 55, a Braford bull, at Lusk one year. I think my nose was draggin' in the dust for the last second. There were only two guys that ever rode him. Spike Bronson was the other one. But there were lots of rodeos when they paid all the money on the ground.[234] The bulls were that tough to get around."[235]

Working with the pen of bulls was always tough. "We had a bull get into the neighbor's Jersey heifers. The rancher wasn't all that happy about it, so Earl Hale and I went to get the bull. Earl was an ornery old guy. He'd pull a joke on somebody and ride it to death. That morning, he was riding a horse named Rabbit, a little white horse that was scared to death of bulls. He couldn't run fast enough to get away from them either. I roped the bull, and Earl moved in to get another rope on him. The bull 'built to' ole Rabbit and he started runnin.' The bull was headed in the right direction so I just gived him a little slack. He'd get his head in old Rabbit's rear end

---

[234] Ground money, assembled from entry fees, is paid to every entry in a bull riding competition if no one is able to ride a bull for the required eight seconds.
[235] Many years later, Melvin said the bull breeding program in the country has now produced bulls that are nearly "unrideable." In the 50s Buzzy Hoover was trying to produce the same type of bull.

and lift him up in the air. Earl would scream and cuss and slap at the bull with his rope or hands, whatever he had handy. We went that way for quite a while. Earl kept telling me he'd kill me if I didn't get that bull off him."

Melvin finally took up the slack, but not until the bull strayed away from the ranch buildings which meant Melvin ended up dragging him the rest of the way to the corrals. It wasn't long after that that Hale had another encounter with a Hoover bull. The animal jumped the fence at a Custer, SD rodeo. Hale, working the arena as a pick-up man, roped the bull, jerked him off balance, and headed back into the rodeo arena, the bull bouncing behind him.

"Earl was pretty proud of himself," Melvin said. "You could just see it. His old buckskin horse was working just right. The bull was comin'. The crowd was cheering. Then—the bull missed the gate. He wrapped himself around the gatepost. The next thing you know, Earl's flat on his back in the arena. That bull jerked the whole front end out of his saddle. He never was too fond of bulls after that."

Earl, like many cowboys of the era, seldom let adversity get the better of him. "Ole Earl sure wasn't a sissy," Melvin said. "He broke his leg one time picking up horses. He came over to the truck poured startin' ether[236] on the leg to numb it, then went back to the arena. That's the way most of the guys going down the road were. Nothing stopped them, or at least not for very long."

Winter months generally meant staying home and taking care of the rodeo stock. Although Melvin said he enjoyed these quiet times with the animals on the ranch, he admitted that his family didn't "always appreciate the stock's qualities."

Most of the bulls at the ranch were quiet when not in an arena.
Thelma said she didn't trust them to stay that way.
Photo: Ridge Hoover Chlanda collection

---

[236] "Starting ether" was used to start diesel engines. It was a common practice in ranch country to spray an injury with the ether to numb pain.

Thelma and her mother, Verna Callaham, were carrying a tub of corn to the chicken house the morning a Brahma cow, corralled nearby, coughed. Verna started running, hauling Thelma and the tub with her. In a few seconds they were perched on a fence, the full tub between them. A few months later, Melvin was trying to capture a Brahma that escaped the corral. Thelma, intent on hanging her wash on the line, heard a snuffle on the other side of her clean white sheet. Cautiously pushing the cloth aside, she came nose to nose with a startled bull. She grabbed her laundry basket and with one wild leap, propelled herself up the ladder of the wind charger tower. The bull stampeded in the opposite direction. Melvin, witnessing the event from his saddle, convulsed in laughter. He said Thelma crawled down from the tower and "gave me a good cussin." She never did explain why she took her laundry basket to the top of the tower.

The ranch was a mecca for cowboys of all types. Thelma said there were a few that needed to be thrown off the place before they arrived.

"Melvin and Buzzy were gone quite a bit. There were a few guys around that just weren't any good," Thelma snorted with disgust. "One of these guys told the men he was going to come upstairs to my room. Tuffy Bridge heard him. He parked a chair in the kitchen and slept there all night to make sure Vern didn't try anything."

Thelma's diary in 1953 provides insight into the couple's life on the ranch. She sewed dresses and shirts on her brand new sewing machine. She visited back and forth with Buzzy's wife, Ridge, who she considered a great friend. The women accompanied their husbands to the Denver Stock Show. Thelma wrote that they visited a booth full of hand-painted scarves, each sporting a huge price tag. Once she returned home, she simply duplicated the design and painted it on one of Melvin's silk neckerchiefs. Then she bought a couple more silk neckerchiefs and made one for her sister, and another for Ridge. She reported that they looked just like the ones at the Stock Show.

At one of the Stock Show venues, Melvin ordered Thelma a pair of shiny black boots, decorated with red leather appliquéd designs. Thelma reported that when the boots arrived, they didn't fit. Heartbroken and knowing that the boots couldn't be replaced, she started a process of stretching them, soaking them in water and wearing them or filling the wet books with sand or packed paper. Eventually she was able to wear them.

Recipes for burnt sugar cake and cinnamon roll dough were tucked into the diary pages between stories of dances in Glen, Andrews, and Harrison. She and Melvin played checkers and Canasta, listened to the radio, went roller skating in Lusk, and to the movies in Harrison.

Even the yellowed pages couldn't quiet contain her glee when she reported Melvin was charged with speeding and had to pay a

Thelma and Ridge.
Photo: Moni Nation, 1962.

Thelma also used her handiwork for a jacket for her daughter, Moni so she could attend the Hoover rodeos in style.
Photo: Nation collection

$14.65 fine. He'd been telling her SHE was driving too fast. On a neighboring page, Thelma reported that her young daughter discovered the un-baked bread rising on the oven door. The little girl kneaded the bread vigorously and told her Dad that night that she'd made the bread, "all herself." A note on the page said the bread was a "bit flatter" than usual that day.

The diary also reported that Melvin had shaved his beard and that Moni wouldn't have a thing to do with him. "Moni recognized his voice, but every time he picked her up, she rared back, looked at him, then started bellering. Never did make up with him tonight."

Earl Callaham, Thelma's grandfather, made many trips to the ranch that year. His brother, Gay, accompanied him on one occasion. Velma, always known as Sis, was a frequent visitor. One evening the pair pierced each other's ears. They spent hours designing a fancy western shirt for Melvin to wear to an upcoming rodeo. In April, Sis brought Melvin a chicken for his 23rd birthday.

"Sis spent as much time with us as she could," Melvin said. "She and that Thelma were the biggest damn 'smartalecs' I'd ever seen. If they weren't teasing someone, they were givin' someone hell. It was never boring when they were around."

Buzzy Hoover and his father quarreled endlessly. In the summer of 1953, the elder Hoover, the money behind the ranch, forced his son to sell the rodeo stock and then put the ranch up for sale.

Leo J. Kramer bought most of the stock and asked Melvin to go to work for him. Melvin agreed. Then Buzzy came up with some more cash. He called Melvin and they started searching for more stock. Buzzy kept some of his horses by pasturing them out with friends. He and Melvin headed south to Brahma Bull country to locate some good bucking bulls. Melvin called Kramer and said he'd changed his mind. A news article in Thelma's scrapbook reported that Kramer was killed in a car wreck in the fall of 1953. Harry Knight and Gene Autry ended up with his bucking stock.

Buzzy purchased Harley Roth's contracting business, but most of the bulls for the reincarnated business came from Texas. A few were purebred Brahma, but most were crossbreeds of various kinds. Nation accompanied Hoover to Houston in the summer of 1953. They bought 100 head of bulls from the Goss Ranch in the Bayou area of Texas.

"We took the bulls to an arena in southwest Houston that was part of a night club called 'N— Roans.' Nation said. "We spent three weeks testing the bulls. Buzzy and I were the only white men in the bunch. When we were all done, we had about 20 bulls to bring home. A

Pat and Wilma Callaham play with their horses in the shadow of a Hoover/Roth truck. Photo: Ridge Hoover Chlanda collection

few years ago I asked a man who lived in Houston if he'd ever heard of 'N—- Roans.'[237] He said they'd turned the nightclub and the arena into a museum for the Black cowboys. I'd like to go back there someday."

Many of the Black cowboys who rode bulls were outstanding hands, but Melvin said 1950's discrimination reached even into the rodeo arena.

"They starved those good colored cowboys to death," Nation said. "There was one boy who finished second in the world, but he turned hand springs to do it. There sure wasn't anything fair about it."

Although more stock was purchased, the situation on the ranch continued to be unstable. Old Buzz threatened on an almost daily basis to close the operation down. In August 1953, Melvin "ran into" Bill Coffee at the Sioux County Fair. Coffee was having problems loading a mare and colt into a trailer. Melvin stepped in to help him.

"Bill asked me what I was doing. I said I was about ready to change jobs, that things weren't working out at the Hoover Ranch. He told me to stop by the house when I was ready for a change. I did. We moved to Warbonnet[238] November 16, 1953. I never regretted it."

---

[237] Although the author tried to locate information about the nightclub, she was unable to do so.
[238] The Warbonnet Ranch, purchased by the Coffees in 1941 was 10 miles north and a 1000 feet lower than Harrison, Nebraska. Built in the Warbonnet Valley west of Hat Creek the ranch's main water supply was the Warbonnet Creek. The creek's head waters were located above the ranch. The ranch was established in 1869 by two early cattlemen, S.F Emmons and Bob Brewster. Eventually the ranch was purchased by John Anderson who had worked for the cattle company. He built a beautiful white brick home on the ranch grounds, but the Nation family always lived in the "cook house" located north of the white house.

The Hoover Ranch had three main tasks, find new stock, train and sell extra stock, and produce rodeos. The operation was successful when Buzzy Jr. and his dad coordinated their efforts, but that was seldom the case.

WARBONNET

"There wasn't a ranch that ever fit me better than Warbonnet.
I loved every inch of it." Melvin Nation.

Although, in time, Melvin considered Warbonnet a great place to live, the first night at the ranch was far from comfortable. The couple was busily unloading household goods and setting up the ranch house when they realized their 18-month-old daughter was missing.

"Babe[239] and I headed for the creek. Melvin took off for the barn," Sis [240] said. "We searched that place from one end to the other. We finally went into the house to call in the neighbors, but first made one more run through the house calling for her."

Moni popped out of the kitchen cupboard.[241] "Here I am, Daddy," she chortled. "I is hiding from you." Sis said she wasn't sure if they wanted to hug the little girl or "paddle her little rear end."[242]

The Warbonnet Creek that had created so much panic for the Nations the night they moved in had been the ranch's primary source of water from the time it was established in 1879. In a 1997 interview Bill Coffee said he told his Dad he had a plan to produce a steady, clean, water source for the ranch house and supplement the livestock water by running a pipeline directly from the Scotty Springs, the headwaters of the creek. The grade was all downhill. It appeared to be simple physics. The task proved more difficult than expected.

"I ran a pipeline from Scotty Springs to the cistern we built on the hill above the ranch buildings," Coffee said shaking his head. "But I couldn't get any water to come out of the damn pipe. Every day at 5 a.m. my Dad would call me and ask if I had water yet. I'd tell him, 'No, no yet.' Finally, I flew to Denver, Colorado and talked to some engineers. They told me to put a vent

---

[239] Velma Callaham always called her sister, Thelma, 'Babe.'
[240] Velma Callaham Rising was always called "Sis" by her family.
[241] A floor to ceiling cupboard on the west end of the kitchen provided a great hiding place. During hide and seek games the Nation children simply pushed the coats aside in the coat-rack portion of the closet and climbed inside, just as Moni did that first night.
[242] Velma Callaham Rising. Personal Interview by Moni Hourt, 2008, Rising home, Crawford, NE.

in the pipe. I did. They next morning when my Dad called I told him, I sure as hell did—eight gallons a minute. It's worked ever since."

When Melvin and Thelma moved to the ranch, sweet water was instantly available across the ranch. However, once in a while an animal would crawl into the cistern. Thelma would complain about an "odd taste," and Melvin would take the men to the cistern to clean it out. A snake managed to trap himself in the cistern. He wriggled his way through the water pipe and dropped into the kitchen sink. After Thelma made sure the snake knew exactly what she thought of him, she chopped his head off with her "carving" knife and threw his dismembered body on the front step. No-one returned to the field that day until a screen was installed—very tightly—on the cistern water pipe.

Warbonnet from Cistern Hill.

The water in the creek was also diverted to irrigation channels, or pumped directly out of the creek bed by a gas-powered generator mounted on a tractor. Much of the water was used to water the trees Melvin planted in the yard. Until pipelines and hydrants were installed in the yard, water for the trees south of the barn, was carried from the hydrant in the barn. [243]

Wind-charger electrical power was installed at the ranch in the early 1940s. A few years later, electrical lines were constructed down Monroe Canyon to the ranch. When the Nations moved into the ranch cook house, the electrical batteries and generators, stored in the two big brick generator houses across the creek, were no longer functioning. The ranch was totally electrified.

---

[243] In his years at the ranch, Melvin planted hundreds of trees. His girls remember it was one of their jobs to string hoses across the yard or carrying buckets of water to water the trees.

Telephone service was also available at the ranch, originally via wires stretched from fence post to fence post, occasionally even climbing up and across pine trees. When the line reached a gate, it was guided up the side of high poles, across a top brace and down the other side. Then the line restarted its fence pole/tree hopping process. By the time the Nations moved in, poles had replaced most of the fence line route, but telephone service was spotty.

"We all got together in the early '50s and rebuilt the line down Monroe Canyon and on into Wyoming. Your Dad could build a lot of line in a short time. That made the job easier," Everett Thomas[244] said in 1996. "We had to cut down a bunch of trees to put in the poles, but we sure had better service after that. Grace[245] had a switchboard in our backroom. People would call her, and she'd switch their calls on to Wyoming. Calls came through all hours of the night, but we didn't have to pay for our subscription, so that was good."

The updated telephone service was delivered across a six-member party line. To call the neighbors, the phone was cranked an appropriate number of rings. One long ring was two fast cranks of the phones magnetic powered electrical generators, a short ring was one quick fast crank.[246] The Nations' ring tone of two short rings and a long ring announced incoming phone calls.

Long distance calls were placed through the telephone office located in Crawford. The switchboard operator took the call, called the requested number, then called the ranch to connect the two parties. "Rubbering," (listening in on phone conversations) was a common recreation for those on a party line. Occasionally, there would be so many listeners on the line that the actual call recipient could barely hear the caller.

"Leona was the worst. I don't think she ever missed a call," Thelma remembered, smiling and shaking her head. "Melvin would finally say, 'Leona, get off the phone.' Sometimes he'd add please. Either way, most of the time, she'd just hang up long enough for us to hear the click, then she'd pick it back up. I thought about slamming the phone into the cupboard to give her an earache, but was afraid I'd break the damn thing."[247]

Moni quickly learned that she could pick up the phone and ask for her Aunt Anita, (Nation) an operator at the Crawford Bell Telephone office. Then she asked Anita to please call her Grandma on the Leeling[248] place.

Early one cold, winter, morning Thelma was surprised when her mother pulled into the yard. The mystery was quickly solved. The car wouldn't start that morning. Moni didn't want

---

[244] Everett Thomas lived on a ranch about four miles southwest of Warbonnet.
[245] Grace (Martin) Thomas, Everett's wife.
[246] Thelma Nation interview 200 with Moni Hourt, Hat Creek Ranch.
[247] Thelma Nation. Interview with Moni Hourt, 2000.
[248] Verna Callaham. Interview with Moni Hourt, 1989, Hourt home, Sioux County, Nebraska. After moving from the Hoover place, Verna and Elmer Callaham moved to the "Leeling" place three miles north of Harrison, about 7 miles south of the Warbonnet Ranch.

to miss school, so she simply called her Grandmother. Verna Callaham had driven 20 miles, round trip, to take her granddaughter the half-mile to her country school.

The family quickly settled into their new life. Melvin said the ranch suited him in a way nothing else ever had. He liked the hard work and took great pride in the ranch itself. "I argue with people that acre for acre, Warbonnet is the best ranch in Sioux County. I loved every inch of it."

Nearly 80 years before Melvin arrived at the ranch, Benjamin Brewster,[249] drew the same conclusion about the land at the base of Monroe Canyon. On April 1913,[250] Brewster wrote that "in 1879, he and his crew drove a herd of cattle to Warbonnet from North Laramie, Wyoming."[251] The ranch coordinates recorded by Brewster's uncle, Samuel Emmons, and Joseph Maurice (often spelled Morris)[252] were recorded in the 1878 Northwestern Nebraska survey. In his handwritten memoir,[253] Brewster described his early impression of the ranch.

> "It is a wonderful sight from the top of the bluffs across the Hat Creek basin for fifty miles to the Black Hills, a low blue line on the northern horizon…Uncle Frank made the elevation somewhat over a thousand feet from the ranch to the top of the bluffs…Warbonnet Creek is formed by five or six small spring branches uniting and the ranch is situated a short distance below the fork. Other creeks to the east and west are similarly formed and they all eventually flow into Hat Creek and the latter empties into the Cheyenne River just south of the Black Hills. The country in this drainage basin is nearly fifty miles square and our range was situated in the southern strip stretching from Hat Creek, twelve miles west of the ranch, to the head of Indian Creek some fifteen miles west.

---

[249] According to a bio located in the Harvard University Class of 1861 pamphlet, Brewster was the nephew of Samuel Franklin Emmons, a graduate of Harvard University who volunteered for the United States Geological Exploration of the Fortieth Parallel and was "regularly attached to the corps as a geologist where he remained until July 1, 1877." According to the Harvard bio, Emmons and his wife moved to Cheyenne, Wyoming in 1877 and established a cattle-ranch, subsequently named the War Bonnet Ranch, in the Hat Creek basin, on the boundaries of Wyoming, Nebraska, and Dakota. He turned his range cattle business at War Bonnet over to his nephew, B.E. Brewster, in 1879.

[250] Clarence Schnurr. "Warbonnet-John Anderson." *Sioux County Memoirs of Its Pioneers*. In this story, Clarence identifies B.E. Brewster as "Bob Brewster." That name may have come from Virginia Cole Trenholm's book *Footprints on the Frontier*. However, there is little indication that his family called him "Bob." Schnurr did not identify the source of his "April 1913" data, but it probably came from Brewster's unpublished memoir.

[251] Schnurr, Clarence. "John A Anderson." *Sioux County: Memoirs of Its Pioneers*. Harrison, NE: Harrison Sun-News, 1967.

[252] Maurice later established a ranch on Sowbelly Creek and became one of Sioux County's first commissioners.

[253] Brewster, Benjamin Brewster. *Benjamin Emmons Brewster, 1951-1935 An Autobiography Covering His Boyhood and Career Raising Cattle*. The manuscript was never published. Its front cover says, "This typewritten copy was made in 1949 from his long-hand draft, which appears to have been written in 1896. It was found in his Boston office about 1925." The informational text was not signed, but did note that by 1925, Brewster was an invalid. Copy provided by Sarah Coffee Radill, now located in Moni Hourt collection.

Uncle Frank had built cabins and corrals on the head of Indian Creek and on Hat Creek to the east. We claimed the range for thirty miles along the bluffs and for fifteen miles north. It was wonderful cattle range at that time, well- watered by hundreds of springs along the bluffs and by numerous small streams thickly lined by trees and bushes forming natural shelter for cattle. The land between the streams was generally well grassed and more or less broken by small flat-topped buttes and ridges. In places were many washes of bad land, a white clay soil—very slippery when wet and quite devoid of grass. The bad land increased greatly in extent the further north you went and the creeks were sunk rather deep in that area, with few good crossings… The Warbonnet Ranch buildings looked quite imposing to me after our rather scanty ones on the north. Laramie. There was a large bunk house 18x30 with sheds, stable, and a stock yard built two or three hundred yards out on the flat to the west of the creek."

Hired by the Emmons and Brewster Cattle Company in the early 1880s, John Anderson came to Sioux County in 1884 to work on the Warbonnet Ranch. In 1887, John and his brother Nels, partnered with B.E. and Paul Brewster to established the Warbonnet Livestock Company. John bought the interests of the last remaining partners in 1907. He increased his herd, further developed the irrigation systems and hay meadows, and improved the ranch buildings. He and his wife, Emma, raised their family in the large three-storied house, built of locally-molded cement brick, on the south side of Warbonnet Creek. They also buried their tiny son in a grave along the creek.[254]

Bill Coffee said the cook house at Warbonnet was constructed from material from the earliest structure on the ranch. Photo: Bill Coffee family.

---

[254] In the mid-1970s a marker was laid at the foot of a giant cottonwood tree in honor of the Anderson's son, but the little boy was actually buried north of the marker. When the flood swept through the area in 1956, a corner of the casket was uncovered. Melvin spent several hours covering the casket. He showed his daughter and granddaughter where the grave was located. Melvin always felt that Bill placed the marker where he did to make sure no one ever "messed with the little boy's grave."

The cook house across the creek from the big house, according to Bill Coffee,[255] was built shortly after the ranch was established in 1879. Massive logs hauled to the ranch from the Monroe Canyon sawmill formed the two-story structure. The house became the center of ranching operations in 1879—as evidenced by photographs of early cowboys lounging near its exterior.

Ranching operations during the years the Nations lived at the ranch also revolved around the cook house. Regularly men met in the kitchen for meals, planning sessions or just to visit. By the time the Nations arrived, the kitchen walls had been plastered, while the living room walls were covered with horizontally placed "lath," then in a vertical wainscoting pattern on two of the walls. The naked chink-filled log walls in the unfinished attic rooms still characterized 1800s construction style. The large kitchen, attached to a south facing porch and "separator room," featured white-speckled, red, tile flooring. A single row of solid squares, decorated at intervals by the ranch's "Square Top Three" brand, ran in a zig-zag path around the edge of the kitchen creating a perfect race track for two-legged kid races.[256] A dining room table that would seat at least twelve, and was the scene of many discussions, stretched across the room. On the kitchen's east wall, a large iron cook stove squatted between the pantry and bedroom doors.

Moni and Robbin in the kitchen with the Majestic Cook Stove. The tile floor was red with white tiles outlining the edge. Moni hid in the large cupboard on the far end of the kitchen the night the Nations moved into the house.
Photo: Nation collection

---

[255] Bill Coffee. Interview by Moni Hourt, 1999, White River pasture.
[256] To the often great irritation of their mother, the Nation children loved to run the white road around the kitchen.

The "Majestic[257] stove" was sparked into action when it came time to cook a massive pot of stew, or to warm little girls and men who spent sub-zero days outside. Often on cold winter days, the oven door was opened and piled with boots, gloves, or even baby calves that needed a quick jolt of warm air. It was also used to render the fat from a butchered hog.[258]

"Melvin always thought the lard that I rendered out was better than anything we bought in town," Thelma Nation said ruefully. "But rendering lard was hard work. When we cut the fat off the hog we left the skin on. Then I filled every damn pan I had, cranked up the wood stove, and watched the fat melt. The lard melted—eventually. The skin broke off and drifted to the sides of the pan. I scooped the crisp pieces of skin out with a spoon and drained it on a dish towel. Melvin would almost make himself sick eating the cracklins."[259]

A few steps south of the "Majestic," cupboards stretched from the floor to the ceiling. Hooks, screwed into the end of the cupboard, held sweaters, coats, and an occasional rope. Boots and shoes were generally dumped underneath. The men seldom removed their boots, but they always scraped them off before they entered the kitchen.

"Thelma was plumb 'irate' if someone tracked mud across her kitchen," Melvin, his blue eyes twinkling at the thought. "I sure didn't have the courage to do it."

Moni, Melvin, and Robbin in their favorite reading chair.

---

[257] The Majestic Stove Company of St. Louis, MO produced stoves from the 1880s until the 1940s. At the 1904 World's Fair in St. Louis, the Majestic Stove exhibition was advertised as a "very popular attraction."

[258] Thelma filled the fire pit on the stove with small chunks of wood; other small branches were stacked in the wood box. She filled large pans and iron skillets with slabs of "back fat" from a hog. The lard was heated at a low heat maintained by adding small chunks of wood to the wood box. Eventually the melted lard was screened through cheese cloth, poured into small containers, cooled and stored in the "separator" room where it was cool. During the melting process, the skin floated to the top and broke into small irregular shaped pieces: "cracklins." In later years, after Thelma stopped making lard, she purchased "pig rinds." Melvin did eat them, but swore nothing was better than her cracklins.

[259] Cracklins in modern cook books are called gratins. They are made from the pork belly section of a hog. They consist of skin, fat, and meat from processed pork. They are not the same as pork rinds.

Mud may have been banned from the kitchen, but toys weren't. The western-most kitchen drawer was filled with toys that were supposed to be stuffed away when the men came in for dinner. If they weren't, one side-glance from their Dad sent the girls scurrying to hide the offending play things. Many winter evenings Melvin relaxed in his large overstuffed chair in the living room, pulled a book from the nearby "built-in-bookcase," tucked his daughters in beside him, and read to them. *The Virginian*, *Black Beauty*, *My Friend Flicka*, and books by western author, Zane Grey, were his favorites.

"The book I remember the most was *Black Beauty*," Moni Hourt said. "He finally told me if I didn't quit blubbering he wouldn't read it anymore."

A "booklady" made regular trips past the Warbonnet Ranch.[260] Moni said she picked the books up at the mailbox, carried them to the house, and arranged them in her Dad's chair. There was generally a reading session that night.

Although some reading sessions were postponed if Melvin was "tired out," he generally read to the girls several times a week. "Our living room walls were covered with Frederick Remington and Charles Russell prints, and invariably he'd connect the pictures to something we had read. A William Henry Jackson photograph[261] of a cattle drive hung above the coach. Dad would challenge us to count the cattle, but we never got very far."

A few of the hired men, primarily the ones that worked year-round on the ranch, spent evenings with the family, but most of them retired to the bunkhouse, that was built perpendicular to the east side of the house. The bunkhouse was prohibited territory.

"You kids didn't need to go to the bunkhouse," Thelma said her lips tightening. "Melvin and Bill got men from all over the place, some even came from skid row in Denver. There were a few of the guys that we trusted, Bruce, Charley Quay, Marvin and Roger Davenport, but mostly the men stayed over there. We didn't let you kids bother them."

There was another reason that the Nation children were banned from the bunkhouse.[262] Bill asked that they not be allowed to play in the building or be there at any time without supervision. To Bill, the building meant incredible grief and loss. In 1947, shortly before his second birthday, the Coffee's only son, Buff, his sister, Twink, and a little girl who lived at the cook house were playing in the bunkhouse. No one is sure what happened, but there was rat poison in the building and some was found scattered across the floor. It was assumed that all

---

[260] The first official "bookmobile" that traveled to area ranches came from the Crawford, Nebraska library in the mid-60s, but a diary entry in Moni Nation's diary on June 15, 1962 said the "book lady" had left some books for them when she stopped at the mail box. The first Sioux County bookmobile made rounds to country schools in 1971.
[261] Jackson was the first person to photograph Yellowstone State Park. He also took pictures of cowboys in the west. The print hanging on the wall at Warbonnet was taken during a cattle drive on the JA Ranch, named by Charles Goodnight in honor of his European financial partner, John Adair, in Texas in 1901. The cattle in the 1902 lithograph covered the prairie and lined the winding river. They were reportedly sold to Corbin Morse of Rapid City.
[262] By the time Moni was 12, most of the hired men stayed at Hat Creek. She was allowed to move into one of the bedrooms in the bunkhouse. A few years later, Robbin also moved her room to the bunkhouse.

The Cook House where the Nation family lived. In the upper picture the attached bunkhouse is on the right. The bottom pictures show the house and bunkhouse from the back yard. The buildings were demolished in 2019.

three children started to eat the poison and that the girls spit it out. The family believed that Buff ingested the sweet-smelling pellets. A short time later he went into convulsions and died that evening. In a 2009 interview Virginia Coffee acknowledged that she was never sure Buff's convulsions had been caused by consuming rat poison. She said that he had fallen and bumped his head a few days before the bunkhouse incident. She also conceded that that her brother, a physician in Alliance, believed Buff had suffered a skull fracture and a brain injury in the fall.[263] Whatever the cause, the little boy's death devastated the Coffee family and always haunted the Nation girls.

Melvin often said death was "simply part of life," then added that it was "sure tough for those who were left behind." In early January 1954, Buzzy Hoover called to tell him that an airplane had crashed southwest of Harrison, somewhere near the Nebraska/Wyoming border. He asked Melvin to join the search party. Melvin was with one of the groups who discovered the accident.

"They were both good men, just out there having a great time, hunting a few coyotes. Someone made a mistake," Melvin said regretfully. "Harry had five little kids. His wife remarried and did a good job with the kids, but it's sad she had to do it alone."[264]

The "Big House," John Anderson's massive cement block home was built to house a large growing family, but his young son, who died at an early age and is buried at the ranch, didn't get to enjoy the large verandas, and second floor balconies. The house was also generally off-limits to the Nation girls, but when Thelma was busy, the girls slipped under the large wrap-around porch and played in the soft, cool, dirt below the porch deck or carried a lunch to the porch. Seated "regally" in the rickety chairs that perched under the eaves they ate their sugar and toast sandwiches. Although Bill and Virginia lived in the house when they were first married, they

---

[263] Buff died shortly before his second birthday.
[264] "Two Men Killed in Plane Crash." *Crawford, Tribune.* January 15, 1954 told the story of the accident.

Melvin's paint horse grazing in the Big House yard.

moved into town after the 1949 Blizzard.²⁶⁵ Most of the time, the big house sat vacant. During the two summers the Coffees did live at the ranch however, the porch rang with girlish laughter.²⁶⁶ As Melvin was also known to say, "Life has to go on."

Warbonnet Barn was the center of the ranch activities throughout most of the year.

---

²⁶⁵ Bill went to Hat Creek at the beginning of the blizzard. Virginia Coffee and her two oldest daughters were stranded at the ranch for several days. They ran short of both fuel and food before a government "weasel" transported them to town to stay with Bill's parents. They moved to town after the blizzard.
²⁶⁶ Bill and Virginia had two older daughters, Twink (Claire) and Sara. Ann was Moni's age and Sue, the youngest daughter was Robbin's age.

THE CYCLE OF RANCH LIFE

> "A ranch revolves around cattle and the work of taking care of them. That suited me just fine. It follows a steady cycle throughout the year, then starts all over again. I liked the hard work and ranching made a lot more sense to me than farming ever did." Melvin Nation

Ranch work ran in cycles. A large part of each winter day was spent feeding hay to the various herds of cattle scattered in pastures across the ranch. For the first year Melvin lived on the ranch, he hitched a small set of mules, Jean and Ellen[267] to his hay wagon then needled sections of the 6 to 8 ton hay stacks onto the wagon to be fed to the cattle. (It generally took three or four trips to the stack yard to load and feed an entire stack.)

Sand Hills rancher, Buck Buckles,[268] said the needling process began by poking a long needle, attached to a chain, through the stack. The chain was thrown over the top of the stack, then the process was repeated three or four times, creating several chain arches over the stack. Once the chains were thrown over the stack, they were all tied to a longer chain located in the middle of the stack and hooked both to the offside of the wagon and to the team. In was important that the chains were evenly spaced in order to tip the hay correctly over onto the wagon. If any of the chains were pulled too tightly, it would tear the stack all to pieces. When done correctly, the horse rolled portions of the stack onto the sled in an elongated tube that resembled a rolled cigarette. Once that load of hay was fed, the process was repeated. Twisting hay onto a wagon was never easy and always labor intensive.

---

[267] Virginia Coffee's two sisters were Jean and Ellen. Bill obviously named his mules after the two women, but did keep the joke somewhat private until a hired man spilled the beans. He encountered Virginia and her sister, Jean, on a train trip to Alliance. Virginia identified the woman next to her as her sister. The man asked if she was Jean or Ellen. Somewhat surprised at the question, Jean asked why he wanted to know. He quickly and with much glee, related the story of the Jean and Ellen mules. According to ranch folk lore, the story, recited on the train, was not considered by the women, as humorous as the hired man thought it was.

[268] Buck Buckles. Interview with Moni Hourt, many times between 2007 and 2018. Buckles was a longtime friend of Melvin Nation. He used horses in the hay field until 2016.

Buck Buckles used a slide stacker to put up his hay until 2016.

A year after Melvin was hired at Warbonnet, Bill bought a small team of horses from Harold Skavdahl.[269] A long cable replaced the needle to roll the hay onto the wagon. Cabling hay took less horse and man power than needling, but still took time and skill.

"To cable a load of hay on to a sled, one end of the cable was tied to the front center of the sled and then looped around the stack," Buck Buckles explained. "Then the sled was usually raised off the ground to a desired height to determine the size of the load. The other end of the cable was placed across the bed of the sled and hooked to the team, be it a two or four horse team. The horses then slowly moved forward, twisting the load of hay onto the bed of the sled. It required a damn good driver, but Melvin was a damn good driver."

Eventually, a tilt bed sled was used in the stack yard which made the process much easier. Melvin said the top two-thirds of the hay stack slid easily onto the wagon bed, but the last 1000 pounds had to be pitched onto the sled.

"I was young and hard work didn't bother me any, but when people talk about the 'good old days' I tell them we are living in the "good old days," Melvin said. "Everything was hard work back then, but I don't think we ever thought it was unfair. That's just the way it was."

Irrigation was another labor-intensive job on the ranch and was directly tied to yearly hay production. In his memoir, B.E. Brewster explained how irrigation systems were developed to produce hay crops to feed the cattle on the ranch. By the time Bill Coffee bought the ranch

---

[269] Oscar Skavdahl established a ranch on the Niobrara River in the late 1890s.

in 1941, those same hay meadows produced enough hay to feed even the thousand-plus herds maintained by the Coffees.

"Putting up the hay" was a constantly evolving process. Bill said they used a modified overshot stacker[270] at Warbonnet when he was a boy. He said the remains were still sitting in the Mike Meadow at Hat Creek., but he never expected to resurrect the device. "It was a little dangerous and didn't work as good as a Slide Stacker."[271] Bill said.

Overshot stackers were used throughout the region.

Video footage[272] shot by Peg Coffee captures several days of haying at Hat Creek. The crew used the Beaver Slide Stacker. In one 16-mm film clip, 10-year-old Bill, seated behind a pair of horses harnessed to a sweep head, deftly maneuvers the team toward a buck[273] of hay. He quickly scoops the buck onto the sweep teeth. After a jaunty wave of his hat, he drives his team

---

[270] The head of an overshot stack head was mounted on two arms fastened to the back of the stacker frame. After hay was shoved onto the head, it was pulled upward with a team of horses. The team stopped as the head reached an upward position and the hay was flung over the top of the stacker cage. It hit a back stop and fell into the cage. Several area ranchers said when an overshot stacker arm broke, it came crashing down to the ground. Several people were killed in overshot accidents.
[271] Beaver Slide Stackers originated in the Big Hole Valley in Beaverhead County, Montana in the early 1900s. A patent for the stacker was awarded to David or Dade Stephens on May 31, 1910. The one on the Coffee Ranches was built by a blacksmith in Harrison.
[272] According to Bill Coffee, his mother, Peg bought a 16 mm camera in 1925. He said the camera cost her over $300. Some of her earliest movies show a young Bill riding on his pony when he was five or six years old. According to the Kodak Company website, Eastman Kodak released its first 16 mmm "outfit," consisting of a camera, projector, tripod, screen and splicer for $335 in 1923,
[273] A buck of hay was gathered from the windrows by the person operating the sweep. A good buck was about three-foot high and eight-foot wide.

toward the stacker, and deftly pushes the buck onto the stacker head teeth. A different segment of film shows a hired hand driving the horses toward the stacker. Once the stack is pushed onto the stacker head, the man waves his hat and smiles at the camera then backs his horse a few steps before heading back to the pasture.[274]

Stacking hay with a slide stacker. Photo: Buck Buckles family

A cut-away shot shows a team of horses standing at a 90-degree angle to the incline, waiting patiently. The horse team backs up tightening the cables that are attached to the stacker head via a set of pulleys. The sweep head moves quickly up the incline. The hay tips over the top of the 30-foot incline into a wire cage located in the rear of the stacker. The man on the stack quickly shoves the hay toward the edges of the stack smoothing it into an ice-cream scoop shape that sheds water. He too waves his hat, just before the second buck plopped on his head, covering him with a pile of dusty, sticker-infused, grass hay.

Melvin said the guy driving the team, or later driving a pickup that was hooked to the stacker head, could control the placement of the hay in the stacker cage. If he wanted the hay to slide down the front of the cage, he pulled the head slowly up the ramp, then stopped smoothly. A good man on the team could also throw the buck to the back of the cage by encouraging the team to take a couple of bold steps as the stacker head reached the top of the incline. A quick stop propelled the buck to the rear of the cage.

---

[274] Ibid.

"If he wanted to be ornery he could dump the hay on a guy's head, or dump the hay all in one spot and the stacker had to work a lot harder to even out the hay." Melvin explained.[275] "Once in a while, a rattlesnake would come up with the hay and fly through the air. That always caused a commotion. It was a dirty, dusty, job. I didn't get on the stack unless I had to, then I got off as soon as I could. Later we didn't put a man on the stack until the stack was almost built, then we'd top off the stack so it would somewhat shed the rain," Melvin Nation explained.

The 16-mm video of Bill sweeping hay also included shots of a hired man using a knobbed-wheel tractor[276] to push hay toward the stack. By the time Melvin arrived at the ranch, the haying operation was all mechanized. The men cut hay with sickle-bar mowers attached to a tractor. The cut hay was then raked and windrowed into long (preferably straight)[277] rows. A tractor with a reversed transmission was attached to the sweep head. Even with mechanization, haying was labor intensive. Four to six men worked from June to late August producing dozens of six to eight ton stacks.[278]

In the fall of the year, the stacks were moved to hay yards for easy access during the winter months. "Down at the Spade Ranch in the Sandhills they had long, straight, meadows. They'd use a 32-horse team to move the stacks to higher ground. It was quite a sight," Bill Coffee said. "But we moved ours with a caterpillar or later with a cable stack mover or tractors. There wasn't any part of haying that was easy, but we always had feed for our cattle."

Norman Callaham,[279] Thelma's brother joined the hay crew at Warbonnet the summer of 1958. He said two other men, Jack and Dick were also part of the crew that year and all of them had trouble "keeping up with Melvin."

"I don't think I ever knew, even after all these years, someone who worked as hard as Melvin." Norman said. "He'd call you about 4 a.m., and he only called you once. I'd head to the barn to help milk as soon as he called me. After breakfast I'd climb up on tractor pulling the dump rake, or sometimes, I drove the side-delivery rake, or the mower. Melvin drove the reverse-gear sweep that was made from an old car or pickup. One afternoon we were hustling to get the hay

---

[275] In 2001, Melvin showed his family the slide stacker retired at the edge of the Hat Creek hay meadow. As he explained the process of stacking hay with a slide stacker he moved around the stacker to point out different sections and functions.
[276] The tractor was probably a Farmall tractor.
[277] Moni Hourt said she could never seem to keep her windrows straight, much to her father's irritation.
[278] The number of stacks produced each year varied. In 1968, Bill promised to pay Moni and Robbin $1 each for every stack they put up. In all 125, 8-10 ton stacks were put up on Warbonnet. Bill gave the girls a $100 savings bond that Christmas.
[279] Norman Callaham, personal taped interviews, 2113, 2017, 2021, and 2022 at Hourt place in Sioux County and at Norman's home in Whittier, California. Although Norman only had a high school education, he became a chief inspector at Rockwell International, a major manufacturing company in California that manufactured parts for America's aircraft and space industry.

up before it rained. Melvin hit a hole; he flew up of his seat and landed on the hood of the sweep, just turned around and kept driving."

The crew moved the old hay stacks from the stack-yard north of the Warbonnet house, before bringing in stacks from the current haying season. Norman was tasked with mowing the yard. He said he jumped off the tractor to pull some wire out of the way of the mower when he realized the ground was alive with rattle snakes that had denned under an old stack. "I supposed I let out a yell, because in a minute Melvin and the men showed up. Melvin grabbed a shovel and started chopping snakes. When the last snake quit moving, he collected the rattles. Thelma put them in a canning jar that she set in the kitchen window. Never did like snakes."

A hay crew's day began at dawn. There were no coffee breaks. Before they left the ranch each morning, the men filled their water jugs, generally Clorox jugs[280] or stone crocks that had been wrapped in water soaked burlap sacks. If they failed to remember their "jugs," they went thirsty until noon or "mooched" off another man. The noon break lasted an hour. At night men could relax once the night chores were done. The bunkhouse featured beds and a shower, but no indoor bathroom. There was an outhouse a few feet from the bunkhouse door.

Although it was the men's responsibility to wash their own clothes, there wasn't a washing machine in the bunk house. The shower made a poor substitute. Thelma, using an electric wringer washer, often did it for them.[281]

"I washed a lot of clothes, because the men got rather stinky," Thelma said with a smile. "One of the men decided to wash his new pants with Clorox. Of course the pants came out with white spots all over them, so he added more Clorox. The pants just fell apart. I did his clothes from then on, but my main job was cooking."

Dinner was at noon; supper was at six. [282] Melvin told the men that his wife had made the meal; they were going to eat it before it got cold. "No one ever went away from Thelma's table hungry," Melvin Nation said with a great deal of pride.

"I fixed breakfast for the guys who were staying over here at Warbonnet, then I cleaned up the mess and started dinner. After dinner, I cleaned up and started supper. I made bread every day. I butchered chickens then put them in the freezer, so I could always make fried

---

[280] Although stone crocks were used, the brown, gallon-sized, Clorox bleach bottles made the handiest water containers. Burlap sacks were wrapped around the jugs, sewn into place, then soaked with cold water. No one wanted to break a jug and go through the process of creating a new one.

[281] Thelma used a broom stick handle to snag the clothes from the washer and push them through the wringer. One afternoon, four-year-old Robbin decided to help. She grabbed a wash cloth from the wash water and poked it into the wringer. The wringer sucked her hand between the rubber wringer rods. Thelma grabbed the wringer rod release bar and before the little girl's hand could be broken, she jerked it free of the wringer.

[282] When Melvin was complimented for requiring the men to arrive at the house at noon and 6 for meals, he said that was John Coffee's rule. He said he just made sure it was followed.

chicken. Sometimes I cooked ham or roast beef. I made some type of desert every day. That was just what was expected of a hired man's wife. Most of us didn't get paid individually;[283] when a man was hired, his wife was expected to do the cooking. At least that was the way it was at Coffee's."

Thelma believed her unofficial job at the ranch was that of "game warden." During deer season, she drove the roads and sometimes—not too gently—told hunters headed for Coffee land, that it was off limits. One afternoon the new superintendent from Fort Robinson State Park drove into the main yard, stopped to open the pasture gate, and climbed back into his car intending to drive into the north meadow where a large herd of turkeys grazed. Thelma was at the car before he could put it in gear.

"He told me he was going to hunt turkey. I told him he wasn't," Thelma said. "He said he had Senators so and so with him. I told him I didn't give a damn; he wasn't going to go down in the meadow."

Returning to the house, she grabbed a shot gun and stepped into the gate. "I may have told him I'd shoot his damn head off," Thelma said. "He told me he was going to take the matter up with Mr. Coffee. About that time, Bill drove into the yard. I told Mr. Big Shot to go ahead and talk to Bill. Bill told him to get the hell off the place. We didn't allow hunting. That was that."

That night when Thelma told Melvin what she had done, he told her the gun wasn't loaded. She said she didn't care; she'd scared the hell out of the son-of-a——.

Open season did exist for one animal at the ranch: rattlesnakes. They were constantly slinking into the yard and up onto the back porch. One afternoon, three-year-old Moni screamed into the house to report that a snake was killing her kitten. Thelma, nearly eight-months pregnant with Robbin, grabbed the gun and "wallered" over the back fence. A large rattle snake, coiled and ready to strike, gently swayed back and forth a few feet from the tiny kitten. The kitten, seemingly hypnotized by the movement, slowly moved toward the snake.

"I kicked the kitten out of the way and blew the snake's head off." Thelma said matter-a-factly. "I'd grown up with snakes. They didn't scare me."

That morning one of Melvin's rodeo buddies, needing a place to sober up, was asleep on the couch. Thelma had tried to shake him awake, but decided he wasn't sober enough to aim the gun.

"Melvin wasn't real happy with him. We had a lot of men around. Some worked for us. Some needed a bed. Most of them were o.k. Melvin kept a pretty close eye on them, and we never had any trouble," Thelma said. "But there weren't many of them that stayed around for very long."

---

[283] In 2009, after Melvin's death, Thelma lamented that she never produced enough income to drawn social security. There were times when she rebelled against what she deemed her "unpaid cook and maid" role at the ranches.

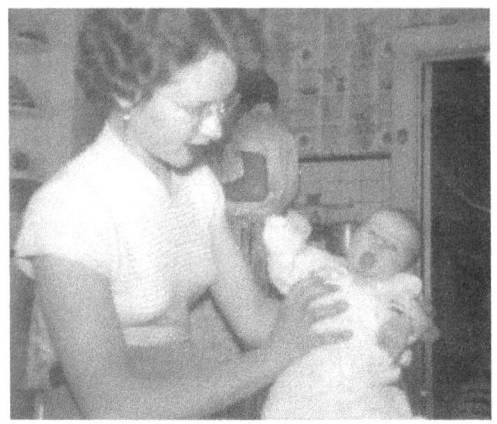
Thelma with Robbin in November 1954.

Melvin and Thelma's second daughter, Robbin, was born November 1, 1954, a year after the family moved to Warbonnet. Melvin insisted that his wife stay with his folks in Crawford for the three weeks before the baby's birth.

"I guess he and Bill were scared I'd have the baby in the middle of a snow storm," Thelma said. "The roads were a mess when it snowed, and I really didn't want them to deliver the baby, so I agreed to go to town. But that was the longest three weeks of my life. Bruce was the only man we had at that time. He and Melvin took turns cooking: eggs, fried potatoes, and hamburger. My iron skillet had three inches of grease in it when I got home; the stove was almost as bad."

Even if a driver wasn't expecting a baby, battling the Monroe Canyon Road, a nearly 1000-foot vertical incline connecting the ranch with Harrison, was a challenge. During periods of rain or snow, the road became a slippery, slimy, quagmire.[284] Thelma's strategy: simply attack it.

"I'd wind the car up as far as I could by the time we hit the bottom. We'd slip and slide and grind our way up the hill," Thelma remembered. "The girls would stand behind the front seat, pushing against it like they thought they could push us over the hill. Eventually we'd bounce over the top and go on to town. I don't remember turning around very often."

Virginia Coffee told Thelma she carried newspapers with her in the years she made winter trips to town. If the car skittered on the slick roads, she locked the brakes, jumped out, and jammed the papers under the wheels. That gave her enough traction to lurch past the icy spots. Thelma said she always forgot to load the papers, so she just hit the hill on a "dead run."

Maybe the fact that Thelma considered the roads an almost-human adversary increased her reluctance to have Norman make Saturday night trips to town the summer he lived with them.

"Thelma and Melvin went to Harrison most Saturday nights, but once in a while, they stayed home," Norman remembered. "Melvin asked me one of those nights if I wanted to take his 1957 Ford to town. Thelma wasn't happy about it, but I didn't wait around to argue. That was one sweet car. It was in perfect shape—except for the fact that it was a little noisy. After Melvin caught the muffler on a rock in the canyon, he replaced it with a straight muffler. I loved the sound. Lew Sheriff, the cop in Harrison didn't. When I'd get to town, I'd slow down and drive real careful down the street so Lew didn't notice me."

---

[284] The road was straightened and partially paved in 1967.

The 1957 Ford Fairlane was more than a mode of transportation.

The car, even if it was a little noisy, was a symbol of pride and fun for the family. On night car trips, Moni and Robbin climbed into the roomy back window, and until they drifted off to sleep, tried to identify the Big Dipper in the star patterns that zipped by. Thelma and the girls spent many afternoons washing and polishing it to a fine shine before trips to town. No one even groused about the car payments on the vehicle that originally cost $2945.

One lazy summer evening Norman arrived in Harrison to the news that a drag race was planned south of the city. "When I got there they started harping on me to race Mel's car. I knew better. First of all, I didn't want to break his trust; second of all, I sure didn't want him mad at me."

Norman turned around and drove back to town. He passed two state patrol cars slipping into town from the east. They'd come to investigate the rumors of Saturday night drag races outside of town. "I came in from the south. I probably hit the outskirts a little hot; the car was rumbling and back firing—making too much noise. Great sound, but the patrolmen didn't like it as well as we did. I headed toward Warbonnet, but it wasn't long before I saw I was being followed."

Norman said he was almost at the top of Monroe Canyon when he saw the red lights flashing. "I just ignored them and down the road I went. I knew the road and the corners; they didn't, so I lost them. I topped the hill above Warbonnet, going too fast, and saw that someone had shut the gate going into the yard. I opened it—with my front fender. I don't think I've ever been as sick in my life."

He said he walked into the living room. Melvin was reading a book. Thelma looked at his stricken face and immediately asked, "What the hell have you done?"

"I thought I was dead, but Melvin just asked me what happened. I told him. He told Thelma to "quit her fussing, that Norm would get it fixed." And, I did. Donny Geer's dad, Ned, had a garage in Harrison. That next weekend, I helped him take the fender off. We straightened and painted it. It looked really like new. Melvin let me drive it all summer, although we generally all stayed home when it rained."

None of the roads across the country were much more navigable than the one going up Monroe Canyon. People avoided unnecessary travel when bad weather was expected, but weather prediction was anything but an exact science. When Thelma started selling Tupperware, she and the girls often made trips across the region to hold "parties."[285] They were headed home from a party in Banner County near Harrisburg, NE when they "ran into" a massive snow storm.

"I was past Agate,[286] and knew I couldn't turn around. I just kept creeping forward," Thelma shook her head at the memory. "We were about 15 miles from Harrison when I saw headlights. I knew it was Melvin. I was sure glad to see him."

Melvin turned the pickup around and slipped and slid back to the car to check on his family. Robbin abandoned the car. She climbed into the pickup, curled up under the dash, and went to sleep. She had enough excitement for one day.

"The snow was so damn thick, you couldn't even see the hood," Thelma remembered. "We managed to crawl back to town. Melvin had one tire on the edge of the road. I followed his tail lights. It wasn't snowing as hard in Harrison; so we headed on home. When we dropped over the top of Monroe, the snow stopped altogether. I was glad when we finally pulled in the yard. It was a long trip."

Even the 10-mile journey between Hat Creek and Warbonnet could get "hairy." Melvin was repairing equipment at Hat Creek, when snow blowing against the shop windows caught his attention. "I didn't notice that the wind came up, but I didn't stick around long once I did," Melvin said. "I threw about a ton and a half of dirt in the Power Wagon and headed home. I followed the REA lines to the main road, but I had to stop ever so often so I could see the wires. When I got out on the county road—if I could see the dead weeds on the edge—I could tell where I was. I drove off the road several times. Snow was blowing clear over the cab. It took me two and a half hours to get home. When I finally got there the cab, except where I was setting, was plumb full of snow."

Although the equipment wasn't always Nebraska-storm proficient, the ranch was considered fully mechanized, except when it came to "cow-work." Horses were always the main mode

---

[285] Tupperware, plastic kitchen ware, was sold during "parties." Guests had the chance to examine the items, then place orders for the pieces they wanted. Thelma was a successful salesman. She crisscrossed her region, generally with the girls in tow. The product was developed in 1946 by Earl Silas Tupper. The product was sold by women through Tupperware parties.

[286] The Agate Springs Ranch was located 23 miles from Harrison and 34 miles from Mitchell, NE. Travelers often stopped at Agate to escape a storm or even to get enough gas to get to the nearest service station.

of transportation for working cattle—no matter how deep the snow or how cold the temperature.[287] When a herd of heavy cows[288] drifted into a corner during an early spring storm, Melvin headed across the pasture to bring them in. He said he was riding a grey horse. Snow blew across the pastures and filled the air around him. The horse's head and ears disappeared into the thick gruel. The pasture's east/west fence line popped up from the snow and he followed it to the gully where he saw the cattle earlier in the day.

"I got to the damn gully. I'm tryin' to see something, then those old cows just come up out of that snow. I can still see them," Melvin said in a 2007 interview. "They looked like grey ghosts. I turned them east, about a mile later they hit a corner, turned northwest into the wind,[289] and headed toward the ranch. I just followed them in. I don't think I could handle it mentally or physically anymore. At that time, I didn't know what fear was. But still—there is nothing that puts chills up your back like a bad snowstorm."

Western Nebraska winter always seemed to find ways to celebrate its vicious reputation. Twisting through the ranch yard, Warbonnet Creek was a kid-restricted area which meant the kids found a dozen ways to explore it. Sis was visiting the ranch with her children one winter afternoon, when Moni, Robbin, and their oldest cousin, Donna, decided to take a walk. "Somehow" they found themselves next to the creek. At first, they just stood and watched the water dipping and bubbling around the small holes in the ice. Then 7-year-old, Moni decided to see if the ice was suitable for ice skating. She bossily told the younger girls they were too small to skate, that they had to stay on the bank. She tested the ice, then started shoe-skating across the surface. Suddenly the ice collapsed, plunging her into the icy water.

"I swept under the ice," Moni Nation Hourt said. "I can still see the white and black snow and ice patterns blinking above me. The water tumbled me down the creek until I hit the water-gap fence about 50 feet from the bridge. I climbed up the fence and wriggled through the opening in the ice. I was cold but mostly scared. I knew I was in deep trouble."

Moni was almost to the house when Thelma and Sis dashed out the front door. The two little girls had run to the house to get help, but neither could speak very clearly. The women thought Donna was telling them that Moni had hit her with a stick. Robbin had finally grabbed her mother's hand and pulled her out the door toward the creek. By that time, a very cold Moni had nearly reached the yard gate.

"When Mom told Dad that night, he nailed me with that blue-eyed glare of his that was worse than any spankin'," Moni said. "During the summer, Robbin and I spent hours under the bridge, building mud pies—throwing mud pies—or just squishing the mud between our toes. But no one went out on the ice again."

---

[287] Up until Melvin's death in 2008, cattle work was never done on a four-wheeler. Both Melvin and Bill had a great deal of disdain for "four-wheeler jockeys."
[288] A "heavy cow" is one that will calve within a short time.
[289] Cattle always move better if they are headed into the wind.

The creek generally trickled down it's gravel bed, but a 1958 thunderstorm above the ranch created a flash flood that surged down the narrow channel. Melvin parked his pickup on the south side of the bridge and fought his way across the narrow bridge that was topped by nearly three feet of water. By the time he reached the house, the water had surged through the front door, filled the porch, and seeped under the kitchen door. Thelma piled what furniture she could move onto the table and chairs. She took her washing off the clothes line and stuffed the clean clothing beneath the doors in an attempt to keep the water from flooding into the house. She was only partly successful. About six inches of water and mud crawled "sluggishly" across the kitchen and leaked into the living room.

"Pat[290] was living with us at the time, and Norm was helping hay," Thelma said. "She started sweeping. Melvin and Norm, and even a couple of the men came in to scoop the mud and water out of the house. About three inches of mud piled up on the north wall of the kitchen. The squares of linoleum on the kitchen floor floated loose and mud seeped underneath. The floor in the living room warped. The smell of that mud lasted for months. It was a damn mess."

The next day, water still whirled six feet above the normal creek bed and lapped the bottom of the bridge. Melvin and the girls tossed a few eggs into the water. They dipped and flipped across the waters cracking open when they hit the debris, a subtle warning against trusting a babbling stream.

Although the ranch dominated Melvin's life, he was also aware of events beyond the boundaries of the ranch. The polio epidemic that raged through Nebraska during the early 1950s was a big concern in the Nation household. When the vaccine was available in 1956, the Nation girls joined most of the other children in Sioux County as they marched down the steps of the Sioux County Court House and received their polio vaccinations.

"Every summer someone came down with polio," Thelma said. "When my good friend Lucy Nelson (Hughes) came down with polio, she was just 23. She had three kids to raise and another on the way. Her youngest son was born while she was in an iron lung. She was paralyzed from the neck down for the rest of her life. Polio scared everyone. It didn't just kill people, it crippled them for life."

When vaccinations were scheduled at the Harrison courthouse, dozens of kids lined up for shots. "They were a bawlin' and carryin' on," Thelma grinned. "The adults weren't. We were all laughing and joking. It was such a relief. I don't think any of us gave our kids much sympathy. The summer before they gave the shots, there were a dozen cases in the area; the next year there were just a few, and those people weren't vaccinated. Polio was a God-awful disease."[291]

---

[290] After her parents moved to California in 1957, Thelma's sister Pat stayed with the Nations and finished her senior year of high school.
[291] According to the Center of Disease Control and Prevention, 13th edition, April 2015, in 1952, 875 cases of polio were reported in Nebraska. That year there were 57,879 cases of polio across the United States. In 1957 after the advent of a polio vaccine there were just 2499. In 1964, there were just 106 cases.

Polio and the vaccine that cured it, filled the front pages of many weekly and monthly publications stuffed in the big silver mailbox just outside Warbonnet's main gate. When the periodicals arrived: *Newsweek, Life, Reader's Digest, Nebraska Cattleman, The Harrison Sun,* and even *The National Geographic,* the issues were stacked on the kitchen table. They migrated through the house from there, creating discussion, and in the case of the vaccine jubilation.[292]

A *World Book* encyclopedia salesman arrived at the ranch house door in 1960. Thelma purchased a 20-volume set, the six-piece *Child Craft* volumes, and the two-book dictionary editions. Cost: $250, paid in 36 monthly installments of $5. The encyclopedias marched across the top shelf of the living room bookcase. Long before the arrival of Google search-engines, Melvin regularly grabbed volumes of the cream colored encyclopedias off the shelves to find information, about geography, history, or even mythology. He and his daughters solved problems and explored the lives of famous mathematicians listed in the math issue of *Child Craft*, and once-in-a-while he would trade the western history stories that he read to the girls for the legends found in the Child Craft Legends' Volume.[293] However, the primary discussion on the ranch didn't originate in the magazines or encyclopedia. It centered around the height of the grass, the condition of the horses and cattle, and always how to get the best prices from the cattle.

Before the 1950s, cattle were generally shipped to the Omaha Stock Yards or to the Chicago Livestock Exchange where commission men would bid on the cattle. Bill Coffee said he took several loads of cattle to Omaha. Before one trip, JT told his son accept only top bids. Bill didn't think the commission men offered him enough at Omaha, so he reloaded the cattle and traveled on to Chicago. There he sold the cattle for $.10 cwt less than what he was offered in Omaha—and had to pay the extra shipping costs. He said his father "often" reminded him of that trip.

Shortly after World War II, sale barns were established across the region, making it much easier to market cattle, but the prices still varied from year to year or in some cases from month to month. When Melvin hired on at Warbonnet in 1953, cattle prices averaged[294] $15.60 cwt, down from a 1951 high of $29.30. By 1957, the average prices had only risen to $16.80 cwt.[295]

"Bill was talking about sellin' everything about that time," Melvin remembered. "There'd been several bad years, and he was faunchin' and fumin' about going broke. I really thought a lot of JT, but he was tough on Bill. And Bill always worried about lettin' him down. There just wasn't anything I could do but wonder if I'd have a job the next day."

---

[292] Many of them ended up in the bathroom magazine rack.
[293] Moni Hourt said that Melvin made the King Arthur stories so exciting that she spent weeks pretending to be a young King Arthur, inserting a willow branch between the trunk of a big willow tree in the yard, then jerking it free and running off to slay any dragon (barn cats) who were unlucky enough to cross her way. (None were ever slayed.)
[294] This average includes cows, steers, and heifers.
[295] "Average Yearly Cattle Prices." United States Department of Agriculture. Washington D.C. www.nass.usda.gov

"That's one of the toughest things about being a hired man," Thelma Nation said. "If the prices dropped or it quit raining we wondered if we needed to look for another job. Melvin and Bill would get into a big fight. Moni would run back and forth listening to them scream and yell. She'd come bawling into the house thinking she was going to lose her horse. I'd just sit there wondering if I should start packing and worrying about where we'd go. Eventually Bill and Melvin just seemed to figure out that they probably should put up with each other."

Cattle prices rose in 1958 to an average of $20.90 and continued to rise for the next 21 years, hitting a high of $65.90 cwt in 1959. The rainfall increased in the 1950s and grass was plentiful. Melvin didn't "go looking for a new job."

Norman said he didn't remember any tension about cattle prices or anything else that summer. "It was a great summer. We moved to California that spring, and I hated it out there. The work kept me busy, and Melvin was really good to me. Sure Thelma was a little bossy, but she was my oldest sister so she always had been."

The tornado that emerged over the butte to the west of the ranch created more concern than tension that June. Moni was celebrating her birthday when Melvin came into the house and told the family they better move to the storm cellar at the big house. Moni and Robbin were ordered inside the doorway while the adults watched the tornado's tail twist and turn lazily across the butte before swooping low enough to obliterate several big stacks of hay in the meadow. Then in a twist it went back up into the clouds and disappeared.[296]

A few days later, the hay meadow was the scene of another unusual incident. Norman was raking hay into windrows when he saw Dick "high tailing it" across the newly cut stubble near the tree line. The tractor that he'd abandoned chugged northward, but Dick was running toward the house as fast as "his short little legs could carry him."

"About then, I saw the mountain lion running in the opposite direction," Norman said laughing. "Melvin and I jumped in the pickup and intercepted the guy. He was scared to death. He didn't know that we saw the mountain lion. He said he was sure the animal tried to attack him. Melvin and I just about laughed ourselves silly. We drove out to the still moving tractor; Melvin jumped out and stopped it. It took some coaxing to get Dick back in the field. That fall, Thelma called and told me the mountain lion returned and killed a bunch of sheep." Norman laughed. "The day we saw him, he just wasn't hungry."[297]

Two construction projects concluded Norman's 1958 summer work: rebuilding the hay loft floor in the Warbonnet Barn and demolishing the open-faced garage to the northwest of the house.

---

[296] Tornados were unusual in the Warbonnet Valley, but in 1955 a tornado devastated the Scottsbluff County area killed two people and resulted in $500,000 in damage.
[297] "Mountain lions seen in local area; plaster cast made of tracks." *Harrison, Sun*, September 11, 1958. The article reported that a mountain lion was spotted in several areas in Sioux County including near the Leo Dunlap ranch which was about 10 miles from Warbonnet.

"The loft floor was actually getting dangerous," Norman said. "The girls crawled up there one day when Thelma came out to the barn, and Robbin almost fell through a hole in the floor. Melvin said it was built in about 1879, so no wonder it was so broken up. It took us about two weeks to redo it."

Even with the loft door open, lighting conditions in the dark interior were inadequate. Melvin hit his thumb twice the first day. Norman said the thumb swelled and bled profusely putting Melvin in a decidedly irritated mood, but Norman said his brothers-in-law irritation really wasn't directed toward the young Bible salesman who showed up that afternoon.

"I was downstairs getting another board when the kid showed up. He wasn't much over 21 and didn't seem too sure of himself. I talked to him a minute and told him that the foreman was upstairs working, but I'd ask him if he had a few minutes to visit. I'd just gotten inside the door when Melvin hit his thumb again. It really must have hurt because he bellered, "You can just kill my dirty old a—. The salesman took one look at the open door, jumped in his car, and drove away. When I told Melvin about the episode, his eyes snapped and popped, but he didn't laugh out loud. He just shook his head and said, 'Bless him.' Then we went back to work."

Tiny winged creatures created the chaos during the demolition project.

Before razing the building to the ground, Melvin asked the crew to remove some wood panels on the inside walls. Pulling a piece of paneling from the back wall unleashed a swarm of bees.

"Poor ole Dick started screaming and slapping at the bees and of course they zeroed in on him," Norman grinned. At one point it looked like the whole hive was swarming him. Melvin was laughing so hard I thought he'd choke to death. He kept yelling at Dick to hold still, but Dick was not about to hold still. He finally ran into the garage and shut the door. Melvin called Jack Snyder."[298]

Jack Snyder's bee apiary, on his family's ranch about three miles north of Warbonnet, supplied most of the area with honey. He arrived with his smoker and large galvanized tubs, but Norman said he didn't seem to need much smoke. "He just talked to them like you'd talk to a scared dog. He peeled the honey combs out of the wall and put them in the tubs; the bees followed. It really didn't take him very long. We could see Dick peeking through the shop window, but he didn't come out until Jack drove away. He [Dick] was sick most of the day from all the bee stings."

The next day, Jack returned with some chunks of honey comb and honey for the family. Norman said whenever he returned to the area, he went to Jack's and picked up a container of honey.

---

[298] Jack Snyder was CF Coffee's nephew. Jack's father, Alva, was the son of Catherine Coffee Snyder and D.H Snyder. The first time he drove cattle up the Texas Trail, CF Coffee, Bill Coffee's grandfather, did so as an employee of D.H and J.W Snyder, Jack's father and uncle who were famous trail bosses during the cattle drive era. The Snyder family, Jack, Alva and, his mother, Georgia, lived on a small place about three miles north of the Warbonnet buildings. He often stopped by the house to bring Thelma fresh honey or the girls' favorite, honey combs.

"That summer was good for me. Moving to California was tough," Norman concluded in the 2017 interview. "Working with Melvin that year made me feel like I was at least worth a little something."

JOHN

> "I had great respect for John Coffee. Maybe he was a little hard on that Bill and didn't give him the due he deserved, but he was a great man and was sure good to my family." Melvin Nation

Melvin officially "took his orders from Bill," but until his death in 1959, John Coffee was still a strong presence at the ranch. In 1902, when John was just 20 he and his father, Charles, formed the Coffee and Son ranching corporation. He purchased one-half interest in the 1,920-acre Hat Creek Ranch for $10 an acre, then paid $40 a head for half-interest in the cattle herd. Although he was a partner in the operation, he continued to draw a $30 a month wage, the same as the other ranch hands. When Charles organized the Sioux National Bank in Harrison in 1925, John became the bank manager. By the 1930s seven Coffee banks dotted towns along Highway 20.

"When Dad decided to retire in 1945, he told me we had to sell the banks or the ranch," Bill Coffee said in a 2000 interview. "There were only two things I ever really wanted in life, the ranch and Virginia.[299] I never cared for the banking business. I just wanted to be a rancher. I told him to sell the damn banks."

John T Coffee. Coffee Collection

"When Thelma and I moved to Warbonnet in the winter of 1953. JT was basically retired," Melvin said. "But he showed up at the ranch almost every day. I respected John Coffee. He was quite an old guy."

Melvin said John traveled the ranch in a car, maneuvering locations that even twenty-first century four-wheel drive vehicles would have trouble conquering. His penchant for

---

[299] Bill and Virginia Kennedy were married in 1942.

chain smoking cigars filled the car with smoke that swirled and patched its way around its occupant who perched in the center of the bench seat. From that perspective, John traversed the ranch, seldom miscalculating the terrain. There were a few exceptions.

"One of the first months I was there, Hat Creek flooded out of its banks," Melvin grinned. "John didn't know that we weren't using the creek crossing. It was all growed up and covered in weeds. He hit it with that old Henry J[300] and stood her right on her nose. He buried it up to the windshield in the muck and mud. That was the end of the Henry J."

John removed the back seats from his cars. He piled the empty backseat area with ranching tools, calves, and even a pony.

"Mom and Dad moved into town when I was about seven," Bill said. "If Dad didn't take me to the ranch, I rode my pony, Tippy, out. I stayed a few days, then I'd ride back to Harrison. It took me most of the day to get to town, but I didn't care. I'd stop and visit people or just poke along. About dark, I'd hit the top of Sowbelly Canyon. About then, Dad would just 'show up.' He opened the back door, Tippy climbed in and away we'd go. I'd put him in Powell's stable, then the next day, I was ready to go back out again. I didn't like town much."

John also seemed to know when a miniature ranch hand was ready to go home. "Mr. Coffee often picked me up when we were done working or moving cattle and take me back to the ranch." Moni Nation Hourt said. "I generally shared the back with rolls of wire, fence stretchers, a tire, or even a calf. He spread a coat or some gunny sacks on the floor for me to sit on. I thought it was a grand adventure."

In the late fall of 1956, John brought lunch to the crew moving cattle from the summer pasture. The country was full of snow. Differentiating between a road and a pasture was difficult. When the crew hit the top of the hill above the Hat Creek Valley, they encountered a set of car tracks meandering out into the prairie.

"We rode past them tracks, then I got to thinkin' about them. It dawned on me that JT might have tried to follow us down the canyon and run off into one of the deep draws running beside the road," Melvin said.

Bill and Melvin reversed direction and followed the tracks. They heard the roar of the car's engine before they reached the edge of the small ravine located about 100-feet off the roadway. John's Chevrolet Bel Air, buried hood down in the bottom of a draw smoked and groaned. Melvin said the car was filled with cigar smoke to the point that John was invisible as he sat in the front seat. Bill rode up to the window and tapped on it. 'Dad,' he said when John rolled down the window. "I don't think you are going anywhere."

---

[300] The Henry J was an American automobile built by the Kaiser–Frazer Corporation and named after its chairman, Henry J Keiser. It was a 2-door sedan.

Melvin rode back to town and picked up the Power Wagon.[301] They used its front-end winch to pull the car from the draw then John drove the four-wheel-drive back to town. "He was stuck tight. The car's transmission was gone. It was colder than blazes," Melvin said. "I was always glad we seen those tracks."

Long after John's death, pieces of automobiles lay scattered across the pastures, a silent testament that John had passed by. They were torn loose when his automobile high centered, scraped between narrow roads, or gullies, or careened down the side of snow filled canyons. It also showed that even as a well-respected banker, he never lost his love for the ranch his family had carved from the prairie on the Wyoming, South Dakota, and Nebraska borders

In his supervisory role, John seldom showed his disapproval, but everyone on the ranch knew he did NOT like to "have his cattle roped." Melvin admits he was young and cocky and a bit "full of himself" the morning he encountered John in the White River pasture.

"There was a calf down there that had lost his mama," Melvin's grin reached his dimple. "John told me to gather him up, but 'not to run him to death.' I was a 'smartalec.' I built to that calf and roped him on a big old high run. Then I turned and headed for the car, the calf running behind me, never losing his feet—but on a run."

Pounding up to the car, Melvin stepped off his horse and hauled the calf to John's car so that the older man could take him back to the ranch. John never said a word—he just bit several inches off the end of his cigar.

Although John had once spent much of his life on a horse, Melvin said he only saw him get "a-horseback" once. The crew was struggling to move a "wallering" bunch of three and four-year old steers up the road. John, on the drag, bounced back and forth with his car, then slammed to a stop. He climbed out of his car, commandeered a horse[302] from one of the hired men and "jerked down about six foot of rope."

"John 'over and undered' Red and helped us get the cattle corralled," Melvin said. "I'm not sure we would have finished it that day without him."

When discussing John Coffee, Melvin always concluded that the man was, 'One of the good ones.' "He helped a lot more people than anyone ever give him credit for. There was a homesteader family that lived above Andrews, across the fence from the White River pasture. They was poorer than church mice. Ever fall when we cleaned out the pasture, John made sure we left a beef over by their claim fence. He gave many a homesteader a boost including my Dad. The bank in Crawford closed Dad out. All he had left was the land, six head of work horses, a

---

[301] Bill Coffee said John bought a surplus Army Jeep four-wheel drive in 1946. When Dodge produced its power wagon a year later, John bought one of the first models. The base price of the 1946 Power Wagon was $1627, about $550 dollars more than a conventional Dodge two-wheel-drive one-ton pickup. The Power Wagon at the Coffee Ranch was bright red and featured a winch on the front and a hitch on the back.

[302] As Melvin told a story, he listed the horses by name. The hired man, Rudy Geike was riding a horse called Hat Creek Red out of Little Joe the Wrangler and Cowboy Sue.

milk cow, and a couple of saddle horses. John lent him the money to get started again. They said before he died, there were a bunch of notes in his safe. He told his secretary to tear them up."

Although Bill didn't want to go into the banking business, he was always proud of the fact that none of the Coffee banks located along Highway 20 closed during the Depression. He said that was because his dad had "guts." In the mid-1930s, anticipating a run on the bank, John telegraphed the Omaha State Bank and mortgaged everything the family owned.

"We met the train, threw gunny sacks full of cash into Dad's car, took it to the bank, and spread it out on the tables behind the cashiers' cages. When the doors opened, people almost ran in. If they wanted their money, we gave it to them. When they saw the tables piled with cash though, most of the them left; some that had gotten their money brought it back. When the run was over, we sent the money back to Omaha. We never mortgaged the land again."

The elder Coffee was determined that his bank survive. He had equally strong ideas about the survival of his cattle herd. Melvin said John was adamant that calves be moved out of the calving lot as soon after calving as possible, saying that he'd rather lose a calf to snow than to scours. He also believed native grass was much more nutritious than even the best hay and refused to move his herds home from winter pasture until after the first snow. Mother Nature did her best to test the validity of that declaration.

John Coffee battles a horse at the Coffee Hat Creek Ranch. Coffee collection

HIRED MEN AND CANTANKEROUS BEASTS

"We had some good men come through the ranch, and some that weren't so good, but they all got acquainted with cattle and hard work. Some just liked both a little better than others did." Melvin Nation

Generally, the men on the ranch coped well with Mother Nature's tantrums. John's decree against moving cattle from the summer range (about 20 miles south of the ranch) until after the first snow, didn't create many major problems. Those first snows—normally—slid through the country in mid-October dusting the area with a warning snow. However, in 1956, it was November 16 when the first snow roared across the region. It filled the White River Country on the table south of the ranch, with several feet of snow. Cattle were trapped away from feed and water. The calves hadn't yet been weaned and struggled to maintain contact with their mamas. The cattle needed to come home.

Gathering cattle from the four-section White River pasture, fenced only on the section lines, was at best a challenge. A bad snow turned the exercise into one of jaw-clenching determination. That November morning, Melvin, Charley Quay, and Chappell Moore unloaded their horses at the "Newman Place" and headed across country. Within minutes of leaving the pasture gate, Chappell's horse fell with him.

"His horse tied his front end in a knot and rolled over the top of him. I can still see Chappie's head hit the ground. I thought he was dead," Melvin said during a 2001 interview. "His horse took off. I knew I had to have the horse to carry a dead Chappie back to town. I ran the horse down and roped him, but when I got back, Chappell was setting up shaking his head. He didn't want to go back, so we went on."

The trio "gathered" the big pasture and shoved the cattle into a smaller pasture from which they'd moved the cattle to the ranch the next day. About 8 p.m. they headed back to town.

"It was one of those nights when the sky melts into the ground. The country was full of snow. There weren't any fences for a long time," Melvin said. "We were angling across the pasture. I was walking—breaking a trail. Chappie hadn't whimpered all day, but he did ask me if I knew where we were going. I told him I sure hoped so, but I didn't know for sure."

Melvin paused and looked out the barn door across the yard. The summer evening light sifted through the cottonwoods along the road producing an incongruous background for the images created by his story. He grinned his half-smile grin, looked up, and continued. "Then we hit a fence. I wasn't sure if we hit the east/west fence or the north/south fence. If we went one direction, there was a gate; the other took us a long way in the wrong direction. I went what I thought was north. In 75 feet we hit the corner. Boy, I was happy to see that gate. If I'd a gone south, I don't know how far we would have gone before I saw I was wrong. Once we got to the gate, we traveled on a ridge. It weren't too bad. We went the other four miles into town without much trouble. The next morning Chappie was hurtin' so bad; he didn't even get out of bed. He was quite a man. I never knew any better."

Chappell Moore came to the Coffee ranches in September of 1954. Initially he and his wife, Violet[303] lived in the bunk house at Warbonnet. About a month after he arrived, he and Melvin engaged into a particularly "intellectual" discussion on beer. They finally concluded that they wanted to brew their own brand. Thelma ordered beer making equipment from Montgomery Wards and found a recipe for homebrew. With the men acting in the supervisory capacity, the women stirred up several batches and poured them into big stone crocks. Finally, the tester[304] indicated the beer was ready to be bottled. The women were capping bottles when Robbin disappeared. They found her curled up in a corner—asleep. She had been dipping a little cup into the vat and testing their product.

"Chappell was at the ranch for 10 years," Melvin said. "He was the best little man I ever knew. He weren't scared of anything. There wasn't any whimper in him, but he had a "tagger[305]" on his back. Sometimes you might work with him for a week, and he never said a word."

Despite his often non-communicative nature, Moore was up for every task on the ranch, including wrangling pigs. For several years, a neighbor's feral pigs had been terrorizing the Hat Creek neighborhood. Boar hogs killed calves and ran several cattle through fences at the ranch. A pig round-up was organized.

The job wasn't as easy as it appeared. Pigs dashed under horse's legs, tore through fences, and often turned and fought with sharp tusks and pure, mean, aggressiveness.

"Bill and I go up there and rope ole' pig and drag her to the corrals. She's a bad dude," Melvin grinned and loosely crossed his arms as he often did when his story was coming to an interesting climax. "She took a run at a bull in the corral and gutted him. We finally decided a gun worked

---

[303] Violet taught the Warbonnet school 1/2 mile from the Warbonnet ranch.
[304] A beer tester or a hydrometer tracks fermentation to determine when it has become a bona fide drink of beer.
[305] To have a "tagger" or tiger on your back means you have something deep seated bothering you.

better'n a rope. We got rid of most of them, even shipped some to market, but I'm not sure we were all that successful."

During the hog-hunt, the crew encountered a herd of half-wild geese. They determined that one big gander would make a "fine" mate for the goose at the ranch. They roped and confined him to the chicken house. The gander soon escaped into the bushes; the once domesticated female followed.

The Hat Creek and Warbonnet Ranches were nestled in a rift valley about 1200 feet below the tablelands where Harrison, Nebraska was established. The valley was ideal winter country for cattle, but the Coffees' summer pastures on the table, featuring buffalo grass, black root, and other hard grasses quickly fattened the cattle. For two weeks every spring and another two in the fall, cattle were moved between pastures or to Harrison where they were shipped to market. Cattle were divided between the pastures that were generally named after the homesteaders who had originally claimed them: the Rohr, the Pullen, the Corbin, the Hunter, the Sheets. The White River[306] pasture was so named because it contained the headwaters of the White River that stretched on through South Dakota before joining the Missouri River. Drives to each pasture presented challenges and produced "mythological" legends.

The headwaters of the White River are located in the Coffee White River pasture south east of Harrison.

Cattle driven to the summer pastures at White River included cow-calf pairs and steers. During Melvin's early years on the ranch, many of the cattle shipped to market[307] or taken to summer pasture were two or three-year-old steers. A lead steer, a Brahma/ milk cow mix, was used to lead herds up and down the "hill." Shortly after leaving the pasture, the steer traditionally shoved his way to the front and plodded up the road. The other cattle, sometimes as many

---

[306] On the hill tops above the headwaters of the White River, visitors can still see the ruts of the Cheyenne to Fort Robinson stage line. Lakota and Cheyenne often wintered along the river and about 100 feet west of the headwaters, the remnants of stone framed dugout stretches almost 25 feet south into the bank Research revealed that the dugout was probably a fur trade store, operated before 1882, when the first settlers came into the region. When asked, Bill Coffee said the Beaver Men, (fur traders) had a store there. Melvin would never let his kids explore the dugout that still included a heavy, iron door frame until at least the 1980s, because he said he thought it would be full of rattlesnakes. In 2016, Moni Hourt, Don Housch, who did extensive research into the fur trade store, and Doug Buckley visited the site and found that the walls that are made of stone framed an area approximately 25 x20 feet, much too large to be an ordinary homesteader's dug out.

[307] The cattle were shipped from the cattle yards at the railroad siding in Harrison. In earlier years the Coffees shipped their cattle from Coffee Siding established by CF Coffee between Harrison and Van Tassle, Wyoming. At that time, the Coffee Siding shipping point offered cheaper fees for cattle than the Harrison shipping yards did.

Left: Don Housch and Doug Buckley stand within the doorway of the stone-lined dugout near the White River headquarters on land that belong to the Bill Coffee family. Above. The dugout itself, lined with stones stretches nearly 30 feet into what was once an outcropping.

as 1500[308] of them, followed behind creating a column that sometimes stretched two or three mile down a country road or across swatches of prairie. About 1200 two-year old steers were being driven to the railroad siding at Harrison the morning the lead steer decided he didn't want to stop at the pens. He turned south—again and again. For nearly two hours, the other steers followed their leader, creating a "mill" [309] that shoved and swirled just outside the stock yard gates. Several of the steers overheated and died before the animals were safely corralled. When the steers were marketed that fall, the lead steer was loaded into the back of a stock truck for his trip to the sale barn. Ernest Pullen, given the unenviable task of hauling the steer who peered imperiously over the top of the truck sides, was certain the animal would "bust through the stock racks" before they got to Lusk. He didn't.

A second set of lead steers, Mike and Pat, did a good job of leading the steers to their destination, but sometimes even the best of help couldn't prevent a wreck. Melvin said a few railroad engineers "seemed to enjoy the mess" created by ill-timed train whistles.

"One morning they blew that damn whistle just as we were coming in the gate," Melvin said. "Cattle scattered in every direction. We gathered them up out of yards and gardens all over town. That engineer got a good cussing, and he deserved it."

---

[308] An average herd was between 800-1000 cattle. Often three to four men drove the cattle: one on the lead, and two working the tail end and /or the center of the line. Cowboys on the drag, the end, pushed the cattle forward.
[309] At times, a lead steer would turn into the herd instead of leading straight toward a destination. The other cattle would follow creating a milling herd of cattle that resembled a whirlpool. The lead steer would have to be extracted from the herd and driven somewhere before the herd would follow the preferred path.

Hired Men and Cantankerous Beasts 151

*Although this picture was taken in 2007, the Sioux County Sale Barns
have changed little since the 1950s.*

Under the best of circumstances driving the steers into the train yards was a touchy business. The cattle trail skirted the edge of Harrison. Dogs, a start of a motor, or an excited spectator's shout, could send them into a frenzy. One spring morning everything went extremely well. The cattle were penned with very little trouble. The crew was still smiling when they went through the gate. "Jaws" [310] music could have warned the crew, but it had not yet been written.

Sorting began to organize the cattle for their journey to market. That's when the Hat Creek crew realized there was a shortage of train engines to pull the number of cattle cars needed to transport the cattle. No problem. Smiles still abounded. It HAD been a great move. While the crew waited for the engines to arrive from Chadron, they decided to visit the local saloon. (Very strong Jaws music should now break forth.)

"Chappie, Charley Quay, Bill, and I got to boozing a little. Pretty quick we were crazier than coons," Melvin said. "For some reason Bill bought us each a jug of wine. When we heard the train whistle blow we headed across the track—each of us carrying their wine. Chappell threw his up in the air. It came down right between his eyes, broke his glasses, cut up his face. We were plumb stupid, but we don't care. We did know we had to get the cattle into the cars, but at that point, it seemed to be a great joke."

---

[310] The John Williams soundtrack for the 1975 movie "Jaws" had not yet been written, but it certainly might have warned the crew that disaster was lurking.

At first the train crew decided to help the ranch crew shove the cattle from the pens into the cars, but the animals' moods hadn't been improved by the forced delay. The ranch crew's jocular mood didn't improve the situation. The train crew crawled up on the fence and watched the show.

"At one point, I looked over. Bill was all hunkered down in the corner. Cattle were going everywhere. I hit one steer in the head with my wine bottle, but was careful to hold my finger in the jug so I didn't lose that wine," Melvin's infectious grin enhanced the story. "We were absolutely stupid, out of control bastards. Somehow we got the steers loaded and got them out of there. By the time Thelma got up there to pick us up, Chappie was passed out on the bar. That was one of the last years we shipped the big cattle. (Two and three-year-old steers.) No, it wasn't the last time we went to the damn bar, but I think that was the last time we went before the cattle were loaded."

A train chugs toward the stock yards at Harrison, NE. Cattle can be seen lounging in the pens.

Visiting the Longhorn Bar after the cattle had been safely loaded onto the rail cars, was deemed an acceptable way to celebrate the crew's success. Despite the fact that the bar definitely made a profit when the cowboys were in town, the bar owner's wife, Clara Grimm, didn't have a great deal of fondness for cowboys, particularly Chappell.

"We'd been in town quite a while that one day. We were all playing pool," Melvin smiled. "When Clara walked by Chappie hooked the tail of her skirt with his pool stick, nothing indecent, but she didn't care. She'd been mopping the floor. She whirled and hit Chappell in the face with the mop. It was the funniest thing I ever saw."

After another late night foray in town, Chappell decided to play trapeze artist using the bar's "chandelier" as his personal swing. He was swaying to and fro, when Clara walked in the door. She took a run at the pool table, grabbed a pool cue, then proceeded to "kill herself a Chappie." Every time she swung the pool cue in Chappell's direction, he "doubled up" and sashayed away from the stick.

"She was beside herself," Melvin said. "I swear if she'd got ahold of him she'd a killed him. He finally jumped down, just like a cat, and danced backwards out the door. He was a handy little guy."

Melvin said he enjoyed moving cattle but said he definitely didn't like the wrecks. "I like to string cattle up and down Sowbelly. There's nothing prettier to me than cattle strung out a mile or two, head to tail," Melvin said. "I can imagine what those old trail cowboys thought. It must have been a helluva sight. I don't make a racket about it, but I never get tired of it. As long as things are going good there isn't anything much better that driving a bunch of cattle down the trail—until it isn't."

The spring moves involved herd of cows and calves or the more volatile yearling steers. It was the latter that were headed up the Hunter Trail Pasture[311] when the lead "balled up" at the gate. Melvin was halfway up the trail, leading his horse on the steep, nearly 800 feet long-incline, when the first cattle surged back toward him.

"The trail winding up the canyon face, was a "bad, old, steep, narrow trail. Bill said they'd carved it out with a bull-dozer. He claimed that once you could drive a jeep up it. But by the time I hired on, it was a journey for a horse to climb it. It didn't take much to cause a wreck."

That spring day, "too many cattle" rammed the front end. Depending on who told the story, a rider blocked the gate; the gate was open but the cattle jammed into it; or "some damn fool forgot to hang it all the way back." The other factor contributing to the "wreck" was the hock-high piece of wire strung parallel

The Hunter Hill Trail ran almost straight down the side of the 800-foot cliff.

---

[311] The Hunter Trail curves over 800 feet from the bottom of the Hunter pasture to the top. Bill Coffee said one of his men used caterpillar to build the road, but weathering eventually made the trail, vehicle impossible. It was so steep that riders dismounted and let their horses up the trail.

to the trail. The wire and the clogged gate combined to create a "bad situation." Melvin said he saw the wreck happening and turned his horse loose. It trotted down the trail before the cattle reached him.

"The steers were coming around and over me. They'd hit that wire and flip. Then down over the bank they' go. I was holding onto a lil' pine tree just over the edge of the bank. I can remember one steer flipping clear over the top of me. He slid a-straddle a couple of pine trees then bounced on down the canyon. When it was over there weren't any crippled steers, but that wreck sure taught us a lesson about driving the cattle up the hill. From then on, someone would take a handful of cattle to the front end. The guys on the back would just leave the cattle alone, and they'd follow the leaders up the hill. Three or four of us put them up there most of the time."

Cows and calves were easier to move than the easily agitated steers, but Melvin said he was always on the look-out for the unexpected that could reduce an ordinary drive to shambles.

Several times a year different groups of cattle were driven up Sow Belly Canyon. One year floods moved quicksand down the Sowbelly creek bottom that crisscrosses the road. A dozen cattle strayed off the road and wandered into the new quicksand pools. The crew spent all day digging the quick sand away from the cattle, freeing their heads and legs, then even their tails before roping them and dragging them out of the sucking mud. Melvin said they broke every nylon rope they had that day.

Other wrecks weren't quite so dramatic. Barking ranch dogs hiding behind Dean Lundy's[312] ranch buildings in the bottom of the canyon, sent cattle scurrying backwards. Their retreat produced a wave effect that spilled over the tail end,[313] driving it back down the road. The cows generally ran a short distance before turning back to find their calves, but the incident delayed the process. A pair of horses ran down a fence early one morning. Their shadows or just the movement in the opposite direction from the cattle's sedate pace, scattered the herd. The yearlings plowed through fence lines on either side of the road. The crew had to "let down the fences," go into the outlying pastures, gather the cattle, and bring them back to the road. If the delays were too long, there was always the chance, even in the early spring, that the cattle would overheat before they reached the top of the canyon.

A wooden bridge near the bottom of the canyon on the West Hat Creek Road often rattled as the cattle tripped over it. Skittish yearlings, or even grumpy old cows irritated because they'd been separated from their calves, often turned on their heels and scattered back down the hill pushing the "drag' over the riders.

"We used to have a lot more trouble with the cows than we do now," Melvin said in 2007. "They're gentler, but mostly we learned to handle them better. People were a rougher people

---

[312] Lundy served as the Sioux County High School Agricultural teacher in Harrison for 25 years. He and his wife lived in Sowbelly Canyon, almost midway between the bottom and the top of the canyon road.
[313] The end of a herd is called the tail end or the drag.

then, just rougher. They didn't handle the cattle very good. They were in too big a hurry, rammin,' jammin' making too big a racket. I've found through the years that the quieter, easier, the slower you handle cattle the better. I know I come a long way in learning to handle cattle. I think it's the damn people that make them wild."

Melvin said a person needed to see things from a cow's point of view. "Know what that cow's going to do before she does it. Let that old cow think she's doing it on her own. Just back off and stay away from her if you can. That works," he smiled, "most of the time."

Cattle stringing across the pasture. Riders on the drag, slowing push the cattle forward.

The worst "wreck" at the Coffee Ranches had little to do with cow management, and was one of the few incidents that resulted in a large number of cattle deaths. Grass tetany, or grass staggers, was documented as early as 1930, but as late as 1949, the book, *Feeds and Feeding: A Handbook for the Student and Stockman,* written by Frank Morrison, a professor of Animal Husbandry and Animal Nutrition at Cornell University, said the reason behind the "disease" that often led to death in lactating cows "had not been determined." Symptoms listed included frantic movements, irrational bouts of staggering gallops, foaming at the mouth, and convulsions that resulted in death, often within a few hours. In western Nebraska, a few cattle deaths from the disease were reported every spring, none on the Coffee Ranch.

"By the early 60s, ranchers knew that the disease, I guess you call it that, was probably caused by lack of magnesium," Melvin said. "There were even cases when ranchers saved a cow by drenching them with magnesium, putting a hose in their stomach or in their juggler vein, but few ever had magnesium on hand. And the worst part was that a perfectly healthy looking cow could go from nursing her calf to dying within a matter of hours. We really paid close attention, but that one spring it just hit us."

Melvin said ranchers knew grass tetany generally occurred in herds that had "wintered hard" on insufficient, low-quality hay. Early "lush grass" years also increased the likelihood of grass tetany incidents because the early season grasses provided less nutritional value for the heavily lactating cows whose calcium and magnesium supplies were drained by their nursing calves.

"Chappel called about 4 one beautiful spring morning," Melvin said. "That was about 1961. He said there were dead cattle everywhere. By the time I got to Hat Creek, Bill was already there pacing around the pasture. A few of the cows were still alive, staggering to their feet before falling back down in convulsions. Their eyes rolled back, heads flopped back over their backbones, feet sticking out from bloated bodies—one helluva sight. The baby calves were running around trying to nurse from their dead mothers. No one said much—14 good, young, healthy Hereford cows, lying there—dead or dying. Wasn't a damn thing we could do."

Later that day, the men gathered the calves. Melvin turned several of them in with his milk cows. The dead cows were buried. When discussion ensued around the dinner table in the months to come, Melvin and Bill decided the incident occurred because of several related events. Soft spring rains followed by warm days had swept the region. Almost overnight, green grass blanketed the prairie. The cattle were still fed large quantities of excellent hay, but they quickly spurned the hay for fresh grass. The large, strapping, calves, some nearly a month-old depleted their mother's nutritional needs and they died.

"Grass tetany ain't the problem it used to be," Melvin said. "Within a couple years, companies was selling supplements with calcium and magnesium that people added to salt. Now they even mix it with feed." He shook his head. "But I'll never forget that day. It was of the worst damn things I ever saw. I felt bad about those cows, but I can still hear those baby calves a-bellerin'—still makes me feel helpless."

COWS RULE

"On a ranch, the old bossy cows rule the roost. And seldom do they do what you want them too." Melvin Nation

Calving season began around March 15 at the Coffee Ranches. Mother cows made their own rules—always. One year the barn was full of Hereford cows with sun burned teats. They had the upper hand, and were obviously enjoyed their power when Melvin arrived. Chappell and Bill were sitting among the rafters in the calving barn. The cows were patrolling below them like so many hungry wolves.

"I drive the cows back into the pens, and we got them doctored." Melvin said. "It was funnier than hell. We had a few of those cattle that you'd swear were a throwback to the old longhorn cows."

Janet Oldaker drives a pair of Hereford cows toward the corral.

CF Coffee, JT's father had driven longhorn cattle from Texas into the northern plains in 1871. In 1878, he and his brother bought a herd of Durham cattle from Oregon. The cattle brought to the Hat Creek Valley in 1879 were a mixture of the two breeds. When Melvin hired on, the pastures were stocked with Herefords.

Hereford were considered great "mamas," but their light-colored bags and teats were susceptible to sunburn. The cows DID NOT like to be doctored for the sunburn and liked it even less when they were forced to allow their calves to nurse their sore bags. One old cow nicknamed "The Bear" made regular trips to the barn. Since hired men came and went, every man was warned that Bear was dangerous. One new man told Melvin he was absolutely sure he could handle the situation. He confidently headed to the barn to doctor the cow. A few seconds later a massive thump vibrated down the length of the small building. Melvin strode to the door and threw it open. Bear didn't even look up. She continued to grind the man against the wall. Two by Fours bounced with each "jam." The next time he doctored Bear's sore bag, the hired man carried a club.

On a yearly basis, the old "crooked-eyed cow" was driven into the corrals for her annual bag repair. One spring, Melvin's new man was designated as "bait." His orders: run past the open chute entrance. In theory, the cow would make a beeline through the chute in her frenzy to pound the offending human on the other side. Her head was subsequently trapped in the head catch thus making her easier to doctor. Melvin swore to the man that he always closed the outside gate quickly enough to prevent the cow's escape. The man could not summon the courage to slide in close enough to catch the cow's attention.

Thelma was drafted to help with the project. She saucily ran past the chute, stopping in the chute gate, to "thumb her nose" at the cow. Bellowing, the cow lurched through the alleyway intent on getting to her prey. She jammed her head through the head catch. Melvin slammed the gate closed. About that time Melvin heard a "yahoo" and looked down the fence line. The hired man was hiding behind the fence waving his arms and quietly "yahooing' apparently trying to show that he was doing his part. He quit a week later.

Generally, the hired men could avoid cattle confrontations—if they listened to orders and paid attention. Many did neither. The Alliance boy swore that he worked in calving pens all across the Panhandle. The wild cow was already doctored. Melvin told the young man to run to the far side of the corral and throw the gate open to turn her into the pasture.

"The kid was wallering down the middle of the corral when I opened the gate," Melvin said a grin sneaking across his face. "That cow ran right up behind him, but never even tried to hit him. He looked back and saw her and finally decided to move a little faster. She was about three feet behind him, her tail straight up, bellering. I know she was laughing. The kid hit the corral fence. He hauled his elbows up to the top plank. His momentum shoved him over the top. He hit the other side with a terrible splat. He didn't think it was as funny as I did. He went to the bunkhouse and packed his stuff."

On cold nights, Melvin would get up several times a night to check on the calves. He said a baby calf generally survived, even on a sub-zero night, if the Mama Cow licked it off and let it suck. If a calf "froze down" Melvin often carried the animal to the house and laid it beside the Skelgas stove in the living room.

"One cold night, he dragged five calves to the house," Thelma said. "They warmed up and started bellering and bumping around the living room. I made him get up and take them outside."

When the calves were totally chilled down, instant warming was crucial. A bathtub filled with warm water worked amazingly well. Melvin dumped the calf into the warm water, more water was added as needed. It was generally Thelma's job to remove the wet, soggy, animal. The girls tackled his soaked hide with old towels.

"Melvin was tough to live with when he lost a calf," Thelma said. "We'd do everything to keep them alive. When it was really cold we'd crank up the old cook stove, open the oven door, cover it with blankets, and lay a calf on the door. We saved a lot of calves that way. The kids thought it was great when Mel brought the calves in. They'd take towels and rub them down. They were always trying to talk me into giving them some milk. I told them that was their mother's job. I wasn't as excited about the calves as they were."

After school, Moni and later Robbin rode the calving pasture and gathered the cows who looked like they were having trouble—then the girls were sent to the house.

"We spent hours in the calving pasture," Moni said. "We knew what was going on, but, we were girls. Dad didn't want us around when a calf was being born or especially when he was pulling a calf."

The girls would drive the cow into the barn, unsaddle their horses, and head for the house. Then they'd sneak back to the barn and crawl into the hay mow above the calving barn and watch their Dad pull the calf.

Although calf pullers were necessary at times, Melvin generally performed the task without them. He stripped off his coat and shirt, then reached into the cow, grab a calf's foot and pull the tiny animal free. If a calf wasn't breathing after the placenta was pulled from a calf's face, Melvin swung it back and forth until it took a breath. Once in a while in a last-ditch effort to get the calf to take a breath, he thumped it on the ground. Once the calf took a breath, he turned it over to the cow to lick it clean and let it suck. Then he washed his arms in the icy water of the cow tank and put his shirt and coat on. He didn't get in a hurry unless he thought he was going to lose the calf, and he ignored the cold.

Strangely, Melvin also seemed to ignored his "spying" daughters. "I thought about that later," Moni mused. "Dad never missed anything. He noticed a fly crawling across the barn wall, but he never heard us crawling around the hay mow and peeking through the big window above the calving shed. I never asked him, but I think now, that even though his "Victorian" upbringing wouldn't let him officially sanction our presence, he knew we were there. Year later, my sister helped her husband calve. Dad was proud of her ability and never mentioned that she was a woman."

There was little doubt that Melvin noticed his oldest daughter's presence on top of the barn. She often climbed up on the flat surface of the corral fence and shinnied up the barn roof. Then she skipped across the flat surface of the barn skirt from one end of the corral to the other. "It was Dale Ray's fault that I climbed to the top of the barn," Moni said smiling. "Well, maybe, I can't blame him entirely."

Dale Ray Rising[314] spent several weeks of his eighth summer at Warbonnet. He and Moni, a year his junior, passed their time "adventuring." She showed him how to climb up on the edge of the barn. He bragged that he could make it to the peak. He slipped off his shoes, rubbed his feet in the corral dirt, then "snugging' his toes in the davits produced by hammering tin on the roof, quickly scaled the roof.

"Dad didn't actually prohibit barn roof climbing, but I'm sure I knew I wasn't supposed to be up there, but I sure wasn't going to let him 'best-me.' After Dale went home, I continued to scale the slippery tin sides. I loved to sit on the peak of the roof and look across the ranch. I was careful, though, that Dad was gone when I went up there."

One afternoon, Moni was perusing the surroundings when Melvin pulled into the yard. He immediately noticed his daughter's location. She said it was one of the few times she received a spanking.

"I can't say I never scaled the roof again," Moni said wryly. "But I made sure Dad was far, far, away before I did."

Getting far away from the milk cows was never possible. Every morning and every night, the cows, bags full and "bellering" with impatience, pushed their way through the milk-barn door. Melvin was waiting, although he never waiting joyously. According to the Nebraska Historical Society,[315] there were 40 percent more milk cows on Nebraska farms in 1920 than there were in 1957. Melvin would have celebrated the statistic, if he read it. Like most cowboys, he hated to milk. He often told his children that everyone should do something every day that they didn't want to do. For him that was milking the cows.

"Milking cows was a bunch of malarkey. Cows aren't meant to be milked. They're meant to be sucked. There isn't a cowboy on earth that likes to milk a stupid cow, unless it's to feed a calf a little bit," Melvin's declaration was tinged with humor. "But we used the milk and sold the cream. It did us a lot of good, so I milked the damn cows," he grinned, "unless there was a hired man around."

In the spring of 1954, one of the hired men talked his buddy into doing the milking, then he left for a Saturday night on the town. He didn't make it back on Sunday morning.

"I went to Hat Creek to help Bill do something that Sunday morning," Melvin's dimple danced. "I could hear him cussing when I pulled up in front of the barn. He was trying to

---

[314] Dale was the son of Marvin Rising, a long-time friend of the Nations.
[315] "Livestock Patterns. Farming in the 1950s and 1960s." *Wessels, Living History-Nebraska.*

milk an ole' cow. Milk was running down both elbows. He kept yelling that he was going to kill Bob for not taking care of the cows—he was flat going to kill him. I about laughed myself sick, then I helped him milk the cows. When Bob got home, Bill never said a word. He shoulda kicked his butt."

One old Brown Swiss milk cow produced a bucket and a half of milk twice a day. She was gentle, came when she was called, and went right to her stanchion, but she also liked to kick. Melvin warned the men to attach the kickers[316] before they settled in to milk the cow. Hank ignored the warning. With a calm vengeance, the cow reached out and nailed the man with a hind foot flinging him into the milking barn wall. He melted slowly down the wall like the wicked witch in the Wizard of Oz and "splatted" into the waste trough that stretched across the barn. He didn't forget again.

Ed Oldaker milks his cow and feeds the cats simultaneously. The "kickers" are wrapped around the cow's hock.

"Once in a while, I milked the cows," Thelma said. "My sister said when we were kids, I avoided milking whenever I could. I didn't change much. I milked only when I had to. One night Bruce and Melvin stayed in town too long. Jean and I ended up milking."

The cow had a huge bag and teats, one with an extra hole that spewed milk across the women as they began the milking process. "We perched on the stools, one on either side of the old rip. We milked awhile, then we smoked a few cigarettes. It took us an hour. We just left the milk in the barn for the cats."

The milk that made it to the house filtered through an electric milk separator located in the wash room off the kitchen. Separated milk was fed to the pigs. Whole milk was fed to motherless calves that hadn't been grafted onto surrogate mothers or to bum lambs.

"We fed the calves from teat buckets hung on the fence. We filled pop bottles fitted with a lamb nipple to feed the lambs. We were pretty good at holding a lamb bottle in each hand and two between our legs," Moni Hourt said. "Then Dad drilled holes in a two-by-four. We stuck pop bottles into the holes and fed the whole herd of lambs at once. We made good use of the cow's milk."

The calves and lambs generally "slurped" the milk with abandon, but sometimes, particularly if the young calves needed to be coaxed into consuming their meal, Thelma added a little "Karo Corn Syrup" the same kind she used in "Dutch Honey,"[317] to the milk, or

---

[316] Kickers are pieces of equipment that are wrapped and fastened around a cow's hocks to keep them from kicking.
[317] Dutch Honey was the syrup of choice at the Nation family breakfast table. It consisted of a cup of fresh cream, a cup of dark Karo syrup, and a cup of brown sugar. The syrup, cooked to a "syrup consistency" was slathered on pancakes, waffles, apples, and fingers.

added a couple of tablespoons of Jack Snyder's honey. Those two sweet tonics could generally convince any reluctant animal to drink its "supper." And of course, if a calf had scours, Melvin mixed a little of the syrup or honey with a raw egg and poured it carefully down the calf's throat. Long before the days of over the counter scour medicine, raw eggs cured many problems.

"We sold the cream and sometimes the eggs we didn't use to the creamery in Crawford[318] or Lusk,"[319] Thelma said. "That was our grocery money. After the kids got older, Melvin still kept milk cows, but he milked them a few weeks, then turned the calves on them. The milk cows raised a lot of calves and again made us some extra money."

Cow's milk was used for many things including feeding baby calves.
In this picture Melvin uses a teat bucket.

---

[318] The Fairmont Foods and Creamery shipped cream all over the United States. A premium was paid for sweet cream.
[319] The curved front wall of Kilmer Creamery in Lusk was covered in glass bricks. When Thelma took the cream to Lusk, she purchased ice cream cones for the girls. While they slurped their cones, they sat in the booths by the glass brick windows and watched the rainbows dancing across its surface.

SUPPORTING CHARACTERS

"Ranchers generally have a few chickens and a pig or two on a ranch, but the sheep Bill shipped in didn't suit the operation very well." Melvin Nation

Although, the primary animals on the Coffee Ranches were cattle and horses, chickens, pigs, and even geese left their footprints in varying degrees.

Chickens roamed most area farms and ranches. They provided the eggs that leavened cakes and flipped happily in morning breakfast skillets. At Warbonnet, they free-ranged long before the practice was lauded by animal rights activists. The only problem chickens presented was that other animals liked them as well as their human owners did. Raccoons used their tiny man-like fingers to rip away screen and sneak into the hen house. The ensuing slaughter generally led to deadly serious "coon hunts." Weasels and foxes lurked around the pen waiting for an unwary hen that could be snatched away to a hidden lair. Even the lowly bull snake made his appearance on a semi-regular basis.

"I was gathering eggs when I saw something move. I knew it was a damn snake," Thelma said. "He had slithered his damn hide into an empty nest. I guess my cussing woke him up. He flopped out of the nest and wallered to the door. He was so lumpy with the eggs he swallowed that he couldn't even slither. He sure didn't eat any more."

Among the several dogs that made an appearance at the ranch, the breed that dominated was a Dachshund. They generally didn't chase the cattle or horses, but they were "hell on chickens."

"We named all our dachshunds, Pooch," Thelma said. "Pooch 2 almost lost his happy home over the chickens. He was constantly sneaking into the chicken house and snagging an old fat hen. Finally, I caught him dragging one out of the chicken house. Gawd, I was mad. I took some twine and tied the dead chicken to his neck, thinking that I'd let him drag it around all day and he would never want to touch another chicken. It didn't work that way; he just used it as an easy to get snack. I finally cut it off and threw it away. I didn't think I should contribute to his chicken habit."

Several Pooch-dogs resided with the Nations over the years. JimBob is pictured here with the first Pooch.

Keeping the chickens alive and healthy was mandatory, because they were an important food source for the family. Thelma bought baby chicks at Norgard Hatchery[320] in Crawford every spring, raised them to "fryer" size, then drafted her children, friends, (often Jean and Sis), Melvin, and unlucky hired men to help on butchering day. The crew generally slaughtered 25-30 head of chickens in a day. A "chicken-head removal" expert, Thelma quickly dispatched a chicken, then tossed it aside and moved on to the next future-chicken-dinner. The feather removal squad moved in. Chickens were quickly dunked into a barrel filled with boiling water. The de-feathering crew "hand-picked" the hundreds of feathers from the carcass. The flames of a Skelgas stove effectively singed the remaining feathers off the now nearly nude carcass. Pin feathers were scraped and picked from the chicken before it was gutted, butchered, and placed in the freezer, the refrigerator, or taken immediately to the stove. Using her iron skillet and a liberal amount of melted lard, Thelma turned each chicken into a friend chicken delicacy that would make KFC jealous.

"Thelma could kill and butcher a chicken faster than anyone I ever saw," Sis [Velma Rising] said. "I sure couldn't keep up with her. Kids today think that's kinda cruel, but a chicken doesn't just jump into your plate and holler, "eat me." Butchering a chicken was a lot of work I guess, but we didn't think much about it. Many times, you went out and grabbed a chicken out of the pen in the morning, butchered it, and served it at noon."[321]

The ducks and the geese that ran free across the ranch never made it the frying pan. In fact, Melvin admitted, he never did completely understand their role on the ranch. "Thelm had peacocks, guineas, and geese over the years. Now the peacocks were pretty. They and the guineas squawked their heads off when someone pulled into the yard, so we could call them watch-animals, or something fancy like that. She always said they ate a lot of bugs, but mostly those damn geese just made a mess. And they didn't even taste good."

A wrinkled, slightly blurry photograph shows the geese preparing for an attack on 2-year-old Moni. Thelma said just as she clicked the camera, one old gander grabbed Moni from behind, snagging the little girl's diaper and flogging her with his wings. "She was screaming and punching at him. The dog was barking. I kicked the damn goose out of the yard." Thelma

---

[320] Norgard Hatchery in Crawford was one of the largest chicken operation in the region. They sold baby chicks, eggs, and young chickens to farmers and ranchers across the state. By the time Moni was married, they also butchered chickens, which meant the Hourts had fresh, home-grown, chickens without the home-butchering circus.
[321] Rising, Velma (Sis). Personal interview with Moni Hourt, 2005.

said smiling. "Melvin made short work of him that night. I did try to cook him, but he was too tough to chew."

One late night, Melvin, Thelma and a group of their "cowboy" friends arrived home to find the cellar in the front yard had collapsed, the geese fell inside, and were squawking and protesting their sudden confinement. Melvin, hobbling around on a pair of crutches supervised as the men crawled into the cellar and threw the geese pell-mell from the gaping hole.

"Yep," Melvin pondered. "Those damn geese weren't worth the trouble."

Pigs, on the other hand turned into bacon and ham and delicious pork chops after they finished their life-cycle. Confined to a pig pen near the creek, the pigs snuffled and rooted through their heavily fenced lair and generally led a "good life" on the ranch. Their love of mud and slop intensified their persona. Melvin often filled a large bucket with grain, added a little water, and let it ferment a few days. The pigs thoroughly enjoyed the distilled alcohol-like treat; the girls loved watching the tipsy, weaving, fermented grain-induced dances. (removed piece.)

By climbing to the top of the pen's back fence and scaling the A-frame pig house, the girls could open the vent at the top of the house and watch the sows and their piglets. It was an interesting, constantly changing spectacle until the day that it turned gruesome and disgusting. The girls ran screaming to the shop to report that the sow was "eating" her newly birthed piglets. Melvin beat the sow off the piglets, but was only able to save two of them. The girls raised the orphaned pigs, Mitzy and Bitzy. The pigs followed the girls around the ranch like a pair of dogs. Eventually though the half-grown hogs were taken back to the pig pen.

"When the girls were older, they slopped the pigs, but they weren't supposed to get in the pen. The sows were just too dangerous," Thelma said. "The neighbor kids rode their pigs and played with them, but ours didn't. JimBob came back to the house one morning without his hat. He finally said he climbed up on the fence to watch the pigs and dropped his hat. The pigs ate it. I spanked his butt for being down there. The pig could eat him as easily as it ate that hat. There were stories floating around the country about people getting eaten by pigs."[322]

David Nation[323] said he thought Melvin was proud of his hogs—to a certain point. "He had this great pig pen with an A-frame hog house. An old hearse was parked at the back of the pen. The glass was still in it, so you could see those big old fat hogs, lounging around in there. The creek ran through the bottom of the pen. It was hog heaven, but this one morning Mel-

---

[322] Thelma and other parents in the region used a story about a Buckley family member getting eaten by a pig to warn their kids away from pig pens. The story became a mythical tale that couldn't be confirmed then in 2019, Moni Hourt was copying interviews taped by Joy Buckley. In the 1976 interview, Opel Buckley said when her father, William Case was a boy, he and the rest of his family headed for church. His father decided to feed the pigs their "swill" before joining them at the Sunday services. He never arrived at the church When his family went back to find out why, they found his foot, still encased in his shoe, inside the pig pen. They never found the rest of his body.

[323] David Nation, the son of Clark Nation worked for Melvin on at least two occasions. He spent almost a year at the Warbonnet Ranch in 1963.

vin stomped into the house for breakfast. He was plumb miffed. He lost a pig. I think he was insulted that the hog even considered leaving that fancy pen."

The hog revealed his whereabouts that afternoon. "He "wallered" into the north meadow and stood mockin' us in the middle of the irrigated hay ground. Mel tried to drive him out of there with a shovel. The hog snuck into the brush," David said in a 2017 interview. "I was sent to the house for a horse," he grinned. "Melvin thought a horse could solve any problem."

David followed the hog's tracks as they meandered into the Badlands west of the meadow then back onto the roadway. Blacky Lantz, also searching for the strayed porcine, eventually found the huffing, puffing, animal waddling down the road. "Uncle Melvin climbed on the hood—to encourage the pig to keep moving and down the road they went. The hog was moving slow—slow—slow motion. Melvin was fit to be tied. I sat on my horse and laughed myself sick."

Tired of the hog driving operation, Melvin, according to Dave, jumped off the front fender and tackled the 800-pound animal. "They wrestled around some. Melvin was getting pretty beat up. The pig squealed and wriggled. He was having a great time. Blacky was having a heyday, laughing, egging them both on—the pig and Melvin."

The hog was eventually wrestled into the jeep, hauled back to the house, and dumped into the pen. The next morning Dave said Melvin was so stiff and sore he could hardly move. The pig was dead—probably from the "heat producing" wrestling match, or maybe he died because he was determined to have the last laugh.

"Melvin just snorted in disgust, said the damn thing probably wouldn't taste very good anyhow," Dave's laughter wriggled through his words.

Area ranchers tolerated hogs. After all, often under the direction of butcher Rudy Hartman,[324] they became slabs of bacon, spare ribs, and massive hams, but few ranchers ever put up with sheep. The sheep herd that arrived at Warbonnet seemed to be a logical answer to a serious problem. Rattle snakes were prevalent on the ranch and hid in the same deep grass that had become the Nation girls' playground. Mowing machines and their long sickle blades were impractical for mowing the 4 to 5-acre yard that surrounded the ranch buildings. People-powered push lawn-movers required maximum effort and more time that Melvin chose to allot to either himself or the hired men. Thelma made it very clear that she wasn't going to "push the damn thing." The small flock of sheep arrived to "keep the grass mowed."

"The sheep did a pretty good job of keeping the grass and weeds down at Warbonnet, but there were problems. For one thing they needed sheared," Melvin shook his head. "Bill decided we could do it. He sent away for sheep shears and an instruction book. We really didn't think it would be hard. We sure didn't read the book."

---

[324] Rudy Hartman purchased the Harrison Locker Shop in 1950 but according to the *Harrison Sun* November 9, 1950, "Rudy has been cutting meat in the neighborhood of a quarter of a century and knows his stuff, even if he says so himself." Rudy arrived at the ranch every fall to butcher hogs and could according to Bill Coffee, "skin and butcher a hog faster than he could drain a bottle of beer."

"We didn't do too well with the sheep business," Bill Coffee said during a 2001 interview. "We thought they'd keep the yard cleaned up, but never did figure out how to build a fence tight enough to keep them in the yard. When it come time to sheer them, we put a picture on the barn door that showed us how to do it. We thought we had it licked. But I can still see the barn. There was blood from one end to the other."

Professional sheep shearers like Jess Wasserburger could quickly remove an intact fleece, a feat Melvin and Bill never came close to achieving.

At first, the novice shearers tried to sheer their "victims" by sitting them on the floor and cutting the fleece away with their new, sharp, "scissors." The fleece didn't come away as neatly as expected.

"We cut off chunks," Melvin said. "Sometimes that included skin. By the time we were done, the sheep looked pretty sad. By noon we were hurtin'. Finally, we put the sheep up on a table. That was easier, but the sheep didn't look much better. We washed away the dirt and smell with a few beers. That didn't help things any."

The chunks of fleece were dropped into a floor to ceiling wool sack attached to access holes in the hay mow. Then Melvin dropped his daughter, Moni, into the wool sack with instructions to "stomp the wool down."

"I'd stomp around inside that itchy bag, then I'd holler. Dad would come up to the hay mow, reach down inside the sack, and pull me out," Moni Nation Hourt remembered. "I can still remember how "cool and refreshing" it felt when he pulled me out of the sack. Stomping wool was definitely not my favorite job."

The wool was sent to the Minnesota Woolen company and turned into blankets and jackets. Thelma even ordered a wool suit from the company representative, Mac Crawford. The woolen products were beautiful, but neither Bill nor Melvin expressed a desire to shear the sheep the next year. They contacted the FFA boys at the Sioux County High School. Under the direction of local sheep owner, Anne Dunlap Quintard, the boys quickly and deftly sheared the herd.

"Anne knew how to sheer sheep. The wool actually came off in one piece," Melvin said. "Those sheep shears hung in the barn at Warbonnet for a long time. We never used them again."

The ranch went out of the sheep business the next year after a roving mountain lion [325]diminished the herd. The lion, with paw prints that dwarfed even Melvin's large hands stalked around a pen where a small dwarf calf was enclosed, but its killing was limited to the sheep pasture. The lion harassed several ranches in the area before moving on to parts unknown. It left the memory of its screams forever etched on the minds of those who heard it.

"Robbin and Moni were layin on the living room floor when the cat screamed," Thelma said. "Some say they sound like a woman screaming. I never thought it sounded human at all, and it scared those two girls to death. It was two weeks before they slept in their own beds."

---

[325] The September 11, 1958 edition of the Harrison Sun reported sightings of a mountain lion across Sioux County including in the Warbonnet Ranch area.

HORSE SENSE

> "I seldom met a horse I didn't like. I sure never met one that I didn't want
> to get to know. Bill was one of the pioneers in the Quarter Horse world, he had
> some good horses. I spent hours working with them—and I enjoyed them—
> most of that time." Melvin Nation

Horses weren't native to the Americas. Columbus brought the first six to the Caribbean Islands in 1493. History shows that the Sioux, Cheyenne, Arapaho, and the Crow commandeered horse herds from the Spanish in the 1600s. By the late 1700s horse mounted Natives crisscrossed the Americas. The horses enabled the Native Americans to become nomadic hunters and warriors who dominated the upper northern plains, Wyoming, and Montana. The majestic animals were also a key component to the cattle industry.

Charles Coffee borrowed a horse when he was hired by JW and DH Snyder to drive cattle from Texas to Wyoming in 1871. The horses he brought to the Hat Creek Valley in 1879 were ancestors of the Spanish horses, tough little Texas cow ponies. It wasn't long before he was using Morgan horses from the Pine Ridge Indian reservation to produce animals that filled specific needs on the ranch. Riding horses were raised on the Hat Creek Ranch. Work horses ran on the Wyoming ranch.[326] In the 1890s, the military, stationed at Fort Robinson, Nebraska, offered area ranchers access to thoroughbred stallions. The concept had a two-part goal. Ranchers would improve their herds, then sell horses back to the military at the remount station. The program gave the military access to good thoroughbred-cross horses without developing an extensive breeding program.[327]

"Ranchers were supposed to keep the stallions and a herd of mares, 10 or 12, in small enclosed pastures," Bill Coffee explained in a 1999 interview. "Dad just forgot to "enclose" them.

---

[326] The combined horse herd, including colts, often numbered over 250.
[327] Fort Robinson was one of the largest remount stations in the country and supplied horses for the Spanish American War, World War I, and World War II. Records show that the number of horses at the Fort reached nearly 5,000 at one point.

We turned them into the Hunter Hills[328] about nine miles from Hat Creek. It was one of the wildest pastures in the country. Most of the mares were never saddled. Once a year we rounded them up, brought them back to the ranch, cut off the colts, and took the adults back to the hills. Sometimes we'd get the studs rounded up," he grinned, "but most of the time we didn't."

The horse roundup in the Hunter Hills was always "complicated." One fall, in the late 20s, the crew crowded a herd toward the single path that stretched over the canyon wall to the valley below. The stallion with the herd fought to turn his brood back to the interior of the pasture, then whirled away from the trap to make his own escape. As the men converged on the stallion, he hurled himself toward the canyon wall, apparently believing he could find a path down the sheer incline. Instead he plunged to his death. Ten mares followed. Fifty years later, Bill stood silently on the rim of the canyon and described the scene. The image still plagued his memory.

During one annual roundup, a large herd of mares and stallions headed down the trail and swept across the valley toward the ranch. The cowboy assigned to turn the herd from the lower Hunter gate into the Hat Creek pasture, failed to get the job done. The horses galloped down the road toward South Dakota. Bill said his Dad hit the gas and raced down the road to get ahead of the horses. It was nearly 15 miles before he could get them turned around.

In 1932, most of the horses were moved from the Hunter Hills pasture to pastures on the main ranch. The horses left on the upper Hunter Hill pasture became the only wild horse herd in Nebraska. Those driving cattle up the trail to the Hunter Hills rarely glimpsed the horses. Even when a deliberate search ensued, the process of finding the horses could be difficult.

Ranchers bordering the Hunter pasture seldom spotted the animals either, but in "Man from Snowy River," style, the stallions often made their presence known. In the late 50s, several horses disappeared from neighboring ranches. An ambitious Hunter-Pasture stallion apparently wanted to increase his herd size.

"I called that Coffee and told him we were damn tired of his horses raiding our herds," Albert Meng[329] huffed in a 1997 interview with Moni Hourt. "He just ignored me until I called him back and told him me and some of the neighbors were going to go up there and take care of it ourselves. He said something about trespassing, and I said something about horse thieves. Wasn't too long after that that we got most of our horses back."

Melvin asked Keal Rising and Bruce Quintard to help him capture another set of wayward animals. Several hours after they arrived in the pasture, the trio corralled a young mare and

---

[328] The Hunter Hills were located on a plateau about 1000 feet above the Hat Creek Valley where both the Hat Creek Ranch was located. It is crisscrossed with canyons and creeks. A windmill in the pasture was over 400 feet deep. At one time the Coffee Cattle Company also ran horses and cattle on the Wood Reserve, a massive piece of timber land between the Hunter Hills and the Fort Robinson Military Post.

[329] Albert Meng, interview with Moni Hourt 1997. Hourt was interviewing Meng as one of the early organizers of what would become the Crawford Old West Trails Rodeo held annually in Crawford, NE. He didn't share Hourt's affection for the wild horses.

gelding stolen from the neighboring DeHaven place. They located a pair of work horses that came from another nearby ranch and pushed them into the corral located at the far end of the pasture. In the process they encountered a young colt that looked like good "riding" horse material. Keal spooked him out of the underbrush.

"Bruce builds a rope but forgets where he's at," Melvin said with a shake of his head that sent a crooked grin sliding across his face. "He's going a bat-out-of-hell when he hits a low branch and is flat flung out of the saddle. I'll never forget watching that loop settle down around his shoulders. His rope was tied hard and fast. His horse was on a dead run. Bruce must have felt the rope, because he reached up and pitched the loop up over his head. It hung there for a split second then closed. That was the closest thing to a halo that that Bruce ever had above his head." Melvin's grin reflected as much relief as humor.

A young stallion became their next target. The horse spotted his would-be captors and dashed across the edge of the canyon then broke toward the clearing. Keal built a loop, and prepared to throw it, then, let the stallion run past him.

"I gave him a bad time about backing off and said if I'd a been closer I'd a caught the horse," Melvin's smiled wryly. "I probably would'uv roped him, and he'd a taken me right over the edge of the cliff. He wasn't gonna be captured."

In the early 70's, Melvin agreed to take his family to the Hunter Hills on a "wild horse viewing excursion." By that time, there were several herds in the pasture, each led by a dominant stallion and lead mare. One herd materialized at the top of the ridge, curious about their observers. In the space of four picture frames shot by a Nikon camera, they slipped back into the trees at the top of the ridge, their tails and heads arched with prideful disdain. The horseback riders followed another worn path in search of the second herd. They topped a hill. Below them the bodies of several dead colts sprawled across the valley. Pickup tracks careened parallel to and around the dead bodies. Bullet holes proved that the animals had been killed with high powered rifles. Melvin reported the incident to Bill. That night, he stomped into the local salon and confronted the men who leased the pasture. Their lease, although not expired, was revoked—-immediately; the lease money was not refunded. Bill made it clear to the entire community that the wild horses were off limits.

The horse herd in the Hunter Hills expanded rapidly over the next 20 years. By the late 1980s, an excess of young stallions ranged the pasture. They hazed the mares and killed several colts. Bill and Melvin decided to remove some of the stallions for the sake of the herd. Bruce Quintard, Jim Lemmon, Mike and Kerry Morava, and several other friends assembled at the pasture. The operation included an airplane, two four-wheelers, walkie-talkies, and several men and women on horseback.

"Dad put me at the bottom of a canyon to keep the horses from going up the trail on the other side," Moni Nation Hourt said. "About 25 horses came over the top of the canyon path. They didn't get past me and go up the trail to the pasture. They ignored me, split in a dozen directions, and pounded their own trails up the canyon walls. I just sat there and watched them go."

After a day's work, a dozen young stallions were corralled and taken out of the hill pasture. The rest scattered across the grassland, melting into the underbrush, and disappearing into the pine-tree covered canyons. Every few years after the 1986 roundup, young stallions were taken from the pasture to keep the population from expanding beyond a sustainable number.[330]

In 2012, there were approximately 20 horses in the pasture when a wild fire swept across the canyon pasture destroying most of the grass and the pine trees that covered the prairies and canyons. Several of the horses were so badly burned that they had to be euthanized. The rest were moved to the Warbonnet Ranch and set free in an isolated pasture several miles from the ranch buildings. After 100 years, the Hunter Hills no longer sheltered a wild horse herd.[331]

None of the horses in the Hunter Hills were pedigreed; the Quarter Horses in other select pastures across the ranch definitely were. A December 1988 article in the *Quarter Horse Journal*[332] explores Bill Coffee's saga from the Morgan/Thoroughbred horses developed in the Hunter Hills to producing some of the top Quarter Horses in the world.

"Our first AQHA stallion was an apron-faced buckskin—Buckskin Moccasin—by Smoky T by Dundee and out of a Peter McCue mare. I've no complaints about him at all, or any other stallion we've owned through the years, but the one that contributed most to the production of Coffee horses was a chestnut. His name was Toad," Bill Coffee told *Journal* writer, Jack Lyn in 1988.

Rancher Keith Zimmerman[333] said Buckskin Moccasin[334] was the first registered Quarter Horse in Sioux County. He added that another one of Bill's early stallions, Rusty Gold,[335] could run a hole in the wind. "In my opinion though," Zimmerman said. "Toad was the best horse Bill owned. He was one of the best Quarter Horses this country has ever seen."

A Harrison Sun article dated July 8, 1948 suggested that the Coffee horses were being watched by the Quarter Horse industry. The short article reported that Mr. Bryson VanGundy, the secretary of the Rocky Mountain Quarter Horse Breeders Association had arrived in the area to inspect Bill Coffee's Quarter Horse breeding program. It concluded by saying "All the colts eligible age were passed favorably by Mr. VanGundy."[336]

---

[330] Melvin conducted his last wild horse roundup three days before he suffered a stroke in 2009.
[331] In 2016, a few of the surviving horses were returned to the Hunter pasture, but the small herd did not include breeding stock.
[332] Jack Lyn. "Because They Were So Bred." *Quarter Horse Journal-Easter/Western. Year in Review*. December 1988.
[333] Zimmerman's land bordered Hat Creek. He attended many of the Quarter Horse sales featuring the Coffee Horses. Zimmerman was a high school student at Sioux County High when he suggested that Ag-teacher Dean Lundy organize the high school rodeo in the community.
[334] An article in the January 25, 1945 *Harrison Sun* reported that Bill Coffee purchased a Quarter Horse stallion at the Western livestock show in Denver, Colorado. That horse was Buckskin Moccasin.
[335] Foaled 1946, was also a descendant of Peter McCue
[336] "Inspects Quarter Horses." *Harrison Sun*. July 8, 1948.

Toad, the horse that caught Keith Zimmerman's eye, was purchased from Harry Wommer of Bayfield, Colorado in 1949. "Bill wanted the horse for quite a while, and gave what he needed to get him." Melvin said. "Then he bought the best Quarter Horse mares available to breed to him. He was a damn good judge of horseflesh."

Long time friend and fellow horse breeder, Tom Norman drew this picture of Toad.

Some of the first mares to arrive on the ranch were daughters of Quarter Horse "greats": Peter McCue, Skipper W, Three Bars, Cowboy, and Oklahoma Star. Bill also purchased Hank H and Wisecamp bred mares. He carefully selected others stallions that, when bred to the top mares, consistently produced the "type" of colts he wanted to populate his ranch.

Most of the mares on the ranch were not ridden, Dusty Star was an exception. She produced champion colts and could "turn somersaults" in an arena or show ring. Melvin also listed NR Jackie and Featherlegs as two notable mares. "We didn't ride many mares, but the ones we did were darn good ones. One mare I called Birdy could slow lope back and forth behind a cow and a calf as we moved them up the road and never shake them out of a walk. She was something."

Bill's stallions dominated the Quarter Horse breed throughout the 60s. Each stallion produced characteristics that Bill valued in his horses: an even temperament, athleticism, and "cowability." Toad,[337] a descendant of foundation Quarter Horse, Peter McCue, was a stallion

---
[337] A 1943 Quarter Horse out of Spencer2 and Goldie McCue, a descendant of the Quarter Horse foundation horse Peter McCue who was foaled in 1895.

with "cow all the way through him." Bull Lighting[338] out of Three Bars, another foundation horse of the Quarter Horse breed, was actually a registered Thoroughbred with "lots of speed." His bloodline was used to produce larger, "stretchier" colts. Shasta Lad[339] was a grandson of Skipper W, while Raw Edge[340] was a son of Toad. The stallions all produced outstanding colts that could turn on the proverbial dime often dumping their riders in the process, but would also stand quietly while the riders they dumped climbed back on. Many of the Quarter Horses on the ranch were sired by Little Joe the Wrangler out of Joe Hancock, a pair that Melvin called "cowboy" horses.[341] The Little Joe horses were bred to exhibit speed and agility as well as cow horse and reining ability. Many were shown under halter and topped horse shows across the region, including those in Harrison, Fort Robinson, Cheyenne, Denver, and Douglas, Wyoming.

"Bill judged some of the top horse shows in the country," Melvin said. "He knew what the best looked and moved like. He made sure his own horses could run with them in the ring."

Melvin said he seldom took a horse into the show ring. His job was to make sure they were groomed to show, to trim and shoe the show animals, and to train many of the reining and working cow horses. Most of the horses shown in the ring were geldings or stallions although a few of the mares like Dusty Star did win trophies at various shows.

Buck Jordan[342] often had the unenviable job of hauling the horses to area horse shows. He'd load six to eight head in an open truck then waddle slowly down the road making sure that the horses didn't injure themselves as they shifted back and forth on the wood-floor box. Eventually Bill bought a two-horse inline trailer, one of the first in the region, but it could only haul two head. Regardless of how the horses arrived, everyone knew they'd win some of the top prizes.

Area ranchers often challenged the superiority of the Coffee horses, but few succeeded. Tom Norman[343] did. Rancher Ray Semroska[344] said Coffee's Rusty Gold was featured at several match races at the Sioux County Fair Horse races. The $500 match-race between Rusty Gold and Tom Norman's horse, Shortening Bread, came down to the wire in three separate races. Rusty Gold lost all three of the 1/8 mile contests.[345]

---

[338] A 1957 stallion out of Lightning Bar by Three Bars who had Man of War in his bloodline.
[339] Foaled in 1956 was out of Spot Cash a son of Skipper W bred by HJ Wisecamp of Alamosa, Colorado.
[340] Foaled in 1958 was also a grandson of Dusty Star.
[341] Foaled in 1935, out of Joe Hancock a 1923 stud colt.
[342] Jordan's family lived in the Hat Creek Valley. He often hauled and showed the Coffee horses. In a July 26, 1956 *Harrison Sun*, it was reported that Jordan hauled horses to three South Dakota shows where the Coffee horses won many classes.
[343] Tom Norman lived near Whitney, NE and raised excellent horses. He also bought many of the Coffee horses. In later years he became a painter, capturing Quarter Horses on canvas.
[344] Semroska, Ray. Personal Interview, 2015. Semroska lived in the Hat Creek Valley about 10 miles from the Hat Creek Ranch.
[345] An article printed in the September 1, 1949 *Harrison Sun*, reported that "Norman's horse nosed Coffee's horse at the finish wire after a slower start." No other subsequent match races were reported.

Before streamlined horse trailers, livestock was carried in livestock trucks that featured a bed that tilted and high wooded slated sides. Cody Oldaker and Bryan Hourt stand in front of the livestock truck transported hundreds of head of horses and cattle at the Coffee ranches.

By the late 1950s, the ranch was producing and training enough horses to warrant a production sale. Some of the sales were held at the ranch. Others were held in Crawford, NE. One sale was held in Fort Morgan, Colorado.[346]

The *News Letter Journal* published in Newcastle, Wyoming on September 27 and October 4, 1956 reported the upcoming "Bill Coffee and Bill Coy[347] Quarter Horse colt sale at the Hat Creek Ranch October 6." The sale offering included, "25 permanent registered blood lines."[348] The advertisement also invited participates to a barbeque at the ranch.

"When they barbequed the meat that first sale at the ranch, the cook they hired used tires for the fire," Keith Zimmerman said. "The meat wasn't any good. Bill made sure it was right the next year. The horses sold good though."

---

[346] Zimmerman, Keith. Personal interview 2015.
[347] Bill Coy sold many horses on the sale. Other area Quarter Horse producers who sold horses included Rex Hagemeister, Tom Norman, and Gordon Moore.
[348] *News Letter Journal*. Newcastle, Wyoming. September 27, October 4, 1956

"The thing that stuck out in my mind was what a great crowd there was at the sales," Ray Semroska said. "Some of those colts went for $500 to $1000.[349] That was too rich for my blood, but I sure would've liked to have one of them."

Worry about the sale's success permeated the ranch in the days before it occurred. "They always sold for a bunch of money, but we sure worried until we heard the hammer." Melvin said. "We were all proud of those horses. We wanted them to make a lot of money."

Hat Creek Dusty became one of Melvin's favorites. [350]"I called the horse Chink. I loved that horse more than I'd ever loved a horse. He was a handy little bugger. They won the Rocky Mountain Futurity on him. There wasn't anything he couldn't do."

Bill sent Hat Creek Dusty to Bill Coy to fine tune his skills before the AQHA reining championship. The horses suffered an injury during the training. He was sold soon after.

"Truthfully, I rode very few horses I didn't like," Melvin said. "The problem was Bill ended up selling most of the ones I liked."

One of Coffee's outstanding colts was given away—to the male All-Around winner at the National High School Rodeo in Harrison in 1955. Coffee had helped establish the rodeo in Harrison and was a strong supporter of the event. He chose a colt with outstanding bloodlines for the All-Around winner.[351]

By the mid-sixties there were over 60 registered Quarter-Horse mares on the ranch, plus the colts, the stud horses, and the riding horses. "In my opinion, at that time, no one had better horses than Coffee did," Melvin said.

During foaling season, the stallions were removed from the herd and housed in a specially designed "stud barn" constructed behind Hat Creek's main barn. Enclosed "runs" allowed the stallions to get some exercise without coming in contact with the other horses. When they were running with the mares, the stallions fiercely protected their harem. Horseback riders entering pastures containing individual breeding herds were always cautious. Generally, the stallions took their mares to the far side of the pasture. Sometimes they decided to run the invaders out of their territory.

"You could handle the horse herds on horseback. That's how we'd bring them into the ranch, but once in a while a stud would become pretty protective," Melvin admitted smiling at his sardonic use of the word "protective."

A ranch-stallion's protectiveness was evident early one spring morning when Melvin, Moni, Chappell Moore, and his son, Lee, rode into the White River pasture. Bull Lightning instantly spotted the intruders and surged to the front of his harem. The group trotted their horses through the gate. Bull Lightning, silhouetted on a nearby ridge, coiled into a

---
[349] One thousand dollars in 1961 is equivalent in purchasing power of about $8500 in 2019.
[350] Out of little Joe the Wrangler out of Joe Hancock. His dam, Dusty Star was a descendant of Peter McCue.
[351] The horse was won by Porky Souls of Newcastle, Wyoming.

lunging run, zeroing in on the crew. Before the men could pull their ropes and repulse Bull Lightning's aggression, he targeted Lee's horse. Mouth wide open, he lunged at the gelding. Lee jumped from the saddle and slid prairie-dog style under the barbed wire fence. Bull Lightning's teeth raked the saddle fender leaving a permanent indention where Lee's leg had recently rested.

"We drove him off before he could hurt anyone, but Lee spent the rest of the morning looking over his shoulder," Melvin said.

Moni and her sister Robbin also had an unpleasant encounter with Bull Lightning. That morning, they were part of the crew gathering the "Boggy[352]" pasture. The men had pushed the stallion and the mares to the far side of the pasture, then set about gathering another section of the pasture. The girls headed to the ranch with a small herd of cattle.

Bull Lightning sensing the presence of "invaders" circled around the pasture. His single-minded dash scattered cattle across the pasture. He focused on Robbin's horse, Sorely. In a journal entry about the incident, Moni wrote that she zig-zagged back and forth between the stallion and her sister's gelding, but Bull Lighting "sure wanted a bite out of Sorely." Neither of the girls carried a rope and could only try to out-dodge and out-run the angry stud. Finally, in desperation, the girls rode their horses into a small dam. Bull Lightning slid to a stop at the edge of the water, shaking his head and rearing angrily. He finally decided he had enough fun, snorted and galloped back to his mares.

"When it was all over we looked up on the hill. One of the men was just settin' there watching us," Robbin Nation Oldaker said. "He didn't even come down and help us. I knew who he was. To this day I consider him a damned coward."

In the spring of 1963, Raw Edge stepped in a gopher hole and injured his shoulder. The horse was confined to a small pasture near the barn to heal.

Another stallion, Hat Creek Bob, was locked in the barn to keep him away from Raw Edge.

"Mona was supposed to get "Bob" out of the barn a couple of times a day, water him, let him get a little exercise, then put him back. But first, and I don't know how many times I told her, she was supposed to make sure the gate to Raw Edge's pasture was closed." Melvin shook his head. "I came home one night and made a run through the corrals to check things out. I knew immediately what had happened. The tracks were easy to read."

In her journal, Moni said she went out to water "Bob" but forgot to check the pasture gate. She was leading Bob to the water gap[353] when Raw Edge burst through the pasture gate. In stallion fashion, he was screaming and pawing at the other stallion. "I knew I couldn't let go," Moni wrote. "I yelled and screamed and hit Raw Edge with the end of Bob's halter. Finally, he went

---

[352] The horses were generally kept in a pasture east of the barns. Since the pasture had a boggy area it was named the "Boggy" pasture.
[353] The water gap, a small corral attached to the main corral complex was built around a small section of Warbonnet creek which made running water available to any animal that had access to the it.

back into the corral. I shut the water gap gate. I took some grain and coaxed Raw Edge back in the pasture then took Bob back to the barn. I was scared to death, but they weren't hurt."

"At supper I asked her how long it took her to get Raw Edge back to the pasture. She sure didn't want to tell me what she did. I doubt if she ever forgot to check a gate again," Melvin smiled at his daughter's discomfort.

Melvin and Bob Jordan bought Hat Creek Bob at one of the Coffee production sales then trained him as a dogging horse. The fact that Bob considered himself a gentleman, probably kept the "corral incident" from escalating. Quiet and well-behaved, Bob played hide and seek with the girls, ducking around the trees, then trotting up behind them with what they considered a grin on his face. When they were in the yard, he followed them like a big sorrel puppy. When he was confined to the corral, he stood sad-faced, waiting for the girls to bring him a treat. The girls weren't allowed to ride most of the stallions; Bob was the exception.

"Bob never acted like a stud horse." Melvin said. "We took him to rodeos. He never messed with anyone. He was small. That made him a good dogging horse, but he didn't produce very good colts. We castrated him, then he was even better."

Since most of the horses were pastured at Hat Creek, Melvin made almost daily trips to the ranch to help Chappell with the additional work created by the horse herd. He also helped with other tasks that needed done on the larger ranch. Early one spring morning, he and Chappell planned to sort cows in the weaning lot south of the Hat Creek barn. Melvin's feeding took longer than usual.

"Chappell went ahead and started by himself. He was riding a barefoot horse and the lot was slicker than snot. The horse fell with him and broke a leg plumb off. By the time I got there he was setting up next to the barn drinking a quart of whiskey. He had about half of it down so he wasn't hurtin' much anymore, but he was in bad shape. I looked down at him. His boot was pointing in the wrong direction.[354]" Melvin shook his head sadly at the memory.

The horse slipped on the ice and fell, smashing Chappell's foot into the stirrup. Chappell told Melvin when the horse finally got to his feet he realized his foot was caught in the stirrup. He admitted he thought he was a "goner." Fortunately, his foot slipped free.

"I caught his horse for him. That stirrup was twisted flat. He had a little foot, but I still don't know how he got it loose," Melvin said. "It really never healed up. He left that following summer, in 1965. I still miss ole Chappie."[355]

---

[354] *Chadron Record,* January 23, 1964. Article says… "Chappell More suffered a compound fracture of the lower bones of the left leg when his horse was frightened by a truck and bolted slipping on the ice and falling on Mr. Moore's leg."

[355] Chappell Moore and his wife , Violet and family lived in Chadron and rural Dawes County for several years. They finally moved to Chandler, Arizona where Chappell operated heavy equipment, a skill he'd also used in the US Military during World War II. He operated heavy equipment until he retired. He died in April of 1995.

That spring, before Chappell left the ranch, an electric storm hit the barbed wire fence in the Get Away[356] pasture. Shasta Lad and 14 pregnant mares stood along the fence line.

"I'll never forget the sight of those horses layin' along the fence, head to tail," Melvin said. "There were some "toppy" mares in that pasture with Shasta Lad. Only Birdy lived, and she was never much good after that. It was a terrible thing. It was hard on old Bill."

"Dad and Bill are just sad." Moni wrote in her diary in early June.[357] "Dad says he doesn't think Bill can get over this. He loved those horses."

"I never did quite get over it. Whatever thoughts I had of going on with any serious breeding died with those horses that had been so good to me. People usually had to talk hard and fast to get me to sell a good mare, but after the storm I sold what was left. I kept Bull Lightning for a few more years and then sold him too. Eventually I sold pretty much everything. Those horses went a long way toward making the Two-Eyed-Jack horses famous in the show world though." Bill Coffee was quoted in the *Quarter Horse Journal*.[358]

The fall of 1965, after Chappell left Hat Creek, the remaining weanling colts were hauled to Warbonnet. "They were the most beautiful animals I ever saw," Moni Nation Hourt said. "There were 50 of them of every color imaginable. It was my job when I got home from Harrison[359] or on the weekends to bring them in for grain, One night they wouldn't go through the gate. They'd get almost to the gate, then spook and head back to the pasture. When Dad got home about dark he came out and helped me get them in. I knew better than to come in without them."

Halter breaking 50 colts was a time consuming process. When a colt was extra stubborn his or her halter was attached to a collar circling a Jenny mule's long neck. The mule went wherever she wanted. The colt quickly learned to follow. It took several "lessons" before the young horses responded to a tug on their lead rope. Once they did, they could be easily led around the corral, they were turned out to pasture to "grow up a little." Within a couple of years, most of colts had also been sold.

"We kept on riding some of Toad's sons until they were about twenty-four or twenty-five. Our custom here, when ranch horses gets too old to work, is to turn them into a retirement pasture where they have good shelter, live water, and good grazing. That's where the rest of the

---

[356] The Get Away pasture was south of the ranch. Cattle being moved up Sowbelly Canyon or East Hat Creek were turned into the Get Away pasture then turned out onto the road from a corner gate.
[357] The exact date that the horses were killed has been difficult to ascertain. Both Bill and Melvin just said it was in the spring of 1965 Moni's journals just indicates that the event took place in the spring of 1965 too, but did not record the exact date.
[358] Jack Lyn. "Because They Were So Bred—I had a Horse Called Toad. *Quarter Horse Journal. Eastern/Western.* December 1988.
[359] Moni was driving back and forth from Harrison with Kenny Osborn, whose family lived in what was the Parson ranch about 5 miles south of Warbonnet that year because she had graduated from the eighth grade at District 76 and was attending Sioux County High School.

horses ended up. About three years ago, the last one died." Bill said in the 1988 article.[360] "For the first time in about 125 years, we're buying our riding horses instead of raising them."

Bob Jordan, with the assistance of his Jenny Mule, halter breaks a young colt.

Many of the newly purchased horses made a trip to the round corral beside the Warbonnet Barn. Melvin would start a horse on the ground, then gradually get it comfortable with a saddle and rider. Eventually the horse would be forged into partnership material.

"Horses have always been therapy for me," Melvin said. "Things would get to weighin' on me. I could get on a horse and ride out across the pasture, ride up on a high ole hill and watch the sunrise. When I turned my horse back home, I knew I could handle about anything."

Melvin said meeting the day a-horseback was his favorite way to start a day.

---

[360] Ibid

NO LOOKING BACK

"I grew up at Warbonnet, become a better man. Worked hard, took care of my family. Maybe I missed the rodeo world a little, but I've never been much of one to look backwards. Yesterday's gone, so you better set your sites on tomorrow."
Melvin Nation

Melvin said riding was always his favorite part of the ranch work, but there wasn't much that he didn't like. He said every day was different although it "fell into a pattern." So in late May 1958, when Buzzy Hoover came to Warbonnet to ask Melvin to become a partner in his reestablished stock contracting business, Melvin turned him down. Two days later on May 31, Buzzy was killed in a car wreck between Van Tassel and Lusk, Wyoming.[361]

"I called Melvin in the middle of the night. They were here within an hour. Thelma stayed here with the kids. He and I went to Lusk to take care of the accident stuff. I don't remember much of that day, but I know Melvin and Thelma never left until my family got here. They were good friends. But you never know how good a friend is until you really need them." Ridge Hoover Chlanda[362] said in a 2017 interview.

That summer Bill and Virginia were living at the ranch with their four daughters. Thelma called a neighbor to come to the house, but the woman hadn't arrived by the time Robbin woke up. Her crying woke Moni. "I know we put on shoes," Moni remembered, "but we didn't change out of our pajamas. I led Robbin across the bridge and up to Virginia's house. If Virginia was surprised to see us she never acted like it."

Virginia fed the girls Sara Lee cinnamon rolls; they'd never seen "boughten" cinnamon rolls before and excitedly told their mother all about the treat when she arrived home that evening.

"The Coffees only lived on the ranch a couple of summers after we came out there," Thelma said. "I was sure glad they were there that morning. I thought I had the kids taken care of,

---

[361] A California couple was also killed in the head-on crash. The couple's son survived the accident. Obituary: Greeley Daily Tribune-May 31, 1958.
[362] Ridge married John Chlanda of Greeley, Colorado in 1959. They had one daughter, Kristie. He helped Ridge raised her two children, Sandy and Randy.

Robbin was seldom without a cat in tow.

but they weren't. Virginia didn't seem to mind any, and there sure wasn't anything I could do about it. I couldn't leave Ridge alone. She and I were damn good friends."

"Buzzy Hoover was one of the handiest men I ever knew," Melvin said. "He could do anything, was a helluva athlete. You'd be walking along beside him and suddenly his voice would drop. You'd look over. He was walking along beside you on his hands. But his Dad never let him grow up; when Buzzy did try to build his own life, Old Buzz would jerk the rope out from under him. He lived too fast, and it killed him. Ridge went on and made herself a good life with those two little kids. Buzzy never even got to know them. Sad how things work out sometimes."

During the summer of 1958, the Nation children played at the big house with the Coffee girls. The older daughters, Twink and Sarah, played "school" with Moni and their sister, Ann, who was Moni's age. Ann and Moni played in the creek, teased Ann's cousins when they visited, and rode Moni's pony. Sue Coffee and Robbin were also the same age. Neither spoke very clearly. One afternoon, both little girls ran into the cook house. Robbin asked for a drink of "Watee." Sue laughed because Robbin couldn't even say "Wado." Thelma gave them both a drink of "water."

"That Robbin was ornery. She was funny as all get out and was always into something," Norman Callaham said. "She loved cats and dragged this one old cat around by his tail most of the day. We were into dinner one day. Thelma opened the refrigerator door and let out a squawk, 'What the hell is that cat doing in there?' Robbin walked over and pulled the cat off the shelf and looked at her Mom like she was seriously overreacting. 'It was 'fweating' (sweating),' she said. Then she grabbed the cat and went out the kitchen door. She was only about three."

"One of my favorite stories about Robbin happened that same summer," Thelma said laughing. "One morning Bill pulled across the bridge in time to see Robbin walking down the road toward the house. She'd left her underwear a few feet behind her. Bill picked up the underwear and leading her by the hand brought her to the house."

"She told me she 'vet' them," Bill said handing the underpants and the girl over to a very embarrassed Thelma. Then without another word he walked back to his pickup and left. Ranch work dominated the Nations' lives, but Melvin's tally books also reported regular visits by family members. His sisters and brothers made annual trips to the ranch. Sometimes they accompanied him as he fed the cattle or checked the cattle. When Sis visited she spent her time in the house or wrangling kids.

"I always thought a lot of Sis. She had her hands plumb full. Keal switched jobs 'purty' regular, so Sis came up here. She and Thelm were good friends," Melvin remembered, then added. "The best of friends."

By January 1959, Sis had four children under the age of five and was pregnant with her fifth. Her two youngest children, Rhonda and Casey, often spent week-long sleepovers at Warbonnet.

Although the "little kids" were comfortable around the family, they were scared of strangers. "Bruce wasn't a stranger, he was in and out all the time, but Rhonda was scared to death of him," Thelma looked back over time. "One night she ran through the kitchen and bumped into him. She just screamed and jerked back. The next thing we knew she was on the floor. She wasn't breathing. That was before anyone knew anything about CPR. Melvin picked her and shook her; that didn't do any good. So he turned on the faucet and stuck her feet in cold water. She was turning blue. Finally, he put his mouth over hers and breathed little tiny puffs into her little lungs. She took a breath and started screaming her head off. I'd never been so glad to hear a kid scream in my life."

Sis, (Velma Rising) Casey, Dixie, Rhonda, Donna Rising, and Robbin Nation.

Melvin insisted that Thelma take Rhonda and Casey to the doctor where they were diagnosed with severe anemia. He said Rhonda's low red-blood count caused the seizure that nearly resulted in her death. He also told Thelma that was why Casey "absolutely loved to eat dirt."

The younger kids spent most of that summer and fall at Warbonnet. In October of 1959, Sis delivered a two-month premature baby girl. Roxanne only lived 30 days later. "Mom and Dad had moved to California in 1957." Thelma said in a 2007 interview. "Keal changed jobs—a lot. It was a tough time for Sis. In the summer of 1960, Melvin thought it would be a good thing if I took her out to Mom and Dad's. We loaded our six kids on a train at Cheyenne. It took us a couple of days to get to Whittier, but we had a big suitcase full of toys and snacks. The kids were pretty good. There weren't many people in the car, and they seemed to think the kids were cute. The trip wasn't bad at all—if you didn't get too serious."

Donna Rising Norgard said she didn't think either her Mom or Thelma were too serious about delivering discipline on the trip. "Mom told me that they knew the kids couldn't get out of the train, and the other passengers were pretty easy to get along with, so I think we were just allowed to have a good time."

A water fountain at the end of the train car qualified as a "kid magnet." Thelma said the older children nearly wore a groove in the rug between their seats and the fountain. At one point Dixie lined water filled paper cups the length of an empty seat. The next curve, sent a deluge of drinking water spilling over into the aisle. Robbin and Donna dumped the toy suitcase, shoved it into the aisle, and fell asleep. Rhonda and Casey preferred to bed down beneath the seats, seemingly soothed by the rhythm of the rails. Moni disappeared. A search ensued. She was finally located in the observation car, bouncing a little Black girl on her knee. Thelma said the parents were both smiling, so she just left her daughter where she was.

"It was a good trip for all of us, but especially for Sis. We laughed most of the time," Thelma said smiling then added sadly. "It was the last time we laughed like that for a long time."

Casey, Sis, Rhonda, Dixie, Donna, Robbin, Thelma, and Moni in California in 1960.

That August, Sis loaded her children in the car for a trip to town.[363] Eighteen-month-old Casey, climbed out of the car when his mother ran back into the house to get her purse. Five minutes later, she found him. He had climbed through two fences, then apparently decided he wanted to touch the water in the bottom of a small cow tank in the corral. When Sis found him he was face down in six inches of water. She couldn't revive him.

"Little old guy didn't even have a chance to live," Melvin shook his head. "What a blow to Sis and to Thelm, to all of them. Life ain't fair sometimes."

Sis with Robbin and Thelma with Donna. The sisters spent their lifetimes sharing every aspect of their lives, including their children.

---

[363] Sis and Keal were working for Shorty Milligan on the Andrew Falconer ranch. They lived in the old Hat Creek Stage Station that was built along the Cheyenne Deadwood stage line trail in the 1880s.

A NEW DECADE

> "The 60s were generally good years in America. The economy was pretty good, cattle prices stayed steady. We were happy at Warbonnet. Maybe we weren't as rich as some other people we knew, but we were a lot happier than most."
> Melvin Nation

Neither Bill nor Melvin were known for great communication skills. In the spring of 1960, Virginia convinced the men to enroll in a Dale Carnegie[364] course in Crawford, NE. She accompanied the men to the weekly sessions that promised to teach its graduates "How to Win Friends and Influence People." During one of the first classes, the instructor asked his students if they had ever seen an unhappy bird or an unhappy horse. He concluded that "The reason birds and horses are not unhappy is because they are not trying to impress other birds and horses."

The quote probably didn't make an impression, but the trio did glean common sense communication skills from the class. Their graduation certificates were signed on May 1, 1960.

"I wasn't very good with people, never had been," Melvin said. "I guess it [the class] helped. It sure didn't hurt anything."

Melvin didn't use his new communication skills very well when his son was born on February 7, 1961, or at least the nurses at the Chadron Community Hospital didn't think so. Thelma told the nurses that she and her husband had named their new son, Melvin. That afternoon, Melvin told the nurse the baby's name was JimBob. Smiling, the nurses suggested that the couple talk it over and decide on a permanent name before they filled out the birth certificate.

"We brought the little guy home," Melvin sat looking at photographs of his young son. "Thelma laid him on the kitchen table. He lifted his head and his feet off the table and just laid there. Looked like a little turtle. He was the strongest baby I ever seen. Sis and Thelma and those five little girls[365] were all around the table. I told them they were going to spoil him rotten. They pretty much ignored me."

---

[364] Founded in 1912, Dale Carnegie Communication Training, focused on self-improvement.
[365] Robbin and Moni, Donna, Dixie, and Rhonda Rising.

Robbin, Thelma, JimBob, Melvin in 1963. Photo by 11-year-old Moni.

Even Dale Carnegie's best communication skills probably would not have alleviated the problem of keeping a ranch crew. Melvin said he never remembers being anything but short-handed. "We needed four or five men around to help with haying, but we never had a big enough crew. One [366]year Bill picked up men from an employment agency in Denver. Most of them lived on skid row. That was like having a revolving door. Most lasted about a week. We hired about anyone looking for a job. There were some good men out here—just not enough of them."

Charley Quay[367] was one man who earned the "good one" label. He hired on in 1954 shortly after Robbin was born on November 1. He was a good hand with livestock, willing to work hard, and did whatever job he was assigned. Plus—he liked the new baby.

"If Robbin was fussing, he'd just pick her up and jounce her around," Thelma said. "She wet on him a few times, but he never got too excited.

Charley Quay stayed around the ranch for several years. No task was beyond his job description. He even helped Thelma clean up the mess created during her infamous skunk hunt.

Unabashedly, Thelma regularly recounted the circumstances surrounding the event. First, she reiterated that she "truly hated skunks." They were a constant problem. They ate the cat and dog food. They set up housekeeping under the house even after Melvin filled the hole with moth balls and poison. Thelma didn't want the skunks around the house—at all. That particular evening, a fat male skunk made another foray into the yard.

---

[366] N/A
[367] Charley Quay worked for Marvin Rising in Crawford many years after leaving Warbonnet.

"He was eating the cat food. I didn't want to hit the bowl the food was in; it was my mixer bowl. So, I just stuck the gun out through the screen about six inches from him and 'blooooey,'" Thelma grinned. "I'd put the gun up against my hip to steady it. It knocked me up against the wall and sure hurt my hip. It blew the skunk all to pieces. We had to scoop him up with a shovel. It took weeks for the smell to go away."

Bill came to the ranch every day, visited with Melvin, and sometimes helped with the work. The day after the "skunk hunt" he stopped at the house. Much to Thelma's relief he didn't mention the smell.

Bruce Quintard had spent many Sundays at the Hoover Ranch. Melvin took the younger man under his wing and hired him in the summer of 1954 to work at Warbonnet. Every evening, Bruce read to Moni and long before she started to school, he taught her to write the alphabet, his name, and to read an old "Dick and Jane" book. He listened to the stories that she scribbled across the paper, and was never too busy to saddle her pony. The day he brought his new bride[368] out to meet the family, 7-year-old Moni, hid under a table in the wash room and refused to speak to anyone.

"Bruce finally crawled under the table and convinced her to come out for supper," Melvin said. "He was a good kid, but he just couldn't hold his liquor."

Saturday nights in Harrison generally meant drinking a little or a lot of beer. Bruce celebrated with his friends then headed back to the ranch often arriving just before sunrise. He scurried up the tree in front of the house, ran across the front porch, and rang the kitchen bell mounted on a pole beside the front door. (No one was ever sure why he didn't just pull the rope tied to the bell.) Invariably, Melvin climbed out of bed, coaxed Bruce off the house, then put him to bed.

"One night he staggered into the house; both eyes were swolled shut," Melvin shook his head. "He got into a fight with a couple guys in town. When the cop tried to arrest him, he escaped to the sale barn, threw a halter on his horse, and took off. He staggered into the house about 2 a.m. He was covered in blood."

While Melvin took care of the horse, Thelma peeled away layers of blood. In an attempt to reduce the swelling on his triple sized eye lids, she applied pop bottles filled with hot water. "That was a dumb thing to do," she conceded many years later. "I coulda cooked his poor old eyeballs. But he survived. The next day, Melvin talked to the cop. Bruce didn't serve any jail time."

"Bruce was a little knothead," Melvin said, "but we was pretty good friends his whole life. He worked for us off and on until he took over his great-granddad's[369] place."

---

[368] Bruce married Jean Fleming of Lusk. She was the only child of Elmer and Ruth Fleming.
[369] Daniel Jordan, Bruce's great-grandfather was 15 when he came to Sioux County. His mother, Sarah, homesteaded north of Bodarc in 1889. Bruce and Jean Quintard purchased the homestead. The family celebrated the 100th anniversary on the ranch in 1989.

The original Jordan homestead where Bruce and Jean raised the fifth generation of Jordan descendants,[370] was only 10 miles east of Warbonnet. Jean and Bruce still spent many weekends and evenings at the Nation's, playing cards or simply visiting. Some Saturday nights were spent at the Buckaroo Bar[371] in Van Tassel, Wyoming where gallons of beer and whiskey skittered down what was deemed the "longest bar-counter in Wyoming." At times, the couple would head for Crawford and spend the evenings at Marv's Bar. Many of those evenings had unexpected endings.

The two couples drove to Crawford one Saturday night. Jean was pregnant with her first child. Thelma who normally drank coffee instead of alcohol, "discovered" screw drivers that evening. She ignored Melvin's warnings that the drink was strongly laced with alcohol and gulped several. Bruce downed "one or more" too many beers. By the time the revelers reached Fort Robinson Thelma was in her words, "sicker than hell."

Moni and Robbin spent the evening at their Grandparents' home on Crawford's Elm Street. They snuggled in between the adults and even managed to sleep through Thelma's regurgitation stops. By the time they got home, the girls were wide awake. They thought it was hilarious that their Dad carried their Mom to bed. They took advantage of his lack of supervision, pulled their tricycles in from the yard, and began racing around the kitchen.

Moni and Robbin using the kitchen as a drag strip.

---

[370] Misty and Casey

[371] The Buckaroo was a popular hangout for the ranching community until the late 50s. It burned down in 1965.

"All at once I heard Moni screaming that Jean needed me—that Bruce was cookin' himself," Melvin said shaking his head.

Bruce had climbed in the bathtub fully clothed and turned on the hot water. He scrunched up in the corner of the tub, the steamy water lapping at his stocking covered toes. Melvin jerked him from his impromptu water bath. He and a night-gowned Jean, managed to dump him on the bed. The next day at dawn, Melvin rolled Bruce out of bed at 3 a.m. so he could help feed the cows. Jean and Thelma slept in.

The calves were weaned, and the cows were carefully secured in various pastures, the fall afternoon Melvin and Bruce decided to go duck hunting. Late that afternoon, in a state of inebriated bravado, they brought a brace of mallards to the house. They were proud of their duck hunting prowess, but neither Jean nor Thelma were thrilled with the prospect of cleaning the ducks. And they weren't happy with their husbands. While the men were out milking, the women hung the ducks to the kitchen light fixtures. Dinner was served under feathery chandeliers.

"Leaving those two alone was never a real smart idea," Jean Quintard declared with certainty. "Never."[372]

Thelma and Jean prepared lunch early one morning, left it in the refrigerator, and made a grocery run to Scottsbluff. The men finished their work and decided to practice their shooting skills, but it was cold outside. Seldom deterred from their impulses, they stacked several Sears catalogs against the log wall in the Warbonnet kitchen. Then they took turns shooting targets that apparently dodged and wriggled across the static catalog pages. Unfortunately, catalogs didn't stop the bullets. Luckily the wall did. The men rearranged the furniture to cover the holes. It was several weeks before Thelma found the honeycombed section of the wall. Melvin very reluctantly explained their existence. The holes were never completely camouflaged, not even by the buckets of paint that adorned the kitchen walls.

"Thelma was always painting the kitchen. Sometimes it was one color; generally, it wasn't," Jean Quintard said. "Bruce and Melvin went pheasant hunting one morning. Thelma ask Melvin what color he thought she should paint the kitchen; he said something smartalecky like 'make it colorful or polka dotted.' We made it polka dotted with a few swirls thrown in. Sure was fun."

Most of the men who worked on the ranch didn't stay as long as Bruce did. Hired men of all types and ages came and went at the ranch. Roy Sharp[373] was a high school student when he arrived. He was a quiet young man who did what he was told. "There wasn't no "give" in Roy," Melvin said. "We were running a lot of cattle them winters Roy was here, about 3000 steers. We

---

[372] Jean Quintard. Personal interview with Moni Hourt. Many times over the years. In 2016, Joe Hourt told Moni that she should asked Jean Quintard's permission to include the stories about Bruce in the book. Jean said they were definitely part of the story and "sure weren't any secret."
[373] The son of Buck and Charlotte Sharp of Harrison.

never seemed to travel together. I catched and doctored 125 head of calves one day. I don't think Roy was far behind."

Before the younger man had headed out to hay the steers, Melvin warned him not to walk over the wagon tongue. But even then when he first noticed the hay wagon standing beside the gate, he wasn't real worried. Thirty minutes later when the wagon still hadn't moved, he decided he better investigate. When he turned into the meadow, he could see Roy leaning against the tractor. The young man had stepped across the wagon tongue and fallen. The front wheel crunched across the full length his left leg.

Roy rolled away from the tire, pulled himself to his feet, "limped" the tractor down, climbed inside, and put on the brake. "It was a couple of weeks before he could do much, but he didn't quit tryin,'" Melvin said. "He was a good fellow."

Some of the men who came to the ranch were "wantabe" cowboys who knew little about ranching or more importantly riding a horse. Hap spent a month telling everyone on the ranch what a good cowboy he was. When it was time to do some cow work, Melvin gave him "Baldy."

"He saddles old Baldy, leads him out of the corral, and crawled on him. Baldy just stands there," Melvin said. "Hap kicked him. Baldy sure did move out of his tracks then. He jumps straight up and turned a somersault in the air. Hap lit in the saddle on his head. Baldy side stepped. Hap hit the ground with a "thunk." That was the end of his bragging.'"

Roger Davenport[374] grew up on a dairy farm in Wisconsin. Every morning, he was told to take Bugger out and gather the horses. Every morning, the horse bucked him off.

"I told him to take a rope and tie himself on," Melvin said shaking his head with disbelief, "but I didn't think anyone in the world was dumb enough to do that. The next morning when he saw me he pulled up his shirt tail and started cussing me. I about laughed myself sick. I'll bet he carried those rope burns the rest of his life. He stayed around though and did learn to ride the horse."

Roy Drillinger ended up riding Bugger the next spring and the horse went through his humping routine before Roy could even get him out of the corral. Melvin told him to spur the horse through it. The horse bucked him off. Roy climbed back on and tried again. The third time he "drove the iron in." The horse decided he'd had enough and headed out to the pasture.

Mastering a horse was necessary, but carelessness or abuse was never tolerated. One new hand was told to gather a bull out of the pasture. He was told to ride the long way around the pasture instead of taking the creek crossing."

"He spurred that poor bay horse off into the mud," Melvin shook his head in disgust. "The horse went in clear to his head. The little old horse got out some way, but it about drowned him. The cowboy lost his hat and his glasses. It scared him some, but we sent him packing. No sense of putting up with stupid."

---

[374] Roy and his brother, Marvin both worked at the ranch.

Melvin, Robbin, Moni, Thelma and JimBob, 1972.

A year later, a second hand missed the crossing. The horse was quickly mired in the quicksand like gumbo. "We was busier than hell. Had cattle scattered all over the place, but I couldn't leave the horse in that mud. I tied onto the saddle horn and finally got him out. By that time, the poor ole guy was covered in blood."

Apparently, the gelding had been lacerated by sharp branches submerged in the mud. The horse was put out to pasture to heal up. The man "went up the road."

The steadiest "hired men" on the place were Melvin's daughters—Moni and Robbin, and later his son, JimBob. "The kids helped me whenever they could," Melvin said. "I probably depended on them too much, but I wanted them to learn to do things. Mostly they was good hands."

Snooper increased Moni's "good handibility." She was three when the family traveled to Dean Lundy's ranch in Sowbelly Canyon to pick out a Shetland pony. Melvin said he gave Dean a "hundred-dollar bill" for the horse and paid Blacky Lantz $5 for the saddle. Ed Oldaker, Melvin's future son-in-law broke the pony to ride. "Sometimes he was a no good little son-of-a-gun, but Mona rode him a lot of miles. He'd throw a fit. She'd go get a bigger stick. He made her sit up and ride."

When he wasn't in work mode, Snooper was a fairly amiable playmate. Thelma would saddle the horse in the morning. Moni would ride him off and on all day, tying him to the yard fence when she wanted a break. However, he seemed to resent it when another rider climbed into the saddle. One of his favorite anti-rider games was to gallop madly across the bridge and duck under the big house porch. He'd shove forward until the swells of the saddle prevented forward motion. Then he stood, listening to his rider scream.

Robbin, Melvin, and Moni with Snooper at Warbonnet.

"The day he took Ann[375] to the big house, Mona had to climb under the porch and shove him out of there. Ann didn't get on him much after that," Melvin said. "He was just an ornery little shit."

The pony terrorized Robbin, who was nearly four years younger than Moni. He perfected several torture routines. He'd run pell-mell for the chicken house and thrust himself through the half open door. Ignoring Robbin's frantic tug on the reins, he'd dash wildly across the yard, then dropped to his knees and roll. One afternoon he lay down in the creek, dumped Robbin into the water, and took off for the barn. She refused to ride him after that.

"By the time she was four or five, Mona[376] went everywhere with me," Melvin said. "The pony had to trot to keep up with the bigger horses. I know her legs had to get sore,[377] but she never said much. She worked a lot of cattle with him. Finally, some people offered us $500 for the horse. Mona was about seven and ready for a bigger horse anyway so we sold him."

The Nation children learned the finer points of horseback riding from "Bill," the horse Melvin purchased many years before from his brother, Clark.[378]

"The first time I threw Ramona up on Bill she wasn't even a yearling. He bucked her off. I had "ahold" of her leg, so I caught her and put her back on. He bucked her off again. She thought it was fun," Melvin grinned. "Her mother didn't."

---

[375] Bill Coffee's daughter.
[376] Although most of the family called Ramona, Moni, Melvin seldom called her anything but Mona or Ramona.
[377] The gall on Moni's legs became so bad that Thelma lined her daughter's jeans with felt. When they had a long ride to complete, Thelma would have Moni put on a pair of her "nylons," then Moni would stick her nylon encased legs into the padded pants.
[378] Bill as a colt, was trapped in a shed during the '49 Blizzard.

Bill treated his role as a kid-trainer seriously. "Bill knew more than the kids did, and he didn't let them get away with much. One morning I told Mona to keep the cows from taking off down the fence line.[379] She was a kid and wasn't paying attention. A cow finally got loose."

When the cow escaped his young rider's control, Bill shook his head, snorted with irritation, and bolted down the fence. He had little patience for cantankerous cows. When the cow gave up and turned back to the herd, Bill did a fancy, very speedy, pirouette. Luckily the big brown horse's young rider was wearing spurs. When Bill sucked backwards, Moni was launched upward. She was snatching at the ends of her bridle when her spurs snagged the edge of the saddle fender. She clawed her way back down the reins into the saddle.

Although Bill's ears indicate he doesn't particularly like being ridden by a year-old Moni, he stayed quiet. Melvin's posture shows that he wasn't too sure the big brown gelding would do so.

Several years later, JimBob rode the 18-year-old Bill to gather calves. The six year-old headed across an irrigation ditch. "I was quite a-ways away, but I saw that damn old horse shake his head. I knew he was going to jump the ditch. He made a couple of nice jumps and threw JimBob over his head. Jim lit on his feet, and the horse stood there looking at him. He was quite an old horse."

Melvin said the horse never dumped Robbin, but came close a few times. A hired man wasn't so lucky. "I suppose Bill was about 21 when Marvin[380] gave him a try." Melvin said. "I warned him not to let the cows get ahead of him. Then one stuck her head out. Marvin went after it. Bill loped along nice and easy for a few strides, then got tired of fooling around. He jumped into a run, got in front of the old cow, and turned back—hard. Marvin spun out of the saddle and out across Bill's butt. I can still see that old horse running and bucking beside him, snorting and laughing at old Marvin."[381]

---

[379] When you're trailing cattle, one will often break free then take off generally veering into the open. If a rider doesn't cut the animal off and return her or him to the herd, then the rest of the cattle will follow. There is an art to letting an animal move out and checking it from moving out toward "freedom." That skill takes many years and generally many "chewings" to learn. It is seldom ever fully mastered.

[380] Marvin Davenport worked on the ranch for several years as did his brother, Roger.

[381] When cattle are moved, one will often break free, then veer toward an open area. If a rider doesn't cut the animal off, the rest of the herd will follow. The skill to keeping an animal moving but not allowing them to break free is difficult and often leads to many "chewings" before the art is mastered.

Melvin on a colt, Moni on Bill. Robbin with Mike the dog.

"There was a time when you couldn't ride him past a cow, then he got sleeping sickness and slowed down some. In later years, I'd drive out to cake the cows and lead him along with me when I was cutting "heavys."[382] I caked the cows and turned the "heavys" down the lane. He walked along behind them until he saw the ranch, then away he'd go, down through the cows. He did it every time just to annoy me."

---

[382] Cows who were about to calve. When Melvin fed the cows he'd sort out the "heavy" ones.

THE BEAUTY AND THE BEASTS

"There was nothing any prettier than stringing a line of cattle down a road; sun just coming up. A good cattle drive was a beautiful thing—until it wasn't."
Melvin Nation

Melvin Nation, cattle strung out behind him, leads a herd out of Sowbelly Canyon in 2000.

Dealing with the egocentricities of the animals on the ranch was an everyday challenge. That realization was the primary reason that Melvin's children were seldom allowed in a corral full of cattle, particularly mama cows.

"JimBob was about four or five. I didn't realize he followed me to the corral until I looked up and there he was," Melvin shook his head. "The crooked eyed cow was right behind him. About scared me to death. I knew I couldn't get to him before she hit him. Jim had a little plastic baseball bat in his hand. He turned and hit the cow right over the head. The bat popped. The cow bellered and fell back. The kids weren't scared of much. I didn't want them to be scared, but I wanted them to be aware of things around them."

Cattle perpetually treated their two-legged stewards with disdain, full-blown disrespect, or dislike. Melvin and Robbin were doctoring calves early one spring morning. Robbin, aboard her horse, hovered nearby as Melvin vaccinated a calf. The cow, calf-protection in mind, snorted her way toward her downed "baby." Melvin yelled at Robbin to get her horse between him and the cow. Her horse decided it was a very good time to head back to the barn. Melvin finally dragged the calf through the fence to finish doctoring it. The old cow tried to follow him. Eventually, using his old battered Stetson, he drove the cow away, finished vaccinating the calf, then went back to his horse who was standing a few feet away quietly watching the commotion. Nothing more was said.

Both girls were helping him move bulls to the upper pasture early one morning. The drive had been a difficult one. The bulls were much more interested in fighting than they were in moving to summer pasture. The trio was nearly to the gate, when the heel flies hit.[383] The bulls, trying to escape the stinging bites of the flies scattered in a dozen directions. "Mona was a little older. We about rode our horses to death trying to get the bulls through the gate. They were hookin' and snortin' at the horses. It was a tough journey."

Melvin tried to convince Robbin to switch horses with him, but she was adamant. No one, not even her Dad was going to ride her horse, Sorelly, that hard. The crew finally turned the bulls loose and went back to the ranch. It was one of the few times the job didn't get finished.

Often Mother Nature intensified the livestock challenges. All three of his children were with Melvin the spring morning that he decided to take a herd of yearlings to the Hunter Hills. "We shoulda never left the barn. By the time we were three miles from the place it was raining like hell. I wanted JimBob to stay at Bud Serres' but he wouldn't stay alone, so I left the girls too. Robbin left the house, climbed on her horse, and followed me. She went with me all the way to the top. We were about drowned by the time we got back to the ranch."

Although, Bill and Virginia and their four daughters, Twink, (Claire) Sara, Ann, and Sue, lived at the ranch a couple of summers over the years, the girls were seldom involved in ranch life. When Ann, Bill's third daughter was an eighth grader she started helping with the cattle drives. She was mounted when the crew headed to the Sheets place, a large summer pasture located about 35 miles south of the ranch. Ann and the two Nation girls were holding the cattle in a corner so they could be sorted into smaller pastures. The girls were laughing and joking, enjoying a beautiful spring day, when Ann's saddle slipped sideways. Out of the corner of his eye, Long Pine, the big sorrel gelding she was riding, spied the saddle and its struggling rider. He snorted, whirled, and started spinning. Ann flew from her saddle; her foot wedged in the stirrup.

---

[383] Heel flies are large, robust flies that resemble a bee and deliver the same type of painful bite. Biting and buzzing, they will attack livestock and often drive them into a run. They generally don't swarm until the "heat of the day." For that reason, most of the cattle at the Coffee ranches were worked before "it got too hot."

"The old horse was bucking and kicking, but he had her on the outside circle," Melvin said as he pushed his hat to the back of his head and rubbed his white un-sunburned brow. "I was pushing cattle over the hill when I heard the girls hollering. I headed down the hill, but I knew I couldn't get to her fast enough to stop a damn bad wreck. Then her boot came off. She flung out of the way. Landed on her butt, didn't hurt her any. I can still see that girl hangin' out at the end of that stirrup. It still gives me shivers." He righted his hat. "We were lucky. The horse never left his circle and started running. We gathered up her horse and went back to work."

A year later, on a chilly spring morning the crew[384] left Hat Creek about 4 a.m., again headed to the Sheets place. The day threatened rain. The cattle trailed quietly up West Hat Creek Road. [385]Moni and Ann were leading their horses and walking behind the drag theoretically to get warm, but primarily to gossip. Ann didn't notice she dropped a rein until Long Pine stepped on it. When the bit pinched his mouth, he reared. When he came back down, the shank of his bridle hit Ann in the forehead creating a deep gash. Bill and Ann rode to a nearby ranch house where Bill borrowed a car and took his daughter to the Alliance hospital. Ann's uncle, Dr. Jim Kennedy stitched her head wound and sent her home.[386]

"It started to rain about the time Bill left," Melvin said. "We didn't have rain coats or any of the stuff we have now to keep us dry. By the time we got to the pasture we was drowned, but those little ole' girls never whimpered. Bill was supposed to pick us up, but he didn't show up 'till we were about three miles from town. I made the girls get in with him, and I took the horses on to town. They sure weren't wantin' to leave me."

"I can remember looking back at Dad. He was loping along behind us, leading our horses. He had his hat tipped into the wind," Moni Nation Hourt said. "His neckerchief was so wet it was flopping against his neck. I wanted to bawl. I knew if his neckerchief was wet, he was cold. That trip to town in the pickup was a lot worse than the trip would've been in the rain."

The most infamous cattle drive involving the unpaid hired help, occurred when Ann and Moni were sophomores. They were given the task of moving 150 head of cows from the Pullen Place, a mile north of Harrison to Warbonnet. Melvin helped them round up the Pullen pasture and made sure they were headed down the Monroe Canyon Road. The girls were told that one was to stay at the front, one at the back—-no variation. For nearly six miles the girls followed the directives, but the cattle were moving easily down the foggy road.

There was a dance the night before. Later the girls swore they only spent a few minutes at the tail end discussing the event. Unfortunately, that was enough time for the cattle to stray off the road at the top of Monroe Canyon. They pushed through a fence and disappeared up a steep hill into the fog. Just five cattle were left on the roadway. On a trot, the girls drove their

---

[384] The crew consisted of Melvin, Bill, Robbin, Moni, and Ann.
[385] The Hat Creek ranch border
[386] Virginia Coffee, suffering from pneumonia, was already a patient at the hospital. One of Virginia's brothers was a physician at the Alliance hospital; one was an Alliance dentist.

shrunken herd on down the hill. They met Melvin about four miles from the ranch. He had come to help them finish the job. He wasn't impressed that they did "such a good job" driving the five head home.

Ann went back to the ranch to meet Bill. Moni wasn't so fortunate. Melvin loaded her horse in the trailer and turned back up the hill. They cut the fence, crawled their horses up the fog-ice covered hill, and gathered the cattle. Melvin left the pickup and trailer at the top of the hill to be retrieved later. He took the lead toward Warbonnet. Moni followed with the drag. They didn't gossip—not even one bit. Ann and Moni hoped the memory of the incident would fade away, but Melvin and Bill never let them forget "the time those girls lost the herd of cattle." For years and years and YEARS, the men used what the girls considered "an increasingly exaggerated story" to whip any audience willing to listen, and most were, into a giggling frenzy.

Robbin, luckily never completely lost her bunch of cattle. She just misplaced them slightly the day Melvin sent her down a rough trail with a small herd. He told her the cattle would follow the road towards Hat Creek, but he did warn her to keep the animals "out of the heavy brush." Then he went back to gather up another bunch.

"Of course they headed straight for the brush. I couldn't get them out," Robbin Nation Oldaker said. "I rode back up to the Pullen[387] place, loaded my horse, and drove home. Mom loaded me back up and took me down Sow Belly where we ran into the herd of cattle."

As Melvin predicted, the cattle had continued on down the road, but when the crew returned to help drive the cattle on to Hat Creek their "drover" was missing. They were all relieved when Thelma showed up. Robbin said she unloaded her horse and finished the drive. Melvin as became his habit over the years, held his tongue. (Except of course when he was extolling a story about a lost herd of cattle.)

A majority of the cattle drives were quiet and uneventful. If they started at Hat Creek, Melvin would back the truck up to the loading chute at Warbonnet and jump the horses into its bed. He and the girls, or just Moni, when Robbin was too young, would climb into the cab of the truck and sputter east across the Prairie Dog road. The heater wheezed and complained before it finally dumped hot air into the cab which generally meant the crew peeled off a couple of layers of clothing before they completed the 10-mile journey to Hat Creek. (At their destination they hustled to redress before they hit the chilly air.)

As they lurched along the county road, Melvin sang songs like the "Streets of Loredo, "Blue Tailed Fly," "Mockingbird Hill" and "T is for Texas."[388] The girls thought he had a marvelous

---

[387] One of the Coffee pastures was located approximately five miles north of Harrison at the top of Sow Belly Road.
[388] Melvin had his own set of lyrics for most of the songs. "T for Texas" was no exception. He always sang, "T is for Texas, T is for Tennessee. T is for Thelma, the girl that ruined me." The girls thought it was great that the song contained their mother's name, and never did quite understand why Thelma generally gave Melvin a smiling glare when he sang the song's lyrics. It wasn't until Moni was grown that she discovered that "T for Thelma" was not part of the song. She was very disappointed.

voice. No matter how many consecutive days they had ridden in the cab of the truck or how early they'd climbed out of bed, they soon started laughing and singing along with the lyrics that Melvin changed as it suited him.

If the dawn threw just enough light across the prairie, the girls could make out the shadow of an abandoned airport hangar, sitting alongside a flat piece of prairie that once served as a landing strip. In a 1993 interview, Bill Coffee said purchasing the plane that once lived in the hangar, was "sorta an accident."

"We went to the Buckaroo one night, and a couple days later there was a plane tied to the fence at Warbonnet," Bill said with a smile. "I'd been drinking a little bug juice up there, and I guess I bought a plane."

Although Coffee didn't know how to operate his winged-purchase he asked his cousin, Rex Coffee, to teach him the basics. A month later he flew into the Chadron Airport and asked the instructors there if they could certify him. After a quick flight, they did. Bill often flew the plane to Omaha or other distant destinations. Checking water by plane also significantly reduced the time it took to get around the mills located across the Coffee holdings.[389]

The June 17, 1948 *Harrison Sun* reported that "Bill Coffee was flying his plane when it crashed near Ainsworth." Although Bill broke his ankle in the crash, he walked to a ranch house for help. Virginia and Connie Jordan were not injured in the accident. Evelyn Jordan, the planes other passenger was slightly injured. The plane was never replaced.[390]

One of the most interesting sidebars of the "Bill's plane" story, at least in the girls' minds, was that Melvin said he was only a few hours away from earning his pilot's license in 1948.[391] The plane stories, and hundreds of others kept the girls awake on the 10-mile trek across Prairie Dog, but once they reached their destination, there wasn't much time for story-telling. Melvin backed up to a slant-floored chute[392] or to a high bank and jumped the horses out of the truck. The crew always headed for the pasture before dawn's full light, so the animals were unloaded in the feeble rays emitted from the truck's tail lights. If the crew drove cattle from Hat Creek they unloaded at the loading chute, then rode south down the long lane from the barn to the Get-Away Pasture where the cattle, gathered the day before, waited. In the semi-darkness of the pre-dawn, stumps and cattle looked deceptively alike.

---

[389] During the summer months when cattle were out on summer pasture in distant pastures like the White River or Sheets Place pastures, "running water" was nearly a day-long job. Vern Hansen, Peg Coffee's second husband checked the water for many years.
[390] Bill said he'd been flying through "pea soup," a limited ground ceiled created by thick clouds and fog, when the accident occurred. The official report said, "the accident was caused by inexperience in flying under instrument conditions."
[391] Melvin took flying lesson from Frank Snook at the Chadron airport. When he contracted "lung fever," probably pneumonia, in 1950, he did not have the money to pursue the lessons.
[392] There was a chute at Hat Creek and the Pullen Place. Generally, however, the truck was backed up to a small truck-floor-height hill, either natural or man-made, and unload the horses.

"The girls always griped because it was too dark, and they couldn't see the cattle," Melvin said, his grin spreading across his face. "But I told them if it didn't move it's a tree. Gather everything that moves."

The yips and hollers of the crew and the waking "bellers" of the cattle soon filled the small pasture. Within minutes a line of sleepy cattle and men trailed across the enclosure heading for the gate located in the southwest corner. They streamed out onto the road and headed west toward the Bodarc Church. Dawn generally danced across the horizon by the time the cattle turned south from the church. Within 30 minutes the birds woke, their irritated chirps drifting in from the trees along the distant creek. Riders moved steadily beside the cattle, shaping them into a long column that often stretched two or three miles up the gravel roadbed. Cows moved back and forth up the column looking for their calves; steers stuck their noses in the air and headed south until something convinced them to go another direction. Only the quiet clump of the cattle's feet and the wakening wildlife punctuated the quiet. Early mornings required layers of clothing that turned their wearers into puffy lumps on slow moving steeds. By noon clothing had often been shed, one layer at a time, and was tied tightly behind saddles.

The drives that ended near Harrison generally included breakfast at the Gateway Café.[393] Moni said being squashed in the red upholstered booth, the morning light filtering through the glass block windows warming her shoulders, always filled her with pride.

"I was the only girl on the crew in the early days," Moni said. "Dad and Bill would tease me and bring up any error I'd made that day. I knew Dad was proud that I could hang with them. That's all that mattered."

On the longer drives to the White River Country, southeast of Harrison, Virginia Coffee met the crew at the top of Sow Belly or East Hat Creek. She opened her trunk and pulled out hot coffee and cocoa, chocolate cake, and sandwiches layered with piles of meat and cheese. The crew would consume as much as possible, waddle back to their horses and finish the drive. The crew always agreed that no one could put together a lunch like Virginia could.

On every drive, as soon as he pushed the first cattle out the gate, Melvin slipped past the herd and began the process of stringing them up the road or across the prairie. He rode back and forth beside the animals until they created an undulating rope slowing blending into the horizon. Several times during the drive he rode down the side of the herd, picked up a few more cattle, and moved them forward which increased the length of the line. On irregular interviews, he arrived at the "drag" and joked with those tasked with keeping the herd moving forward. His journey, often at a trot covered several more miles than that of the rest of the crew. When the job was finished, the crew rode back to the trailer laughing and visiting about the drive. The only time the laughter ceased was when something went wrong. Then bad moods were prevalent.

---

[393] The Gateway Café and Restaurant in Harrison was owned by Laurence and Rosetta Lewis.

Cattle string across the pasture-land south of Highway 20 on the way to the White River Pasture.

"Most of our wrecks were caused by someone being in the wrong place or doing something stupid," Melvin said crossing his arms. "I hated stupid mistakes. I did way too much yelling when they happened."

"We had a bad week one spring," Moni Hourt said. "We lost yearlings in Sowbelly. Dad and Bill were on us all week. They'd be a half mile across the pasture from us and start gesturing. We were supposed to understand what their hands said. If we didn't, we were in trouble. I was 16 and full of righteous indignation. So I quit."

Moni said that early morning, Melvin told her to go to the barn, saddle her horse, then head to the pasture to gather cattle. When Melvin and Bill arrived at the barn, her horse was still in the stall.

"Dad asked me what the hell I was doing. I screwed up all the courage I had and told him that I quit. They both looked at me like I'd grown two heads. Then Bill told me I couldn't quit because I'd never been hired. Dad added that it was a good thing I'd never been hired because then I couldn't be fired. Then he told me since I'd never been hired and couldn't be fired, to get my butt in the saddle and head to the pasture. I was mad as blazes, but I saddled my horse. Many years later I read this story in my journal. I realized that episode mirrors life. You weren't hired into life, and you can't be fired. When things get tough, you might as well get back in the saddle and go back to work. I told that story at a banquet one time. Bill and Dad were both there. They gave me a "bad time" about quitting the best job I ever had."

SOMETHING NEW EVERY DAY

"On a ranch, there's generally something new going on every day. People talk about being bored. I don't think I was ever bored. We made our own kind of entertainment." Melvin Nation

Although Ann only helped with the cattle drives, Moni and Robbin were considered year-round help. After the cattle were moved, they were shifted to the hay field. Robbin was an exceptional hand with a sweep. She could sweep a buck of hay onto the teeth of the slide stacker without losing a fork full of hay. Moni couldn't seem to get the knack of picking up a buck of hay on the sweep teeth and pushing it into the stacker. She was much better with the rake, although, her windrows were never as straight as Melvin demanded.

Robbin on the hay sweep helps Everett Thomas fill his hay mow with hay. Also picture Ed Oldaker, Vern Holtz, and in the hay mow window, Everett Thomas. Joe Hourt had the unenviable job of "mowing back"

"Robbin was a good hand in the hay field," Melvin said. "She could sweep as much hay as a man. The other one didn't get along very well. She'd rather be on a horse."

Although the girls helped in the hay field, neither were expected to pick up any of the 10,000 small square hay bales that scattered across the fields one year. "Don't know what that damn Bill was thinking, but he suddenly thought we needed small bales," Melvin said shaking his head. "We had bales everywhere. He finally hired Indians from Pine Ridge to help get them picked up. We did that two years. That was two years too much."

Bob, Melvin, JimBob, Gary, Robbin, Moni the summer Gary and Bob came to Nebraska.

Gary and Bob Pliley, Melvin's sons happened to choose one of those summers to visit. They were quickly sent to the hay field. "We spent days pickin' up those bales, taking them across the pasture on a flat-bed trailer, then piling them up in big stacks," Gary Pliley,[394] Melvin's oldest son said. "Then a pickup backfired and started the stack on fire. The whole stack burned down. The next day, we just went to another field and picked up more bales."

"By the time we went home, I decided I never wanted to look at another bale of hay," Bob Pliley said. "I don't think I ever have. The only good thing about being in the bale field was the meal Thelma brought out to us. She brought everything out in crocks and iron skillets. I ate so

---

[394] Gary and Bob Pliley spent part of the summer of 1963 at the ranch.

much I couldn't move, but we didn't have any choice. Melvin gave us about an hour to rest then we were back at those damn bales. I had blisters on my blisters."

The Lakotas who worked at the ranch those summers didn't do much complaining. They camped in the north meadow and several times, invited Moni and Robbin to have supper with them. The girls had eaten few camp-fire cooked meals. The trips to the meadow were great adventures.

Ranchers seldom embraced adventure. They preferred ranch life to run smoothly in a cyclical sequence revolving around the needs of the cattle. In the fall, cattle were driven to winter pasture or sold at market. During the winter months, providing hay and water for the cattle was top priority. Many cold blustery winter days were spent in the shop repairing the haying and ranch equipment. In the spring, cows were calved out, fences were fixed, and the cattle were moved into summer pastures. By early summer, the grass and alfalfa was ready to be transformed into winter feed. In the fall, the cycle began again.

Controlling water sources and maintaining fence lines were year round endeavors. Both tasks could generate tensions between neighbors.

As one of the regions earliest settlers, CF Coffee had obtained the water rights to watersheds in the Hat Creek Valley. In a 1966 lawsuit, several ranchers downstream from the Coffee ranches claimed that Bill was restricting downstream water flow to their lands. The lawsuit ignored the original landowner's historical "riparian rights," and Bill was required to allow free-flowing downstream access. During dinner and pickup-tailgate discussions it was obvious that neither Bill nor Melvin ever agreed with the ruling.

Fence line squabbles never led to court battles, but did result in very loud discussions and fractured friendships. The Coffee crew diligently kept their fences in good repair. It wasn't an easy job. In the days before hydraulic post hole diggers, the men dug all the holes by hand, then tamped the posts in place. Corner posts and braces were built and gates repaired and tightened on a continual basis. The major fencing period generally stretched across two-weeks. Neighboring landowners shared the responsibility of maintaining fence lines—but some failed to keep their portion in good repair. Those who didn't were treated with disrespectful disdain.

Fencing was never his favorite job on the ranch, but Melvin said it was one that just needed done, so he did it. He added that every job had its benefits, (except maybe milking) if you just looked for them. Only someone with a slightly warped sense of humor would have considered the "White River Pasture Fencing Incident" anything but bizarre.

Early one spring morning Melvin said he was checking fence lines along a particularly hilly section of the four-section pasture. Suddenly he noticed a shimmering ball rolling jerkily down a long butte-covered hillside. Every few seconds a section of the ball peeled free and curled twisting through the air. Melvin drove little closer. Then he realized the ball, wriggling and pulsating through the new grass consisted of hundreds of rattlesnakes. Shortly after it reached the "flats" the ball melted into the grasslands.

"The snakes weren't moving very fast, and by the time I got there most of them had slithered into the grass," Melvin's grin widened. "I heard that snakes would "ball up[395]" to keep warm in the winter, but I never seen it before, and I never saw it since. Yeah, I'd call it a little strange."

The girls seldom helped with the fencing, but the year Thelma was hospitalized for an emergency hernia operation, Melvin took them with him to fence the lower Hunter Hills. That morning he braided the girls' hair in five strand plaits in the style he used to make braided bridle reins. He packed a lunch—peanut butter and chokecherry jam sandwiches—then headed toward the hills. While he fixed fence the girls explored the old Hunter homestead. He took a couple of quick breaks to show them how to pick pine gum from the pine trees and make chains from dandelion stems. They took a short hike to the top of a small hill and ate their lunch. When the girls tired, they lay beneath the pine trees and listened to the wind singing through the needles.

They knew better than stray far from their father's line of sight. A few years earlier, one of the hired men who was fencing in the Hunter Hills, had meandered away from the fence line. He lost his bearings in the rough terrain and wandered around in the canyons for most of one day before Melvin finally located him. The girls weren't about to repeat what their Dad had deemed the "damn dummy's" stupidity.

"The next day Jean took us home with her," Moni Hourt said. "We had a great time with Dad, but I don't think Dad actually did much fencing. We thought we were pretty special though. We wouldn't let Mom unbraid our hair for a week."

Several times a week, the girls climbed into the pickup to "help" Melvin irrigate in the North Meadow. He took his shovel and walked down the earthen ditch, closing pieces of the ditch wall to stop the water from flowing onto sections of the alfalfa field, or opening a new hole to water a different segment of the field. The girls stayed behind on the ditch wall to make clay dishes.

"We took several pieces to the house and Mom put them in the oven, but they generally broke," Moni Hourt said. "Sometimes we ran down the ditch looking for badger holes, but most of the time we didn't even pretend that we were helping."

Building the two-horse trailer wasn't considered work either. Nearly every night, the winter of 1962, Melvin would crank up the wood stove in the shop. It would be glowing red by the time Bruce Quintard or sometimes Bob Jordan arrived to help with the project. The girls' job was to fetch tools and hold pieces in place. When the bright red trailer was finally completed, everyone swelled with pride.

---

[395] *Current Opinion*, vol 23, page 17, 1898. According to the author of an article on strange animal behaviors, southern snakes seldom rolled themselves into balls like those in the north. The article said, sometimes the snakes were mating within the ball, but generally they formed the interlaced sphere in an attempt to stay warm during the winter

Robbin sitting on the frame of Melvin's homemade horse trailer.

Although building the horse trailer wasn't technically ranch work, it did occur on the ranch, which meant Melvin was close by if something needed done. Leaving the ranch on a "real vacation" was a rare event. Once in a while, though, he and Thelma loaded their kids into the back seat of a car, padded with blankets and pillows, and left the ranch.

"We went to Yellowstone a couple of time. We even rented a boat and went fishing. When we went to Estes Park, we stayed with Buzzy Hoover's folks and went fishing on the Big Thompson River. We visited my brother Clark in Miles City and even went to Missouri to see my sister," Melvin said. "We didn't leave the ranch real often, but we had a good time when we did."

One year, the cattle were in the summer pastures. Haying equipment was ready, but the hay wasn't quite ready to cut. Melvin and Thelma were in Crawford, when they suddenly decided to go camping. They stopped at Earl and Iva Nation's home and borrowed a stack of blankets. Then they headed to the Black Hills.[396]

"We spread our blankets out on a hillside and hunkered down under the stars," Melvin said. "Robbin kept rolling down the hill. Every so often we'd have to go down and get her."

The next morning Moni crawled out from under the blankets and followed her Dad up the hill to a small fishing point. He was seated against a pine tree, his hat tipped against his brow,

---

[396] The Black Hills of South Dakota was a popular vacation spot even in the early 60s. The family generally made a quick swoop past Mount Rushmore, completed in 1941, when they drove through the "Hills," but they seldom spent much time at the Monument.

the early morning sun tracing the contours of his face. As he had on many days of his life, he was watching the sunrise. He told his young daughter that he never understood people who didn't believe in God. He said all a person had to do was look around them, God was everywhere, but he was especially near at sunrise. Moni said they never did fish that morning. They watched the sun tiptoe over the water as the fish leapt and dived among the ripples. A doe and fawn watered at the edge of the lake and a bald eagle soared overhead. Later they hiked around the lake, and she and Robbin chased the chipmunks. In a story she wrote for her high school English class in 1965[397], Moni called it the "best day ever."

The following year a trip to the Black Hills included an early morning visit to Mount Rushmore. "They knew what they were doing when they carved those faces on that mountain," Melvin said when he discussed the trip many years later. The early morning sun kinda crawled across the faces of the presidents lighting them up like a giant spot light. It was pretty impressive. There really wasn't much there at that time, not much of a museum or anything like that, but you sure had to appreciate the work that went into it. Years later we went back up there. The place was swarming with tourists. I enjoyed it more when it wasn't so popular."

"We drove along the Needles Highway," Moni wrote in her 1965 essay. "They call it that because the rocks are so sharp. Twice we saw President Washington peeking out between the tall rocks."

That afternoon the family stopped at the Hot Springs Plunge.[398] "Mom and Dad rented swim suits," the essay that eventually earned its writer an "A" continued. "I didn't even know they could swim! It was scary to go down that long slide, but Dad was at the bottom. He yelled at me to let go, he would catch me. He did. I went up and down 10 times."

The essay revealed that the family "didn't get home until really late, almost10 that night, but it was ok, Jim (the hired man) did the chores."

Wednesday nights the family generally drove to the Harrison Fair arena, the unofficial home of the "Sioux County Roping Club." Melvin dogged steers and the girls joined their friends on rides around the arena.[399] One evening shortly after the left the house, they heard a thump. The horse trailer popped free of the car hitch and bumped down the hill toward the creek. Melvin jumped out of the car and sprinted to the trailer loaded with his dogging horse and Moni's barrel horse. He put his shoulder into the trailer and brought it to a stop.

---

[397] The essay entitled, "Our Family Vacations" was recorded in a plaid-covered notebook, one of many Jean Quintard bought for Moni over the years.
[398] Evans Plunge in Hot Springs South Dakota was established in 1890 and features naturally heated 87-degree water. It is only about 60 miles from the Warbonnet ranch, if you take all the back roads.
[399] Those at the weekly "Roping Club" nights often became generational friends. Moni spent hours riding around the Fair Grounds with Jim Fox. Her children were friends with Jim's children, while his grandchildren became friends with Moni's grandchildren. Robbin's family's developed generational connections with the Keith Zimmerman family.

"I decided my Dad was the bravest, strongest man in the world," Moni said. "I knew that trailer was going to tip over and kill the horses, but he stopped it. We hitched it back up and went to Harrison. Years later when I mentioned it he said he just pulled the brake lever. I never believed it was that simple."

Over the years many people commented on Melvin's strength, but an entry in Moni's 1965 journal that discussed a father/daughter volleyball game in which Melvin played alongside his daughter, further expanded the concept. "Dad really is pretty much the strongest guy in the country," She wrote. "He had to take off his boots and slipped and slid some, but he still hit that ball so hard it hit the other wall with a splat. Just split it plumb open. We had to get another ball. Good thing Jess[400] ducked."

Strength wasn't needed for the family's weekly Saturday night grocery and movie trip to Harrison. But the event did give everyone a chance to show off the outfits that Thelma whipped up on her sewing machine. While Melvin was milking she braided the girls' long hair, and unwound the sticker-encrusted curlers that tamed and shaped her curly brown hair, then they'd slip into homemade ensembles that rivaled any of those found in the Sears catalog. Thelma couldn't take credit for the new Levis that Melvin saved for town visits, but she created the sharp crease that stretched the full length of each leg. She also sewed his bleached-white shirt, one of dozens that she constructed over the years. Once his good hat was in place, often a Silverbelly Stetson, he tucked his tally book in one front pocket of his shirt and a can of Skoal snus in the other. He filled the car from the gas tank, watching as the gas gurgled through the glass cylinder of the tank that stood between the granary and the shop then whirled back to the house to pick up his family. He knew better than to honk, but his family was generally waiting when he pulled up to the door.

The can of snus that always inhabited his right front pocket had a tendency to work its way through the pocket's bottom stitching. Thelma found a solution: she created inside shirt pockets. The pockets were topped with a placket-type opening that resembled that of a buttonhole. The pockets could be made as large as necessary to accommodate any Snus can.

"I put on this one new shirt and stuck the Snus can in my pocket," Melvin said. "It went clear to my belly button. The damn pocket was as long as my shirt. That Thelma thought she was pretty funny."

"I'd get so damn mad when he wore a new shirt to the Roping Club and dog steers," Thelma said. "Half the time, a horn would snag the front of the shirt and tear it. I'd throw a patch on it and make him wear it for work, but I generally made a new one for town." She grinned. "Didn't want him looking like a slob."

---

[400] Although the diary entry does not identify the player, it was probably Jess Locker, whose daughter, Jolene was in Moni's freshman class.

During the 50s and early 60s, Harrison merchants remained open on Saturday nights, generally until the last customer walked out the door. Rudy Hartman manned the counter at his butcher shop so that ranch wives could pick up their butchered beef or buy extra meat for special events like brandings. When Tress Powell wasn't waiting on customers at Powell's Hardware, he was perched on a stool near the back of the store. Every kid knew the bowl beside him was filled with hard, cellophane-wrapped candies. Levis, pearl-snap western shirts, Stetson hats, and women's blouses were carefully arranged in Whiteaker's front window. Every Stetson hat, and most of the Levis Melvin owned were purchased at Whiteaker's.

By 7 p.m. the area's "young people" had congregated at the Summit Theater where a quarter would buy a movie, a bag of popcorn, and Coca-Cola served in large paper cups. The Koch Furniture and Variety Store[401] next door offered almost as much entertainment as the theater. Although Melvin seldom entered the labyrinth of aisles that contained every type of merchandise imaginable, Thelma and the girls regularly maneuvered the product-packed aisles or simply visited with the Kochs. Nearly every Saturday night visit to town included a visit to the Corner Market to buy groceries. Leslie DeKay carefully recorded charged purchases in a wooden file box that he kept on a shelf behind the counter. Once a month, after pay checks were distributed, accounts were to be settled.[402] Moni and Robbin generally spent their time in the store examining the bins of candy arranged next to the front door. Thelma always let them pick out one piece; Beulah DeKay added another piece to the grocery sack "for later."

Like most of the men in town, Melvin preferred to wait at the Town Top Bar[403] while his wife shopped or the girls attended the show. Most of the ranch women, including Thelma, sat in their cars parked alongside Main Street and visited. The country kids played on the sidewalks or in the neighboring vacant lots. The older kids met with their town friends. Flirting seemed to be the primary occupation, but once in a while a fight would ensue. The fights were quickly curbed by irate mothers. Some of the men stayed in town until the bar closed. Their families would eventually climb into their cars and go to sleep. Melvin knew better. Thelma's "curb sitting patience" only lasted so long.

---

[401] The north side of Koch's, as the store was called, featured furniture; the south side contained a variety of products. It was owned and operated by Minnie and Martin Koch until 1970.
[402] It was rumored that some did not keep their "bills paid up," but Thelma never let her monthly account go unpaid.
[403] Johnny Broderick owned and operated the bar, which he called "Johnny's Bar" from 1947 until 1956. It was then sold to Charles Kuhnel. Clara and Bill Grim bought the bar in 1959 and operated it under the name "Town Top." Connie Jordan renamed it the "Long Horn Bar when he purchased it in 1968. The business was moved from the east side of Main Street to the West side and back again several times over the years, but neither the name, the location, nor the ownership really mattered. It became and remains to be a meeting place for country people and townspeople alike.

Robbin and Moni in front of Johnny's Bar in Harrison. The camera in the picture is the one that Thelma's used to take many of the pictures in the family collection, but the mystery is who took the picture. Chances are Verna Callaham took many of the others.

Sundays were often spent at Bob Jordan's ranch on the South Dakota border south of Warbonnet. Bob built an arena featuring electric lights and a chute. He and Melvin practiced dogging steers and their kids raced their horses around the barrels or rode across the ranch.

Jackpot rodeos across the region gave local cowboys another chance to exhibit their skill in the rodeo arena. Bob and Melvin often hazed for each other in the dogging event and helped each other's children compete in the junior events. One year at the Saddle Rock Riding Club Rodeo held at the Crawford City Park, Bob missed his steer and Danny Jordan tipped a barrel. But Melvin won the dogging buckle; Moni won a similarly styled buckle in the barrel race. The pair cherished their "matching" buckles throughout their lives. [404]

Although Melvin said he wasn't sure "Thelm" enjoyed following him around, she didn't "complain any." "Sis was generally there and they never gave up a chance to gossip," He grinned. "Those days was a way to blow off a little steam and keep our horses tuned up. Bob and I shared a dogging horse, Hat Creek Bob. Sometimes I won on him; sometimes Bob did, and sometimes neither one of us did. I don't know that we really worried about it much."

---

[404] Winners listed in the *Crawford Tribune*, October 8, 1964.

"Bob was one of the best friends I ever had. We spent a lot of time over there—and—," Melvin smiled sardonically, "he visited us quite frequently."

Bob never needed much sleep and often showed up at a Melvin's house long after he went to bed.[405]

"We'd hear Bob open the front door and clump through the living room," Thelma[406] said. "By the time he got to the bedroom, I'd already gotten out of bed and gone into the living room. I'd hear him say, 'Move over Melvin.' Then I'd hear the clunk of his boots as they hit the floor. The springs of the bed would squeak as he settled in on my side of the bed. He and Melvin might sit there in the dark and visit until daybreak."

---

[405] Bob's penchant for late night visits encompassed his entire acquaintance group and lasted throughout his lifetime.
[406] Thelma Nation. Personal Interview by Moni Hourt, 1996.

THE DAWNING OF A NEW ERA

"The only sure thing in life is that things are probably going to change. Change isn't real easy for most of us, but we can't stop it, so we might as well put up with it." Melvin Nation

In the early 60s, space flights splashed across the Nation's newly purchased television screen. On May 5, 1961, when Astronaut Alan Shepherd became America's first person in space, making a flight that lasted 14.8 minutes, Melvin made sure his morning coffee stop, coincided with the well-publicized event. In a scrapbook that Moni kept about the space flights, she made a notation about her Dad's interest in the flight.

"Dad says a man will be on the moon in 10 years, and someone will be living on the moon by 2000," She wrote. "He said he wasn't going to leave Nebraska."

The space race with Russia and the Cold War created a big push for improving education. The government funded large numbers of projects to gather information for a wide variety of educational programs.

Gerald, Jerry, Parker, a geologist from Denver, supervised a program to determine the rate of erosion at the Badlands east of Warbonnet.[407] He and his wife moved into a small trailer house in the "Big House" yard in the summer of 1962. He spent his days at the Badlands and didn't seem to mind taking his children and the Nation children with him on his fact gathering excursions. While he set gauges and stakes, the children would climb the gumbo hills poking out of the badland floor, then slide down them in a cloud of dust and cracked earth. Rainy days were the best. The badland hills turned into piles of goo that provided hours of slick fun. On a regular basis the children returned to the small headquarters hut with petrified turtles, ammonites, shells,[408] and trilobites. Parker accompanied them on their fossil hunts returning with a

---

[407] "Erosion Studied in Sioux County Project." *Chadron Record*. November 13, 1961. The article says that the "Warbonnet Project" supervised by Parker, was chiefly concerned with "dryland hydrology and the water cycle in the arid and semi-arid portions of the western United States." It goes on to say the badland region on the Coffee ranch land was ideal for the study due to the fact that "it has the right type of soils and grasses required for the studies.
[408] Brachiopods or lamp shells.

wagon loaded with giant fossilized turtles. When Parker left that fall, he taught Melvin how to read the gauges and record the data at the project site.[409]

"I always told the kids they should learn something every day." Melvin said. "I thought the government survey was a little silly. The hills had eroded for hundreds of years, but it was interesting to read all the gauges and notice how they changed according to the weather.[410] I taught Mona how to read them. She drove over there and did it when I couldn't."

The Parkers spent part of the next summer at the ranch, but funding for the project was eliminated that fall. When the project was abandoned, so was the equipment. The monitoring house and platform were easily dismantled but small, cylindrical, metal stakes driven into the ground throughout the badland area were left behind. For years, horsemen carefully avoided them when they gathered cattle running in the Badlands pasture.

Melvin may have believed in learning something new every day, but that did not apply to the "new math. An adept mathematician, he performed mental math calculations quicker and more accurately than the new calculators that finally arrived at Sioux Sundries.[411] When the girls returned from school with homework in the fall of 1963, he was furious. That year, the school district adopted the "new upgraded science/math" curriculum. The books included concepts like Venn diagrams, algebra, and binary addition and subtraction.

"The night I showed him the binary equations and explained that one and one was not two, he quit helping me with homework," Moni Hourt said. "I never did conquer the new math. Dad didn't even try."

Earl Nation died on July 9, 1964 of complications from a ruptured appendix. Iva stayed in her home in Crawford for a short time, then moved to Chadron near her daughter, Eva. A full-time nurse was hired to supervise daily routines. On April 14, 1966, his 36th birthday, Melvin wrote in his tally book, "Mama died today. I was holding her hand. Death is part of life, but that doesn't make it easy to deal with."

In 2006, a television reporter asked Melvin if he had any regrets in life. He said he had just one: he wished that he had spent more time with his family. He told the reporter, "Thelma raised a great set of kids—the only thing I did done was put food on the table."

His children never felt neglected. Like most ranch kids of that era, they realized the ranch was priority. On the other hand, they firmly believed they spent a great deal of time with their father—-just not always in a conventional way.

---

[409] Information from Nation's geological notebook was shared with Parker on his regular visits. The notebook carefully lists the precipitation, air and soil temperature, and wind speed and direction that was recorded on seismograph machines enclosed within a small building at the observation site.
[410] Melvin's research data booklet included meticulous records recorded during the two years he tallied information from the research station.
[411] Moni Hourt said the first calculators sold at Sioux Sundries in Harrison in 1966 cost $10-12 dollars and were far from accurate. She said every problem was done at least twice to double-check an answer.

The family excursion to the Davis Canyon pasture south of Scotty Springs, was deemed as a "fence checking" episode. The family piled into the pickup and meandered over the "cow trail" road south of Whitman Road checking fences along the way. Deep into the canyon, next to the escarpment that created Monroe Canyon, the arrived at an abandoned homestead surrounded by tall stately aspen trees. While Melvin checked the surrounding fences, Thelma and the girls explored the cabin, which was still in relatively good condition. A large upstairs room accessed by a tall staircase that flanked the outside of the building, contained several books that were left behind by the previous occupants. They gathered up several including *A Girl of the Limberlost*[412] and an old cookbook.

The year Halloween fell on a Saturday night, Melvin came in early and told Thelma they should take the kids "Trick or Treating." Thelma cut holes in an old pillow case and turned Robbin into a miniature ghost. Moni dressed as a bandit, complete with Melvin's old black hat and a red handkerchief mask. The Nations climbed into the pickup and headed across country stopping at several area ranches. *Trick or Treaters* seldom trekked into ranch country, but the ranchers were delighted when they appeared. The first stop was the Geike place secluded in a glen accessed by what had once been a meandering narrow wagon trail.

While Eva Geike piled apples, picked from their apple trees, into the pillow case sacks, Paul told the Nations that the day he put the apples in the cellar, he rounded the corner and came face to face with a mountain lion. He laughed heartily and said he must have been a homely old cuss, because that lion turned tail and ran back to Coliseum Butte.

When the Nations arrived at the Thomas ranch, Grace Thomas was already dressed to go to a Square Dance party that night in Harrison. The skirt of her bright orange dress, all trimmed in black rickrack draped over a many-layered crinoline petticoat. Her husband, Everett, dressed in a matching orange and black shirt grinned when Melvin told him he sure wished he had a shirt like that. Grace gave the girls one of the cherry pies she baked for the Square Dance luncheon. It rode the rest of the route on the dashboard. Leona Dout told them they had to do a trick before she would give them a treat. Moni pulled her hat down and quickly did two somersaults: one for her treat and one for Robbin's. The chocolate chip cookies were well worth a dozen somersaults. Darrell Atchison was tuning his guitar in preparation for a Halloween Party gig. While the girls watched, he strummed a few chords of the song his band planned on playing that night. Leone Atchison, quickly whipped up a sack of popcorn while Melvin and George discussed cattle prices. Moni Hourt said the family giggled and laughed

---

[412] *A Girl of the Limberlost* written by Gene Stratton-Porter, published in 1909. Bill told Thelma she could keep the books and anything else she found up there, but most of the items had been removed long ago by the former occupants.

their way home. Melvin lustily sang new and improved verses (Appendix 5) for "We Went to the Animal Fair"[413] and his audience enthusiastically joined in.

"His favorite song was "T for Texas, T for Tennessee," Moni said. "He sang it all the time. That night every time he sang his original phrase, "T for Thelma the girl who ruined me" Mom would reach across Robbin and I and thump him."

The Asian Flu[414] that swept across the country in 1957 produced neither laughter or merriment. Several feet of snow and below-zero cold blanketed the ranch in early March when six-year-old Moni contracted the disease that eventually killed 80,000 US citizens. The doctor told Thelma to keep her daughter at home instead of trying to make the 50-mile trip to the doctor's office. In the first few days, the little girl's temperature hovered between 105 and 106 degrees. Thelma immersed her young daughter in bathtubs of cool water or sponged her body with cool water in an attempt to keep her temperature from continuing its upward spiral.

"Melvin stopped by the house every little bit," Thelma Nation said. "We had Moni on the couch in the living room where it was warm. He sponged her off, but he never completely wrung all the water from the rag. It ran down her face and got her clothes wet, but I didn't say anything. He was as scared as I was. We really thought we might lose her. As it was she didn't really get over it until late spring. She was one sick little girl."

Moni Hourt said she remembers being confused that her Dad stopped at the house during the day. But she didn't complain when her Dad, smelling like the outdoors and cattle, sat down beside her. He'd take his gloves off, and softly lay his hands on her face.

"His hands were cold and rough on my hot skin. They were so big and so very gentle. There was a basin full of water by the couch. He dipped the rag in the water and wiped it across my face and neck. The water ran over my chest and under my arms. I can remember thinking that it felt so good. To this day I can feel the touch of his hands."

Despite her parents' best efforts to conquer the disease, Moni was eventually confined to the Crawford Memorial hospital for several days. Thelma said she and Robbin stayed with Doris and Tom Hamaker.[415] She and Doris, who arrived with a bag of books and games, took turns staying with Moni. Becky Benson,[416] the hospital cook also made regular visits to the little girl's room bringing vanilla milk shakes and chicken soup. Moni said her mother brought her home

---

[413] The song, "We Went to the Animal Fair" was printed in the *Life* magazine in 1941. Melvin took great pleasure in singing the whimsical verses.

[414] The Asian Flue (Influenza A H2N2) killed nearly 80,000 people in the United States. Pneumonia and influenza related deaths occurred primarily in elderly and young children.

[415] Keal Rising's sister and the wife of Tom Hamaker, Iva Hamaker's nephew.

[416] Becky Benson and her husband Jimmy were the only Black family in Crawford. Becky was well-known as a kind, caring presence in the hospital who always delivered extra treats for hospital patients.

Monday afternoon. Melvin was at the barn, his horse saddled, ready to check the cows. He rode to the horse first and carried Moni into the house.[417]

Moni's diary entries, beginning when she was eight, further refuted Melvin's statement about spending an insufficient time with his family. Granted some of those hours may have been classified as work, but in his children's eyes the hours were well spent.

Helping to gather and feed calves before school every morning was reported with pride in the Moni's little white diary. "I drove all the way to the bunks," the page labeled February 10, 1959 reported. "Daddy didn't holler once." The next day she hit a bunk and moved it out of its neat row. "I got too close to the bunks. Daddy put them back. He says I'll get the hang of it."

Sometimes the tractor ended up sideways in the gate. Other times she hooked the pickup box on a feed bunk as she turned the corner. By March, though, she reported that her Dad let her drive all the way back to the house on her own and that she had NOT hit anything in a week.

If the job was caking calves, Melvin would bounce into the back of the pickup, open the burlap sakes filled with cake, then as Moni drove alongside the bunks, he poured the cake from the sacks into the long line of bunks. When he pitched hay, he climbed up on the stack of hay that towered eight feet above the bed of the wagon. If he performed the task himself, he put the tractor in first gear, jumped on the wagon, scrambled to the top of the stack, and pitched the hay off both sides of the stack until the pile was reduced to a few scraps. If the tractor strayed in the wrong direction, he jumped off the stack and climbed back on the tractor to realign his path. The hay ground changed every day because Melvin said the cows didn't want to eat off a dirty plate any more than he did. Putting his daughter in the tractor seat eliminated the manual path correction, but didn't always eliminate the stress of the situation.

"Sometimes there was some frantic hand gesturing behind me," Moni remembered. "But he didn't yell—very much. I remember how badly I hated to go back to the house and get ready for school. It didn't matter how cold it was, the second I heard Dad say my name, I was out of bed and ready to go. He only called us once. I don't think we ever let him walk out the door without us."

Moni admitted she never-ever-ever forgot a driving error she made one early summer morning. Melvin told her to drive his brand new pick up from the shop to the barn. In order to do that she needed to drive past a tractor parked on the bridge. She hit the tractor which left its imprint on the pickup's bright yellow paint.

"I was so ashamed of myself. I couldn't face Dad. It was a brand new pickup, and I had ruined it. I jumped out of the pickup and ran all the way to the North Meadow. I stayed there all day."

---

[417] *Harrison Sun*. March 28, 1957. "The Warbonnet News" section of the newspaper reported that "Ramona Nation was a patient in the Crawford hospital from Saturday until Monday.

When she finally returned to the house Melvin was in bed. She wrote him a letter of apology and left it on the stove where he cooked his morning eggs. Nothing more was ever said about the incident. Melvin never fixed the front door.

"To this day, the thought of scraping up that pickup makes me sick," Moni said. "We never wanted to disappoint Dad."

Robbin Nation Oldaker said her job after school was to help Melvin dehorn calves. She said she was furious if she arrived home a few minutes late, and he was already headed to the pasture.

"I'd saddle my horse and lope out to help him," Robbin said. "I was pretty proud if I thought I was doing something to make life easier for Dad."

There was little doubt that the everyday task of "raising the kids" was primarily Thelma's domain, but Melvin's influence was always apparent and often reflected the time period. He seldom showed emotion and often reminded his children that they needed to be tough. "Bawling" was discouraged with the admonition, "Quit that damn snotting, or I'll give you something to bawl about." Although spankings were almost non-existent, Thelma's threat that she was going to "tell your Dad," generally yielded altered attitudes.

"All Dad had to do was give you one of his icy blue-eyed glares and you decided misbehaving wasn't worth it," Moni Nation Hourt said. "He always agreed with Mom and sassing her in his presence was a major offense. I never remember getting spanked, but when you committed a particularly grievous offense, he'd deliver a very low-voiced, quietly worded lecture, that always ended with "let your conscious be your guide." Long before I actually knew what a conscious was I certainly knew I had to let it guide me. When I was about 10-11, I attended Bible School classes with a neighbor. The minister asked for the definition of a conscience. I replied, "That's when God thumps you on the head and makes you listen." Dad never thumped me on the head, but I guess I decided God probably did. Dad's admonition about letting a conscience guide you definitely made an impact."

CELEBRATIONS

> "We worked hard, and we played hard. Sometimes we mixed the two."
> Melvin Nation

Branding day couldn't actually be labeled a celebration, but it was a major event in ranch country. Melvin strove to manage the day as a well-oiled "machine" in which the calves were quickly branded, vaccinated, and in the case of many male calves, castrated then returned to the pasture "before their mamas even miss them." Kids vied for the honor of wrestling the most calves. Ranch women took great pride in making tasty meals that would give even the biggest crew seconds and thirds.

"There was only one year that I was ever worried about having enough food," Thelma said. "Sara[418] was gonna get married, the day after branding, to a guy from Omaha. I think every one of the guests decided to show up to see what a branding was. I cooked about everything in the house. Finally, Bill told me to quit worrying about it. He said if we ran out of food, they could go to town. I didn't run out of food, but it was close."

On branding day, the girls helped round up cattle then Melvin would send them to the house where their mother and the neighbor women were involved in the dinner preparations. By the time they were 10 or 12 they were relegated to the branding pen.

"It was a great day when Dad let us wrestle calves instead of helping in the house. We—well I—never really helped Mom make dinner," Moni Hourt said. "I'd rather help round up the cattle, then in later years, go take pictures. Robbin helped Mom more than I did particularly after we were older."

Alcohol was not permitted in the branding pens, but branding dinner was generally followed with a few beers, or maybe more than a few beers. The men plucked the beer cans out of the water tank where they'd been cooling all morning then sat around and visited—and drank. At times, wives and children drove the branders home.

---

[418] Bill Coffee's second daughter.

After one Hat Creek branding, Melvin decided Robbin was more capable of driving him home than he was. She said it rained that afternoon. Prairie Dog Road was slippery. The pickup hooked to a two-horse trailer wasn't four-wheel drive.

"I looked over at Dad. He told me to keep going, so I did," Robbin said. "I left some pretty awful tracks, but we made it."

Christmas Day outranked even branding as the major event of the year. The day was dedicated to family.

Moni started kindergarten at District 76, ½ mile west of the Warbonnet Ranch in 1956. From that point, Christmas began with the school program. Thelma made sure the "girls" were dressed in bright new dresses, and Melvin never failed to attend. The plays were often repetitive, and many former students used distorted faces, rude sounds, and ill-placed giggles to distract the young thespians on the stage. However, the event generally ended with a full-throated rendition of "Joy to the World" or some other Christmas song and was enjoyed by the entire community.

Christmas program after Moni's kindergarten year at District 76. Students: Ray Doug, Linda Chlecq, Jolene Locker, Bruce Wickersham, Becky Wickersham, Moni Nation. Front: Pre-schoolers, Robbin Nation and Scott Wickersham.

"Daddy said Robbin and I looked pretty fancy tonight and I did a good job with my poem." Moni Nation Hourt wrote in her journal in 1960. "Teacher gave me a book."

"Melvin's family never celebrated Christmas," Verna Callaham[419] said. "That first Christmas he and Thelma were married, he was just like a little boy. He ran over and looked at every present that was opened. He didn't want to open his though. He didn't want Christmas to be over."

Throughout his lifetime, Melvin continued the practice of being the last one to open his gifts. Then he always said, "It's been another beautiful Christmas. You're a bunch of spoiled damn kids."

Christmas Eve the family often made a trip to town so Thelma could pick up anything she still needed to

---

[419] Verna Stockton Callaham. Personal taped interview by Moni Hourt: 1994.

produce Christmas dinner—and to buy the canned oysters for a Christmas Eve supper of oyster stew. Dozens of canned oysters floating in a sea of fresh cream were the stars of the once-a-year treat that was eaten with tiny, crisp, oyster crackers.

When the family returned from their Christmas evening journey, they generally found an envelope propped on the branches of the Christmas tree. Melvin would pull the money laden envelope from the tree and empty its contents, his Christmas bonus from the Coffees, into his hand.[420] Then he returned the envelope to the tree. If Bill happened to deliver the envelope personally, Melvin brought it to the house and wedged it among the tree branches. He didn't remove it until the gifts were opened Christmas morning.

Early Christmas morning, generally before the sun was up, Melvin woke his family so they could discover their "Santa gifts" then he fed the cattle. He always told the kids that the house had to be clean, really clean, before they could open any gifts. By the time he came in from feeding, the house was scoured to an Excited-Christmas-Morning-Shine. Even then breakfast was eaten before the gifts were opened. Many Christmas Days were spent with Sis and Keal's family or with Elvin and Frances Nation. Sometimes, the family simply stayed home alone or shared the day with whatever hired man was working on the ranch that year. No matter the scenario, Melvin never worked Christmas Day. The Day was reserved for family.

One Christmas picture shows Melvin diligently bottle feeding Robbin's new doll. There are no pictures of him trying to examine a hair under Moni's new microscope or taking Jim-Bob out to shoot his new BB gun. And there aren't any pictures of Melvin carefully explaining that the whole set of doll clothes that Moni found in her mother's sewing box before Christmas were actually contracted by Santa Claus.

An old car hood towed by a pickup enhanced several Christmas celebrations. "My Dad and Uncle Melvin knew how to swing the hood out just enough to dump us," Donna Rising

Christmas at Sis and Keal Rising's house in Wyoming in 1959. Thelma, Robbin on Thelma's lap, Melvin, Casey, Sis, Donna, Keal. Moni and Dixie in front.

---

[420] Melvin never told his children the amount of the bonus, but he was always proud that he had received it.

Ed Oldaker and Bryan Hourt square off in a Christmas Day skeet shooting competition. Joe Hourt, front, mans the skeet thrower.

Norgard[421] said. "It didn't matter how hard we tried, we couldn't stay on."

Shooting matches took place Christmas afternoons. Thelma wasn't real thrilled that the targets were often the clothes pins on the clothes line. Eventually a skeet shooter and a box of clay pigeons provided hours of good "red neck" entertainment. Everyone was sure they could top the "rifle man" competition that day if "the wind was right."

Although he excelled during the "clothes pin competition," Melvin seldom hunted the wildlife around the ranch. An exception was Thanksgiving and Christmas. On those occasions, he believed it was his job to shoot a turkey for dinner. The turkeys were accessible. They roosted in the trees behind the house. They were fairly fat, because they ate the cake from the feeders, but Thelma did not relish the task of digging buckshot out of the turkey carcasses or picking and butchering the many-feathered animals. One Thanksgiving, she "accidently" left the turkey on the porch. The cats discovered it. She ran to town that afternoon and bought her first *Butter Ball*.

"Your Dad wasn't too happy with me," Thelma said, "But he admitted the town turkey tasted good. That was the last year we had wild turkey."

"Actually, I thought we should kill more of those turkeys," David Nation, Melvin's nephew, said with a twinkly-eyed sneer. "We were all out to Melvin's, us and uncle Elvin's, one Sunday not long before Thanksgiving. The turkeys come in to roost like they did every night. Melvin convinced me that I could climb up a ladder and snatch one of those turkeys right out of the tree. Said, the turkey would flop a little, but he was sleeping and wouldn't be much of a problem. I was about 12 and worshipped Melvin. But I should have known better. I knew he wasn't above pulling a good joke. Anyway, we go out and get a big ladder. I crawled up that damned cottonwood. About the time I reached out to grab the first turkey I come to, he decided to let go. I had poop in my hair, my hands, on my clothes. Those guys

---

[421] Donna Rising Norgard. Personal interview, 2015. The daughter of Keal and Velma (Sis) Rising, Donna and her sisters spent many Christmases with the Nation family.

about laughed themselves stupid. I climbed back down the ladder, and By Gawd, they made me put the ladder away."

Once in a while, Melvin's somewhat twisted sense of humor backfired. A big snapping turtle, crawled belligerently out of the creek, daring the girls to step close enough so he could take a bite. They ran to the house and convinced the rest of the family to come look at the giant creature, "the biggest they ever saw!!!" Everyone was impressed. The turtle chomped on to the branch Melvin offered him and shook it frantically breaking it in half. When he let go of the branch, he lunged forward toward Mike, the family dog, who quickly ran toward his mistress. Mike was apparently scared "to death" by the turtle's antics. At least that was the only excuse anyone could find when he suddenly lifted his leg and wet up and down Thelma's leg.

"I fell on the ground and laughed until I thought I would cry," Melvin grinned. "Thelma didn't laugh. She marched to the house cussing me every step of the way. The dog, the kids, and I followed. We made quite a damn fine parade, and I really did try to quit laughing. I really did. She didn't think I did though. She slammed the door in my face and broke the window out. She slammed the bedroom door. I don't think she talked to any of us that night. We even fixed our own supper." Luckily it was Sunday night. Thelma had already made the Sunday-supper pie.[422]

Thelma did get her revenge a few weeks later. On their anniversary, Melvin went to town. He explained later that he was visiting with the "Staudenmaier boys[423]" and lost track of the time. About 2 a.m. Thelma, scared to death that something had happened, headed up Monroe Canyon looking for him. She met him at the top of the canyon, yanked the car around in a neat circle, and sped toward home. At lunch the next day, she served a new dish: a pile of angle worms and a note that proclaimed, "Happy Anniversary, Worm." The hired man, probably a little pleased that Melvin had finally been on the other end of a "joke," broke into a mighty guffaw.

The family seldom missed the celebrations at the Sioux County Fair in Harrison or the Fourth of July Rodeo in Crawford. For many years, Melvin walked out of both arenas with a check.

"He never rode many bulls after Robbin was born, but he rode pretty steady for a couple of years after we were married," Thelma said. "He didn't have as much style as some of the cowboys, but he was stronger than hell."

---

[422] Sunday supper generally consisted of pie and fresh whip cream. Thelma purchased 25-gallon tubs of frozen cherries and peaches from the grocery store which became the basis of many desserts. Fresh apples were used during the summer, but Melvin's favorite was Thelma's chocolate custard pie topped with meringue. Sometimes the pie became a pudding, if it didn't set up properly. Then whip cream topped the luscious dessert. Melvin's culinary skills consisted of making fried eggs and toast.

[423] The three bachelor Staudenmaier brothers, Jim. Junior, and George always spent Saturday night at the bar in Harrison. They loved to visit. Many husbands blamed them for late nights in town.

In 1953, Verna Callaham, who admitted that Melvin was her "absolute favorite," disapproved of the score Melvin received for his ride. After the rodeo she marched into the arena, hands firmly on her hips, and headed toward the judge who awarded the low score.

"I told him he was a dumb son-of-a-b—-," Verna Callaham said defiantly. "About that time, I heard Moni behind me. She was waddling along with her hands on her hips. She didn't talk very well yet, which was a good thing. I grabbed her and hustled her out of the arena before the judge realized what she called him. I decided I better start watching my mouth."

Although he won several hundred dollars riding bulls at the Sioux County Fair rodeo, one year Melvin was left with nothing but a dimple. The bull flung his rider over his head shortly before the 8-second whistle and proceeded to maul his two-legged opponent.

"He flat wanted to eat me," Melvin said. "He wallered me across the arena and rammed his horn through my face. He knocked me plumb out. The ambulance gathered me up. About the time, we hit the gate I woke up and jumped out the back door. I wasn't really hurt, just lost a couple of teeth. The hole in my cheek healed up, but it never went away."

"When a stupid woman sashays up to him and tells him he has such a cute dimple, I tell her he wasn't born with it. They don't have guts enough to ask how he got it, but I think a few of them give me the credit. Doesn't matter; they back off." Thelma's glare substantiated the fact that Melvin's dimple wasn't any other woman's business.

In later years, Melvin switched from bull riding, to dogging steers: jumping off a horse at 15 miles an hour, diving onto a longhorn steer speeding between Melvin's dogging horse and a hazing horse, and twisting the steer to the ground. It wasn't illogical that a couple of years later he even tried his hand at chariot racing.

The sport had gained popularity at regional rodeos in the late '50s. Maurice Keel, who lived on a ranch about eight miles west of Warbonnet, won consistently. Melvin was determined to beat him and win the $100 purse. Keel's chariot, painted bright yellow was pulled by a pair of powerful bay thoroughbreds. Melvin built his chariot in the Warbonnet shop, but didn't bother to paint it. Using a grinder, he smoothed the sides of the chariot until it was a burnished silver color. He topped it with a heavy iron rod that clamped around the ¾ circular chariot body and helped maintain its "C" shape. With considerable effort Melvin, Bruce, and Bob Jordan, hooked green-broke geldings that were "wilder than March hares" to the chariot.

"I kept them in the track the first race, and we crossed the finish line in front of the other team," Melvin said. "Keel won his race so the two of us squared off in the final race."

The 3/4-mile race started on the west side of the Harrison Fair grounds arena. Melvin managed to slow his horses down enough for the starting gun to explode. By the time the teams hit the final corner all four horses were crowding the middle of the track. Melvin's team took the outside edge riding the side of the track at a nearly perpendicular angle. Down the final stretch, the team of wild gelding pulled into the lead. Liberally applying the buggy whip and slapping the reins over the top of the unpadded rim, Melvin drove the team and the silver chariot over the finish line. They edged past Keel's chariot beating him by what many spectators said was less than six inches. The team made two more trips around the track before it came to a stop. The crowd in the grandstand cheered wildly as the horses careened past, making what the crowd thought to be a couple of victory laps. Keel took his horses to the horse barn.

"My arms were black and blue for a month," Melvin said. "And old Maurice was mad at me for the rest of his life. He was sure I'd cheated him somehow."

Many of Melvin's rodeo experiences occurred in the Crawford, Nebraska arena. In 1947,[424] the 17-year-old discovered that being a "mugger"[425] during the wild cow milking contest was a profitable occupation. He and future brother-in-law, Keal Rising, brought in nearly $600 during one rodeo by mugging for different teams. That amount of money soothed the bumps and bruises the pair incurred as human stanchions. Their job: keeping very unhappy mama cows in a holding position long enough for the team's "milker" to deposit a few squirts of milk into an empty beer bottle. The pair competed in the wild-horse race a few times too, but Melvin said he "got pretty damn tired of that damn Rising falling off the horse" after he went to all the trouble to hold the animal down long enough for him to be saddled.

Many years after Keal and Melvin topped opponents in the wildhorse race, Keal's nephew Randy organized teams that won competitions across the Panhandle.

---

[424] The rodeo was held in the fall in 1945 and 1946, but 1947 it was held on the Fourth of July a practice that continues.
[425] A mugger in a wild milking contest is tasked with confining the cow so that the one milking her can get a few squirts of milk into a bottle. The muggers wrapped their arms around a cow's neck in an impression of a human stanchion.

Although Melvin participated in many "wild cow milking competitions he never mentioned saddling the cow and trying to ride it over a line as required of this pair, photographed in about 1930. Photo: Hourt collection, no attribution.

By 1949, Nation decided that bull riding was probably safer that trying to conquer mad mama-cows or unruly wild horses. The bull he climbed on at Crawford that year was only the second he tried to cover.

"He were a bad chute-fighting son-of-a-gun," Nation said in 1999. "He kept setting me back off my rope every time I'd try to get down. Lawrence Tate had the stock. He told me I might as well turn him out. He said I couldn't get him ridden, 'no how.' Marv Rising was helping me down. He told me if I wanted the bull, I could take the rope and jump at him when they opened the gate. That's what I did. I tied for first. That was one of the biggest days in my life."

In a 1997 interview, Marvin Rising also recalled Nation's 1949 ride. "He sure didn't have much style. He were just a green kid, but he was stubborn as hell and as strong as a young ox. He squared his jaw, called for the gate, and jumped into his hand. I don't think you 'could'a' pried him off. After he quit riding bulls, he started dogging, and he was good at that, too. He's always been one of those guys that when he set his mind on something he just did it. I have a lot of respect for Mel."

The Crawford Rodeo was always a good one for Melvin. In 1951 he won the bull riding. He also won part of several other rodeos that week and pocketed nearly $1000. "I thought I was rich. I paid up the '51 Ford we'd bought, and took a vacation to Washington to see my brother."

In a diary entry dated July 3, 1951, Thelma Nation wrote that Melvin had done very well at the Crawford Rodeo the night before. "He's cleaning up," she wrote. "He's placing in both the bull riding and the bareback riding. We went to the bar tonight and saw some guys we hadn't seen for a while. We had a good time."[426]

In later years Melvin moved beyond the competitor's bucking chute. He served as pickup man for Bernice Johnson and Fred Dorenkamp. He also opened bucking chutes, hazed dozens of steers, and competed in the bull-dogging and team roping. Sometimes he simply went to watch. One year he and Keal Rising, suffering leg injuries sustained during bull dogging incidents, balanced on crutches, and watched from the sidelines. However, although his viewing location may have varied over the years, he seldom missed the Fourth of July Rodeo in Crawford.

If the cut hay was stacked, the men at the Coffee Ranches took the entire Fourth of July as a vacation day. Melvin and his family drove to Crawford for the annual parade then picnicked in the park before attending the Fourth of July Rodeo that night.

Melvin in 1975 as a pickup man at the PRCA Fourth of July rodeo in Crawford, NE. That same year Melvin's son-in-law, Ed Oldaker placed second in the dogging.

"That year Chappie and his family met us down there. We set up the table and were having a couple of beers when the man at the next table decided he didn't like the way Chappie looked at him. He was one of those drunks always looking for a fight," Melvin said.

Chappell told the man he and his family were eating and that he sure didn't have anything to against him. The man bellied up to the table. "Chappie gets up and dances around the man poking him at will and laughing every time he connected. He wasn't mad, but wasn't going to let the man bullying him none either," Melvin recalled with a head shake. "Finally, he knocked him on his a—. The drunk's wife gathered him up, and we ate our dinner."

In the 50s, while the adults picnicked in the park or visited with friends, their children walked downtown to Chewie Wilson's junk shop to buy fireworks. The fireworks, scattered willy-nilly across the top of foggy glass-topped counters that contained pipes and tobacco, offered tantalizing choices.

---

[426] Thelma Callaham Nation. Diary 1951-52.

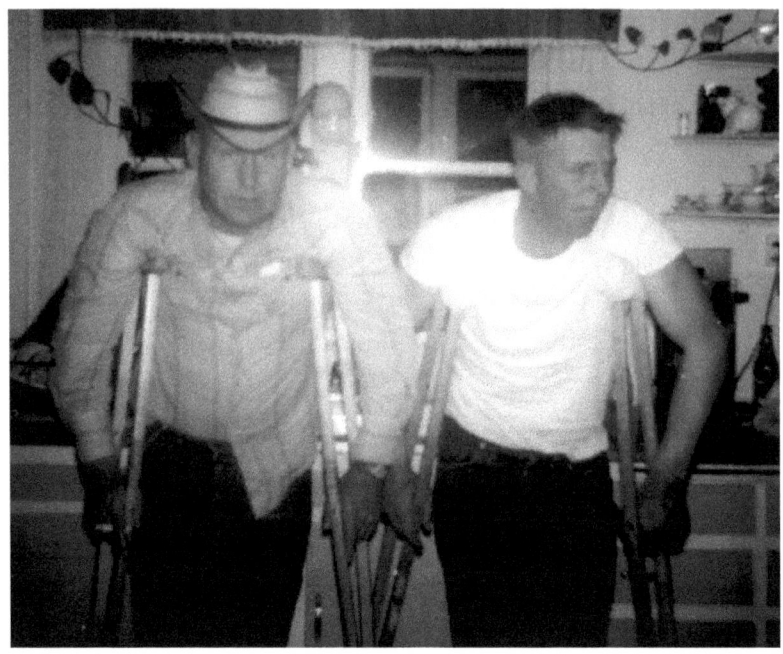

In 1963, Keal Rising broke the Crawford arena record with a 2.0 in the steer wrestling. Melvin, who was hazing said he shoved Keal down and Keal "got er done." When the dust cleared, Keal had broken a bone in his leg. Melvin broke a bone in his leg when a horse he was breaking fell on him. Both men spent most of the summer hobbling around on crutches. In 1965, Melvin returned to the Crawford arena to win the first round of the steer wrestling, and place 3rd overall.

Thelma and Robbin walk across the Crawford Rodeo arena. Spending the Fourth of July in Crawford, NE, became a family tradition.

Sparklers and snakes were the favorite fireworks. The desire to light the foot-long sparklers before dark tested the girls' patience, but most of the time, a few survived until the end of the rodeo. Thelma used her cigarette lighter to ignite the "sparklers." Melvin lifted them onto the roof of the pickup. They flopped and circled the sparklers across their narrow band of sky until they fizzed out, then they stretched out on the windshield and watched the fireworks explode in the sky above the rodeo arena. If the night was warm, the girls, wrapped in blankets, climbed into the bed of the pickup for the ride home. Generally, before they reached Smiley Canyon, Thelma reconsidered the idea and bundled them inside.

MOVING ON

"The late 60s and early 70s were good years for ranchers.
Maybe we were fooled into thinking they'd stay that way." Melvin Nation

Between 1950-1970, driven by increased meat consumption and rising prices,[427] beef production more than doubled on the Great Plains, constituting three fourth of the agricultural income on the Prairie.[428] Melvin said the Coffee ranches benefited from the agricultural economic upturn because Bill improved every part of his ranching operation including cattle production, but still maintained the integrity of the land.

"He never overgrazed, especially in the dry years," Melvin explained. "He left 40 or 50 percent of the native grass in a pasture. That way if there's any moisture at all the grass comes back. He improved irrigation at both ranches and was always looking to produce that better cow."

In the days before the internet and data bases full of breeding stock information, Bill frequented area sales searching for what he considered the right-kind of animal. "He wanted a bull with a good hind end, deep in the body, with a good straight back and was 'pretty haired,'" Melvin added. "The cows he bought complemented the bulls. Long before most ranchers did, he paid attention to birth weight. He was careful to update bloodlines and kept his bulls fresh. He always wanted better, more efficient cattle, that produce strong calves. He was a damn good cow man."

Forming a partnership with Pete and Joe Nunn in the mid-sixties, Bill purchased a "damned good looking set of cattle" from the Perkins and Prothros ranch in Boise City, Oklahoma. Dubbed the Ps because they were branded with a P-backwards P brand, the cattle could have graced the front cover of "Cow Beautiful" magazine. Their attitude mirrored that of a spoiled diva.

"We never worked those cattle that we didn't have a wreck," Melvin said grinning and shaking his head. "They bought a couple thousand head of those calves. When they spooked, it sure seemed like they went in a thousand different directions at once."

---

[427] Cattle prices averaged $24.20 in 1952. By 1972 they averaged $42.40
[428] "Cattle Ranching in the United States." Pamphlet US Department of Agriculture. January 1973.

Joe Nunn agreed. "We were gathering at the Atterbury[429] one fall. My Dad was driving the pickup with a couple of sacks of cake in the back. The twin Brown Swiss steers that we used as lead steers followed the cake. The rest of the herd trailed along. All seemed to be good—solid drive. Then one of those Brown Swiss tried to jump up in the pickup. He hit the tail gate. It bounced. The P cattle spooked. They went clear to the backside of the 300-acre shipping pen."

"Talk about exploding," Melvin added. "I looked over my shoulder and the only thing left trailing Pete was the Brown Swiss steers. It was "pertinear" three miles before we got them stopped. We never did get them gathered back up that day."

Although the Coffee crew was nearly always short-handed, 23 men congregated one morning to bring 1500 "Ps" into the shipping pens at the Nunn Ranch. Melvin said most of the cattle had to be roped and dragged through the gate.

"Those cattle were good doing cattle, so we kept buying them," Joe Nunn said. "But I think every year we wondered if it was worth it. Right in the middle of one wreck a steer ran right under the belly of Old Joe, the horse Bill was riding. I thought sure it would upend him, but it didn't. My Dad pulled up about that time. He blew up. Bill blew up. Bill loaded his horse and his crew went home. That was about the only time I saw my Dad mad."

As part of his wage, Melvin ran a designated number of cattle on the Coffee Ranch. Although he still believed that the Hereford cow was the best "Mama," he said breeders, trying to produce a bigger cow "fooled around and bred the milk out of them." He purchased "a little herd of black heifers" and ran them on the ranch.

"You'd look out across the pasture and see big calves sucking those little old cows. They just raised a bigger calf. And the black cows didn't get pink eye or sunburn bags," Melvin said. "Bill looked them over. Didn't say anything, but that fall he bought a set of black cows from Jim Christian."

Although Melvin still loved the Warbonnet Ranch where he and Thelma had lived for nearly 20 years, change was in the air. Moni was married in 1969. That same year their country school, District 76, closed. A freshman, Robbin drove into Harrison for school; JimBob enrolled in the Harrison Elementary school and traveled with her. When Robbin married in 1971, Thelma found a job at Sioux Sundries in Harrison and drove JimBob to school every day. Melvin leased the "home place" after Elvin moved to Washington in 1966. He bought the place in 1974.

"I was having trouble getting everything done at the Home Place, and at the ranch too. But that wasn't the only reason I thought we should leave," Melvin said, "Bill thought Warbonnet was bad luck for boys.[430] He didn't want JimBob working at the ranch. I thought he was getting cheated. I wanted him to learn how to do something like the girls had."

---

[429] The Atterbury pasture located in south-central Sioux County was named after its original homesteader.
[430] John Anderson's son died at the ranch as did Bill's son.

By 2000 most of the cattle on both Hat Creek were Angus or Angus cross. In 2003, Two big Angus cattle created a momentarily frame for Buffy Hourt, Melvin Hourt, Carinna Sias, and Bryan Hourt.

Thelma made it clear she didn't want to move. From the time Elmer Callaham moved his family to "Spud Ridge[431]" she hated the plateau where the Home Place was located. Her feelings had not changed. Melvin remodeled the house. She agreed to move. As she had done her entire life, she made up her mind to "make the best of it."

"We moved down there in the spring of 1973," Melvin said. "Land values were high. Money was cheap. The banks were willing to lend you anything you wanted. When I left Warbonnet, I thought it would work, I really did. I thought the future was ours."

---

[431] "Spud Ridge," so named because potatoes grew well in the plateau soils is a high plateau located approximately 1000 feet above Crawford, Marsland, and Scottsbluff, Nebraska. It is southwest of Crawford, west of Marsland, and northeast of Scottsbluff. In later years it was known as the Hill View community.

THE HOME PLACE

"I thought it would work, and it did for a while, but it would have been better if I would have never left in the first place." Melvin Nation

When Melvin and Thelma moved down to the Home Place, they had been married for 22 years, most of it spent on the Coffee Ranches. Their oldest daughter, Moni and her husband, Joe Hourt, lived in Crawford, Nebraska, where he worked as an auto-body repairman. Their second daughter, Robbin, and her husband, Ed Oldaker, were employed on the Herb Geike ranch three miles west of Warbonnet Ranch. The Nation's oldest granddaughter, Buffy Hourt[432], was three-years-old, Annette Oldaker and Bryan Hourt were both just one-year-old. That fall 12-year-old JimBob enrolled in District 51, the rural school Melvin attended when he was a boy. His classmates sported many of the same last names that filled the class rosters 30 years before.

Melvin with Buffy, Janet, Bryan, Craig Norgard, (Sis's grandson,) and Annette in 1975.

---

[432] Buffy Hourt, May 9, 1970; Annette Oldaker, September 1, 1971; Bryan Hourt, March 11, 1972; Janet Oldaker, November 28, 1973; Amy Oldaker, November 24, 1976, Melvin Oldaker, August 11, 1981.

When Ed and Robbin visited, Melvin took Ed, Amy, Annette and Janet for a spin around the place in his small chariot-wagon.

In the years they lived on the Home Place, three more grandchildren, Janet, Amy, and Melvin Oldaker would be born. For the grandchildren, the Home Place was an adventure, but the time period often made the "new adventure," a tumultuous one for the adults.

Change and unrest dominated the '70s in the more populous regions of America, but just as during the Depression era, the events in the Panhandle of Nebraska revolved around making a living and tackling everyday life. It was obvious from his tally book entries that Melvin was aware of the larger world around him.[433] He wrote that he "sure felt bad" for the families of the athletes killed in Munich in 1972. He thought the US should use force to rescue the 52 hostages taken by Iran,[434] and he was disgusted with the fighting in Northern Ireland, but his greatest concern revolved around the Vietnam War.[435] He was concerned that JimBob could be drafted and have to fight what Melvin believed was an unnecessary war.

"There weren't any reason we should've ever gone into Vietnam," Melvin said in a 1999 interview. "As far as I was concerned, those poor boys over there died for no reason. I worried that Jim would be sent over there. When Elvin went overseas, we were in a battle for our country. That wasn't the way it was in Vietnam."[436]

Some current events directly impacted life in western Nebraska. The oil embargo of 1973,[437] sent oil and gas prices skyrocketing.[438] Melvin, responding to the problem with logic, stepped back in time. He broke a team of horses to pull the hay sled that he used every morning to feed his cattle. He built a two-wheel cart resembling the chariot he had raced in the Sioux County Fair. The cart was big enough to hold several bags of cow cake that could then be dumped into troughs for the yearlings. It also ferried passengers. The grandchildren cherished excursions in the cart. Even the smallest riders remember zipping across the hill side on the way to cake the yearlings or check pastures.

---

[433] Melvin, like most ranchers, carried a tally book. In it he recorded the daily operations on the ranch, cattle prices, and often personal comments. During the years on the Home Place, facts and figures dominated its pages.
[434] The 52 American diplomats and citizens were held hostage for 444 days from November 1979 to January 1981.
[435] The Vietnam War lasted for nearly 20 years. Approximately 58,220 Americans were killed in the war that was deemed a "police action" by the American government.
[436] The draft was discontinued in 1973. The Vietnam War ended with the fall of Saigon in 1975. The American draft that began in 1940 ended in 1973.
[437] Imposed by the Organization of Arab Petroleum Exporting Countries.
[438] The price of oil shot from $3 to $12 a barrel. At the pump gas prices rose from a national average of $.38 cents in May 1973 to $.55 cents in June 1974.

"Granddad could build anything. He even built a car-battery powered, horse-drawn wagon that could pick up bales," Bryan Hourt said. "What he built may not have been fancy, but it did what he wanted done."

According to Melvin's tally book, in April of 1972, a year before he moved to the Home Place, he branded 31 steer calves and 34 heifers calves. He also listed 70 range cows, 21 yearling calves, 2 bulls, 3 fall calves, 1 dry heifer and 3 cows still to calve that were pastured at the Home Place. On the same page, he listed the fact that there were 60 range cows, 50 calves, 9 dry cows, 3 milk cows with calves and 2 bulls at Warbonnet. He wrote that 3 cows at Warbonnet had yet to calve.

At the end of 1973, his tally book recorded the fact that he sold 61 heifers for $1486.35, two cows for $536.16, $7638.65 worth of wheat and $4183.69 dollars' worth of oats. A short time later he sold a single cow for $230.73 and 123 more calves for $34,739.30. He made payments to the FHA and the Sioux National Bank then purchased more cattle. The 55 calves he bought averaged 325 pounds and cost an average of $184.25 each. He purchased 4 cows at an average cost of $230. The two black bulls he purchased cost $3300. Although he was rapidly trying to replant all the farm land back into pasture land, his tally book reported he planted 56 acres of wheat, 60 acres of Millet-Sudan grass, 100 acres of oats, and 50 acres of corn. He reported there were 50 acres of wheat to plant. He did custom haying, sold wheat and oats and listed trucking fees charged for the trucking services he provided for area ranchers. He also bought cattle on shares and calved them out for a share of the calves. He was determined to make the move an effective one.

"We spent most Sundays out there," Joe Hourt said. "I tried to help in any way I could, generally that meant holding onto a horse, welding something together, or staying out of the way. I had my own job, but on the weekends I worked with Melvin." And of course everyone showed up for branding.

Bryan Hourt shows off his roping skills to his sister, Buffy, and cousin, Annette Oldaker.

"We put up hay with a tractor and loader. Melvin built a sweep on a jeep frame. We swept the hay into bucks, then dumped the bucks into a cage with the tractor and loader," Gary Witt said. "I helped him hay for several years. I sure liked that better than picking up bales."

Witt said Melvin's small round baler produced what looked like millions of bales that stretched across the hillsides. He and his brother, Mike, hired on to pick the bales up off the fields. JimBob joined the crew and eventually 794 bales were stacked at the house. The boys were paid five cents a bale. Later that summer they were paid eight cents a bale to pick up an additional 1,184 bales.

"Melvin used to say if you get the Witt boys pulling in the same direction, they can move the world or in this case a couple thousand bales," Gary Witt[439] added. "He liked to have us both in the branding pen at the same time, too."

The three teenage boys didn't spend all their energy working. Gary admitted between moving cattle and haying, they hunted rabbits and coyotes and produced their share of trouble. "One afternoon Melvin caught us smoking and drinking a little beer," Gary said. "He wasn't a bit happy."

The piles of bales became a maze and a "stickery" jungle gym for the grandchildren. They climbed to the top of the bale pile, then slid down the inclines. Before long they realized they could navigate the gaps between the piles during wild games of hide and seek. Worried that the bales might collapse, Melvin banned the kids from the pile, much to their chagrin.

Although money worries were looming on the horizon, for the first time since he was a kid, Melvin could concentrate on training horses. He had purchased a stallion and several mares before he bought the family operation. He trained the colts that were produced and quickly sold them. Several other horses were broken to pull a wagon or his homemade chariot. Chris Hamaker said Melvin's "stud horse" didn't always show his well-trained side.

"I was helping Melvin sort some yearlings. I was on one side of the high corral fence; he was working cattle on the other side," Chris Hamaker[440] said with a chuckle. "All at once I heard him cussing. His horse bucked up above the windbreak, then sank out of sight. Four of five jumps later, Melvin flew above the fence line. I didn't see him hit the ground, but I heard it. He wasn't hurt, but he sure was mad."

Old Gray never did any bucking which made him the perfect choice to teach a kid to ride. Buffy and Bryan Hourt spent many Sundays riding the horse first around the corral, then out in the calving lot, and finally down in the canyons.

---

[439] Gary Witt and his brother Mike lived on the Witt place two miles from the Home Place. Their father Jerry and Melvin had grown up together and attended school at District 51. Gary was in high school by the time the Nations returned back to the ranch, but JimBob and Mike attended school together.

[440] Chris Hamaker, the grandson of Dave Hamaker, "Uncle Dave," was the third generation on the homestead his grandfather claimed in 1906. The farm/ranch was two miles west of the Nation ranch.

"Once you dropped down into the canyons, it was like you were in another world," Buffy Hourt Allred remembered. "You couldn't see the house, or fences, or another person. It was like I was a pioneer. What I didn't realize was that Granddad could generally see us from the corrals or the sheep pasture. On time Granddad was riding with me, and he showed me where his Mom and Dad lived when they first came to the place. I told him I thought it would be a great place to live because the wind didn't blow as much down there."

Iva Nation's scrapbook recorded her hatred of the wind and the loneliness she felt living on the Home Place, but she raised eight children on the hill and infused them with love and toughness. Thelma Nation also hated the wind that beat around the house built on the crest of the hill, but she built flower beds, planted trees, and spent hours creating music on her organ.

"Grandma's feet would pump the pedals, and her hands would just fly across the keys. The house would almost sway back and forth with the music," Annette Oldaker said. "We sat there being really quiet and listened. We were afraid if we were noisy, she would quit. She didn't play when other people were around, just us kids."

At Warbonnet, chickens produced meat and eggs. The exotic chickens that filled the chicken house on the Home Place were a strange mixture of the unusual and the bizarre. They produced eggs in all sizes and colors, the chickens never made it to the family table.

"We loved Grandma's fancy chickens," Buffy Hourt[441] remembered. "Some had feathers on their feet, some had fluffy head dresses, some of them laid green eggs. Grandma could identify every breed. We spent hours going through the McMurray catalog picking out chickens to buy to increase the herd, or replace the ones the coyotes snared."

Coyotes generally left healthy calves alone, which gave the Nations more to sell that fall. Prices in 1972 averaged $42.40 per hundred weight. That next year they rose to $53.10. Melvin and his sons-in-law carried a new organ into the house that Christmas morning. That afternoon, Thelma actually played her gift for her family. In his tally book[442] that evening he noted that "Thelma could make that thing jump up and dance a jig." He added that. JimBob's Christmas program was "pretty damn funny." The last notation on the page declared that "it wasn't a bad year."

Although Thelma could read music, primarily she played by ear. If she could hear a piece of music she could play it.

---

[441] Years later, Buffy's children, Brylee and Mahayla raised fancy chickens and showed them at the Fair.
[442] Nation, Melvin tally book, 1972.

In 1973, Gary and Frank Pisacka purchased the Crawford Sale Barn from Wright Lathrop. Thelma was hired as bookkeeper and began traveling to Crawford several times a week. She was not a trained bookkeeper, but as with everything else she tackled, she soon became proficient.

A tally book entry dated January 15, 1974 recorded the fact that Melvin had 111 range cows, 12 bred heifers, 94-1973 calves, 7 bulls, 4 milk cows, and 40 cows on shares. He recorded the pasture where each animal was located and the date the bulls were put out with the cows. Since he leased pasture for some of his cattle, he took the time to calculate the number of acres required and compared costs. One entry said he needed about 1600 acres of land to pasture 130 cows. Land leases ranged from $2.25 and $7 an acre. His left-handed scrawl carefully estimated costs and noted the owners of the cheapest pastureland, per head, in the region.

Thirty more calves, averaging 271 pounds apiece were unloaded in the lot below the house in November 1974. The cost: an average of $59.90 a head. He also paid $55 for a baby calf to put on his milk cow.

A few days later, Melvin purchased 70 ewes and a ram. Buffy and Bryan decided it was their job to herd them, and, in Bryan's case, wrestle them down when it was time to doctor them.

"Bryan wasn't very old, but he tackled sheep twice his size and held on until one of us could get there," Joe Hourt said in 2015. "Buffy was always worried about hurting them, but Bryan wasn't. They dragged him around some, but he seldom let go."

Melvin told Bud Hamaker[443] he thought he bought the sheep to feed the coyotes, but Gary Witt said it wasn't the coyotes that damaged the herd. Melvin corralled the animals every night. The coyotes didn't bother them. The wild dogs, however, weren't scared of invading "people space."

"One night a bunch of dogs got into the sheep and killed 10 or 15 of them," Gary Witt said. "JimBob, Mike and I went hunting. We caught them in the dump. We had a 22 and a couple of shot guns. The dogs had killed livestock all across the country. We didn't show them much mercy."

The spring of 1975, a crew, consisting primarily of Melvin's family, branded 150 calves, some calved-out from the 34 cows he purchased from neighbor, Leslie Vantine. He sold calves, wheat, and oats that fall. In order to further increase his cash flow, he worked the sale at the Crawford Livestock Market on Fridays, penning back cattle or moving them to the loading pens when the sale was over.

Bob Jordan had partnered with Melvin on several "doggin'" horses over the years. That winter, the pair loaded the current partner-horse in the trailer and headed for one of the biggest rodeos in the country: The Denver Stock Show. Melvin dogged both of his steers but not quick enough to get to the pay window.

---

[443] Bud Hamaker's father, Jerry, was the son of Paul Hamaker, Iva Hamaker's brother. His family continues to own and operate the ranch his great-grandfather, RSQ, homesteaded.

Melvin dogging. Hazer, Keith Zimmerman. Photo: John Bilby, 1976

"That arena wasn't very big. By the time I cleared the barrier, I were half ways across," Melvin recalled the weekend. "I made two good runs. They were both under 10 seconds, but the "tuffs" were all under 6. A 4.5 won it."

Fourth of July celebrations continued to be held in Crawford. In 1970, Joe and Moni had purchased a home in Crawford. Two months later on July 4, they invited the family to a picnic at their new home. Melvin invited the stock contractor, Bernice Johnson and his crew to come along. Even after the Hourts moved to a small place outside of Crawford, the Fourth of July picnic was held at their house and generally included stock contractors, bull fighters, clowns, and anyone else Melvin invited. Family celebrations always included more than blood relatives.

Cattle prices began a downward spiral in January 1975. In 1974, calves averaged $50.20 per hundredweight. At the end of the 1975, the average price was $27.20 per hundred weight.

"Seventy-three was a good year; seventy-four was even better—as far as cattle prices went. Seventy-five didn't hurt us real bad," Melvin said. "Even in '76, the cattle prices weren't too bad, but the cost of operating was starting to kill us."

The economic crisis that sneaked into the Midwest in the late 1970s was unexpected. In 1970, a great future for agriculture was forecast as demand for farm products increased. That year exports of agricultural products were $6.7 billion (approximately 11 percent of US farm production); nine years later exports rose to $31.9 billion (nearly 22 percent of US production). [444] Soviet Russia bought large quantities of farm products including cattle. As a result, agricultural prices rose much quicker than expenses, which increased farm income. In 1973, farm income reached a record high of $92.1 billion, nearly double the $48.4 billion in 1970.[445] High inflation in the 1970s meant that real capital gains of farm real estate rose about 25 percent a year.[446] Farmland was an attractive investment; demand for it grew rapidly. Many agricultural bankers based their loans on collateral value rather than cash-flow analysis. Much of the time, the land couldn't produce enough to justify the amount of money borrowed against it.[447]

Farm income continued to yo-yo back and forth. Farm income took a massive jump—-from $4900 in 1970 to $12,200 in 1973. Income however, declined to $7800 in 1977, rising to $13,300 in 1979.[448] Credit continued to be almost unlimited through the mid-70s. Agribusinessmen were encouraged to buy new equipment, expand their land holdings, and buy more livestock.

Iowa's Senator Tom Harkin was quoted in 1977: "We had bankers going up and down the road like Fuller Brush salesmen during the 1970s. They couldn't get farmers to borrow enough."

The "day of reckoning" approached.

Melvin was raised to believe hard work paid its own rewards. He thought he could "ride out" the economic depression that was slowly settling across the prairie. He continued working the weekly sale in Crawford on Fridays. He bought calves and fed them in the winter. He calved out his cows and rode and sold horses. He pulled and fixed wind mills. On the weekends, he had time to enjoy the visits of his children and grandchildren. He was particularly determined that Buffy and Bryan, who lived in town, weren't going to be "city kids."

Bryan spent most of his time on a tractor, albeit, in his early years, on one that wasn't always moving. He was about three when he decided to remedy the "static tractor" problem. He climbed into the seat and managed to turn the key. The tractor was chugging towards the side of the shed, when Melvin and Joe noticed it. Joe won the foot race to the runaway machine. He shut the tractor down about two feet from the shed. Melvin shook his head and pocketed the key.

"Granddad never complained about money or anything else. As far as we were concerned, the Home Place was the greatest place on earth. I spent all my time outside with the men. All I really wanted to do was ride in the tractor and drive in the meadow. Grandma had terrible headaches," Bryan Hourt remembered. "In the spring we stopped and picked her sweet peas

---

[444] C. S. Thompson, "Effects of Farmland Market," 19. The statistics in this article were derived from the U.S. Department of Agriculture, *Agriculture Statistics* (1983), 517.
[445] History of the Eighties—FDIC. https://www.fdic.gov/bank/...259_290.
[446] "Land Boom in the Farm Belt," *Forbes* (April 15, 1977), available: LEXIS, Library: NEWS, File: FORBES
[447] C. S. Thompson, *Effects of Farmland Market*, 20. Banking and the Agricultural Problems of the 1980s-FDIC.
[448] C. S. Thompson,. *Effects of Farmland Market*, 19. Banking and the Agricultural Problems of the 1980s-FDIC.

when we went through the canyon. That seemed to make her feel better. She didn't let on that those headaches were really bad, but we knew. We could tell from looking at her eyes. Generally, though, we were sure everything was great."

In hindsight, economists admitted the warning signs were there, but Michael Fitch, vice president of the Wells Fargo's Agribusiness Affairs Division, noted that everyone "concluded that never again were we going to experience depressed farm prices; our biggest challenge was to gear up our productive capacity. As a result, there were tremendous resources placed in agriculture, one of which was credit." [449]

Life in the Nation household, "went on" despite the growing concern gripping agricultural. When Melvin's second son, Bob, married in 1975. Melvin and Moni traveled to Riverton, Wyoming for the wedding. Tucked among carefully recorded figures about costs and gains, Melvin noted that the pair "had a great time. Even took time to stop at 'Hell's Half Acre'[450] to look around."

Janet, Annette, Amy, Buffy, and Bryan in 1979.

---

[449] "In Search of a Solution to the Farm Crisis," ABA Banking Journal (April 1985), available: LEXIS, Library: BANKING, File: ABABJ.

[450] Hell's Half Acre is a steep drop-off about 40 miles west of Casper Wyoming. In historical documents it has been known as "The Devil's Kitchen," "The Pits of Hades," and "The Baby Grand Canyon." A cowboy is credited with naming it "Hell's Half Acre" because it is full of boggy areas and alkali. When Melvin and Moni stopped a small gift offered "touristy" items from its position above the 320-acre area. They didn't buy anything, just looked.

Melvin pulling a Christmas tree up out of the canyons.

Christmas continued to be an important event. Thelma decorated the house. A Christmas tree hunt produced trees for every family. The cedar trees, wind tossed for years on Nebraska hillsides, all featured one flat side. Placed against a wall and decorated with bright baubles and bubble lights, it still exuded the Christmas spirit. Joe and Moni spent Christmas Eve at the Nations. Santa Claus never failed to deliver Buffy and Bryan's presents to the ranch. The Oldakers arrived Christmas Day morning. The adults took the grandkids sledding; then they shot blue rocks. In his tally book, Melvin reported, "it was a good day."

Although neither Thelma nor Joe ever spent much time on a horse, they were convinced to take an excursion to the Hunter Hills in 1976. The goal: an encounter with the wild horses.

"We drove cattle up the hill for many years, but few ever saw the wild horses," Moni Hourt said. "We shoved cattle through the gate, and if we were lucky we saw a flash of color through the trees. We knew we "almost saw the horses, but that was as close as we ever came. I had a new camera. I wanted to get pictures of the horses."

Moni called Bill Coffee. He said they were welcome to go up to the Hunter Hills. Melvin agreed to be the tour guide. Thelma packed a lunch. Melvin found horses for everyone, and they headed across the tree-studded plateau.

"The horses actually found us," Moni Hourt said. "They came out of the trees to check out the strange horses. I shot three or four pictures, then they were gone again. Dad said they were a crooked-legged bunch, but all of us, including Dad, thought they were beautiful. They had been there since about 1890 and were the only wild horse herd in Nebraska. No one cared if they were a little crooked legged."

The horses faded off into the trees, then in a burst of color and noise, the entire herd plunged down into the canyons. The crew headed across the countryside to go out on the point above Coffee Wall. As they came over a small hill, they saw several colts scattered, dead beside a meandering track. Someone obviously chased the horses down and killed them.

"Dad called Bill; he confronted the men who were leasing the pasture," Moni Hourt said. "He gave them a week to get their cattle off the ridge. They didn't remind him that they still had several years left on their lease."

Thelma rented a house in Crawford[451] the fall of '75 and boarded a local high school student. That winter she quit her job at the sale barn, but continued working at the Eagles Club. Melvin

---

[451] The house, on the east side of the viaduct, was located about ½ block north of the house that Iva and Earl Nation owned in Crawford.

Melvin, Thelma, Ed, Robbin, and Joe riding away from the Hunter Mill in 1976 and visiting during lunch.

The wild horse herd in 2008, before many were destroyed by fire (left). (Right) Horses in 1976.

said Thelma played her organ at *O'Doherty's*[452] several times that winter. He was pleased that people liked listening to her.[453]

The "town house" was a convenient "stop off" for the family. Buffy and Bryan visited regularly. JimBob spent several nights a week in Crawford, then drove to Harrison for high school classes. Melvin came in when he wasn't busy. However, Thelma moved back to the ranch after Melvin's accident.

"He was ridin' a colt, checking the cows in the north pasture. The damn thing "blew up," Thelma said an edge in her tone. "Sure as hell a good thing, it wasn't 20 below."

---

[452] Thelma took her organ to town with her. Melvin and Joe transported it to O'Doherty's, a restaurant in Crawford, so she could play it. The O'Doherty's restaurant was established by Tom Spence in the old Midwest Hardware building on Main Street. His family had originally owned the building and produced an early version of the *Northwest Nebraska Post*. The KKK met in the basement of the building. Their robes, masks, and pamphlets were on display in the basement next the Spence's wine cellar.

[453] One year Thelma also played her organ at the Crawford Fourth of July rodeo.

The horse bucked in a small circle, punishing his rider by slamming him back and forth between the horn and swells. Melvin finally threw himself free, but not before he tore the groin muscles in both legs. It took him nearly two hours to crawl back to the house. Thelma said it was easier to drive back and forth instead of worrying all the time.

That summer, the Nations went to California to visit Thelma's parents. According to Melvin's tally book, the weeklong trip was a "good one," but he was glad to be home when it was over. "Too damn many people out there, reminds me of a bunch of ants."

In the fall of 1976, cattle prices rebounded. Melvin noted that he sold JimBob's heifers for $46.80. His heifers averaged $37 and his steers sold for $42. He reported he sold $50,000 worth of cattle that year and bought calves to replenish his herd. He planted more wheat, corn, and oats and brought the hay, cut on shares on the Fort Robinson pastures, home to feed the stock. Interest rates stayed around 7 percent most of the year.

Leather work filled brightly wrapped Christmas boxes that year. Thelma and JimBob stamped the leather. Melvin used the same technique he used to braid endless reins for bridles, to create braided handles for the purses Moni and Robbin received. He used an awl to make the holes that fastened them together. Buffy excitedly wrapped her hand-tooled belt around her waist. When Melvin remarked it was a little big, she swore she would grow into it. Thelma's knitting skills produced sweaters that neither Bryan nor Annette would remove, even for a nap. In his tally book, Melvin remarked that it was another good Christmas with all his family there.

JimBob (far left in jacket) and members of his FFA class constructing greenhouse.

JimBob's Sioux County High School FFA class constructed a greenhouse at the ranch. Thelma filled it with flowers, garden produce—-and doves. The doves soon produced eggs and baby doves. In time, several generations of doves called the greenhouse home. In one tally book entry, Melvin said the doves "sang all the time, but didn't bother him any."

Most weekends, the couple traveled to JimBob's high school rodeos and watched him spur several bulls into the winning circle. Melvin reported that JimBob "set a tough bull." He, himself, competed in area Old Timer's Rodeos that summer. He didn't win anything, but

Melvin and Bruce Quintard helping JimBob draw his rope at a Crawford, NE steer riding in 1977.

enjoyed "visiting with old friends." Several times that year, Melvin was asked to pick-up bucking horses when young cowboys were trying bucking horses. He also picked up bucking horses at the Fourth of July Rodeo. The Fourth of July picnics at the Hourt's house continued and gave Melvin and Thelma time to visit with old friends, many with whom Melvin had competed in year past.

Woven between the mundane entries about family and friends, Melvin's tally book revealed his worry. By 1977, record crops sent prices into a downward spiral; the cost of fuel, feed, and taxes rose rapidly. Calf prices averaged $37 nationwide. Agriculture income in Nebraska dropped to $20 billion. The value of land, the "equity" that farmers used to secure loans dropped. The interest rate continued to creep upwards. In August the Sioux National Bank in Harrison called Melvin and said they could no longer lend him money to buy cattle.

"Things weren't very shiny, but I couldn't quit," Melvin crossed his arms, momentarily looking back with sadness, then he sat up straighter and reached for his coffee cup, "besides, there was a good hay crop that year."

Complete dispersals of several cattle herds took place at the sale barns across the region that fall. Some three and four-generation farms and ranches faced bankruptcy. One Nebraska rancher died after falling from the top of a windmill. His death was deemed an accident, but rumors swirled that the family ranch was facing foreclosure. In the eastern part of the state, nickel auctions were organized to save farms. Law enforcement moved in but the sales continued.

That winter, Melvin agreed to winter 500 calves for Windy Connell of Whitney. Bud Hamaker said he helped move cattle between pastures.

John Vantine, Elvin Staman, Melvin Nation and Bud Hamaker drive cattle near Crawford, NE.

"When my Dad died in 1969, Melvin helped me work my cattle all one spring," Bud said. "I really hadn't trailed many cattle, so he taught me a lot. That winter, when I had time, I helped him and JimBob move the calves around."

Bud wasn't with Melvin the day he and JimBob encountered the low- flying plane, but he heard about it—in great detail. Melvin was grinning when he told Bud that the 300 yearlings were within 10 feet of the gate when he noticed the plane flying about 100-feet off the ground. The pilot fluttered his wings as if waving, then circled and dove toward the cattle, scattering them to the "four winds."

"The plane was low enough that Melvin saw the ID numbers," Bud recounted. "He said he memorized the numbers so he could report the pilot when he got back to the house. But it took another hour to gather the cattle. And by that time he was "over his mad." He just grinned when he told me he probably would have done the same damn thing if he'd have been the pilot."

When JimBob wasn't working or spending his time with his friends, he was willing to lead his nieces and nephews on adventures into the canyons beside the sheep pasture. One afternoon the explorers found a meadowlark's nest. They watched the nest for several minutes until the meadowlark returned, a grasshopper clenched in her bill. Buffy Hourt said the hike through the canyons to the dam seemed to take forever. Once they reached the water, they strolled around it and even skipped a few rocks across it, then JimBob reminded them that they should never, ever, come to the dam alone. Buffy said they couldn't have found it anyway, not at least, until they gained a few years.

JimBob also showed his nieces and nephews how to climb up on the gas tanks beside the chicken house, "clammer" onto the chicken house, then run across the shed to the barn. They were never able to climb on top of the barn, but they could scale the narrow steps inside the barn, throw open the loft door and look out over the place. Their lofty perch seemed to be thousands of feet above the ground; it was barely 10.

Despite the condoned adventuring, there were areas of the farm deemed off limits. Buffy Hourt said she was walking on planks across the pig pen, when her granddad caught her. "He yelled at me," Buffy said. "It scared me so bad that I almost fell into the pen. Granddad never yelled at me. I was devastated. He helped me down and explained that the pigs were dangerous. I never went to the pig pen again."

The picture of Bryan and Melvin in Melvin's wheat field in 1978 appeared on the cover of the Nebraska Farmer magazine.

Paying down the debt and maintaining the ranch dominated Melvin's life. He carefully recorded costs and gains and sale information. He purchased livestock that he felt could turn a profit. Then he and a partner contracted to buy a pair of combines and started doing custom combining. He saw the combines as a solid investment, one that might "balance this thing out."

The 1978 front cover of the *Nebraska Farmer* magazine featured a picture of Melvin and his grandson, five-year-old Bryan Hourt, kneeling in a partially-cut wheat field. The image captured the pair busily discussing yield and quality. In his tally book that summer, Melvin noted that Bryan spent entire days riding in the combine with him and "never let out a whimper."

"I never tired of it," Bryan said. "I was so fascinated with the machinery, the movement, even the sounds around me. I sat there beside him and went 'round and 'round. Grandpa always explained how everything worked. Between him and Dad, they could fix anything. I can remember going to town for part, but I don't remember taking things to town very often to get it fixed. We tore it apart and made it run again. They seldom told me to get out of the way." He grinned. "I did get into trouble for laying stuff down instead of putting it in my pocket where I could find it."

Joe Hourt and Melvin examine a pipe at the Home Place. When Melvin went to Crawford he generally stopped at Joe's Body Shop.

Janet Oldaker Victory drew this picture of Ed Oldaker and Melvin in 2009. The original photo was taken by Connie Nunn Brost.

Years later, Cody Oldaker[454] said Melvin told him he "lucked out with his sons-in-law." "He said he liked both of them, and they were always there when he needed help," Cody remembered. "Grandpa said Joe could fix any machine; Ed was good 'ahorseback.' He said they "got along." He was really proud of that."

Although the tally pages continued to record everyday life, outside its pages, the economic crisis continued to threaten. Most of the agricultural loans across the nation and in Nebraska were issued on a variable rate. The Prime Lending Rate[455] in May of 1973 was seven percent—up two percentage points from the year before. By September of 1977, it rose to 10 percent. The Federal Reserve Board tightened its monetary policy to fight inflation in 1979. Higher interest rates resulted. By October of 1979, interest rates reached 14 percent; by December the rates were 15.25. The soaring rates shattered an already ravaged agricultural economy.

"The bankers told me I had nothing to worry about—that rates had only varied a fraction of a point since 1970," an Iowa farmer who was forced to declare bankruptcy was reported to have said. "My rate went from 7 percent to 18.5 percent in less than a year."[456]

Cattle prices rose from $36.50 in the early 70s to $74 in 1979, then fell to $69 in 1980. The unstable cattle prices made it difficult to make a profit—unless you owned a crystal ball. To make it even more challenging, by February of 1980, the prime interest rate hit 16.75. Some farm loans renewed at 20 percent. A hundred years earlier, in 1878, pioneer rancher, CF Coffee, reported that interest rates were 24 percent in Texas. He said he was glad to pay that because interest was 36 percent in Cheyenne.[457] However, he was paying $5 a head for cattle and sold them for $25 or more in Cheyenne. A profit margin was possible. The same was not true in 1979.

---

[454] Melvin and Thelma raised Cody Oldaker, the Nation's oldest great-grandson.

[455] Prime lending rate is the term applied to bank loans to favored customers, ones with good credit, or ones who borrow millions of dollars. Most of the rates in Nebraska in the '70s were higher than the prime rate.

[456] Easterbrook, Making Sense of Agriculture. Atlantic Monthly Archives, July 1985.

[457] Letter from CF Coffee to Harry Crain. *Letters from Old Friends and Members of the Wyoming Stockgrowers Association*. Wyoming Stockgrower's Association: 1923.

"My grandfather died in 1978," Gary Witt said. "By that time, we were already in trouble. The banker promised Dad[458] that he'd be ok, that he'd stay with him, then he called him in and told him he wouldn't give him any more money—to do anything. Dad sold the cow herd he put together for us boys in 1975, his, a couple of years later. In 1979, the folks' house burned down. By 1980 he was out of options. He sold out."

Standing: Clark,, Melvin, Elvin, and Merlin Nation. Seated: Mildred Widel, Frances Roberts, Eva Gray, Anita Robison, (nephew), Ronnye Widel. The cake, created by Moni Hourt was built in the shape of the house at the Home Place.

Despite the financial instability that swirled through the country, Melvin reported that he thoroughly enjoyed the Nation family reunions held over the years. The 1978 reunion, as did many family events, ended in a wild water fight—Melvin's specialty.

The event alleviated the worry—for a few hours. "Good time with my brothers and sisters and their kids," Melvin wrote. "We never forget we're family."

Although many area ranchers paid more interest, Melvin reported he was paying 14.5 percent at the end of 1979. Thelma helped him produce a spread sheet that listed every expense and every sale. It showed that his heifer calves averaged $337.09, his steers $400.19. Cattle profit increased by $10 a head that year. Costs doubled.

---

[458] At the turn of the century, Art Witt homesteaded about a mile from the Nation farm. His grandsons, Mike and Gary were the third generation on the farm.

JimBob on a bull in 1985.

JimBob graduated from high school in 1979. Melvin remarked that his son should go to college and thought he would succeed if he applied himself. A line later he wrote that he was afraid JimBob preferred rodeoing to books. Many weekends, Melvin joined his son, Bud Hamaker, and Rocky Rising as they traveled across the state to weekend rodeos. JimBob's love of rodeo increased exponentially as wins increased. He placed in enough competitions that summer to qualify for the Nebraska State Rodeo Association Finals.

Labor Day weekend, 1980, the family skipped the rodeos and watched Bryan's first motorcycle race. In a photograph printed in *The Crawford Clipper*, Bryan can be seen topping a small hill. Leaning against a nearby fence, Melvin was caught mid-smile, enjoying his grandson's efforts.

Moni started working for the local newspaper in October 1979. Melvin suggested she do a story on Bill Coffee and his Brangus cattle and was pleased when it was published not only in the newspaper, but also by a cattleman's magazine. He further supported her efforts by

JimBob, Melvin, Bob Pliley, Joe, Thelma, and Buffy watch Bryan top a hill.

allowing her to shoot a set of pictures for a two-page spread entitled, "What is a Rancher?" The battle to keep the ranch solvent continued, but in Melvin's words, "life also goes on."

President Jimmy Carter declared an embargo on grain sales to the Soviet Union in January 1980. Grain prices instantly plummeted. Farmers organized strikes. Although the embargo became the symbolic cause of the farm crisis of the 80s, US grain exports actually rose during the embargo because grain sales to other countries increased. Carter also promoted the development of ethanol as a power source, which produced a new market for corn. But whatever the positive effects that may have actually occurred, the psychological impact of the embargo increased fear in the agriculture community.

In 1996, Everett Thomas discussed the cattle industry of the 1980s. "Prices for cattle go down about every 10 years. But in the '80s, cattle prices weren't the only problem. The cost of operating went up. Interest went up. Taxes went up. People had borrowed on their land and land values fell. They couldn't repay their loans. You heard more about the farmers than the ranchers, but a lot of ranchers didn't survive either."

The Sioux National Bank in Harrison changed ownership in 1979. The new owner immediately launched foreclosing procedures against several area ranchers. He often demanded that they sell their herds and in some cases their land.

"The new owner was a bastard," Joe Whiteaker, a former Sioux National Bank employee, said—forcefully. "He seemed determined to destroy agriculture in our area. Many ranchers left the bank and went to Chadron or to the Valley.[459] In one case, the bastard banker lined up trucks and men to go get a rancher's cattle, but the rancher declared bankruptcy before the trucks could get there. That stopped the hotshot banker in his tracks. Two years later, the rancher sold his cattle and paid the bank everything he owned, then he told the banker what he thought of him. His ears were ringing for a month. Served the bastard right."

Although he continued to work the Crawford sale, Melvin bought few cattle. He did sell several dry cows and a few yearlings, but decided training and selling horses could possibly offset the falling cattle prices. He sold two young geldings that year for $1000 each.[460] For the first time in his adult life, he wasn't working "24-7." In the spring he decided to run for a political office.

Melvin said he ran for the Commissioner's seat because he had a little time to work with.

---

[459] Many area ranchers started banking in Scottsbluff, Mitchell, or Morrill, Nebraska.
[460] Equivalent to $3586 each in 2020.

Melvin, second from right, and Randy Rising stand at attention for the national anthem.

"I feel like Sioux County residents deserve to make a change if they want to," Melvin was quoted as saying in the March 27, 1980 issue of The Crawford Clipper. "If I am elected, I'll do as good a job as my ability and the county budget permits." With that statement, Melvin filed as a Republican for the Sioux County Commissioner's seat. His opponent, Republican Elmer (Tug) Pullen, recently retired from a ranch near the Home Place. He was running for his ninth term as a county commissioner. Melvin garnered the most votes during the primary race. During the general election Melvin received 668 votes. Pullen received 125 write-in votes.

"I really didn't understand how the county was run," Melvin said. "I had a little time on my hands, so I thought I might as well learn."

That Fourth of July Melvin and JimBob, during an exhibition, helped Randy Rising get down on his first PRCA saddle bronc horse. Randy didn't make the whistle, but Melvin said he "put out the effort."

In the fall of 1980, before he became too involved in his newly-elected political position, Melvin, Steve Reece, and Harold Glendy and his son, Tim, organized an elk-hunting trip to the Ruby River, west of Yellowstone National Park. Gary Stansbury joined them as the "camp cook." The hunters each threw 200 dollars into a bread sack to pay for expenses. They hooked onto a couple of camping trailers, loaded their horses in stock trailers, and headed toward Hog Back Mountain near Livingston, Montana. Their destination: grazing association land near the west entrance of Yellowstone National Park. The Association grazing permit on the land belonged to Nate Todd's parents.[461] The Todds offered to host the elk-hunting crew. In return the hunters agreed to help move the Todd's cattle off the association land.

"We spent the first three days moving cattle," Tim Glendy said during a 2019 interview. "Altogether we were up there about 10 days. There was about three feet of snow on the ground; several nights the temperature dropped to six below. Steve and I slept in a tent. Melvin and Gary slept in the one camping trailer, Dad and two of our friends from Lincoln stayed in the other trailer. Most of the elk had already moved down out of the mountains, but we had a great time looking for what was still there."

---

[461] Todd, moved to Crawford to open a saddlery shop in 1979. While building Melvin a saddle, he and Melvin struck up a friendship.

Melvin told his grandson, Bryan, that even "elkless" jaunts across the mountain trails were incredibly beautiful, but after a week, the human odor rising from the nightly campfire was 'pretty rank.' "Grandpa took a bath about every night; after a week, he couldn't stand it. He grabbed a bar of soap and headed for the river."

"Steve filled a dishpan with water and washed some of his stink off; Melvin just stripped down and plowed into the river. It was damn cold. The water started freezing around him. We pulled him out before he froze solid. He was pretty shrunk-up, but he smelled better than we did," Tim Glendy laughed.

Trees and brush densely covered the mountain side; huge boulders forced the hunters to veer from paths partially obscured with piles of snow. "Melvin always knew where he was," Glendy added. "At the end of the day, he made a "bee line" toward the camp. We learned not to question him. We never did figure out why the kid that stumbled into our camp one night got lost, but he sure didn't have his directions straight."

The young teenager, part of a group of hunters camped below the Nebraska crew panicked his way into the Nebraskan's camp late one night. "He was scared to death. He'd tied his horse to a tree somewhere on the mountainside, but didn't know where. He was cold, terrified, and positive he was facing death. We gathered him up and took him back to his camp," Glendy said. "They'd been looking for him for hours, but hadn't even run into us. It was easy to get lost up there. Gary went to town to get supplies and spent a day wandering around trying to find us again. Melvin was about the only one who always knew where we were and how to get back to camp."

On the last day of the hunt, Melvin spotted a buck standing hidden in the trees. He didn't dismount. He grabbed his Remington 700-270, poked it in the right direction and fired. The horse, probably a little shell-shocked, chose not to throw a fit. The elk tumbled off the ridge, slid to a stop against a large pine, and bled out. The men gutted the animal. It was two miles to camp.

"I tied a rope to the elk's hind legs, but my horse couldn't pull him. Melvin was riding a big red sorrel. He pulled his rope down, took a couple loops around the elk's horns and took off down the hill," Glendy recounted. "I climbed on top of the elk to help guide him through the snow. Sometimes it was a wild slide. Ever so often, his horns would catch in some brush. It took a while to get back to camp. That was the only elk we shot, but it was sure a fun trip."

Melvin had the hide tanned and gave each member of the expedition a pair of elk-hide gloves. They shared the meat and the ivory from the elk's teeth. Bessie Ward[462] said Melvin brought her a sack of the elk venison to thank her family for the use of their Airstream camping trailer.

---

[462] Bessie Ward, Benny Ward's wife, personal interview with Moni Hourt, 2019.

"Grandpa talked about that trip a lot," Cody Oldaker said. "He was the only one that got an elk. He loved the mountains, but that was the only time he ever spent much time in them."

A feature story in the October 1980 *Northwest Nebraska Post* didn't mention the elk hunt. It focused on Melvin's 40-mile cattle drive from the ranch to the Crawford Livestock Market.[463] "The cost of fuel has driven the price of trucking sky high this fall," Melvin said in the article. "The cattle market is low. We took it slow and easy and except for the last few hundred feet, the trip was an easy one. I think they arrived in better condition and didn't shrink as much as they would have if we would've trucked them in. It took a little more time, but the extra time made us money."

The trip stretched over two days, so the men spent one night in the pasture supervising the 125 yearlings. Kenny Daugherty told the *Post* reporter that, "It got a little chilly before morning and that ground wasn't padded too good. Luckily the cattle didn't drift too bad, and we caught the horses pretty easy the next morning. Melvin always said he would have liked to have been a drover on those long cattle drives from Texas. I wouldn't."

Melvin discusses the drive with Doug Strotheide of the Crawford Livestock Market.

When the cattle entered the city limits, they weren't sure they wanted to complete the journey. Melvin said it was a good thing extra riders had joined them that morning. "When they

---

[463] The Livestock Market had recently been purchased by Doug Strotheide who accepted the cattle at the stock yards.

caught the scent of town they stopped. One spook and we might still be riding the town looking for strays. The extra help made a big difference."

At the conclusion of the story, Melvin said many people told him the trip couldn't be done. He took a great deal of satisfaction in proving them wrong.

Melvin refused to be intimidated by the times. In December, he and Chris Hamaker drove their horses to old District #33 at the top of Deep Creek, and for the third year in a row took the neighborhood children and their parents Christmas tree hunting. Thirty-five people attended the event that was recorded in the December 24, 1980 issue of The Crawford Clipper.

Buffy Hourt said it was about 20-degrees that day, but the temperature didn't matter. "What I remember most was the ice frosting the trees. Even the sky seeped a shimmering veil of frost. I wished the ice would stay on our tree after we took it into the house, but of course, I knew it wouldn't."

In search of Christmas trees, Melvin drives a team across a ice-frosted prairie.

On December 19, 1980, the Federal Reserve instituted a tight-money policy in an attempt to reduce inflation that had hit 12 percent. As a result, the US Prime Interest rate hit a historic high: 21.50 percent.[464] The value of agricultural land in Nebraska fell 46 percent.[465] The farming crisis of the 1980s accelerated the reduction in farm population in the Great Plains. In 1935, there had been 6.8 million farms. By the mid-1980s there were 2.2 million. Farmers across the nation hauled their tractors to their respective state capitals and even to Washington D.C. and

---

[464] In 1985, the prime rate fell to 10 percent, but throughout the mid-80s if fluctuated between 20 and 12.75 percent. In 1991, the rate hovered between 6 and 10 percent, but it would be 10 years later before the rate stayed below 10 percent.
[465] Timothy B. Clark, "Borrowing Trouble," National Journal 17, no. 36 (September 7, 1985), available: LEXIS, Library: NEWS, File: NTLJNL.

rallied to support a nationwide farmer's strike. Several men in Great Plains states committed suicide; two men killed their families before taking their own lives. Subsidies for farmers were increased.[466] Farm Aid concerts led by Willie Nelson heightened public awareness of the family farmers' plight and raised money for farm support groups. The concert in Lincoln in 1987 raised nearly 1 million dollars to help farmers across the state

Ranchers seldom participated in the strikes, received few subsidies, and did not benefit from Farm Aid. Farm sizes are measured in hundreds of acres. Ranches in the Great Plains are measured in thousands of acres. Few outsiders realize that it takes 10-20 acres to sustain a cow-calf pair for one year, or that insurance plans (at that time) didn't cover the loss of a dozen calves or cows that died in a blizzard. Most city dwellers did not understand that ranchers often borrowed thousands of dollars a year to buy land, cattle, and to maintain their operation. Many saw the "thousands of acres" as an asset without realizing the only way to really "cash in" on the land was to sell it, which of course, destroyed the ranching operation and its place in the agricultural community.

Across the Great Plains, many ranches became hunting operations, summer retreats for wealthy city dwellers, or tax write-offs for investors who took advantage of the low land prices. Ted Turner began his acquisition of nearly two million acres[467] of ranch land in 1987 with the purchase of 23,000-acre Bar None ranch in Montana. In the next 30 years he acquired 290,000 acres in Nebraska. After paying nearly 17.6 million for an 88,000-acres ranch in the Sandhills, The Church of Jesus Chris of Latter-day Saints became the second largest landowner in the state.

A *North Platte Bulletin* article published in 2007, quoted John Hansen, president of the Nebraska Farmers Union of North Platte. He said, "The deep pocket of out-of-state interests put smaller landowners—who need to borrow money to buy land—at a disadvantage. Smaller ranches are not able to make as much of a profit while paying off debt. That leads to some ranches being consolidated and ultimately the disappearance of rural communities."[468]

Rural communities not affected by investors like Turner, were still affected by the financial struggles in the agriculture industry. However, many rural businesses like Brewster's Market, Harrison's only grocery store, continued to support their agricultural customers. Robbin Oldaker said Milford Brewster "carried them" for six months. He never indicated that the extended credit was an imposition.

---

[466] Unfortunately, it was often the big farmers who received the major portion of the subsidies. In 1980, it was determined that 17 percent of the farmers received 60 percent of all agriculture subsidies. 26. "Farm Policy," *America*, v151, September 22, 1984-138.
[467] He is the largest land owner in Nebraska with 290,000 acres. The state has 50 million total acres. The Mormon church is now the second largest land owner in Nebraska with nearly 228,000 acres.
[468] Ducey, James. "Ted Turner snags up more Nebraska land." North Platte Bulletin, October 4, 2016.

"We were working for a rancher north of Harrison. He ran our cows for us, paid our utilities on our house, and paid us a small wage," Robbin Oldaker remembered. "We were able to sell our calves to an organic feeder that year and made some decent money. The man who we worked for held his cattle; the market went to pieces. He couldn't pay us. We couldn't find another job. We didn't even have the money to buy groceries."

Milford Brewster greeted them with a smile and more importantly, respect, every time they came in the store. He recorded their grocery costs on a card that he placed in a file box. Six months later, Robbin said they sold some calves and paid the $600 bill.

Joe Hourt started his own auto-body business in Crawford in April 1985. He said he quickly learned that rural customers who needed a broken door handle fixed or a horse trailer rewired were every bit as important as a customer with a big insurance job. In 2014, he told a high school careers' class that the farmers and ranchers were the backbone of a small agricultural community like Crawford. "When someone comes to work for me, I tell them if they aren't willing to work on an outfit covered in a little mud or manure, they might as well keep on going. When finances were really tough during the 80s, sometimes farmers and ranchers paid their bill a little at a time. Sometimes I'd wait until they sold some cattle. Sometimes they didn't have the money to get an outfit fixed. When that happened, we didn't make any money either. We're an agricultural community. We all depend on each other. That's every bit as true now as it was when I started in the business in 1969."[469]

Ronald Regan became president January 20, 1981. That same day, Iran released the 52 Americans they'd held in captivity since November 1979. Geologist discovered uranium under Crawford. Melvin's tally book didn't record any of those events. He was much more worried that there wasn't any rain that year until the last week of May. "Don't know how Dad had the courage to keep planting wheat," Melvin wrote in his tally book. "I guess you just do."

Logging hundreds of miles across Sioux County to evaluate the conditions of the roads, Melvin concentrated on being a county commissioner. His 1981 calendar reported bi-weekly, fact-finding trips. He attended county commissioner meetings and often made a trip to Scottsbluff or Chadron to get parts for the road crew. He mentioned how much he was learning about county finances and road conditions.

Later that summer, he and Thelma drove to Riverton, Wyoming. They visited Melvin's son, Bob and his family, then went on to Lander where he competed in an Old-Timer's rodeo. The next week he noted that he competed in Hyannis. His family cheered him on, but he said he didn't compete well either weekend. In his tally book, he mentioned that he saw Tuffy Bridge[470] at the Lander rodeo and that they had a "good visit."

---

[469] Joe was hired by Ed Petersen in 1969 and worked for Ed's Body Shop in Crawford until 1985.
[470] Tuffy Bridge rodeod with Melvin and at one time worked at the Hoover Ranch.

After throwing a successful head loop, Melvin waits for Keal to snag the steer's heels.

There was no one home with whom to visit the Sunday afternoon the Hourt and Nation families made a friendly neighborhood call at the "Hippie Cabin." Few in the region had talked to the man who built the cabin located in a deep canyon a short distance from the "Walker Hill's" pasture. Court House personnel told Melvin that the man wore his long hair in a ponytail and generally wore a denim jacket and jeans. The cabin itself, resembled a stereotypical fairy cabin of angled walls and tilted roof panels. Stained glass covered a few of the lower windows, other panes were tinted a pale yellow. On the Sunday visit, the family knocked dutifully at the door, examined the cabin's exterior, then explored the trampled clearing in which it sat. Finally, their curiosity satisfied, they returned to the pickup parked beyond the fence line that created the boundary between the small acreage and Melvin's pasture. Several years later, the cabin's owner, a drug dealer who owned homes in Hawaii and other areas of the United States, including Sioux County, was arrested and charged with federal drug trafficking charges. A diary found in one of his homes, provided directions to hidden stashes of money and gold, some of it on the Nebraska land. When drug agents explored the cabin area, they unearthed several plastic tubs filled with gold coins and bullion worth thousands of dollars.[471]

Despite enjoying a few "lighter" moments that year, Melvin's primary focus was turning a profit. In the fall of 1980, he bought 50 bred heifers, 220 head of heifer calves, and 121 steer calves. In the spring of 1981, he branded 125 calves. He also paid 16 percent interest that year.

---

[471] On the front page of an October 31, 1985 *Crawford Clipper*, the local reporter wrote that a Denver man, William Munson, 41, "who owns 640 acres in Sioux County" had hidden a fortune of gold on the grounds where he had also built a small cabin. The gold packed tightly in "Tupperware" containers had an approximate value of $49,000. The man was eventually sent to prison.

When a flower shop on Crawford's Second Street came up for sale in 1982 at 10 percent interest, Thelma purchased it. Her family helped her move it across the street to a recently vacated building. Patty Staman, the business's previous owner, spent two weeks teaching Thelma the basics of flower arrangement. In a June 10, 1982 newspaper article about "Baskets and Bokays" Thelma said she would be getting assistance from her granddaughter, Buffy, and her sister, Velma Rising.

Baskets and Bokays advertisement in The Crawford Clipper.

She added she was really excited about developing the new business. In his tally book, Melvin noted that he and Joe had a "helluva-journey getting the damn cooler moved," and he "sure hoped she could make this work."

"Grandma made incredibly beautiful arrangements," Buffy Hourt-Allred remembered. "They were very unique. It didn't take long before she built up a good business. She showed me how to make corsages and arrangements. I'm sure I wasted more flowers than I was worth, but she just encouraged me to keep trying."

"When we came to Crawford, we always went to the flower shop," Janet Oldaker said. "Grandma would let us play with the left-over flowers. We thought we were pretty big stuff."

The flower shop provided some entertaining work experiences, but the Friday livestock sale

During the Fourth of July parade in Crawford, Annette Oldaker, to advertise "Baskets and Bokays," drove a three-wheeler attached to a wagon full of siblings. They threw flowers and candy to the parade goers.

In 1982, Melvin took his team to town and gave wagon-rides to local residents. Kenny Daugherty, a long-time friend and hired hand, rode shot-gun.

produced some interesting ones for the Hourt children that fall. Melvin continued to work the sales—most Fridays. If the price was right, he'd buy a calf or two and drop it at the Hourt's small place west of Fort Robinson. [472]

"We hurried home from school Fridays because we were anxious to see how many calves were in the corral," Bryan Hourt said. "We paid $25 for some of them, but they were generally sickly or really young. They were hard to keep alive. The $50 to $75 calves were a lot healthier. We got up every morning and fed them, then fed them again before supper. Amazingly most of them survived. We ended up with 12 calves that first winter. I still love the smell of calf manna."

"I suppose we tired of feeding calves, but mostly I remember how much fun they were," Buffy Hourt-Allred smiled. "I always thought cows produced calves; that fall I discovered that calves were the product of Granddad Nation and a Friday sale."

The Crawford Jaycees scheduled a hayride the Saturday before Christmas, 1982. Melvin, Chris Hamaker, and Arnold Johnson hauled their teams to town to provide wagon rides to area residents. The newspaper reported the wagons stopped at the Ponderosa Villa nursing home and gave nearly 75 rides during the night.

Although Thelma rented a house in town in the fall of 1982, Christmas was held in the country. That afternoon, Melvin saddled his horse, tied one end of his rope to an old car hood, then dallied the other end around his saddle horn. He spent the next couple hours pulling his grandchildren through the snow. Then anyone who wanted to test their marksmanship skills, shot blue rocks. Melvin won hands down, but Robbin did very well. In her journal, Moni admitted that she didn't think the local wildlife or the blue rocks had anything to fear.

JimBob enrolled in college in the fall of 1982, but decided he wasn't cut out to be a student. He left college after the first semester. The Sioux County road crew hired him as part of their maintainer crew. He found that he loved the challenge of driving the big machinery and producing wash-board free county roads. Melvin reported that Jim "was good with a maintainer."

Land foreclosures and farm sales continued to fill newspapers. In an attempt to preserve the family farm and prevent large corporations from establishing mega-farms and ranches, the Nebraska legislation proposed Initiative 300. The Nebraska Livestock Feeders' Association

---

[472] The Hourts purchased seven acres two miles from Fort Robinson in 1982.

lobbied for modification or dismissal of the Initiative, but it was placed on the ballot in the fall of 1982 and carried by a margin of 60,000 votes. The establishment of large cattle and hog feeding operations in the state was curtailed. [473]

The cost of feeding his own cattle and using extra feed to winter calves for other ranchers was penciled on the lines of Melvin's tally book. Despite his dislike of farming, he continued to raise wheat and oats. In addition to haying his own fields, he did custom haying. Bryan Hourt said he was 10 when Melvin started taking him with him to the fields.

"If we were in the hay field, we stopped by the house and fixed ourselves some lunch," Bryan Hourt said. "Grandad made sure we arrived at the house in time to watch his soap opera, "As the World Turns."[474] I didn't think that was strange, because Grandpa did it. I figured anything he did was what should be done."

Combining oats or wheat occupied several weeks of Melvin's summer calendar. The fields were located across the Panhandle. At times, Melvin and Bryan packed a lunch on the way to the fields, but most of the time they just threw a cooler in the pickup.

"Granddad threw a 50-pack of hot dogs and some beer in the cooler," Bryan remembered. "He brought a water jug for me, but he drank beer and ate weenies. He told me once that he really loved weenies. I preferred a sandwich, but I ate a lot of weenies when I was with Grandpa."

Bryan skipped school in March of 1983 to help Melvin move cattle from land near Andrews, Nebraska, to the sale barn. Photographs identify several other riders on the trip including John Vantine, JimBob Nation, Ed Oldaker, and Kenny Daugherty. Joe Hourt, who seldom rode a horse, was also convinced to make the journey. He said he "walked funny" for a week.

The agricultural communities surrounding Crawford and Harrison were teetering on disaster, but as often happened during their lives, the Nation family took one day at a time.

Before Mother's Day in the spring of 1983, Thelma and Buffy filled orders until 4 a.m. The shop was in a shambles. Melvin wrote in his tally book, that Joe and Bryan slipped into the shop early Sunday morning and cleaned the work room. When Thelma arrived, dreading the shop cleanup, she found it was spotless. Until she sold the shop in 1986, Bryan and Joe continued to clean the shop for her as their Mother's Day present.

"We couldn't very well send her flowers," Joe Hourt explained looking over his glasses. "But I think she liked having a clean shop better than she wanted flowers."

"I learned to drive a stick shift that next summer," Even after thirty years, Bryan Hourt's voice was edged in pride. "Granddad would take me out in the fields and turn me loose. JimBob used to give me a bad time when I missed a gear, but Grandpa always told me I'd get it."

---

[473] "Crisis in Agriculture, 1975-1999." nebraskastudies.org.
[474] "As the World Turns" was an American television soap opera that played on CBS for 54 years, ending on September 17, 2010. Melvin came to the house at 11:30 a.m. to watch it as often as he could.

JimBob's criticism came back to "bite him" the afternoon he drove the sweep back to the ranch. He failed to slow down when he topped the hill south of the house. Melvin watched from the hill top as the sweep tipped sideways then rolled happily the full length of the slope, skidding through the fence running parallel to the road, and throwing pieces of itself across the prairie. It rocked to a stop in the canyon. JimBob escaped injury. The sweep never left the canyon.

The stress and helplessness of the period was reflected in the rows of figures that filled Melvin's tally book pages. Some rows of numbers were duplicated several times, as if the writer hoped that he made an error in calculations, but the eventual sum didn't change; it teetered toward a negative balance.

After Verna and Elmer Callaham moved to California in 1957, they made regular trips back to Nebraska, generally in the summer months, but in 1983, they returned for Christmas. The next day, Melvin wrote that "poor ole Elmer fell down the damn steps. Got him out of the hospital for Christmas day, but he's buggered up some."

Verna Callaham takes aim at a pool ball while Melvin waits his turn.

Keal and Sis also arrived at Thelma's rented house on Coates Street in Crawford to celebrate Christmas. Pool balls clashed across the pool table. Gossip and laughter permeated the air. "Good day, lots of family," Melvin reported, "sure are a noisy bunch. And that Melvin[475] has more damn energy that a March Hare. Poor ole' Elmer probably didn't feel too shiny, but he seemed to get along ok."

---

[475] Melvin, the youngest grandson was two that Christmas.

Harold Keener challenged Melvin for the County Commission position in the May 1984 primary election. "I feel it's taken me four years to learn the procedures of the office and get an idea of how it is run and what it involves," Melvin was quoted in the May 1984, Special Election Supplement of The Crawford Clipper. "I'd like to work towards better road conditions if funding is available. When I was elected to the position four years ago, I had no idea how much money it takes to maintain and build our roads. I didn't realize how many roads must be maintained in the country. I feel keeping them in top condition is very important but the fact is, there isn't always enough money to do as good a job as we like. There are many other things that must be taken care of also. "

In conclusion, Melvin said that he'd like to finish what he started. When the final vote was cast, Keener ended up on the winning side of the tally. Melvin's political career was over.

In 1980, Cattle prices had averaged $62.40, almost double their average in 1977. They stayed steady for the next four years, but fell drastically to $54.90 per hundred weight in 1985.[476] Ranchers struggled to keep ahead of the market, but so did agriculture lending-institutes. Thirty-three Nebraska banks failed in the 1980s. Many banks changed hands.

The First National Bank[477] in Chadron built its reputation on a commitment to agriculture. Established by rancher, Bartlett Richards, in 1877, the bank was traded to CF Coffee in 1895 for, 2000 head of cows, calves at side, as well as Richards' home in Chadron. In 1985, the First National Bank was no longer owned by the Coffees, but the financial institution perpetuated the idea that its employees protected and guided those with whom they made loans—particularly those in agriculture.

Melvin's daughter Robbin and her husband, Ed, were the first in the family to realize the value of the former "Coffee bank." In 1977, the Oldakers were hired at the Clarence Schnurr ranch north of Harrison. Schnurr ran their small herd of cattle as part of their wages. The interest rates and the volatility of the market made it difficult to "keep their heads above water," but their small herd grew. They managed to meet their financial obligations. Then, in April of 1983, a violent spring blizzard swept across the country. Cattle drifted with the wind and hunkered down under trees above a dam. When the storm abated, Ed, Clarence, and Robbin started looking for their cattle. At first, they thought most of the cattle made it safely through the storm, then they saw the" tromped-out" trail leading toward the dam. In the water below, cows floated. It was soon apparent that nine of the Oldakers' cattle herd of 30 and nearly 20 of Schnurr's drowned in the dam. The dejected crew spent the next few days digging the carcasses out of the water so that the water source wouldn't be contaminated.

---

[476] United States Department of Agriculture.
[477] The Bank in 202 was renamed the Homestead Bank.

"We started pulling the cows out of the dam and realized the calves were tromped into the mud," Robbin Oldaker said. "I wasn't there when they went out in a boat and drug the cattle out of the water. I couldn't stand it."

Robbin admitted that financially, it was a terrible blow, but she said that wasn't the uppermost thought in her mind at that moment. "I didn't think about that then. I don't think Ed did either. I just thought of how terrible it had been for those cows and calves. We had worked for a long time to build up our herd, and in one night a third of them were gone."

"We were banking with the Sioux National Bank in Harrison, but every time you went in there to get a loan, you felt like you were begging. That got old damn fast," Ed Oldaker said with irritation. "One day a new loan officer shows up. He wants to see my cattle. Before I could even get to the pasture, somehow, he gathered them up and shoved them into a pen. He picked out 12 head that he was going to sell. We weren't even in trouble, but he'd decided we were."

Ed took the cattle to the sale, but "no-saled" all but two head. The next day he went to the First National Bank in Chadron. Bank president Steve Irwin came out to inspect the Oldaker cattle. Ed recalled the visit. "When we were done driving through the cattle, we went past the hay yard. We had a good hay crop that year. Steve asked me if I could feed some cattle. He sent me 200 head. I fed them all that next winter and made good money doing it. That's the way Steve was. He looked things over and generally found a way to help you make money."

Melvin moved his business to the First National Bank that fall. He too, benefited from the bank president's knowledge and faith in his customers. Instead of demanding that ranchers sell off most of their assets, the bank followed a strategy that kept their customers solvent. Irwin made it possible for Melvin to buy some cattle that winter.

Joe Hourt said his father-in-law was just too stubborn to give up. "He kept hoping things were going to turn around. He thought if he worked hard enough, he could make things work."

"JimBob and I did the haying that summer while Grandad was combining," Bryan said. "JimBob rodeod almost every weekend. Once a week, when we went to the house for lunch, he called the radio station to deliver the "Rodeo Report." He was good at it. I was impressed. Granddad must have been too. When we were out combining, he always tuned the pickup radio to the "Rodeo Report."

Sometimes JimBob picked Bryan up on the way to the hay field, but Bryan said Melvin often stayed in town and swung by to "gather me up." "We whipped up through Corkscrew Canyon as fast as he could drive, the back end of the buckskin pickup sliding sideways most of the time," Bryan said, delight still edging his word. "That's where I learned you could drive really fast on country roads. He drove like a mad man everywhere he went, but he was never out of control. There were two big dips in the road past the top of Corkscrew. We'd catch air on about every hill. He unloaded the springs pretty good when we were flying up through there."

Trail rides, with Arnold Johnson and his wife, Myrna in the lead, traversed the prairies between Deepcreek Road and Andrews several times during the 1980s. In a 2018 interview,

Johnson said Melvin often joined the caravan. "Melvin would show up the morning of the trail ride. Most of the time he had his grandkids with him. I think he had a good time. Well, all of us did. Melvin told me one trip, that he hadn't spent much time relaxing in his life, that he thought it was time that he did a little more. I don't think he relaxed too much, though."

Joe Lemmon said he was riding a green colt during one of the Johnson trail rides. He snubbed his horse to a friend's horse, but they weren't far down the prairie trail when his horse jerked free. Lemmon said for the next 20 miles, Melvin helped him herd his horse—in the right direction—toward Andrews where they were holding a campfire supper. "No one could get close enough to my horse to snub him down again. It could have been a wreck. But Melvin made sure I got through the gates and that my horse didn't head back to the Fort. He herded me along just like you do a bunch of cattle. That was quite a ride. We did have a great time when we got to Andrews though."

"Melvin always found something to do, even if it was riding back and forth down the line visiting," Johnson added. "When we got to camp, he went out and gathered wood and set stuff up." He laughed. "I'm not sure he was real good at relaxing."

Maybe Melvin wasn't very good at relaxing, but in an essay he wrote in 1984, Bryan Hourt said his grandfather was really good at teaching him 'stuff.' Melvin spent several nights a week in Crawford. Many weekends, or on rare occasions during the school week, he picked Bryan up to help with the many tasks that needed done on the Home Place. In his seventh grade essay entitled, "My Grandpa," Bryan said when the buckskin pickup drove into the yard, "I just climb in. I can always catch up on math. Going with Grandpa is more important." The essay went on to explain that Bryan learned more than school work from his grandfather, including, "the best story I ever heard: the story of the Wampus Cat."

"A little kid was talking to his Granddad. He asked him what was the meanest animal he ever saw. The Granddad said it was the Wampus Cat, a strangely weird creature with a head at both ends," Bryan wrote in his essay. "So the little boy says, 'How does he poop?' The Granddad says, 'He don't; that's what makes him so mean.'" Years later Bryan admitted that he still loved "that dumb joke."

The two-wheel buckskin pickup could outperform any four-wheel drive, at least in the pair's estimation. One Saturday afternoon after a big snow storm, they "hit" four-corners, flying through the intersection and landing in the snow packed road beyond. The pickup buried itself in a snowdrift. Melvin backed up and hit the drift again. Finally, the pickup trudged its way through the drift and headed back down the road. Bryan said he believed his grandfather was invincible.

Unfortunately, the financial roadblocks for area agribusiness men were also becoming more and more invincible. In another quest to increase his cash flow, Melvin joined the Fort Robinson winter crew in the fall 1984. The former military post had changed radically from Melvin's boyhood days. In 1948, the military turned the Fort over to the USDA for use as a beef research center. In the late '50s the Game and Parks Commission and the State Historical Society took control of the former military post and turned it into a popular tourist attraction. Several herds of livestock including longhorns and buffalo, were purchased in the late 1970s. Jim Lemmon asked Melvin if he would manage the livestock. Jim's son, Joe, became Melvin's "gofer" that winter.

The Fort Robinson stables shine in the background as Melvin drives a team of mules across the grounds. Joe Lemmon pitches the grass hay off to the livestock.

Every morning, Melvin hooked up the four-team hitch of mules and backed up to the hay wagon. Joe and his brother Roy pitched the hay to the cattle. Joe said the process went smoothly, but he wanted to drive the team. One morning after they reloaded the hay wagon, Melvin showed Joe the basics.

"We headed across the Fort. He warned me to avoid the cement car barriers in the parking lot, but of course I plowed into one," Joe Lemmon said shaking his head. "It tore the reach[478] out from under the wagon. Melvin didn't say anything. We climbed into a pickup, headed for the river, cut a piece of cottonwood, shaped it into a reach, and attached it to the wagon. There wasn't any screaming or hollering. We just took care of the problem. Before the winter was over, I learned to drive the horses."

---

[478] "Farm Collector." The Versatility of Early Farm Wagons. http://www.farmcollector.com/equipment/versatility-of-early-farm-wagons. A reach connects the front gear to the rear. It is usually a 2x4 piece of wood with a hole in front of the king bolt. A series of holes are situated about two-thirds back from the reach bolt. When the reach bolt is removed the rear gear can slide forward or backward thus adjusting the length of the wagon gear to accommodate wagon beds of different lengths.

A few weeks later, Jim Lemmon[479] sent Joe and Melvin to the stable to saddle his horse. The pair completed the task then mounted their own horses and headed across the pasture to gather cattle. When Jim arrived at the stable, he discovered that his horse was sporting a saddle that was definitely facing the wrong direction. He apparently repositioned his saddle, because he showed up a few minutes later—cussing profusely.

"I don't know what he was thinking, honestly I don't, when a few weeks later he sent us to saddle his horse—again," Joe Lemmon laughed. "Of course, we put the saddle on backwards. After that, Dad decided it was easier to saddle his own horse than continually turn the saddle around."

A few years before Melvin arrived at the Fort, several horses were killed in the horse pasture. Each carcass featured an elongated wound that ran under the rib cage and punctured the horse's heart. Rumors circulated alternately blaming a "depraved horse murderer, an alien, or a blood-thirsty cult member." After an early morning stake-out, the real culprit was identified. The horses were sharing the winter hay-ground with several longhorn bulls. One of the bulls mastered a horn-tip thrusting maneuver to reduce competition for the best hay. (Although verifiable proof is limited, it's alleged that the bull's head, still wearing his long horns, is hanging-out in the upstairs dining room at Fort Robinson's Main Lodge.)

That winter of 1984, horses and longhorns did not share the same hay ground, but there were plenty of other interesting problems to be mastered. The crew was tasked with calving out several head of Hereford cows that came from the Bowring Ranch.[480] They erected an electric fence near the mare barn to confine the cows. One of the men became the designated tester—for six separate cross posts. "Melvin definitely thought it was hilarious that the guy was willing to take six hits from an electric fence," Joe said. "That Melvin sure could laugh."

Buffalo presented their own challenges. During one roundup, Jim Lemmon sent a snowmobile rider to shut gates in the winter pasture. The man jumped the snowmobile across the creek, but didn't make it to the other side. He mired down in the creek bottom. Water sloshed between the tracks and splashed across the handle bars. The rider jammed the snowmobile in gear. The engine roared. The vehicle rocked its way toward the creek bottom. By that time, the buffalo, impatient to get to their winter pasture, reached the creek bank. The animals didn't even slow down; they simply jumped over or shouldered their way past the water-spouting snowmobile. The driver "hunkered down" in the mud. After making sure the driver was "still alive," the crew finished driving the buffalo to the pasture. Eventually they returned, tied their ropes to the snowmobile and jerked it out of the river.

---

[479] Jim Lemmon was the superintendent at Fort Robinson. He became one of Melvin's best friends.
[480] Bowring Ranch near Merriman is a Hereford demonstration ranch, donated by former U.S. Senator Eva Bowring in memory of her husband.

"Dad sent the snowmobiler back to the pasture to shut another gate he forgot to shut," Joe's voice was filled with incredulity. "He stuck that damn snowmobile back in the creek again. Melvin just shook his head."

The buffalo drive from summer to winter pasture and back always challenged riders. Melvin and Ed Oldaker joined the crew whenever they could, partly to help Jim, but also because they considered the "wild ride" great fun.

Jim Lemmon, riding one of his mules, said the buffalo drove better if they were on a "dead run"— unless they decided to change direction.

Ed Oldaker said he didn't think they ever successfully drove the buffalo anywhere, particularly in the early days. "We tried to keep them going the direction we wanted them too," Oldaker said. "If they didn't want to go that direction, they didn't go. Many times, we ended up going to the back of the pasture and starting all over again."

During one of the first years of the "buffalo drive," Moni Hourt decided to cover the event for the local newspaper. Attaching three cameras[481] to her neck, she mounted Melvin's grey gelding and headed across the pasture. The buffalo came over the hillside, a molasses flood against a textured landscape. The gelding allowed about 10 pictures, before deciding the buffalo

---

[481] One camera was loaded with black and white film, one with color film, and the third with Kodachrome to produce color slides. In the days before digital cameras, every film had its particular uses.

were too close and much too scary. He went into a spin. Melvin said he saw the wreck unfold, but couldn't do much about it.

"The gelding 'quit the flats.'" Melvin grinned at the memory. "Mona grabbed her cameras and bailed. She ended up on her butt, but saved her cameras. I caught her horse. She got back on and finished shooting her pictures. She took a lot of pictures over the years—a lot."

Dozens of photographs recorded family Christmases. Melvin's tally book generally included the written story—1984 was no exception. He said everyone was home, although JimBob left in the early afternoon to work at the Chadron truck stop. Then as he did many times, Melvin added, "It was a good Christmas. Always is when we're all together."

No one ever imagined it would be the last one that they all spent together.

Building on his success with the "Rodeo Roundup," JimBob hired on full time as an KCSR advertising salesman in January of 1985. He seemed to like the job. Thelma spent March 30 with him at KCSR's Home Show.[482] Her son spent the day moving from booth to booth interviewing business owners and discussing the items they were selling. He bought Thelma lunch and introduced her to his friends and colleagues. The next morning, March 31, 1985, he was killed in a car wreck. He was 24-years-old.

JimBob Earl Nation 1961-1985

Melvin asked Joe Hourt to make sure JimBob's car was hidden away so that no one could "stare at it." All day, he carried 10-month-old, Kayla Pelton, around in his arms, taking comfort in her smiles. He paced through the house. He tried to console his family. Then he went to the ranch; the chores still needed done.

On the second anniversary of JimBob's death, Melvin wrote in his tally book, "It's been hell on Thelma. I keep wondering when the hurtin' stops."

In the next year, Melvin continued to work at Fort Robinson. He fixed fence and fed the cattle. He spent many hours driving the back roads. He planted seed on JimBob's grave.

"He put one foot in front of the other," Jim Lemmon said in 1996. "There wasn't anything else he could do."

Cattle prices continued to fall. Bankruptcies increased across the state. On June 6, 1985, three months after JimBob's death,

JimBob's graduation picture taken in 1979.

---

[482] The Home Show was sponsored by KCSR and featured businesses across the region. The event held at the Assumption Arena in Chadron, showcased many different products.

Melvin and Thelma traveled to North Platte and declared bankruptcy. The bankruptcy lawyer asked Melvin what stipulations he would be willing to accept. Thelma told her daughter many years later that Melvin said—very quietly, "I'll do whatever you want. There isn't much of anything more anyone can do to me. I'm already in hell."

"I had great respect for Melvin," Dick Herren[483] said. "He was a proud man. He came in shortly after he got back from North Platte. He told me that he'd pay every penny he owed if I carried him a little longer. I told him his word had always been good. It wasn't easy for him, but he went and talked to every creditor. He paid me off the next year. He didn't have to, but he did. That's the kind of man he was."

Melvin returned to the Fort that fall. Bryan Hourt drove to the Home Place every morning that fall and winter to feed his Grandfather's cattle.[484] That spring Melvin sold them to pay off part of his bank loan.

In 2014, Joe Hourt discussed the first year after JimBob's death. "Melvin stopped at the shop about every afternoon that year. We'd have a beer and visit. He never talked about Jim-Bob. We didn't talk about anything much. We didn't need too; we both knew the road ahead wasn't easy."

On Christmas Day 1985, Thelma Nation gathered her family and told them she'd had enough of their snottin' and bawlin'. She said it was time, they "pulled their heads out of their a—es and went on with life."

"People aren't going to say that my son's death destroyed his family. That's not how he's going to be remembered," she declared, then turned and stomped back into the kitchen to put dinner on the table.

On March 28, 1986, a year after JimBob's death, Melvin said he ate his pride and called Bill Coffee.

"I asked him if he had any place on the ranch for an old man," Melvin said. "He told me to come up that evening, and we'd talk it over. He said he needed a care-taker at Hat Creek. Thelma and I moved back up there on April 1, almost 34 years after we had the first time. It's been our salvation."

---

[483] Herren, Dick. 1987, During a personal interview by Moni Hourt for a story on the Herren business, Dick said he wanted to tell Moni something about her Dad, then related the story.
[484] Bryan was supposed to be back to school at the Glen rural school by 9:30, but often became sidetracked. On a regular basis his teachers called to say Bryan was late again. Joe Hourt finally told his wife, that as long as Bryan's grades stayed up there was no sense of getting excited, that he probably learned more feeding the calves than he did going to school.

The Hat Creek road stretches west across the prairie. Fred Huhn and Melvin visit by the West Gate.

HAT CREEK: THE RETURN

> "I was 56 years old. I was past the prime of my life, wasn't really worth much anymore. I figured I had two choices: give up and sit on a bar stool or start over. Thelm was never real fond of me sitting on a bar stool. We started over."
> Melvin Nation

In the 1986 tally book, strike-outs slashed across the bills listed in the pages. The rows of relentless negative balances that marched across the pages during the last years on the Home Place were increasingly replaced with anecdotes about family members. On his birthday, Moni made him a cake and everyone showed up to help him celebrate. On Buffy's 16th birthday, Melvin wrote that he borrowed the four-mule team hitch from the Fort and took "Buffy and some of her giggly friends" for a hayrack ride. Bryan spent a week at Hat Creek helping him fix fence. One Sunday night, he said Ed and Robbin and their kids stopped to visit. Starting over meant taking one step at a time.

Bill had leased the ranch during the years Melvin lived at the Home Place, but he had continued to buy and sell cattle through his partnership with Joe Nunn. In the mid-1980s, a cattle buyer offered the partnership a price for their cattle. Bill didn't like the offer, so they turned it down.

"That fall the market broke," Joe Nunn remembered. "We got the cattle sold, but had one heck of a time doing it and lost money on every head." The partnership was dissolved later that fall.

Despite the partnership cattle loss and the agricultural market's roller coaster economy, the Coffee Ranch maintained financial stability throughout the '80s. Cattle still grazed on the Warbonnet Ranch that was managed by Ed Hospodka[485], but the pastures at Hat Creek were empty. As Hat Creek's new caretaker, Melvin's duties were not very well defined, so he defined them. His first tally book entry mentioned that there was "a lot of work" to do around the place, that it was pretty run down.

---

[485] Ed Hospodka from Harrison worked on the ranch for several years before and after Melvin's return to Hat Creek. He also, much to Thelma's irritation developed a hunting operation on the ranch. Thelma snorted every time the hunting operation was mentioned. She said she never did like hunters running around killing stuff; she never would.

"Ever fence around here needs fixed," he wrote. "Need to get stuff cleaned up. Haven't irrigated for years; pipes full of dirt." Ed's[486] got a few head left at Warbonnet, but Bill needs some cows over here."

The next Sunday he wrote that he went down to the Home Place. "The old place looks sad, just sad. Not wanting to be there."

In the fall of 1986, Melvin and Bill attended several area livestock sales. Bill bought 300 head of bred heifers. That winter Melvin straightened and cleaned the bent pipe; in the spring, he "strung the pipe out in the south meadow." The hay field sprouted back into production. He calved out the cows, "only lost a few." Ed Oldaker, Joe Hourt, Bruce Quintard, and Jim Lemmon helped him brand.

Jim Lemmon, Neil Nunn, and Bruce Quintard visit with Melvin at the "new house" at Hat Creek. They men were always willing to help Melvin with any chore including working cattle and branding.

Years later, Bill said he and Melvin "put Hat Creek back on its feet."[487] The men spent the rest of their lives together working the ranches they both loved.

Christmas 1986, was celebrated at the Hat Creek cook house. It was a gorgeous day and the kids spent the day riding Buffy and Bryan's new three-wheeler. That night Melvin wrote in his

---

[486] Ed Hospodka managed the Warbonnet ranch.
[487] Bill Coffee. Personal interview with Moni Hourt, 1994.

tally book that everyone was there, everyone but Jim. He said it would never be the same without JimBob, but "life goes on."

New facts and figures started to fill Melvin's tally book pages. The hay grinder was there and worked late into the night. The cows ate an average of 24 pounds of ground hay a day. In early January of 1987, he wrote he needed to fill the feeders and break the ice almost every day. He wrote that someone made an offer to buy the Home Place for $125 an acre. He added he needed to know who made the offer before considering it. He said Bill made daily stops at the ranch. Bruce Quintard and Bob Jordan were frequent visitors. One entry said they all went "coon hunting." He also remarked that the day was a beautiful one with frost covering the trees and fields.

In January 1987, he mentioned that an old friend[488] died. On the next page, he said three kids were killed in Harrison that afternoon.[489] "Bad, bad, old journey," he wrote. "Doesn't make much sense. My heart goes out to all their families."

Frequently, the tally book pages emphasized the relationship Melvin maintained with his brothers and sisters. During the months that Elvin struggled with the debilitating effects of leukemia, Melvin recorded their almost nightly phone calls. He flew to Seattle and spent several days in Elvin's hospital room. "He'd like to quit. His ole mouth and throat is full of sores. I think he's tough enough to beat this thing."[490]

On JimBob's birthday, Melvin mention that his son would have been 26 that day and added that it had been a "bad day." For the rest of his life, the tally books commemorated both JimBob's birthday and the day he was killed. As the years went by, he often wrote, "Time is supposed to heal, and it does a little. But it never goes away."

Another entry declared that, "It never quits hurtin' and oh, how we miss him." Years later, Thelma would say she survived JimBob's death with the help of her sister, her mother, and her family. Melvin never talked about his feelings; he seldom mentioned his son's name except in his tally book. He used his book to support his statement that the "ranch was his salvation."

Everyday ranch work occupied much of Melvin's waking hours. He built a cake sled, constructed a chicken pen, and "ran his water." He and Thelma accompanied friends to the Rapid City Stock Show. He worried about foot rot in his yearlings. He proudly mentioned that Bill brought him a new pair of boots. When Bruce came to visit he wrote that he sent him home with eggs and milk.

"Them old cows are eating a lot of hay, but they sure look good," he wrote in late February. "They'll be calvin' soon." A few days later, he said that there was 10 inches of snow on the ground. He added that he was really glad he hadn't been getting any calves.

---

[488] Grace Thomas, the wife of Everett Thomas, had lived about five miles from the Warbonnet Ranch.
[489] An accident outside of Harrison by the Coffee "Pullen Place" killed two Harrison girls, Kim Jamison and Cori Martinson. The driver of the vehicle, Brian Root of Crawford died at the scene of the accident. His death was listed as suicide. Two other girls, Ashley Rising, and Tina Bauersachs, survived the accident.
[490] Elvin was able to beat the cancer. He lived until 2004.

As the winter wore on, Melvin started checking the cows on his grey horse. He worried about getting them in before the storms hit, but he also commented on the beauty of the mornings or what a nice day it had been.

"Melvin and I became friends when he was at Warbonnet. I bought his calves every year when he was on the ridge, but we became even closer friends when he moved back to Hat Creek," Joe Nunn said smiling at the memory of his old friend. "Almost every time we met, he'd say, 'It's a beautiful morning.'"

Neil Nunn, Melvin Nation, Joe Nunn in 1987 at the Home Place auction.

Carefully constructed sentences in the book that lived in Melvin's pocket, recorded those beautiful mornings. They also celebrated the successful birth of every calf and lamented every death. And he never failed to appreciate his family.

"Bryan cleaned the barn for me today. He sure does me a lot of good," he wrote on March 11, 1987. "He's 15 today. He'll be a good man."

"It was always fun to hang out with him," Bryan Hourt said. "There was a mystique about him. John Wayne had nothing on Melvin Nation. After I moved to Ohio, I told people that I grew up in ranch country. I brought my friends back to meet Grandpa. I introduced him and instantly people would want to get to know him better; they wanted to be like him," he smiled, "I always said if I wanted a girl to fall in love with me, I just introduced her to Granddad. They instantly fell in love with him and decided I was somewhat cool because I was his grandson."

Despite the support and love of his family, there were days when grief seeped across his tally pages. At 2 a.m. one morning, Melvin sat at the kitchen table recording his daily tabulations.

The wind howled across the ranch. Snow piled in drifts and sifted across the pastures. He kept his horse saddled that night and rode through the calving lot every two hours. He worried about calves "freezing down." "I finally figured out why I don't enjoy calving like I used to," he wrote. "Life was all ahead of me when I was here before. Now there is very little to look forward too, more the pitty."

Two days later he compared a couple of calves that were born the previous night. "I got two calves since midnight, had to pull them both. One little bull calf was big; he chilled down in the shed—just laid there. I had to get him under some heat. The other calf was born outside the barn. He was all right this morning: standing up sucking. Lot of differences in calves, in men too. You gotta be tough, keep going."

After talking to a bankruptcy specialist in April of 1987, Melvin reported that he could use Chapter 12[491] to "hold onto" the place—if he could make it pay for itself. The next week he contacted Lonnie Lemmon of Lemmon Auction Service and set up a Farm Sale for May 9. He said he was ready for it to be over.

Joe and Ed went to the Home Place every weekend to help get ready for the sale. At the end of the sale, Melvin reported he made enough to pay off most of his major debt. He leased the place in May. By 1990, he paid off every creditor.[492]

Melvin leads one his well-trained geldings through the throng of bidders.
Most of the horses sold well, a point of pride in a tough time.

---

[491] It took several months after a petition of bankruptcy was filed, for a court to approve the request. Chapter 12 allowed land owners to keep possession of their land, but required them to make regular payments to satisfy the debt on the land.

[492] Because so many farmers and ranchers suffered financially during the 1980s, the government established Chapter 12, a bankruptcy program only for farmers and fishermen. Duft, Ken D. "Chapter 12 Bankruptcy in Retrospect; Its Impact on Agribusiness Firms." *Agribusiness Management*. College of Agriculture, Washington State University,1990.

That summer he reported that Bryan and Moni entered one team penning with him, Ed Oldaker and Kenny Daugherty entered another. "Didn't win, but had a good time."

Friends visit while Melvin lays a heel rope around Thelma's feet. Instead of responding with a flippant remark, she accepted their long-time game with a smile.

Joe Lemmon visits with Merlin Nation who traveled from Washington for the sale. Melvin's grey horse sold for over $5,000, nearly $14,000 in today's market.

New pages were turned. In the fall of 1988, Melvin wrote that he wanted to buy some calves and carefully calculated the projected profit of a purchase. He figured 400 pound calves averaged $.90 a pound. Interest for 10 months at 11 percent interest would add $33.66 to the cost of each calf. The pasture bill for 10 months would cost approximately $120. Each calf would eat approximately 13 pounds of hay a day. He added a $5. veterinarian cost for each calf. Projecting a 2 percent death loss, Melvin figured he would have approximately $525 in each calf. If the calves gained 1 1/3 pounds a day, at the time of sale a calf would weigh 800 pounds. By selling the 800-pound calf at $.80 a pound the profit on each calf would pencil out at $115. Melvin calculated the break-even price at $66 cwt or $528. In November, he bought 43 head of calves from Bruce Quintard.

On April 14, 1988, Melvin's 58th birthday, he wrote that his mother had died 20 years earlier. "It was Easter Sunday, Bill and I were greasing sunburn tits. About 1 p.m. I told Bill I was going to see Mama. She died about 3 that afternoon with me holding her hand. I'm grateful that I was there."

After branding in 1988, a total of 425 cows were turned out on grass. Melvin remarked that they had a great crew, Thelma fixed a good meal, and no one went hungry. He added that Bill wouldn't let me "drag them," but "we got them done in good time anyways."[493]

When the branding was completed, Melvin and Thelma's family and several friends helped them move from the cook house to a house built on a hillside overlooking the ranch. The three-bedroom, three-bathroom, modern ranch-style structure, built during the years Melvin and Thelma lived at the Home Place, faced Five-Points, a landmark that loomed about 1000 feet above the valley floor. Thelma immediately ordered a variety of irises. They soon pirouetted around the house splashing color across the prairie-grass lawn.

The previous fall Thelma mentioned she'd "sure like to have some peacocks at the ranch." Shortly before Christmas, Melvin discovered that rancher who was willing to sell a pair. He called his granddaughter, Buffy Hourt and asked her to pick up the peacocks before she drove to Hat Creek Christmas morning. She hid them in the chicken house until after dinner, then Melvin revealed their surprise. By the time the irises were blooming, the peacocks were strutting freely across the yard adding a swish and sway of purple and blue to the scene. For the next 25 years, peacocks inhabited the Hat Creek Ranch.

That spring Melvin carried a tiny abandoned fawn to the house. Thelma mixed up a "deer formula" bottle and fed her tiny charge. He snuggled under the hedge surrounding the back of the house. When Thelma stepped out the door, he bounded to her side and followed her around the flower-studded yard. A year later, the deer joined the herd in the nearby meadow, but returned every few days to check in on her "mother." The next spring the doe returned with her twin fawns.

"I don't know how many fawns that deer raised in the yard," Melvin said. "I know I paid attention when I mowed. TL would have killed me if something happened to them."

---

[493] At most area brandings, after the calves were sorted, they were roped by the hind leg and dragged to the branding fire. Wrestlers undid the ropes, then quickly wrestled the calf to the ground so they could be branded. Bill didn't believe in roping the calves; he thought it was harder on the calves and took longer. Wrestlers at the Coffee ranches, "farmer branded," wrestled the calves by hand.

Ann Coffee Wachman snapped this picture of Moni Nation Hourt and Melvin near the Hat Creek Ranch. Most of the time, Moni was on the other end of the camera lens.

As often was the case, Melvin's family became his main "crew." Ed Oldaker was the "go to" man when cow work needed done, but other family members quickly responded to an evening phone call seeking "a little help." In late May, Robbin helped push the cattle up the hill. The grandchildren, Bryan, Buffy, Amy, and Janet regularly joined his crew. He wrote that Moni helped move cattle up Sowbelly, but he also reported, later that spring that she was hiding in the bushes along the East Hat Creek road to get pictures of the drive and "spooked the cattle." "The knucklehead should have known better, but it didn't hurt a whole lot. They didn't go too far. She's always takin' pictures."[494]

After Ed Hospodka left Warbonnet, Lynne Zolnaski moved to the ranch. He and Melvin shared jobs as the men on the ranches always did. Zolnaski's daughter, Brenda, a friend of Janet and Amy's, often joined the cattle-moving crew. Melvin commented that when the three of them were together, "They are a noisy lot."

Amy Oldaker Swisher admitted the all-girl crew may have been "a little noisy" once in a while, but she said they also knew when to keep their mouths shut, "One day, we loaded some bulls in a trailer to take them to the pasture," she said. "We got a flat tire. Grandpa was down on his knees trying to change the tire, when one of the bulls pooped down the side of the trailer."

Amy said the manure slid down across Melvin's face, onto his collar, and down his back. He pulled his ever-present handkerchief out of his pocket, wiped the side of his face, the brim of his hat, then stuffed the handkerchief back in his pocket.

"He never said a word; I didn't either," Amy said. "But I sure wanted to tell him that handkerchief didn't do much good."

---

[494] Moni earned her first camera when she was 11 by selling subscriptions to the *Quarter Horse Journal*. Photographs she has taken appeared in numerous magazines across the United States. Her photography and articles appeared in *Pro-Rodeo Sports News* for several years, and she was named Contributor of the Year for the magazine in 1984. She has also worked part-time and full time for the *Crawford Clipper* newspaper as a photojournalist since 1979 and photographed every Crawford PRCA rodeo since 1975.

Laughter often accompanied any job on the ranch—unless it didn't.

Amy, Janet, Bryan, Melvin, and two of the Oldaker girls' school friends, Wendy Dunn and Brenda Fotheringham, showed up to move the cattle to the White River pasture about 4 a.m. one foggy spring morning. The seven-person crew barely left the "get-away" when the rain started.

Janet Oldaker Victory said everyone "was shivering" by the time they hit the pasture gate. She said they could have left the cattle in the Schnurr pasture, about 12 miles from the final destination, but "Grandpa could be really stubborn."

"We finished about 4 p.m. When my legs warmed up, they itched like crazy," Janet said. "That's how cold they were. I asked Grandpa later why we didn't just wait until the next day. He said he didn't think he could get that 'big a crew' lined up again that week. We were always short-handed, so he was probably right."

At the conclusion of another long drive, the crew headed for the pre-designated pick-up spot expecting to find the pickup and trailer. It wasn't there. "It was eight miles to town, about 15 to the ranch," Janet said. "Grandpa just headed down over the hill. He said riding 15 miles would take less time than going into town, loading our horses, and then going back to Hat Creek. We rode most of the way home in the dark. We stayed at the ranch that night. He woke us up at 3 a.m. the next morning to gather another pasture."

While Melvin was living on the Home Place, Bill partnered with Florida rancher, Etter Usher, to establish a herd of Brahma/Angus cattle. An article of the breeds' 1000-pound yearlings was featured in a cattleman's magazine and in the October 1979, *Northwest Nebraska Post*.[495] Coffee eventually returned to raising Angus and crossbred cattle, but the Brangus bloodline produced massive offspring.

In his tally book, Melvin reported they delivered the heifers that morning. "The cattle averaged 920," he wrote. "That's unheard of."

---

[495] Hourt, Moni. "Harrison Brangus Cattle Head Home." *Northwest Nebraska Post*. October 1979. Hourt also wrote the article in the Brahma/Angus magazine, but could not locate a copy of the article.

Generally Bill manned the scales at the Harrison sale barn scales, but on this morning, Melvin busily tallied the average weight of the steers loaded onto the scale.

He and Bill seldom missed Crawford's Friday sale and regularly brought a fresh load of cattle to the ranch. Melvin also increased his own herd. In the fall of 1988, he reported he bought some more cattle from Bruce. The cattle averaged 419.3 per head and cost $.90 cwt. He also bought another milk cow for $900 and talked Thelma into helping him sort cattle. The gate hit her in the head.

"Every time TL helps me, she gets banged up," he reported. "Not her fault, just happens."

"Grandma was always willing to help, but she just didn't do it a lot," Cody Oldaker said. "Sometimes Grandpa would ask her to help, then he started hollering because she didn't do it quite right. He didn't holler much; he really didn't, but Grandma didn't take any of his "shit"—that's what she called it. One time, she went down to help him salt the cows. The salt blocks were in the pickup, and Grandma was driving. She didn't do something right and Grandpa, he throws a fit, so she just drives off—left him right out in the pasture," Cody laughed. "He had to walk in. It was about a mile. Of course, Grandpa didn't like to walk if he didn't have too. When he told me about it, he said it was his own damned fault. He said Grandma set him straight ever once in a while."

Buffy Hourt and her grandfather share a joke during one of the Hat Creek brandings.

The personal observations that lined the tally book pages never included the salt-block story, but between remarks about grinding hay, moving cattle, and dehorning. he expounded on his grandchildren's personalities or characteristics. Melvin Oldaker came home with Thelma after a field trip. His grandfather reported he was a "good boy, although a little on the wild side." Buffy spent the weekend helping her grandmother. He said she was "full of sunshine." The next weekend, Bryan showed up to work cattle. Melvin said he was a "handy young man."

He reported that Amy was full of the devil, Janet was "sure a good athlete," and Annette worked too hard. Melvin's non-family crew of Jim and Sandy Lemmon made regular excursions to the ranch. Melvin always noted their assistance and said he "was sure glad, they were willing to help." He never took his friend and family for granted, but a few times he did misread their signals.

Jim and Sandy Lemmon, Bruce and Jean Quintard, and Melvin and Thelma made annual trips to Rapid City for the Rapid City Stock Show. While discussing the upcoming trip in late January 1989, Jim announced that Sandy was with foal. Melvin let the remark slide by. Finally, during a break in the action at the Stock Show rodeo, Jim admitted that he hadn't been talking about his sorrel mare when he made his foal announcement. His son, Robert was born six months later.

"Damn dummy, sure thought he was cute," Melvin said. "They'd been married for a long time. I really thought he was talking about the mare."

As the ranch cattle herds increased, larger crews were needed to handle them. One week, Melvin reported most of his grandchildren, Amy, Janet, Buffy, Melvin and Bryan served as "drovers" during the past week.

At the top of the Sowbelly road, Amy Oldaker and Melvin wait for the tail end of the cattle drive to catch up with the front.

"I don't know how many times we went up and down East Hat Creek and Sowbelly with Grandpa," Amy Oldaker said. "As often as we could, I guess. We didn't carry any food or water. We were on horseback all day. We'd get to a tank; sometimes there would be things floating in it, a dead frog, a bird, moss. Grandpa would scoop it out, then he pulled his hat off, and filled it up to take a drink. He offered me the hat. I never hesitated, didn't even consider hesitating. I just took a big drink—and swallowed—fast. When he asked us to help, we all said, yes."

Increasingly the tally book pages recorded those everyday events in Melvin's life; economics had been relegated to secondary importance

When Melvin's mother-in-law, Verna, bought a house in Harrison, he listed the price—$10,000, the location—across from the grade school, and its practicality in his tally book. "Verna ain't gonna spend much time here, even though she thinks she will. She actually don't like Nebraska much. She was soured on it a long time ago."

On March 31, sandwiched between remarks about cattle and their pasture placement Melvin said he visited JimBob's grave that afternoon. He added that his son was killed four years before. He said he dreamed about him nearly every night, but was determined to "keep goin on, goin on."

And of course branding always took top billing often covering two or three pages that included numbers—steer, heifer calves, costs—even of the beer—, and of course the number of men who showed up to help. Jim Lemmon ran the branding iron; Bruce Quintard wielded the castrating knife; the "Nunn people, on horseback made things simple."

When Melvin had difficulties finding a branding crew, Buffy Hourt invited the Chadron State College football team to participate. Many did. In this photograph a CSC player mans the hind end, Buffy controls the front-end of the calf while Melvin lays on the brand and Joe Hourt waits with his vaccine gun.

The expansion of the cattle business on the ranch did make branding less simple every year. Many of the neighbors spent several weeks sharing branding duties, the Coffee crew always limited their work reciprocation to the Quintard, Schnurr, and Nunn ranches. As a result, Melvin struggled to find a sufficiently large crew to brand the now, nearly 800 calves on the two ranches. In the spring of 1989, he told his granddaughter, Buffy, that he was having problems getting a branding crew together. She volunteered to help. A freshman at Chadron State College, she was a cheerleader for the football team and was also dating offensive-lineman, Shawn Allred. She drafted a portion of the team for the branding pen. In a *Crawford Clipper* newspaper story published in 1994,[496] members of the squad related their experiences.

"I slept with my boots on one year," said Travis Koltiska of Sheridan, Wyoming, who was an offensive guard for the '95 Eagles. "When we drove into the place, I thought we'd arrived at Bonanza. I expected Hoss to come out of the barn. By the next year, I knew what I was doing. Well, at least I knew when to get out of the way."

The branding operation at Hat Creek developed into a well-oiled machine. Melvin's horseback crew left the ranch by 6 a.m. and gathered the cows and calves in neighboring pastures.[497] They pushed the cattle into the ranch corrals by the time the college crew arrived at about 7:30 a.m. One group of calves were quickly separated from their mothers, and funneled into the branding pen. Bill often gave the crew an annotated set of instructions. Then the wrestlers marched into the pen and grabbed for the nearest set of hind feet. As soon as the pen's last calf was marked with a smoking hot Square Top Three brand, they were returned to their mothers; mounted horsemen and women escorted them back to their pastures. By that time another crew had pushed a second pasture full of calves into the corrals. The process started all over again.

Head football coach, Bill O'Boyle, and assistant coach, Todd Auer, hold a calf steady so that Amy Oldaker can administer the Square-top 3 brand. Ed Oldaker wields the castrating knife.

---

[496] The Chadron State College football team continue to make up the nucleus of the branding crew. In appreciation Bill donated several thousand dollars to improve the CSC stadium.

[497] Generally, his grandchildren, the Fort Robinson crew, often his daughter, Moni, his son-in-law, Ed Oldaker, and the Nunns gathered the pastures. Joe Hourt would take the day off at his body shop, fill his coolers with beer and water to quest the thirst of the branders, then spend the rest of the day running the vaccine gun. Thelma, Jean Quintard, Sandy Lemmon, and Robbin served as the nucleus for the lunch crew. Often Sis joined them. Moni admitted she generally spent most of her time taking photographs.

Janet Oldaker easily flipped her calf into "branding position."

"We never branded cattle in Wisconsin where I was raised, but I've been at several brandings since I came to this area seven years ago," CSC Defensive Coordinator Todd Auer said in the article. "This was by far the smoothest operation I've ever seen. As soon as we emptied one pen; the next set of calves was ready to go. I think we can say we came out on top."

One defensive back, who spoke only under the veil of anonymity, said it was Auer who kept the crew from posting a shut-out against their four-legged opponents. "He got between the calf and the branding iron," the player confided. "He'll still be wearing that brand when he's 80. I'll bet the calves are still snorting about that."

Averaging 200 calves an hour, the crew dispatched the branding duties in less than four hours. After lunch, they loaded up in pickups and traveled the 10 miles to Warbonnet, where they branded another 200 in just over an hour.

"These are good boys," Melvin said in the 1994 article. "We appreciate them. They aren't afraid to get their hind ends on the ground and get dirty. They go after it. I need to get to one of their games. If they plays as hard as they work out here, they can't be beat."[498]

Pat Nickodemus helped with numerous brandings before graduating from CSC and moving to California. He even talked Melvin out of one of his cowboy hats and hung it on the wall of his city apartment as a memento of his experiences at Hat Creek.

"The players learned to appreciate the Sioux County ranchers and cowboys as a whole," Nickodemus said. "When you're an athlete you tend to think you are pretty tough. But we aren't anything compared to ranchers like Melvin. I never understood what a rancher or a cowboy really was before I went out to Hat Creek. The whole experience gives you a reverence for what's on your plate and respect for those who have a hand in putting it there."

For the rest of Melvin's life, the Chadron State College football team continued to "man the branding pen." He often remarked on his "football team" branding crew and generally added that his grandchildren were the foundation of the crew. In 2005, he reported in his book that all of his grandchildren, even his new week-old granddaughter, were at the branding.

On September 26, 1988, Melvin delivered his steers to the Crawford Sale Barn. They averaged 965 pounds. He went to the bank the next day and paid off his cattle loan. He reported he even had some money left over and might not have to "borrow operating money."

---

[498] Melvin did make it to several of the Chadron State football games. When he died Coach O'Boyle and Coach Auer presented Thelma with a football helmet signed by all the 2008 football players.

Members of the Chadron State College football team even convinced Melvin to wear a ball cap—at least for a minute. Wrestling crew members celebrated job well done. Pictured—Tommy Potter, Pat Nikodemus, Melvin, Andy Nikodemus, and Todd Biggs.

Bryan Hourt and Melvin Oldaker share a laugh at the 2005 branding. Bryan flew in from Ohio for the event and Buffy and her two daughters came from Illinois. The Oldaker children still lived close by. Most of the grandchildren made branding day a priority.

The pride he felt in his September cattle deal was tempered by his worry about Bill. "Bill had a bad spell today and fell off his horse. Hurt his ole' head. Been worrying about him."

A bolt of lightning speared the edge of the timber country of the Petersen Special Use area approximately three miles west of Fort Robinson on July 8, 1989. Thick mats of tangled grass covered the un-grazed area. Within a few minutes, the tinder dry prairie exploded into flames.

"The kids and I rode horseback across the Petersen place on a regular basis," Moni Hourt said. "A few days before, Dad and I talked about the dry conditions in the area and the fire danger on the Fort because the land wasn't grazed. The grass, across the area, was so thick and matted that our horses sank into it. That morning, I was looking out the kitchen window when I saw the lightning strike. The smoke immediately stretched to the sky. I grabbed my camera and headed up Smiley Canyon.[499] By the time I reached the turnout area at the top of the canyon, I could see the flames on the south side of the road."

Fire dashed across the prairie at an incredible pace. The crews at Fort Robinson, including Buffy Hourt, were sent out to fight the fire. Fire had not ravaged the country for many years. No one could envision that nearly 150 firefighters, 30 departments from Nebraska, South Dakota, and Wyoming, and hundreds of area residents would be needed to battle the blaze. Eventually 50,000 acres—nearly 22,000 located within Fort Robinson State Park, lay charred and smoking.

"Buffy was out fighting fire with the Fort crew; Moni was riding with Joe[500] and taking pictures. Ed was with the Harrison Fire crew. There wasn't much we could do," Thelma said. "Every little bit, Melvin would stop at the house to find out if the kids had called. No one had cell-phones then. It was pretty nerve-racking."

Fire sweeping through the canyon on White River Road a mile west of the Hourt residence.

The fire came within a mile of Joe and Moni Hourt's place at the foot of Smiley Canyon. Bryan, who was working for Alan and Earl Soester, left work, loaded the horse trailer with his horse, dog, paintings, photographs, and mementos. He parked the trailer on Main Street in Crawford, unloaded his horse and let him graze in Donna and Roy Norgard's back yard. His dog, climbed into the back of the pickup. Bryan returned to Soester's while they decided their plan of action against the fire. Messages were delivered between the family members and the fire department, and sent on to the Nations waiting at Hat Creek.

---

[499] Moni and Joe lived about two miles east of the turnout at the top of Smiley Canyon road. The lightning struck the canyons on the south side of the turnout. Within an hour it burned across the turnout and muscled its way into the trees and grass alongside Old Smiley Canyon Road.

[500] Joe was a member of the Crawford Volunteer Fire Department. The Fire chief agreed to let Moni ride along on his truck if he promised to take responsibility for her. He said he told the chief, he'd been responsible for her for over 20 years, he thought he could keep track of her. Moni was allowed to spend the next two days traveling on the fire truck.

The fire finally burned down, but in an interview in 1990, Melvin remarked that nothing would ever be the same again. "These old fires are natural, but those trees along those ridges are a pretty sight. I'll never see them looking like that in my lifetime."

Several pages of tally book recorded cattle transactions the fall of 1989. The ranch shipped 350 steers. They averaged 960 pounds. Melvin noted that the steers average gain for 90 days was 2.58 pounds a day. They were worth $82.50 cwt or $775.50 a head. Bill shipped the rest of his steers two days later. They averaged 998 pounds and sold for $82.50. From Jun 6 until August 17 the steers averaged a weight gain of 2.93 pounds a day or an average of 485 per head. The average selling price was $801 per head. A month later heifers shipped. They gained an average of 2.12 a day for 97 days or 207 pounds per head. At shipping they averaged 897 pounds. The heifers made $660 apiece. When Melvin shipped his own heifers the next week, the heifers had gained 2.10 pounds a day from May 1 to September 11—400 lb. from November until the following September of 1990. The cattle grossed $642.22 a head.

The November "Buffalo Drive" at Fort Robinson became an annual tradition for Melvin and son-in-law, Ed Oldaker. Arriving from the Wildcat Hills in May of 1973, the small herd had grown to 100 cows and bulls. They re-acclimated to the Pine Ridge country that was their ancestral pastures, but were slow to accept domestication. Even the large experienced crew that arrived to help handle the buffalo often found their efforts thwarted.

"Later the buffalo were easier to handle, but then we just tried to keep them going in "kinda" the right direction," Veterinarian Butch Sahara said. "One afternoon Ed and Melvin were both trying to get them turned. They were riding from different directions. Their horses collided. Ed ended up on the ground. Melvin just kept going."

Sahara said sometimes, the men worked in 25 or 30 below-zero temperatures. "Neither Jim nor Melvin covered their ears. They were from the tough old school. I'm not sure men are that tough anymore. I never wanted to be."

The buffalo crew spent their spare time trying to "one up" their compatriots. Sahara said after lunch one day, Melvin disappeared. Following a hunch about his friend's whereabouts, he stepped outside and looked over the banister of the Fort Robinson lodge. "That darn Melvin was stuffing my coveralls with snow. He looked up at me and grinned. Those blue eyes of his were just snapping. When those eyes looked like that you knew you were in trouble."

The next year, Sahara mounted his own attack. He stole Melvin's headstall and took it home with him. He hung it on the horn of his roping saddle, one Melvin wouldn't recognize, and photographed it. Then he mailed the picture to Melvin's hired man. The man delivered the picture to Melvin who reportedly, "cussed a blue streak." For several weeks, Melvin tried to determine who had his headstall. One day it simply appeared in the barn.

"It was a couple of years before I finally told him the truth," Sahara said. "I sent it to Thelma, and she sneaked it back into the barn. He said that was the only time his wife had ever 'pulled one over' on him."

Although the headstall prank was extremely satisfying, Sahara said Melvin's best reaction was elicited before-dawn early one morning. Many members of the buffalo crew gathered at the Hat Creek Ranch to help move cattle. Bruce Quintard slipped into the barn. When Melvin reached his arm into the barn to turn on the light, Bruce grabbed him. Sahara thoroughly enjoyed the stream of cuss words erupting from the barn, but was already planning his next prank. A few weeks later he climbed the ladder and hung Melvin's chaps on the windmill tower behind the Hat Creek barn, he admitted he had second thoughts. He finally called Thelma and told her where the chaps were "hidden." Melvin had already retrieved them.

"Melvin noticed everything," Sahara said. "I should have known he would spot the chaps, even hanging on top of a windmill tower 30 feet in the air."

Cody Oldaker swore that Melvin spent a whole year planning his revenge. "We drove out of the yard early one morning, Grandpa circled back and ran into the shop. His was a-grinnin'. I knew he was up to something."

Melvin returned to the pickup with a fully loaded grease gun. Sometime during the afternoon, he slipped away and liberally greased Sahara's windshield wipers. The snow was drifting heavily across the landscape when Cody and Melvin pulled away from the stables. Sahara had turned on his windshield wipers; they were busily smearing the windshield with fresh black grease when Melvin drove by. He rolled down his window, smiled and waved gaily. Sahara turned the air blue with his curses.

On April 12, 1991, Melvin mentioned that 44 years ago that day, he left the country for Washington state. He said he never intended to come back to Nebraska, but he did.

"I wasn't gone much over a month. I'm glad I came home. Nebraska has made Thelma and I a good home."

Fishing on the Puget Sound where they built their home became a common occupation for Merlin and Lucille's family, but Melvin seldom went fishing—unless Joe Hourt talked him into it. On a semi-regular basis, Joe showed up with a pair of fishing poles, a tackle box, and dug a few worms out of the flower beds. Then he convinced Melvin to accompany him to the ponds north of the Hat Creek barn.

"Once Melvin slowed down, he settled in and drowned some worms." Joe Hourt said. "We didn't catch a whole lot. Once in a while we took them to the house and Thelma and Moni cooked them, but most times we just throwed them back. Mostly we just sat there, relaxing. Sometimes we talked."

Joe seldom helped with the cattle work, but he did help Melvin in the ranch shop. The calf sled they build could be attached to a saddle horn and pulled to the house, but generally Melvin used the four-wheeler to drag the calf-filled sled to the barn. Joe took great pride in the fact that he made Melvin's work "a little easier."

Sale days in Crawford generally found Melvin and often Bill, on the bleacher seats in the sale bar. Sometimes they bought a few head of cattle. Sometimes they didn't. But almost always, whether with Bill or alone, Melvin stopped at Joe's Body Shop. They visited or Joe fixed something for him, mostly wiring.

"When he came to Crawford he generally stopped at the shop to visit awhile." Joe Hourt said. "He was pretty proud of the wiring tester I built.[501] If someone came in the shop with him, he made me get it out and show how it worked. I thought as much of Melvin as I did any man. I considered him a friend."[502]

"Grandpa had friends of every age," Bryan said. "We grandkids were always around. He talked to each one about what interested us individually. He made each of us feel like we were each important in our own way. That's probably why we were always more than willing to help him when he asked us to."

Throughout a portion of their high school years, Amy and Janet became his summer hay crew. When they attended sports' camps, Buffy filled in. "He called me the Mario Andretti of the hay field," Buffy said. "It didn't take me long to get around the field."

"Amy and Janet put up a lot of hay. They were good at it, darn good. That damn Buffy, could get around a field three times as fast as anyone else," Melvin said. "Her windrows weren't real straight, but they worked. And the thing about her was she was always smiling. She never did any complaining."[503]

A massive raincloud centered over the tableland of northwestern Sioux County on May 10, 1991. Melvin sold calves at the Crawford Sale Barn that day and reported that he "made money on them." Moni was finishing her last day of college. Bryan and his friend, Nathan Painter, out of college for the summer, drove through the rain storm and then found themselves battling through a massive hail storm that punched holes in the windshield and waffled the body of Bryan's pickup. They pulled into the yard about five minutes after Joe.

"The road was washed out by Charles Mack's so I went around and came into the house from White River Road," Moni Hourt said. "My horses were across the river, so I grabbed the halters and was heading out to get them when Joe, Bryan and Nathan pulled up. headed out to get them. They went with me."

---

[501] Joe constructed a machine that tested the wiring in a horse trailer or vehicle. The machine saved him hours of work and made it much easier to replace the wiring, particularly in a horse trailer. He told a group of Crawford seniors in 2013, that he had seen something similar for sale in a one of his body shop magazines that past summer. He said he should have patented the "damn thing" like his father-in-law told him to.
[502] The year Joe and Moni celebrated their 30th wedding anniversary, he told his wife that Melvin had been his father longer than his own father had been.
[503] In his journal he called his oldest granddaughter "his shining light."

The group traversed the lower pasture below the house. They were crossing the railroad track about one-half mile from the house when they heard a muffled explosion. Within minutes a 12-foot wall of water rolled down the track toward them.[504]

"I had my camera with me because the boys said the river was really high. I stopped to take a picture," Moni Hourt said. "Joe grabbed one arm and Bryan grabbed the other. They started running toward the house, dragging me with them."

The water raced the group to the house, turning the lower pasture below the house into a churning mass of debris and muddy water. Diverted by the corral fence, water gushed around the alfalfa field bordering the yard. The four jumped into Joe's pickup. The rising waters blocked the roadway. Bryan and Nathan jumped from the pickup and cut the west fence that bordered the alfalfa field. Joe gunned the pickup and they lurched across the flooded field. Water lapped at the top of the tires. Reaching the hill about 100 feet from the house, they sloshed free of the whirling water. Slipping and sliding, they traversed "Chalk Hill"[505] west of the house, then took White River Road back to Highway 20.

"When we got to town, we stopped at O'Doherty's to get something to eat. The sale barn crew was there. We told them there was a bad flood coming up White River," Joe Hourt said. "But no one had any idea how bad it really was."

It wasn't until the next morning that Joe and Moni knew their house was still standing, saved by the accidental flood-dike created by the debris caught in the fences surrounding their yard.

Joe and Moni Hourt's house lay surrounded by flood water the day after the Flood of 1990. Photograph: Crawford Clipper by Deb Kennedy

By that time a man had drowned in the water. The city park was underwater. The golf course, slated to open the next day, was submerged in debris and tangled rivulets of muddy water. The flood ravaged the sale barn, filling the pens with water, and trapping and drowning several hundred cattle. Water pounded its way into homes located along the White River, upending several and damaging others.

"The next day Mona graduated from college," Melvin said "We had to go through a couple roadblocks to get to Chadron. It was unbelievable to see that much water in this

---

[504] The city dam was located about a mile above the Hourt's place. About 12-foot-deep, it provided the Hourt children with a great swimming hole. On May 10, 1991, water from the cloud burst above the dam rushed into the old concrete structure. The explosion the Hourt's heard was the walls of the dam breaking open. Later Joe and Bryan measured the sign that they saw the water surge over when the dam broke. It was nearly 8 foot tall.
[505] Chalk Hill located on Vogl Loop to the north of the Glendy Road turnoff, is made of slick almost gumbo soil. Many drivers have struggled to maneuver their vehicles down or up the steep hillside.

country. We made it to watch her get her diploma," Melvin added with just a hint of pride. "She was the first person on either side of our family to get a college diploma."

The day after the flood, Buffy Hourt found 35-year-old "Poca," the horse she and Bryan had ridden in dozens of 4-H and rodeo competition, buried besides the river in the mud left from the flood. "Sparky," Buffy's pole bending horse and her colt were in the pasture with Poca. They swept down the river. Buffy found them tangled in brush and rubbish about a mile from the house. The mare's leg was broken; she had to be euthanized. The colt survived only to be struck by lightning the following spring.

"Tough ole deal. Those kids liked their horses. When they retired Sparky, they turned her out into the Hunter Hills. She had six colts. I saw her about every time I went up there. She'd stick her nose in the air and take off. She was a wild little rip."

Melvin said the fall before the flood, he pulled into the pasture. Sparky brought her colt to the trailer. The baby was small, too young to make it through the winter. Melvin opened the trailer door and the mare jumped inside; the baby followed. "The kids babied those horses all winter. They looked really good. Strange how things work out."

Thelma celebrated her 59th birthday January 18, 1991. Melvin commented their life was a good one—never boring. Later that year he wrote it took "the whole crew" to unload "TL's" new kiln. He added that Thelma drove to Pine Bluffs, Wyoming, to buy some more of her "things." It wasn't long before Thelma used her new kiln and her "things," ceramic molds, greenware, and paint to produce unique pieces of ceramic art. The ceramics sold well at Sioux Sundries[506] in Harrison and at Fort Robinson State Park.

That summer the figures were also featured at the Casper, Wyoming, airport gift shop, thanks to Melvin's daughter-in-law.

Beth Pliley, Gary's wife, managed the gift shop at the Casper, Wyoming airport. During a visit to the ranch, Beth told Thelma she thought she could sell the Native American figures, that were Thelma's specialty, at the gift shop. When Beth returned to Casper, she took a variety of the ceramic pieces, including a Native American Nativity scene, with

Thelma Nation sold numerous Native American sculptures at sites across the United States and in France.

---

[506] Sioux Sundries was a cross between a general store and a soda fountain. Delores Wasserburger, the owner of the business created the Coffee burger, a gigantic hamburger that she said was designed to satisfy the appetites of Bill Coffee's men.

her. Within a few days, she called Thelma and ordered a dozen more pieces. Thelma said there were a few times when the men who came into lunch, had to slide ceramics out of the way before they could eat. They didn't seem to mind.

"One day she gets this telephone call from a French lady who owned a art shop outside of Paris," Melvin said in an interview in 2003. "This lady and her husband had been in the Casper airport and saw the ceramics. They really liked them."

The art dealer ordered 40 pieces. The community became involved in the logistics involved in the transaction. Joe Whiteaker at Whiteaker's Clothing Store[507] in Harrison helped Thelma communicate—via a fax machine—with her French customers. The UPS man made sure the packages were picked up and delivered to the shipping point.

The French market became a lucrative one. The art dealers even came to America to meet their supplier. After the group was finished with what Melvin called their "art stuff," Melvin took them all to dinner.

"They could talk better American than we could. They were pretty impressed with Thelma's Indians," Melvin said. "I think I'm always surprised about what Thelma can do, but I guess I shouldn't be."

In August of 1991, Melvin proudly recorded the fact that the heifers averaged 975 pounds while steers averaged 1,090. He said the heifers had gained an average of 2.75 a day while the steers daily gain was 2.83. He reported that they'd taken 3900, 1200-pound, big round bales[508] off Hat Creek that summer and nearly 1000 were still scattered in various pastures on the two ranches waiting to be picked up. The Home Place, that he often identified as a "sad old place" was leased. Visits to JimBob's grave elicited loneliness. But slowly life settled into a new normal.

Dan Jordan said after Melvin returned to Hat Creek, he often called him and asked if he had time to move a "few head of cattle." "I always went," Dan said. "I'd do about anything for Melvin. When I was a boy, he was my hero. I even wrote about him for a freshman writing class. No matter what I did, when Melvin was there, I tried a little harder. At the Sioux County Fair one year, Melvin set me on a calf. That was the first calf I ever rode to the whistle. Later I heard Melvin tell my Dad, 'Danny rode the crap right out of him.' He always made me feel bigger than I ever was."[509]

Although counting cattle accurately might not sound like a difficult job, Jordan said it was one that few men mastered. Melvin was one of them. He said Melvin situated himself at a gate and as the cattle came through he "counted" them with a swooping twist of his left hand. "We

---

[507] A western clothing store in Harrison. Melvin always bought Levis and his Stetson hats at Whiteakers'.
[508] When Melvin returned to Hat Creek, the old slide stacker had been replaced with large-bale bailers that created bales that were between 600 and 1500 pounds apiece. The ones at Hat Creek averaged about 1200 pounds. The bales were always picked up from the hay fields and taken to hay yards.
[509] Dan Jordan, interview by Moni Hourt, 2016.

didn't have to recount if Melvin was at the gate. It was like he had a calculator in his brain. He taught me a lot of things, patience, 'try,' confidence, but he never could teach me to count cows."

Jordan went on to say that Melvin was pretty handy on his feet too—'just like a cat.' "We were cutting a colt. Tied the dang thing to the hitching post. The colt jerked free. He whirled around the post and the rope caught Melvin about ankle high. He jumped, caught the rope, and hauled the colt in. I was all tangled up. He helped me get untangled. Didn't say anything, just pulled me to my feet. I grabbed hold of the colt again. He went to the next one."

When he was 15, Gary Pliley discovered that age hadn't dimmed Melvin's athletic ability much. He visited Warbonnet that summer to get acquainted with the father he never knew. Full of spit and vinegar and the cockiness of youth, Gary decided to "take Melvin DOOOOOWN."

He reached out to pop the older man on the jaw. A split second later Melvin deflected Gary's slap and delivered four or five almost-slaps to Gary's cheeks. Gary responded by aiming another slap at Melvin's jaw— same results. Melvin's slaps never really connected to Gary's face, but definitely left the impression that they could. Gary backed off, laughing that he didn't want to wear the "old man" out.[510] Several years later when Melvin was nearly 60, Gary repeated his "assault" with the same results. He decided not to risk it when Melvin was in his late 70s.

A habitual "bar-stool percher" also discovered that Melvin didn't fit the stereotypical image of "Old Man." Janet Oldaker said she watched transfixed as the perpetual drunk boorishly swaggered up to Melvin. He reached out and snapped the brim of Melvin's hat and mocked the older man's "shit kickers."

"The drunk was young and had a very big build," Janet said. "I heard people saying that he'd been beating everyone at arm wrestling that day. I was so nervous. I didn't know what would happen. Grandpa never let anyone touch his hat. I could see the cords on his neck tightenen' up. I was pretty scared."

Janet said Melvin told the man to back off and added, "Don't touch my hat, boy." The kid just wallered in closer and asked Melvin what he was going to do about it.

"I'm not going to fight you," Janet remembered her grandfather saying through clenched teeth, then he challenged the boy-man to an arm wrestling contest.

"He demanded that the kid apologize and leave the bar if he lost. The kid agreed, puffing his chest out and prancing around like a drunken parrot. I was so scared that Grandpa would lose. But he didn't," Janet said her voice edged with pride. "He didn't win easy, but he won and the drunk slunk out the door. I never seen Grandpa do anything like that before. He drank a couple more beers and went home. I don't think he ever told anyone else about it. He was mad, but he didn't let his temper take over."

Temper flares between Bill and Melvin in the second 30 years of their "partnership" certainly didn't result in arm wrestling exhibitions; they seldom evolved past grumbling glares.

---

[510] Melvin was 32 at the time.

"The men developed a relationship based on mutual respect, friendship, and a love of the ranch. Bill respected Melvin, not only because he was such a hard worker, but because he could read a cow. Melvin believed, rightly so, that Bill was a great manager," John Skavdahl, Bill's long time lawyer, said in a 2017 interview. "Neither one of them talked much about their relationship, but they were good for each other."

"Bill gave us a bonus yesterday. He treats us right. Don't know what we would do without this outfit," Melvin wrote on January 1, 1992. "We have lived to see another year, 41 of them for Thelma and I. We spent the day alone yesterday, weren't so bad. We had a good time."

The price for heifers that February ranged between $80 and $95 cwt. Steers were 10 dollars higher than they were the year before. Bred cows and heifers sold from $800 to $1000 a head. Melvin bought a calf from Bert Oetken for $280. "I just don't think this thing can work," he wrote. "A lot of damn money for a cow."

When Bill bought bulls in late February, Melvin accompanied him. The pair became a regular sight on sale barn seats across the Panhandle. Years later Melvin said Bill was one of the best cattleman he knew, although he wasn't the greatest cowboy. "A cowboy can ride the hide off a horse. He can gather up a herd of cows and drive them down the road. A cowman can tell you all about those cattle, which ones will make money, and which bull and cow will produce a good calf. Bill was an outstanding cowman. Most of my life, I just wanted to be a good cowboy, but I think I learned how to be a cowman over the years."

A college essay entitled "Grandpa's Canyon" written by Melvin Oldaker, explained that his grandfather was more than a cowboy or a cattleman: he was a role model worthy of following.

Oldaker wrote that for 50 years his grandfather led herds through the White River Canyon making sure they arrived safely at the summer pasture then returned them to the ranch in the fall. "Grandpa is a steward of this land, of these cattle. He reaches the top of the ridge and pauses, silhouetted against the skyline. The image is branded into my memory. I'm glad I was part of it….Grandpa has had a huge impact on my life. I often wonder if I can follow his footsteps as I have through this canyon. I guess that's a goal I'll set for myself."

The respect, admiration, and help that Melvin's family gave him could not always alleviate the problems of every-day ranch work. He often remarked that he didn't want "to lean on the kids any more than I have to." "Bryan was here most of the week, but he had to go back to school," Melvin wrote one April morning, his left-handed scrawl more pronounced than usual. "I played "plum out" today, just need some sleep. Had 30 calves a couple of days this week. Need a good hired man, but they're not easy to find."

"Good day today," he wrote a day later. "Thelm helped me pair out. We had a really good time." A few days later he reported that TL helped move the pipeline. There was a smile woven through the words when he added. "She didn't even break anything." Then he added. "This afternoon she went up town to gossip."

Every Wednesday, Thelma, Sis, Jean, and Bea Semroska, met at the two-lane bowling alley in the basement at Sioux Sundries[511] in Harrison. Their goal: record the best league-bowling scores of the season. Melvin was right about one thing, there probably was a little "gossiping" going on too.

Sioux Sundries was a general store, a soda fountain, a bowling alley and the home of the Coffee Burger. Delores Wasserburger said she created the Coffee burger, because Bill Coffee said she needed a burger big enough to feed his hungry crew. Melvin said he always ordered the regular burger!

The fact that Melvin quit chewing that spring wasn't included in gossip topics. Melvin didn't think his wife even noticed. He wrote in his tally book that he "sure as hell noticed—every damn day." In the ensuing years, he admitted that he dug the "snus" out of the freezer at least "a hundred times," but he always put it back. "I quit smoking, and I quit chewing. It was a lot tougher to quit chewing. There ain't a day goes by that I don't reach for my pocket to take a chew." [512]

Trips to the pastures were generally enjoyable. He unloaded his horse at the head of White River early one June morning to "string out some bulls." The solitary trip to the pasture was uneventful; the trip back wasn't that easy.

"I took my sorrel horse down there. Let him buck me off. Thought he'd killed me for a while. Did break a couple of ribs," He scribbled across a page. "Damn fool thing to do."

---

[511] Punk Fitch built a two-lane bowling alley in the basement of the Sioux Sundries building in the early '70s. It was in almost continuous use for many years.

[512] He was proud that he quit chewing, because he'd beaten his own weakness, but he never quit craving the "Key" that he'd chewed for 30 years. After his death in 2009, when he had been laid in his casket, his granddaughter tucked a can of "Key" in his pocket.

Despite the injury, he and Thelma drove to Lakeside, Nebraska the following day to help Bill and Virginia celebrate their 50th wedding anniversary. Three days later, he joined his crew in the hay field. He admitted the ribs were "pretty sore," but added, "I'll live."

Joyce Grooms[513] said she drove her parents back to Nebraska that summer. "I got up early one morning and cooked breakfast for Uncle Melvin and Dad. We sat there and visited for about an hour. That was pretty special. Uncle Melvin didn't sit still very long. Dad went around with him for a couple of days. It was good for both of them."

On July 22, 1993, Cody Oldaker, the Nation's first great-grandson, was born. When the great-grandparents visited Cody and Annette, his mother, in the Scottsbluff hospital, they had no idea that the little boy would change their world.

"Cody hasn't replaced my kids any," Melvin said after Cody began living full-time with him and Thelma. "But we've been able to enjoy him a little bit more, because of the time element."

Thelma was 63; Melvin was 66. At first Cody just visited, then he was stayed with the Nations during the week and attended school at the nearby Bodarc Country-School. It wasn't long before the little boy spent most of his time at Hat Creek. Bill Coffee asked Melvin if he was sure he wanted to take on the responsibility of a kindergartner. "I told him the boy was going to have a chance to be a good man," Melvin said. "And by God he has. He's an interesting little boy."

"He gives us a reason to get up in the morning," Thelma added.

Cody Oldaker unofficially joined the Nation household when he was two. He quickly acquired his great-grandfather's sense of humor and story-telling ability.

Cody marched through the Hat Creek Ranch house with Farmer Ed, his imaginary farmer, companion and spent hours constructing elaborate farmsteads where he and Farmer Ed worked. He nicknamed his granddad, "Fat Boy" because he said his grandad "was not fat." In a letter written for a school assignment, he wrote that his grandma was a "good ole gal" and added, "That's what Granddad said too."

"He's an ambitious little shit," Melvin said. "If he can't find something to do, he'll pick up sticks or pile a load of wood. We sure don't regret having him here. We miss him like hell when he's not here."

Cody said his granddad taught him—everything: how to drive the machinery, gather cows, put up the hay, and weld stuff. "Just everything a rancher

---

[513] Joyce Nation Grooms, youngest daughter of Merlin and Lucille Nation. Personal Interview with Moni Hourt. 2017.

does. Granddad trusts me to get stuff done. I never want to let him down. I hayed all this summer. I'm learnin' to be responsible."

A typical day in Cody's world—according to Cody—revolved around school only when necessary. He said his main focus was the ranch and outlined a "ordinary day." One fall Saturday he and "Granddad" saddled their horses, gathered the Marsteller pasture, put the cattle into the corrals, and sorted them. They shoved the cattle into the trailer, 22 head at a time, then hauled the cattle to Warbonnet. When they were done, they scooped grain, set up bunks, and loaded hay with the tractor. The pair filled the bunks then hayed the calves. That night they locked the cows in the shed, put 10 head of calves on them, then shut up the chickens. Finally, they went to the house for supper.

"He's just not going to quit until he dies," Cody said in 2008. "He's going to be 78, and he probably has slowed down some, not much. His knee hurts when he rides, but he rides anyway. I don't think anyone can work like Grandpa can—not any of the hired men—that's for sure."

Before Cody was twelve, he learned to pull a well, hooking up the well rig, pulling the pipes out of the well, repairing them, then threading them back into the well hole. He helped irrigate, fence, and even paint. By far, his favorite job on the ranch was working with cattle.[514] He told a ranch visitor that he learned something new every day: the techniques of identifying a good cow, how to produce a great calf, what breeds he and his granddad liked the best, and how to handle even tough cattle. He also admitted that his granddad's techniques weren't always traditional.

"One time Grandpa went after a bull with a horse," Cody said. "He always did everything with a horse, but that day he couldn't do nothing with the bull. So he went after the bull with the four-wheeler. The bull hits the four-wheeler. By this time the bull and Grandpa was mad. Grandpa gets the tractor and goes in there at about 20 miles an hour. He hits ole bull in the head. That time, that bull never stopped until he got to the barn."

A tractor or even a pickup might have been a useful tool the afternoon Cody and his great-granddad were "kicking out pairs." Cody said they were vaccinating and tagging the calves, "shoulda been an easy job." One cow pawed the ground so Melvin rode between her and her calf. The hired man quickly tagged the calf. An hour later, he and Cody encountered a cow with a newborn calf. The cow was quietly chewing her crud.

"Grandpa gets the calf down to give him a shot. That cow came right over the top of the calf and knocks him down. She just camped on him, broke a couple of ribs, knocked his boot heel off, and stepped on his hat. She got right down on her front knees and grinded her head into him. My horse was scared to death. I couldn't even get up to the calf to help him."

---

[514] Cody preferred doing his riding on a four-wheeler instead of a horse.

Melvin managed to knock the cow off of him and rolled under the fence line. When the cow ran off, Cody rode up to his granddad. "Grandpa, reached up and grabbed my stirrup. I drug him about 400 yards to the corral. He was kinda unconscious for a while, but he never did stop. He fed [the cows] the next morning."

The previous year, Melvin's injuries sidelined him—at least for a few days. He was working cattle when his "paint horse" fell with him, tossing him to the ground. After he regained consciousness, he crawled over to the horse and pulled himself into the saddle. Shon Whetham and Ed Oldaker moved the cattle that week. "Bill came out to find out how bad I was hurt. Told me to get some help. He said it was time to get a new horse. First time I didn't make a cattle drive since I been here—all these years. Doctor said I broke some ribs and my shoulder. It took some time to heal up."

A week later, Melvin drove cattle to White River, a 25-mile drive. "Hard riding, but we made it,"[515] he wrote. That spring Bill bought Melvin a new horse.[516]

"Grandpa says you have to watch yourself all the time," Cody explained. "You have to know your cattle and what they'll do before they do it. You have to pay attention when you're a-horseback, but sometimes things happen. You can't do much about them. You just go right on; you don't set around complainin' about it. Grandpa isn't much on complainin'."

The previous winter, snow buried calving season. Cody said he and his grandfather spent several days in the saddle, checking calves and moving them into the barn if necessary. "Our boots froze right to our socks. We'd come in, get thawed out, then go back. He didn't do any complainin' then either. I didn't do much."

There might have been a bit of complaining by both Melvin and Cody the day they were caught in a hail storm. Melvin said the hail drove them into the cistern at the Rohr Place. By the time they made it home they were "froze plumb through," and even had a few "knots" on their heads.

Even the worst weather fails to dissuade prairie dogs from building their massive cities of deep hidden burrows that destroy grasslands and lay a treacherous trap for any unsuspecting horses. City dwellers may see prairie dogs as cute little dog-like animals, but prairie ranchers see them as invaders who must be eliminated. At the Coffee ranches, various methods were employed to keep the prairie dog population "at bay." Cody said his granddad's methods were more effective, but not nearly as interesting as his grandmother's.

---

[515] When Melvin was hospitalized in 2009, X-rays revealed dozens of breaks, including the shoulder and collar bone breaks that he sustained when the horse fell with him. Those breaks had never fused completely, presenting a pictures that resembled an incomplete jig-saw puzzle.
[516] Melvin quickly nicknamed the new horse, Rip. The 16-hand three-year-old overo Paint, was registered under the name, Otoe's Game Dancer. The horse opened corral gates, ripped open bags of cat and horse feed, and generally made a nuisance of himself, thus he was renamed, "Rip." After Melvin's death, Thelma gave the horse to Brylee Allred. She rode him to many 4-H championships.

"Grandma and me was going down Pants Butte[517] and this darn ole' prairie dog heads across the road," A crooked smile lit Cody's face. "There was a great big lake of water in the road. Grandma, she was going about 30 miles an hour; she was goin' run right over that ole' prairie dog. But he jumps in that lake, and he swimmed to the other side. We lost the prairie dog. He didn't get runned over. It was a good old day for that dang dog.'"

A discussion of the "Good Old Days," in Melvin's presence, (the exception might have been the prairie dog's good day) always resulted in a snort and a firm declaration that the "Good Old Days" were "right now."

"These people are always crying over the lost "good old days," he shook his head in disgust. "Even an old man like me can get a lot of work done today. We climb into a tractor, hook up the bail feeder, and feed cattle in a fraction of the time we did 50 years ago. We don't fight the cold or the heat in the summer. Those weren't the 'good old days.' These are."

By the time, Cody and Thelma chased prairie dogs across the Pants Butte road, the pants shaped formation that gave the road its name had eroded into a small hump on the hillside.
Photo: Cecil Avey-1960

The Pants Butte road stretches north and south toward the Hat Creek Valley.
This picture was found in Thelma Nation's photo box, but there is not attribution available.

---

[517] NA

In a 2017 interview, Cody said his grandfather said time had taught him to work smarter instead of harder. "The last four or five times we moved cattle down from on top, we led them cows down with the caking pickup. The calves were off them, and they just wanted to go home. We used the horses to get them started, then the ole' cows just trailed on down the road. Someone would follow with the pickup and horse trailer. We unloaded a horse if we needed too, but sometimes we didn't even get the horses out. That was sure better than freezing down."

When a corner lot next to the house Verna Callaham purchased in Harrison came up for sale, Melvin bought it. The house on the lot was demolished. A double wide trailer, purchased for $5,000, was winched onto a flat bed and moved from Harrisburg, Nebraska in Banner County to Harrison where it was settled onto a newly dug basement on the corner lot across from the library.[518] In September of 1995, *The Harrison Sun* reported that *Sioux County Floral* was open from Monday to Saturday. The "fully equipped flower shop was located in the house on the corner lot across from the library." The house also became a convenient lunch stop for Melvin and his crew when they moved cattle "up the hill."

A May 1996 tally-book entry, sandwiched between reports of a "good dinner" at the town house, information about a cattle drive, and a notation on the amount of vaccine used during branding, Melvin said that he sold the Walker Hills and paid off all his debt. The bankruptcy order was discharged. He said he felt like a load was lifted off his shoulders.

Mad Cow Disease, Bovine Spongiform Encephalopathy,[519] first identified in 1986 in dairy cattle in the United Kingdom, resulted in the death of several hundred cattle. Humans also contracted the disease after consuming infected cattle. Over 180,000 cattle were eventually diagnosed with the disease. It decimated the cattle industry in Europe. During dinner conversations, Melvin and Bill discussed the disease that was, as yet, limited to dairy cattle. They fretted that the disease would affect the rising beef prices in the United States. At first, disease-generated fear didn't affect prices that rose steadily through the mid-1980s. In 1993, beef cattle averaged $73.90 per hundred weight. For the next ten years, prices were erratic ranging from the high of $78 to a low of $62.80 in 1998. In 2003, BSE was discovered in Canada. Prices in the United States rose to $97.30 cwt; they rose to $114 a year later. After BSE was confirmed in home-grown cattle in the United States in 2005, prices fell to $103 and continued a downward path for the next five years.

"Mad Cow Disease was one of those stupid things that affected the market," Melvin said in 2008. "It never got into beef cattle herds, but most people don't know the difference between a milk cow and beef cattle, so it hurt the market some. As I got older though, I didn't worry about it like I had. I finally realized there wasn't a damn thing I could do about it."

---

[518] Thelma operated the flower shop about a year before she sold her coolers to Misty Skavdahl. Years later she said she just couldn't handle the pain people brought into the shop when they were shopping for funeral flowers.

[519] Colin A Carter, Jacqueline Huie. *Market Effects of Searching for Mad Cows*. Giannini Foundation of Agricultural Economics.

Throughout the '90s Cody's presence continued to slip into the pages of Melvin's books. In April of 1998, he reported that his great-grandson told him he had to take a day off. "He went over to Robbin's for the weekend. It's pretty quiet around here when he's gone. But he left "Farmer John" to keep us company."

Farmer John, Cody's imaginary sidekick, seldom left the house, but he was a good companion and shared great ideas with his visible partner. It might have been his scheme to ransom Melvin's handkerchiefs.

"Thelma bought some colored handkerchiefs. I didn't like them much," Melvin said in a 2005 interview. "But I couldn't leave the house without a handkerchief. That little scamp stole my white handkerchiefs and hid them, then he sold them back to me. He never touched the colored ones, just the white ones."

The handkerchiefs came in handy during the great cat roundup. Cats, in dozens of colors and sizes, most wilder that Melvin's concept of a March Hare, congregated at Hat Creek. They often found their way to the house. Thelma made sure they were well-fed. Several sneaked into the garage, but only two ever made it into the house.

"Grandma must have left the door open. The cats got in the basement. We couldn't catch them, no-way," Cody said giggling at the memory and slapping his thigh. "We finally sets us up a trap and got one out the door. But the other one ducked into the basement. In a couple minutes, he came boiling back out and ran into that there back bedroom. Grandpa told me and Grandma to chase the cat toward him, and he'd catch him.—He didn't have his hat on."

The cat, rousted from the bedroom, dashed toward the basement steps. Melvin poised, ready, half-way down the stairs, a determined glint in his eyes. The cat sprinted over the top of his head and slid—tearingly down his back.

"Scratched up his old bald head," Cody said trying to suppress a grin. "Blood's running down. There's claw marks on his back. He grabs that cat and stretches him out. Grandma is yelling, 'Don't kill him.' Grandpa opened the door and threw him right over the bushes. The last time I saw that cat he was headed south, his tail just a ringing."

Melvin pulled the handkerchief out of his pocket, wiped his head and went back to his recliner.

He was sitting in a kitchen chair at the dining room table, the night Thelma's dog discipline techniques went awry. Pooch, the latest in a long line of dachshunds that lived with the Nations, killed chickens—just for the fun of it. When the chickens started squawking, Thelma would head for the dining room window. If Pooch was dashing back and forth in his best chicken killing mode, she grabbed the pistol, poked it out the window, and fired into the air. Pooch, wisely scared of the gunfire, whipped back to the house.

"One night, those chickens started making a fuss. Pooch was having a heyday. Feathers were flying. The peacocks were screeching. Grandma grabbed the pistol and headed to the window," for a second, laughter stifled Cody's tale. "She hadn't got to the window yet, when that damn gun goes off. It blows a hole into the dag-burned wall—right beside Grandpa's chair. He just got up—didn't say a word. He took the gun from her, and heads to the back room to put it away. He didn't yell, but you could sure tell he wasn't real happy. 'I don't care if that dog kills every damn chicken, you're not shooting this gun again,' he says. Then he locks the gun in the cabinet, sits back down, and picks up his paper."

Cody shows one of the chickens Thelma saved from Pooch's clutches, to judge Bill Wilson, at the Sioux County Fair in Harrison.

COWBOYS AND CATTLEMEN

"Fifty years goes faster than we can talk about it. Like the song goes, 'Don't blink.'" Melvin Nation

When Crawford Nebraska's Fourth of July-Old West Trail Rodeo celebrated its 50th anniversary in 1997, the committee invited Melvin and several other cowboys who competed in the first rodeo, to serve as the Fourth of July Parade's Grand Marshals. They met for dinner at Moni and Joe's house, before the event.

Dale Greenwood, Melvin, Bob Jordan, Pat Drinkwalter, Marvin Rising, front Bruce Quintard, Keal Rising, Hank Kappen met at Moni's house in 1997 to share their Fourth of July Rodeo experiences. All the men rodeod together over the years.

"During the afternoon, the men shared photographs and stories," Melvin said then added he didn't know if they deserved to be Grand Marshals—"all we did was stay alive." He admitted he was glad that they had a chance to get together. "Once upon a time, we were all young and probably a little stupid. Most of us got a little smarter, or we think we did. The guys that were here today, made the most of their lives. Some of the other guys we knew fell by the side of the road. Just goes to prove that life is what you make it."

"I was so proud of the fact that my Grandpa was a cowboy. When I was little, I didn't run around saying I wanted to be an automotive engineer.[520] Like most of my friends, I wanted to be a cowboy. Unfortunately, we can't all be cowboys, hardly anyone could be as good a cowboy or as good a cattleman, as Grandpa," Bryan Hourt, Melvin's oldest grandson, said in 2008. "Way into his 70s, he could ride the hell right out of a horse, but he also understood every aspect of a cow. He taught me about cattle and horses, and he taught me the importance of home and family and knowing who you really were. I left, but I always come back."

As the world prepared, with some trepidation for the Millennium, Melvin's life continued to be dominated by the sequential rotation of ranch duties. Calving in the spring, haying in the summer, weaning in the fall, feeding in the winter. In between there was branding, fixing machinery, irrigating the fields, working cattle, and the endless job of fixing fence. Cattle work continued to be done, primarily on horseback, but most of the other work had been mechanized.

"Grandpa rode the four-wheeler from the house to the barn, 'cause he don't think walking is necessary," Cody explained to the NPR reporter in 2007. "But he mostly just hops on a horse and does what he needs to do. He likes bein' on a horse about more than anything else he does. Bill doesn't ride anymore, but Grandpa sure does."

When Bill quit riding, he gave Melvin his saddle, a gesture that traditionally signifies respect. But the pairs relationship was still complicated at times. In a 1998 interview Bill Coffee said Melvin Nation was one of the stubbornest men he ever knew and that he had a terrible temper. One entry in Melvin's book said Bill had been a "complete ass" that day. When vaccine ran low at a branding, both men were furious. But after Bill fell from his horse and was hospitalized in the spring of 1998. Melvin drove to Rapid City several times just to "check on him." Bill and Virginia were among those who helped Melvin and Thelma celebrate their 50th wedding anniversary in 2001. Several times a week, Bill came to the ranch, generally eating dinner before he went back to town. At one branding Melvin and Bill proudly raised their beers in a mutual "job well done" salute. Bill told one of the CSC coaches that Melvin was his partner, and added, "I'm the better looking one of the two."

---

[520] Bryan Hourt graduated from the School of Mines in 1996 with a degree in Mechanical Engineering and became a safety test engineer for the Honda Corporation.

"We're partners," Bill exclaimed at the conclusion of one branding. "Take our picture. I'm the better looking of the two."

"The day I climbed off that hay stack, (1951) I never hated a man more than I hated Bill Coffee," Melvin told Olive Bucklin in one of the many interviews she did with him in 2007. "But we've become friends. We really have. We've grown old together."

No one ever admitted that friendship resolved the problem of the Warbonnet dog. Bill often declared that he never liked dogs. He tolerated the ones at the ranch—if they stayed away from the barn, but when the young blue-heeler showed up at Warbonnet in late August, Bill had a change of heart. He started buying dog food; he made sure a water dish was always filled. He was caught several times sitting comfortably on the steps of the Warbonnet Barn with the dog's head in his lap. Then shortly before Christmas the dog disappeared. Melvin drove the roads looking for the dog. Thelma was sure someone had shot it. Bill groused around the barn throwing out comments, like, "Damn dog sure as hell didn't know how good he had it."

As it turned out, the dog belonged to a hired man on a local ranch. The dog had been missing nearly a year before the man saw the animal sitting beside the Warbonnet road waiting for Bill's arrival. The man drove into the yard and took the dog. Thelma discovered the identity of the "dognappers" and called the hired man's wife. She said she asked very "friendly like" for them to return the dog. The conversations went downhill from there. Melvin called and talked to the rancher. The rancher, not a "Coffee fan," said he'd sell the dog for $300. Bill declared that no dog was worth $300. Melvin agreed, but a few days later, the dog was sitting on the road when Bill pulled into the ranch. No one admitted that he or she paid the ransom, but Thelma was heard to say that she sure wasn't going to let some "Damn redneck push her around."

A phone call in 1998 solved the mystery that had haunted the family for 13 years. A Valentine, Nebraska resident called Sioux County High School in Harrison. He told secretary Carol Mumby, that he found a ring inscribed with the initials "JBEN" and the school logo "SCHS 1979." Carol discussed the call with custodian, Misty Quintard Skavdahl. They both knew that JBEN, JimBob Earl Nation graduated in 1979. Misty called Thelma. Thelma called Valentine. The man said he married a girl JimBob dated before his death in 1985. His wife told him that shortly after JimBob's death, his sister called begging her to return her brother's ring, but the woman told her husband she never had the ring. After the couple divorced, the man cleaned out his former wife's closet. In a box stuffed behind a pile of clothes, he found the ring. Thelma and Melvin drove to Valentine and retrieved the ring. In his tally book, Melvin simply noted, "We got Jim's ring back."

Many other events slipped across the pages of the tally book. On October 30, 1999, Melvin reported that he received a phone call from Bryan.[521] "He won the National Rally title in his division. Guess that means he did pretty good. Told me everything he learned about driving country roads, he learned from me. Said I could beat any of those guys. Damn knucklehead kid."

The pocket book also recorded details of the world around him: a rainbow, a beautiful sunset, cold humid days that iced the trees with frost, the height of the grass, struggles with calving. As the years marched on grandchildren competed in basketball and football, graduated from high school and college,[522] and made regular visits.

As the world prepared to celebrate 2000, some with frantic predictions of massive computer crashes and others sure the world would come to an end, Melvin continued to record the world around him. In early December he said that Janet was "going to have a baby." Shortly before the turn of the century, on December 24, 1999, Bryce Oetken became the couple's second great-grandchild.

---

[521] Bryan Hourt graduated from the School of Mines in Rapid City, South Dakota as a mechanical engineer in 1995. He became a safety test engineer for Honda in January 1996. He raced on the SCCA Pro-Rally circuit as a member of the Team Honda Research Team. He was the National Champion in the Group 5 Division in 1999.
[522] There were no college graduates on either side of Melvin and Thelma's family until Moni Hourt graduated with an education degree in 1991. That was just the beginning. Annette received a CNA degree. Buffy, Amy, and Janet earned Master's Degrees in education. All three coached high school sports: Buffy in swimming; Amy in volleyball and basketball, and Janet in volleyball. Amy's husband, Barry and Buffy's husband Shawn are also educators and coaches. Melvin received his degree in criminal justice; Bryan in mechanical engineering, and Lindsey, Melvin's wife is a physical therapist. Melvin was extremely proud of their educational achievements.

Bryce Oetken was born on Christmas Eve in 1999. Thelma and Melvin enjoy his company during one of Melvin's basketball games.

Additional great grandchildren[523] were born; family reunions held; special events were organized. One entry said Earl Cherry, an old friend, called and told him he really liked 'Mona's book.'[524] "I read it. Not too bad. Pretty darn straight." Another entry said he and Robbin talked cattle that night, "She knows a lot about a cow." He wrote.

But the importance of the tally book entries, at least officially, were that they kept a count of every animal on the ranch and at the Home Place. Losing a book was tantamount with the major crash of the state department's computer system.

"I lost my damn book," Melvin recorded in the middle of a new book. "Don't know what happened to it." The next few pages were filled with cattle locations, sales, purchases and prices that Melvin reported were copies from the old book. A year later, a quick scrawl said the book was found at the bottom of a cow tank. He said the book was mush—but—he still put it in his dresser drawer.

Jim Lemmon frequently warranted notations in the tally books. "Grandpa told me that Jim Lemmon dragged him off the bar stool after JimBob was killed and put him to work. He said he probably saved his life. They were good friends," Cody Oldaker said in 2017.

---

[523] Cody Oldaker, 1993; Bryce Oetken, 1999, Bailey Oetken, 2001, Brylee Allred, 2003, Mahayla Allred, 2005, Landen and Logen Oldaker, 2007; Brady Swisher, 2008; Donovan, 2010; Damien, 2013; Katelyn, 2015; Weston, 2017; Jaden, 2022

[524] Earl Cherry collaborated with Moni to write his autobiography, *Memoirs of a Wrinkled Bellied Kid*. Cherry had 1000 copies of the book published and printed. He presented one of them to Melvin and Thelma.

Using his left-handed scrawl Melvin recorded most of the important events, including deaths and births in his tally book.

When Melvin returned to the Coffee ranches, Jim often came to the ranch to help work cattle. He handled the branding iron during brandings and brought his crew to help out. He and his wife were part of the group that annually attended the PRCA rodeo in Rapid City, SD. The Nations joined him and Sandy at the head table at the Fort Robinson Christmas dinners. Jim also counted on Melvin to help with the annual buffalo roundup, declaring him, "One man who wasn't afraid a buffalo was going to run over the top of him."[525]

At the end of July in 2001, Jim died unexpectedly. Melvin's entry was longer than usual. "Death is never easy. It's hard to understand. I think about Robert. Doesn't seem fair that he lost his Dad. There's a reason. We just can't question it. You just have to go on."

---

[525] Discussion between Jim Lemmon and Moni Hourt in 1998. Recorded in Hourt Journal.

UNTIL YOU CAN'T

> "One day you look around and most of your friends are in the cemetery. That's when you know you're getting old. Getting old isn't for sissies. You have to enjoy those people in your life, cause someday you can't" Melvin Nation

Thelma was watching television when the jet planes crashed into the twin towers on September 11, 2001. She went down to the corrals and told Melvin. He came to the house and watched the news, shaking his head in disgust. Thelma said he stopped by the house several times that day and was watching when the first tower collapsed. Then he went out, and maybe in an attempt to find some normalcy in the day, saddled his horse and headed across the north pasture. That night he called Moni[526] and asked her if her school kids watched the news that day. He told her he hoped none of them would ever forget what happened and how important it was that, "we protect this old country of ours."

"We'd been attacked just like we had by the Japanese," Melvin told Olive Bucklin in 2006. "We had to go after them, but I had two grandsons that were military age. I sure didn't want them involved. I've never understood why it happened, but evil's been around forever and will be long after I'm dead."

By the following summer, the United States was involved in what became known as the "War on Terror." The Army invaded Afghanistan. The draft was eliminated in 1978, and neither of Melvin's grandsons joined the military.

Although the war was a common topic in northwestern Nebraska that year, in June the people that filled the yard at Warbonnet had one major goal: to celebrate Bill and Virginia's 60th wedding anniversary.

"Good day," Melvin noted. "Annie[527] did a beautiful job. Sounds like Virginia did years ago."

In a 1999 interview, Bill admitted there were only two things in life that he ever wanted: the ranch and Virginia. Virginia (Kennedy) was a Chadron State College graduate when she married Bill in 1942. She said the first few weeks of marriage, "for a city girl" were challenging. Bill

---

[526] At that time, Moni Hourt was teaching at District 2, Glen, a rural school in Sioux County Nebraska
[527] Ann Coffee Wachman, a talented soprano presented several musical selections at the event. Virginia also sang soprano at many local events.

Melvin and Virginia Coffee enjoyed each other's respect and mutual admiration.

agreed with her assessment. During the party, he repeated his favorite "Virginia" story. He said were married about three weeks when the ranch cook quit.

"Virginia made a great chocolate cake, but that was about all," Bill said. "I told the men I'd fire the first one who complained about the meal. No one got fired that day."

"I told Virginia that day that she was a saint to stay married to that man all these years," Melvin said with a grin. "I meant it, and she actually agreed with me. Enjoyed the day. Got to see a lot of people that have stopped at the ranch over the years."

The following month, Melvin was diagnosed with prostate cancer. "The girls are takin' this awful hard, but it's just the way it goes." He wrote. "It'll cost $10,000. Start treatments tomorrow. I don't know about all this."

Every other day, he traveled to Scottsbluff for radiation treatments. He reported that Moni went with him and asked a lot of questions. Robbin went along on other trips. Thelma made the 200-mile trip on a regular basis. and Most of the time, he simply drove himself, then returned to run the windrower or to perform the many chores that needed done.

On December 2, 2001 Melvin and Thelma took a break from the worry about the cancer treatments and celebrated their 50th wedding anniversary with a small contingency of friends and family. Melvin remarked in his tally book, that "it was just right, nothing big and elaborate, just a great get-together with friends to mark an important milestone. Time sure goes fast."

Nine months later, on September 26, 2002, the tally book reported that Melvin took his last treatment. "We made 40 trips down there, 6,649 miles back and forth. They say its gone."

Melvin and Thelma celebrated their 50th anniversary in 2001.

The colts pulled out of the Hunter Hills in 2002 kept Melvin and his hired men busy most of that fall. "We got some good colts out of there," Cody said in a 2007 interview. "Ole Hunter has been a good horse. Grandpa kinda felt bad because he took the horses out of hills, but there were just too many up there. And Hunter has a great life. I take good care of him."

"It's taking a long time for them to trust me," Melvin wrote in his book that fall. "I have a three-year-old that loves me, but doesn't want to get along with anyone else. Horses are a lot like people. They just want to be treated fair."

Many times over the years Melvin compared raising children with work on the ranch. He said raising kids was like working with horses. You had to be consistent, and make the right things easy and the wrong things hard. He said it was very important that you listen to both a horse and a kid—that they would both tell you the direction they needed to take. Snubbing a horse too tight would make them rebel, same was true with a kid, but you couldn't let them have too much slack, because they'd get in trouble.

"When a kid gets to be 12 or 13, I think you have to let them make a lot of their own decisions," He said. "If you fuss and feud at a string of cows going up the road, they're going to fight you, but if you let them meander a little, just steering them away from the bar pits, they'll find the middle and generally just keep going up the road. When kids get a little older, you have to let them have some of that meandering space."

There was more panicked motion that meandering at the annual Christmas programs held at District #6, Bodarc School. The tradition of attending the annual country school Christmas program reconvened for the Nations when Cody started school. Not much had changed from the years they had watched their children perform on similar country-school programs.

White starched sheets, safety-pinned over a telephone wire, stretched across one end of the one-room schoolhouse, muffled the nervous giggles of the K-8 thespians. Invariably a youngster peeked between the curtains, then creating a "snapping turtle" effect, popped back behind, reluctant to face the eyes of the friends and families filling the room. Melvin generally reported in his book that Cody "did fine" and the kids had a good time. In one entry, however, he admitted that he "hadn't understood one damn thing except the Zimmerman girls[528] on the piano."

Rural School Christmas programs changed little from those performed at District 76 when Moni and Robbin were small. Left to right: Scott Wickersham, Bruce Wickersham, Robbing Nation, Zanya Geike, Becky Wickersham. Accordion player, Moni Nation

---

[528] Austin and Chelsea Zimmerman, the children of Dee and Shelley Zimmerman were outstanding musicians and entertained guests at the program.

Christmas continued to be a time of mixed emotions. Only a few gifts: a William Henry Jackson print in 1982, Amy's gift of one of Clark Nation's wood carving—an elk in 2003, and the "fifth of Yellowstone whiskey that Joe delivered on a yearly basis, appeared in his tally book. However, he always recorded the day as one spent with family. "Had a good time." Many times, there was also a notation about JimBob's absence.

"Sometimes memories are hard to live with," Melvin wrote early one Christmas morning. "I should be thankful for today, for all I have, but I'm sitting here totally alone in my mind. It gets lonesome. I can't help but wonder what he'd be doing if he were here."

"Sometimes you knew Melvin was a little sad, but mostly he just looked at life with a twinkle in his eye," Shon Whetham[529] said. "When I first met him I just thought he was a man who deserved my respect." He grinned. "I didn't realize he had such a 'twisted' sense of humor. Then he stole my horse—the first time. He didn't drink as much as the rest of us did, so we were fair game. He'd leave the bar before we did, unload our horses, and take off with them. They'd be at the sale barn, or at the rodeo grounds, or tied to a tree somewhere. If Melvin was around, you checked your trailer before you went home."

Shon Whetham and Melvin discuss the latest prank.

A favorite trick targeted horse trailers parallel parked on Main Street. Melvin would quickly unhook the trailer and laugh in anticipation, knowing the trailer's owner would pull away without the trailer.

---

[529] Shon Whetham and his wife, Kathy, operate the Jerry and Judy Engebretsen place in southern Sioux County. He and Melvin became friends when Shon started helping him work cattle in the early 90s. Kathy is the granddaughter of one of Melvin's longtime friends, Pat Drinkwalter.

Revenge for all of Melvin's jokes looked within reach one afternoon. Shon's crew already finished their meal at the Village Barn in Harrison, when Melvin came in for lunch. They paid their bill, stepped outside, and immediately headed for Melvin's trailer. They had just unloaded his horse, when he popped outside.

"He knew what we were up to and caught us in the Act," Shon said laughing at the memory. "He cussed us a little, and we finally left. We just couldn't stand it though. We parked at Bob York's and rode our horses back up to the restaurant. We grabbed Melvin's horse and took him out to the Pullen Place. We were sure hopin' he'd get all the way home before he noticed the horse was gone, but that damn Bob, couldn't stand it. He went back and told Melvin where his horse was."

One night Melvin stayed a little later at the bar, and Shon finally won the prank game—at least temporarily. He and a couple of friends slipped outside and unloaded the ton of salt Melvin purchased earlier that day. They transferred the salt to the cab of Melvin's pickup. Melvin spent nearly an hour unloading and reloading the salt back onto the trailer. Shon said he heard Melvin had invented some interesting and very colorful cuss words that night.

"A couple weeks after I went to work for Melvin, he told me he didn't think he'd like me much, but he said he'd changed his mind," John Reece[530] said. "I took that as a compliment. I found out over the years, that Melvin was always willing to change his mind—unless he wasn't."

John said Melvin seldom hollered or yelled and contended that almost any problem could be solved, given enough time. However, the missing rope problem didn't have a good solution. Melvin forgot to tie his rope on his saddle early that May morning. The cattle moved fairly well, but all morning John said his boss "fussed" about his missing rope. Finally, John told him if it bothered him that bad, he'd let him borrow his rope. Melvin disgustedly replied that he didn't want John's rope.

"What if I get mad and decide to hang myself," Melvin snorted. "I'm not going to hang myself with your damn rope."

"He was always laughing about something. We rode for miles and miles. When we were headed back to the barn, we visited. We talked about rodeo a lot. That was something we both had in common. He didn't discourage or encourage me, but he did tell me if he and Thelma wouldn't have gotten together, he'd have been a rodeo bum his whole life. He liked the lifestyle, not the uncertainty."

John said Melvin was one of the toughest men he ever knew. "He'd joke that when it got too tough for everyone else, it was just right for him," John said with a smile. "Then he'd grin like he did and say that maybe he wasn't as tough as he used to be."

---

[530] John Reece, the nephew of Keal Rising grew up in the region. He won numerous saddle bronc riding saddles over the years.

John said when he worked for Melvin he was 75 years old and still getting on a horse every day. He added that the day Melvin suffered a stroke, he's been working cattle all morning long. "I think his toughness, mentally and physically really rubbed off on me. I've learned to laugh things off when they go to hell, and when I can't do nothing else, just pick up the wreck and go on."

Victor Klug[531] said he was 40 years old when he applied for a job on the ranch, but he said Melvin gave him a chance. "He told a great story. They all had lessons, if you listened. He'd take time to teach a person. Not everyone could teach, but Melvin could. There were times when he just stood back and let you do your own thing. To this day, I'll do something, and I'll think about the way he did it."

There were times when even Melvin's best teaching methods verged on failure. One journal entry said he let his hired man lead the drive up East Hat Creek that day. "He ran off and left us," Melvin wrote. "We scattered cattle all the way up the hill. Tough ole day."

Very few were entrusted with the job of "taking the lead up the hills." When his daughters were young, Melvin generally acted as an outrider giving him the chance to check on the drag where the girls were perpetually stationed. Bill took the lead up the hill during many of the Warbonnet years. In later years, although he did let his granddaughter, Amy, take the lead a few times, he generally stayed at the head of the herd, making sure the cattle tromped across the bridges, didn't "ball up," and meandered slowly along the center line, avoiding the "bar pits."[532] He rode back and forth along the edges of the herd gently "shooshing" the cattle to keep them moving and following those on the "front-end."

Although Melvin said he was almost always short-handed on the drives, most went remarkably well; primarily because the help he had was, in his words, "pretty damned adequate." Ed Oldaker, Shon Whetham, Neil Nunn, and Bruce Quintard often manned the roadways. Jim Lemmon and his Fort Robinson crew made dozens of early morning trips to the ranch to drive cattle up or down whichever trail was designated that day. Melvin surrounded himself with people he could trust.

"I always hated to lean on those guys, but if I needed help, I'd give them a call. They knew I'd return the favor. I never had a lot of really close friends, but I had a few, and those I had forever."[533]

To Melvin, death was simply part of life. He told a NTV reporter in 2007, that he hated "like the dickens" to lose a baby calf, because that calf was depending on him to keep it alive. He added that sometimes death was kinder than life, with animals and humans.

---

[531] Klug, Victor personal interview with Moni Hourt 2017.
[532] The ditches on either side of the road were called "bar pits." As roads were constructed, the sloping ditches on either side of a road were called barrow pits. The term was soon shortened to bar pits. There is no proof that the term described the practice of throwing empty beer cans in the ditches.
[533] Melvin Nation, personal interview by Moni Hourt 2000.

Bryan Hourt was rally racing in Maine on July 23, 2001, when Moni received a call from Melvin telling her Jim Lemmon had died suddenly that day from a heart attack. He reminded Moni of the hours he and Jim had spent together, his sorrow for Sandy and her young son Robert. "Never know, just never know if you're going to get to see the next sunrise," his voice was sad as it stretched across miles of telephone lines. "You gotta appreciate every day we get, every damn one."

In 2002, he wrote in his book that Keal Rising was fighting cancer. "We went down to see ole Keal today. He's just not going to beat this thing. Tough on that Sis." A few months, in an entry dated February 26, 2003 he reported that Keal's grandson traveled from Lincoln to be with his grandfather. "Craig left. He was gone about 20 minutes when Keal died. Funny how things work out." A strong believer in predestination, Melvin added, "The day you're born the good Lord sets a day for you to die. That's just the way it is."

Bruce Quintard[534] succumbed to cancer in April 2003. He was 15 when Melvin hauled him to the Warbonnet Ranch and put him to bed to sleep off a bad case of inebriation.

"Bruce was one of the best friends I ever had—when he was sober,"[535] Melvin explained in a 2005 interview. "When he was drunk, he wasn't worth a nickel. He was one of those guys that never shoulda touched it. When he died, it hit me that most of my old friends, those guys I rodeoed with, and laughed with, and yeah, drank with were gone. I miss them all, but I especially miss that damn Bruce"

Bruce was one of the standards at the ranch and seldom missed a branding. He castrated[536] thousands of calves, and often "grossed out" visitors by walking around the pen with a raw mountain oyster hanging from the side of his mouth.

"I about lost my breakfast that first year I was up there." Pat Nikodemas, one of the Chadron State College wrestlers said. "I never ate a cooked mountain oyster,[537] let alone a raw one. After a couple of years, I figured out he was just doin' it for shock value."

---

[534] The Quintard homestead, a few miles from Hat Creek, was established by Bruce's grandparents Dan and Barbara (Wasserburger) Jordan in 1889. Barbara Jordan babysat Bill, and he never forgot her kindness. Throughout his life, he extended that kindness to Bruce.
[535] Melvin Nation, personal interview by Moni Hourt 1998.
[536] Bull calves that weren't needed for breeding were neutered by hand in the branding pen. It took a quick and steady to hand to make the procedure as painless as possible.
[537] Rocky mountain oysters or prairie oysters is a dish made from calf testicles. The outside membranes are peeled from the testicles, coated in flour, milk, eggs, pepper, and salt and deep-fat-fried. They can also be made of turkey testicles but true gourmets prefer beef or lamb fries.

Nearly every elementary student in Sioux County attended Ranch Day at Hat Creek. Bill Coffee welcomed the students.

Sixty-five Sioux County elementary school students gathered at Hat Creek on September 28, 2005 for the region's first "Ranch Day." The event, organized by Moni Hourt,[538] was designed to teach Sioux County students about ranching and its importance. Bill opened the event by welcoming the students then turned it over to Melvin, telling the crowd that, "He knows what's going on around here."

Sioux County School students load into a horse trailer for tours of the ranch. Melvin stands by the back gate. Lori Windsor and Tony Johnson help load the students.

---

[538] Moni was teaching at the Glen rural school when one of her ranch kids told her his town friends didn't know anything about the ranching industry. He was talking about Sioux County Nebraska friends who lived in a community that had been totally based on agriculture. She built a curriculum on the industry, asked numerous speakers from the ranching and agricultural community to speak at the event and convinced Melvin and Bill to allow the entire student population of Sioux County to converge on the ranch. The program continued until 2012.

Melvin loaded the group into horse trailers and shepherded them from place to place across the ranch. He spoke to the students about the changes he had seen in the nearly 55 years since he arrived as a "snot-nosed boy." Joe Nunn, speaking about his penchant for writing cowboy poetry, read a poem about "Ole Mel." Melvin quickly realized he needed to check on something at the corrals.

"We were all eating dinner down at Joe Nunn's the first time Joe read that poem," Shon Whetham said. "Melvin had to get up and leave then too. It was hard for him to get any recognition, particularly from a friend."

Although Bill's health wasn't good, he and Melvin were busy that fall adding to the cow herd and working on a plan to improve Hat Creek's water system. Fresh, clear water had always filled the cistern above the ranch buildings at Warbonnet. The cistern was cleaned regularly and except when a snake slithered out of the kitchen faucet, the water supply was problem free.

Water wasn't that easy at Hat Creek. The Hat Creek Valley, a rift valley, was created several millions years before the ranch was established. Water ran between the rock layers of the valley walls, but there was little surface water. CF Coffee intentionally located his ranch on a creek. It supplied water for livestock—and for the ranch house. The cattle didn't seem to mind the water's slightly alkaline taste or the mud that often tainted the tanks. But after a bad rain, the mud infused creek water also poured from the faucets, filled the toilets with a brown sludge, and even clogged the washing machine.

"There was a good spring at the base of the Hunter Hills. We talked about piping water from up there for several years," Melvin said in 2007. "I went over to the pond and put a level on the hood of the pickup, then I sighted in on the ranch through a gunsight. Sure enough, the land went downhill. It was only about three miles to the ranch. Bill called the Natural Resources District, and they began to work on a plan to improve the water situation."

The pair discussed the system most of the afternoon on October 8, 2005. Virginia called Hat Creek about an hour after Melvin left. She said after Melvin left Bill laid down for a nap and never woke up.

That evening Melvin sat down at the kitchen table and wrote a short letter about the afternoon. The missive is indicative of the relationship the pair developed over the years.

> I hauled a load of open heifers down to the Hergert feed lot Sat the 8. On the way back, I stopped to see Bill, hadn't seen him for a week and I wanted to tell him how many open heifers we had and what they weighed. We had a good visit. He said I've been thinking a lot about the bull deal with Hergert.[539] I think the thing we should do is go ahead and wear our bulls out at the price we have set and when we need to

---

[539] Dave Hergert leased the ranch two years before Bill's death with the agreement that Melvin would be allowed to live and work on the ranch as long as he chose.

replace them let Hergert buy them. My only concern is the quality of the bulls he buys, but he said we can't do anything about that. He said we wouldn't have to buy all the heifers. we know we have quite a few light heifer calves. we could sort them off and let Dave have them if he wants to do it that way. He asked me about the new pipe line we are putting in and said he didn't care if we went into the north pasture. He had some concerns about the Hunter place. He ask me about the new horse I bought a couple of weeks ago. He was interested in everything. I will be forever grateful I stopped and seen him.

In Bill's will he left $10,000 to "his friend" Melvin Nation. A year before, he brought Melvin a bonus check telling him, "Virginia and the girls think you deserve this," then added a little reluctantly, "and I do too." It was as hard for Bill Coffee to give a compliment as it was for Melvin Nation to receive it.

"Grandpa and Bill, they was friends, but boy they'd get into it once in a while. Grandpa just wouldn't take anything from Bill. I think that's why Bill respected him," Cody Oldaker said in a 2017 interview. "After Bill died, Grandpa really missed him. He said they'd been young together, and they'd grown old together. He just missed him, that was all."

That August, for the annual Sioux County Fair parade in Harrison, Melvin helped Cody decorate his four-wheeler with a stuffed dog and a sign that read, "Modern Day Cowboy." He sent Cody to line-up, then mounted his horse and leading a riderless horse behind him, paid tribute to Bill Coffee in a time-honored manner.

Melvin led a riderless horse saddled with Bill's saddle and draped in the Square Top Three brand the Coffee family made famous in Western Nebraska.

The next year the Sioux County Fair faced cancellation. On July 30, 2006, on their way home from Hat Creek, Buffy Hourt-Allred and her two daughters, Brylee and Mahayla stopped to watch a small spiral of smoke that lazily snaked into the bright July sky. Brylee carried her small camera with her to take pictures of the chickens, the cats, and the tire swing that bounced between the cottonwood trees. Buffy used it to record the smoke, never realizing that the tiny column would erupt into a fire that would ravage Pants Butte, East and West Hat Creek, and Sowbelly Canyons. The 2006 fire burned nearly 80,000 acres in the region, 47,000 in Sioux County alone.

"It won't come back in our lifetime, probably not in our grandchildren's lifetimes, but in the spring, the grass will grow. They say this country didn't even have trees 100 years ago. It was only when settlers came in and started fighting the fires that the trees were able to grow," Melvin's voice was full of sadness as he described the scorched hillsides that led out of the valley. "It looks pretty tough right now, but they'll be grass everywhere in the spring. And no one was hurt."[540]

The fire in the Hat Creek Valley began with a lightning strike. Buffy Hourt captured its beginning on a small child's camera.

The fire threatened the city of Harrison. The black smoke looming over Whiteakers' cabin east of Harrison originates in Sowbelly Canyon.

---

[540] Melvin Nation, personal interview with Moni Hourt, 2006.

Trees and grasslands on both sides of the East Hat Creek Road made the familiar path, on which many cattle meandered, almost unrecognizable.

When Nebraska Educational Television producer, Olive Bucklin,[541] arrived in western Nebraska later that fall to explore an angle for a documentary on the beef industry, she too was shocked by the devastation caused by the fire. A month earlier, Bucklin attended a presentation Moni Hourt made about the Ranch Day programs and the importance of teaching students and teachers about the agricultural industry. The fire and its impact on western Nebraska and its ranchers were some of the subjects Hourt discussed, but Bucklin said she had never imagined that the fire stretched over thousands of acres.

"I was looking for ranchers to tell the story of the Beef Industry. Moni's presentation about the many fallacies people embrace about the industry made sense. She made a point of telling the group that the ranchers took great pride in being the stewards of their land. She spoke about the interviews she did with ranchers in western Nebraska after the fire and how it impacted them. I asked her to introduce me to some of those ranchers and act as a consultant on the documentary," Bucklin[542] said in 2006. "She introduced me to Melvin that next week. He was one of the most intelligent, articulate men I ever met. I knew I wanted him to be part of the story."

Thousands of acres of grassland were burned during the fire. Ranchers quickly helped other ranchers move cattle out of danger and after the fired shared the grass that had been spared. Melvin and his crew spent most of the next week after the fire helping area ranchers that weren't as fortunate as the Coffee ranches had been.

---

[541] Bucklin produced many documentaries for Nebraska Public Television before embarking on the "Beef State" production.
[542] Bucklin, Olive, discussions with Moni Hourt 2006-2010

Melvin said he didn't have time. Bucklin convinced him that he did. For the next year, Bucklin made regular visits to western Nebraska and traveled to several ranches including Hat Creek and Warbonnet. With Moni serving in the adviser capacity, Bucklin and her cinematographer shot footage of brandings, calving, and cattle drives. They taped hours of interviews.

"I didn't realize how dedicated ranchers were to their land, to their animals, to their families," Bucklin said. "In the eastern part of the state, we see more slaughter houses and large confinement operations. Ranchers in this region gave us a totally different concept of the industry."

Cinematographer Brian Seifferlein, and sound director, Erin Green tease Melvin during a quick break while they were shooting footage of Melvin and his crew as they moving cattle down East Hat Creek.

"The "TV people" are here again today," Melvin wrote in his tally book. "They don't hurt anything."

One of the most poignant pieces in the documentary was shot early one April morning just as the sun tinged the horizon above the Hat Creek barn. Melvin had been up all night. A backwards calf had died shortly before the crew arrived. Melvin and Cody were in the process of pulling a second calf. In the subsequent interview, he admitted he was tired, worn out by the process of calving out 1000 head of calves. He told the television crew that he didn't count the dead, he just concentrated on the living. He snorted when he was asked about a schedule for calving, telling Bucklin that he sure wished the cows would get on a schedule, but he didn't think that would ever happen. Then he said, that particularly in the past, calving had always been the highlight of his life.

Melvin and Olive Bucklin visit after a particularly difficult night of calving. Even then Melvin's sense of humor prevailed.

"I love to see those little old calves hit the ground and run and kick. I like young life. We used to run a lot of colts. There's nothing prettier than those little old colts, getting up on those wobbly legs and rompin around. It's a beautiful sight. Spring is full of young life. You look forward to that and try to move past the ones that don't make it."

Bob Jordan was also interviewed for possible inclusion in the documentary. He died unexpectedly in April of 2007. Although Melvin cherished his friendship with the young men he had mentored through the years, he said it was difficult to lose the men with whom he'd spent a lifetime. "One day you realize most of your friends are dead." He said. "It isn't a very good feeling."

"Melvin told me a lot of stories about Bob and Bruce and Jim Lemmon," John Reece said. "He told me stories about Bill Coffee. He said they argued some but he hadn't regretted coming back to Coffee's. He loved the ranch. And boy no one ever said anything bad about Bill. That would've resulted in an ass chewing. But I think Melvin was lonesome sometimes, too. He didn't talk about it, but I think he was."[543]

In 2007, cancer once again, turned Melvin and Thelma's lives upside down. A massive storm dumped nearly two feet of snow on the ground shortly before Christmas 2007. Melvin called Moni early that morning and told her they weren't coming down for Christmas as they had the last few years. Robbin received the same phone call, but neither girl was willing to break the tradition of spending Christmas with their parents. They loaded food, presents, and their families into four-wheel drives and headed to Hat Creek. Annette Oldaker arrived with her twin sons, Logen and Landen. Everyone expected to have a great time.

---

[543] John Reece interview 2017.

Picture of Logen and Landen with Thelma, Buffy, and Mahayla Thelma performed her traditional stretching routine with Landen as Mahayla watched. Buffy visits with Logen.

"Bryan drove off the road and got stuck, three times," Three-year-old Brylee Allred's dominant memory of the day involved the journey out of the ditch and through the pasture. For the rest of the family the dominant memory was Melvin's announcement that on Christmas Eve, Thelma's doctor called to tell her she had been diagnosed with terminal small-cell lung cancer.

"It wasn't a good Christmas." Melvin's Christmas Day entry was abrupt and devastating. "We made it through. That's all."

On January 18, 2008 Thelma's 75th birthday, she started chemotherapy. For Melvin, the event was almost debilitating. The entries in his tally book refocused on facts and figures. Remarks about his family and surroundings were tinged in sadness and helplessness.

"Thelma's had her first treatment today." Melvin wrote. "Helluva journey. She shouldn't have to go through this. She's having trouble coping with this. She shouldn't have to."

Although the prognosis had been dire, the chemotherapy was effective. As she had always done, Thelma handled the adversity with flint-hard resolve. When she started losing her hair, she had the nurses shave her head. Melvin and Cody had a tough time accepting her new look, so she donned a wig—for a while. Finally, she told them both the "damn wig itched." She threw it in the corner. Her first CAT scan that spring showed that the cancer had shrunk.

Melvin wrote in an early May entry. "The day is beautiful. Moni took Thelm to the doctor. She's doing better. Doctor is surprised."

Bryce on Irv, Brylee on Rip, Mahayla on Wonder, Bailey on Teddy in 2011.

Filming for the documentary continued into early 2008. One of the last pieces of footage, shot at the shipping pens captured four generations on horseback: Melvin, Moni, Amy, and Cody. The finished product premiered in May of 2008 at the Haythorn Ranch near Arthur, Nebraska where some of the footage for the documentary was shot. Melvin was asked to be a special guest. He didn't attend. He said he had work to do.

Bailey's Oetken fills her great-grandfather's lap with horses. He gave her first horse, a sorrel named Barney.

As Thelma's condition improved, ranch events redominated the tally-book pages. A wind storm scattered cattle all over the ranch. The grass was growing, but the cows were having trouble mothering up. In May he reported that Moni helped drive the cattle to the Hunter Hills and added that Cody spent the day working on machinery. He wrote that Bryan had flown in from his home in Columbus, Ohio, to join the branding crew, that Amy and Janet were there. He remarked on his cattle partnership with Robbin and Ed and that Cody had gotten $491.21 for his calf. That fall steers averaged 1130 pounds.

The tally book remarked that the next generation of Nation offspring continued to follow the tradition of "loving a horse."

Brylee Allred rode her pony, Wonder, in the Harrison Fair and Melvin remarked that, "She doesn't ride too bad." As he had with all his own kids he checked her cinch before she competed. After his death she inherited his horse Rip.

Photograph: Shari Packard.

Wil Packard became a family friend during the months that he treated Thelma's cancer. At the last minute shortly before his wife took this picture, he was coaxed into adding his presence. Pictured with him: Back: Amy, Brady and Barry Swisher, Annette and Landen Oldaker, Greg Oetken, Janet Oetken Victory, Cody Oldaker, Robbin and Ed Oldaker, Bryan, Moni, and Joe Hourt. Front: Melvin Oldaker and Annette's son, Logen, Melvin, Thelma, Bailey Oetken, Velma (Sis) Rising, Brylee, Mahayla, and Buffy Allred.

Thelma's cancer seemed to be under control. Oncologist Wil Packard and his wife Shari joined the family in early November to celebrate Thelma's improving health.[544] A family pho-

---

[544] Buffy Hourt, who was teaching in Cody, Wyoming. She spent her summers at her parents' home and spent many hours visiting with her grandparents at Hat Creek. During one of those visits Thelma mentioned she'd like to get everyone together and wondered if Dr. Packard might come. Buffy said she'd get things organized and call Dr. Packard. The entire family except Shawn Allred who was coaching football that weekend came to the ranch. Dr. Packard and his wife were also in attendance.

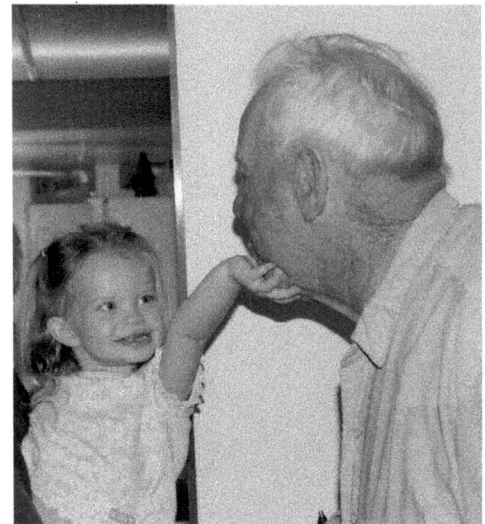

No one ever had the courage to explain to Sis the exact meaning of reincarnation, but Melvin said there was never any doubt that Mahayla Allred was full of Thelma's particular brand of spit and vinegar.

tograph captured the smiling face of every member of the family. Sis had joined the group and Wil Packard stretched out on the ground, smiling happily. The photograph captured a moment in time, a moment that was destined to change.

"Another Christmas came and went. It was a good one," Melvin wrote on December 25, 2008. "Its strange what a year brings. Last year we found out Thelm had cancer. She has luckied out." He added another line. "That Mahayla is an onrey little cuss. Sis says that she is the reincarnit of her Grandma. I think that's acuritte."

In the 20 years that Melvin and Thelma had lived at Hat Creek many changes had taken place in the world. Although reception wasn't perfect, cell phones had made communication in the region as little easier. Shortly after they'd become available, Melvin purchased a bag phone and an antenna that he fastened magnetically to his pickup cab. He said he didn't make many calls. He even scoffed at the crazy things, but he told Joe Hourt that Moni's bag phone worked pretty good. She called him every morning on the way to school.[545] He added that he was sure glad the trip wasn't much longer, she about talked his ear off.

"One morning you must have called him when you rode up to that stone house out there above Glen" Joe Hourt told his wife after Melvin stopped at the shop that afternoon. "He said he could hear you clear as day. He didn't like cell phones much better than I did, but he was still interested by the technology."

The love hate relationship with technology extended to computers. He was proud that Thelma had mastered a computer and was able to trace his family's genealogy past the family myths, but he often remarked that she "spent too much time on the damn thing."

On the other hand, although he never believed four-wheelers should be used to work cattle, he fully embraced the evolution of new farm and ranch equipment. He said that damn four-wheeler saved him "a lot of steps."

---

[545] Moni was teaching at the Pink Schoolhouse, District 43. She said she had very spotting service, but was able to talk to her Dad about 6 every morning as she drove through Corkscrew Canyon, a 15-minute segment of her 30-minute drive. She only had two other points on the road that enabled conversation.

"Sometimes I think these kids should have to do things the way we did years ago, feed with a pitchfork and a sled, hay with a stacker and a sweep, no air conditioning, not even a shade on most of the tractors. We chopped a lot of ice. One of the hardest jobs we had at Hat Creek was chopping the damn ice. I'm not sure many men could do that today," he paused and smiled. "But then it isn't necessary either. We don't have to work ourselves plumb to death."

He had formed a cattle partnership with Robbin and Ed and dutifully noted payments and profits. He said that Robbin knew as much about a cow as Ed did.

He branded a few calves each year with Cody's brand, determined that Cody would have a good start in life. "If I had a couple of men like that Cody, I could get a lot done. I worry about the future of ranching. It'll be men like that Cody that keeps it alive, if that is even possible. That Cody, he's going to be a good man someday. He's a good sucker, the little hammer head. I wish he was as good a student as he is a hand around the ranch, but he's a good one."

Melvin and Robbin spent hours discussing cattle and the world of agriculture. Both enjoyed their conversations immensely.

Cody Oldaker became Melvin's right hand man at an early age.

"He loved his family," John Reece said. "I don't think he gave them a lot of praise to their faces, but he talked about them to the rest of us. He'd never had much of an education, so it tickled him to death that the grandkids went on to college. He also said there wasn't a lazy one in the bunch. He was really proud of that."

He seldom talked politics, but he had a great love of his country. In a 2007 interview he told Bucklin. "We're pretty independent out here, but that independent thinking gets out of control if you aren't careful. If you run your head against a stone wall, better back off and take a look at it. There is some people that want to fight the government. They scream and holler and won't pay their taxes. How do they figure on running the country without paying for it? That's a small price for what they got. I worry that people don't love our dear old country like they used to. It makes me sad."

He didn't consider himself a religious person, but he believed firmly in a God. "I'm no church goin person, but I've lived pretty close to God. I really have," Melvin added during an interview in 2007. "There's a better place after this one. Don't have any idea what it will look like, but don't doubt it's there. My mama and daddy, boy they believed in the Good Lord, and they lived it, too. They lived it a lot better than I have."

In most ways Melvin was a forward-thinker, always looking to the future, always wanting to improve both the ranch operation and his family's lives. On the other hand, he looked at life from a logical perspective. He had a great respect for women, and considered men who mistreated a woman, "filthy dogs." But he also felt it was a woman's responsibility to avoid trouble. He didn't think the statement was sexist, it just made sense.

"Some men are dogs," He told his oldest daughter when she was 14.[546] "You have to watch out for them. "You prance around in tight clothes and short skirts you're just asking for trouble. And don't let yourself be alone with a man like that. You're smarter than they are."

One evening during the State High School Rodeo in Harrison, in 1968, Moni angrily told Melvin that while waiting on a young local cowboy's table that afternoon, he had reached up under her skirt and pulled her "half-slip" down to her knees. Melvin told her that her "dress was too damn short." But he added that she should've, "knocked him off his damn chair and stepped right in the middle of him."

Many years later, the boy, now a man, told Moni that Melvin had "discussed" the incident with him. Melvin hadn't gotten mad or yelled, he just expressed his deep disappointment in the boy's action. He'd told him that he wasn't a man at all if he couldn't treat a woman right. "I'd known Melvin my whole life. I'd looked up to him. I was totally ashamed of myself," the man said in 1985.

Although he said he was not a great "talker," many of the people he met including the NETV crew admired his ability to evaluate various events and draw a clear comparison without bias.

"I asked him about homesteaders versus ranchers." Olive Bucklin said. "Many of the ranchers that I've met saw a homesteader as an interloper, even an enemy. Melvin saw both sides of the story."

---

[546] Moni Hourt journal August 14,1965.

"I can see the farmer's viewpoint. I can't blame him for wanting a piece of ground. If I'd lived in that era I don't know what side I'd leaned toward. I'd probably leaned toward the farmer, because I tend to lean toward the more helpless. You couldn't blame those homesteaders for wanting to have their own land. I don't know how you could fault them. I sure wouldn't," he told Bucklin in a taped interview, then added, "I probably would have analyzed it pretty good before I came out here and plowed up that ole ground. Boy it took tough people. The government was wrong sending them out here to this big old grass country. Probably 80 percent of this land shoulda never been plowed up."[547]

He went on to say that the homesteaders, should be admired, that they were gutsy people. "Them that survived have to be commended. I don't think I ever seen the day I was stout enough, tough enough. They were up against everything you could think of—nature, grasshoppers, no money, too much rain, not enough rain. If the government woulda given them, say five sections, that mighta worked, but even a section wouldn't work here like it did in the east. It was plump stupid the way it was managed."

On the other hand, Melvin said, no one could blame the cattle men for standing against the homesteaders. "Those guys who were using the land to run a cow, was more in sync with the land. I'm always in sympathy with the cowman. Sure, the rancher he got belligerent, and got overbearing. Maybe he got hoggish. But they were here 10-20 years before the homesteaders come in. They fought for what they had."

Melvin used the Coffee family to support his ideas about homesteading. "The Coffees, they'd have died for their land if they'd a had to, but they were smart. CF Coffee, he looked around and knew most of the homesteaders wouldn't make it. He used the Homestead Act to claim the areas with water so he could take care of his cattle, then he opened a bank. He lent money to the homesteaders, and he bought the ones out who couldn't make it. I don't think he cheated any one, he just used his head. He took his fences down and ended up with the land legally. He weathered a lot of storms to get control of his country."

The story about rancher, Barlett Richards, contrasted with the logical intelligence used by CF Coffee, according to Melvin. "Richards, now he tried to fight the government. He wouldn't take his fences down. He thought he could beat them, [the government], but he couldn't and he ended up losing everything. Coffee knew he had to join them to beat them. Sure this is cattle country. Shoulda never been plowed, but I can see why the homesteaders tried to make

---

[547] Samuel H Aughey a professor at the University of Nebraska developed the theory that "rain would follow the plow." His concept was included in Charles Dana Wilber's 1881 book *The Great Valleys and Prairies of Nebraska and the Northwest*. One paragraph in the book exclaimed: "God speed the plow…. By this wonderful provision, which is only man's mastery over nature, the clouds are dispensing copious rains … [the plow] is the instrument which separates civilization from savagery; and converts a desert into a farm or garden…. To be more concise, *Rain follows the plow*." Unfortunately, thousands who came to the Northern Great Plains found that the rain did not follow their plow.

it work.⁵⁴⁸ As with most things in life, the homesteader/rancher question just doesn't have a black and white answer."

"He read all the time and was always evaluating the world around him," Bryan Hourt said. "In my career as an engineer, I've only met a few people that could match his intellect. One of the Honda presidents from Japan really impressed me. He reminded me of Grandpa. Some people would think that was a crazy thing to say, but Grandpa would understand, because he knew I'd thought about the idea before I said it, just like he always did. He told us that we all needed to learn something new every day. I doubt if any of us ever forgot that advice."

Three generations, Bryan, Cody, and Melvin enjoy a discussion at Hat Creek.

Although his children and grandchildren and even his great-grandchildren recognized his impact in their lives, Melvin told Olive Bucklin in 2007, that the only regret he had in his life was that he hadn't spent enough time with his family. "I let the ranch come first." He told Bucklin. "As long as your family is safe and taken care of, the responsibility of the ranch takes priority. You're supposed to be a steward of the land, a caretaker. You're supposed to take care of those animals, because they can't take care of themselves. But—I was too engrossed in the job. Thelma, she raised us a good family. I did what I could to put food on the table and shoes on their feet. They never went hungry. That was my contribution, but she raised our kids. And she did a helluva job."

---

⁵⁴⁸ Melvin Nation, recorded interview with Olive Bucklin October 18, 2006.

At times, Melvin may have questioned his role as a rancher, a cowboy, a family man, but his actions earned great respect in many circles. Tanner Whetham was about eight when he attended a presentation at the Coffee Gallery.[549]

Moni Hourt, who was giving the presentation, said she and the students spent about an hour doing projects revolving around ranching and being a cowboy. They watched a short video about haying in the Sandhills, then she showed them an excerpt from the "Beef State" video.

Tanner excitedly raised his hand, "I know that man. I know that man," he proclaimed as he watched the segment featuring Melvin. "He's a real cowboy, I mean a real one. He can ride a horse almost better than my Dad."

"I told him Melvin was my father," Moni Hourt said. "Up until then he'd been very attentive, respect-

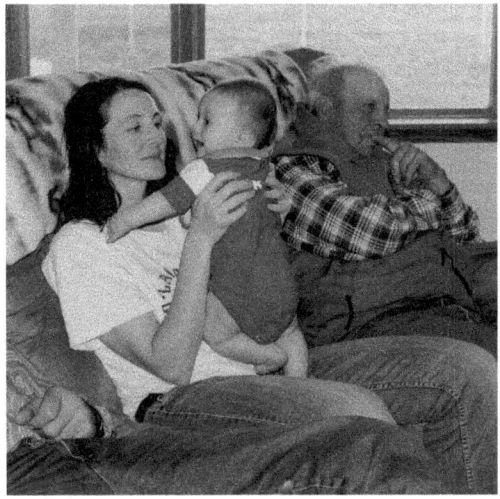

Brady Swisher was born in 2008. His mother, Amy, spent many hours accompanying her grandfather around the ranch. Brady's younger brother Donovan was born in 2010.

ful, and involved with our discussions and our projects, but suddenly I became a "cool dude" because after all my Dad was Melvin Nation. I was 55 years old. I'd been teaching for 15 years, but suddenly I was a little girl, just proud of my Dad."

New Year's Day 2009, dawned bright and cold. Coliseum Butte shimmered above the brown toned prairie that surround Robbin and Ed's home in northern Sioux County. In his tally book, Melvin commented that the great-grandkids were sure fun to watch and that Amy was there with her baby, Brady. He added that Thelma was looking pretty good, and that it had been a beautiful day.

Later that month, he wrote that Joe fixed a door handle for him. He'd stopped by the bar to have a beer and visit before he'd headed home.

It was 25 degrees on January 27. There was a foot of snow on the ground, but he and his crew worked the heifers. On January 30, he reported that it was a beautiful day and that they'd gotten a load of corn at Hat Creek. He added that the day before, he'd finally gotten the fatty tumor taken off his neck.

Six months earlier, he'd seen a surgeon in Scottsbluff and scheduled the tumor's removal. At the last minute, he decided to cancel the procedure. The tumor's growth eventually affected the movement of his neck and generated considerable pain. Finally, he decided to go to a doctor in

---

[549] The CF Coffee Gallery funded in a large part by the Coffee family, was opened at the High Plains Sandoz Center at Chadron State College in 2007. Moni Hourt was the education director for the program for several years.

Chadron to see what he could do. The doctor, a GP, chose to remove the tumor in his office. The procedure seemed to go well and Melvin recorded the fact that he was glad it was gone.

The following Monday, he spent the day gathering wild horses in the Hunter Hills. "Took a four-wheeler out there. Dumped it in a hole, but I stayed on. Plan to get the replacement heifers sorted Wednesday."

By noon on February 5, the crew had nearly finished sorting the heifers. Melvin had ridden "Cat" all morning. "He'd sorted all the cattle; there didn't seem to be a problem,"."John Reece said. "We were sitting there eating dinner, when I noticed his coffee was spilling out of the side of his mouth. I knew he'd had a stroke. I called Robbin, then I called 911."

"This is what happens, John, when you outlive your time," Melvin told him when the ambulance arrived. "I wished I'd just have fallen off my damn horse and ended it."

The medical helicopter picked Melvin up on the highway. Robbin and Thelma followed. By the time Moni arrived at the Scottsbluff hospital, the doctors had determined that Melvin had indeed had a stroke. However, since the stroke affected Melvin's right side and he was left handed, he had not lost his ability to speak or write.

"I wish I'd broke my neck when I hit that hole," Melvin told Moni referring to the almost four-wheeler wreck that he'd described to her during a Monday night phone call. She knew what he was saying.

For the next 18 days, Melvin fought to overcome the paralysis to his right side. He never complained. He treated the doctors and nurses with respect. He did whatever the medical staff ask him to do. He continued to manage the ranch from his hospital bed, organizing the upcoming calving season, talking to Joe Nunn about buying bulls, giving instructions to put in a new tank. He lived his life as he always had, with dignity and courage.

He visited with Virginia Coffee and the Coffee lawyer, John Skavdahl. They assured him he'd still have his job when he got back on his feet. Virginia told him that he and Thelma could live on the ranch as long as he wanted. He told his children, he hadn't really been worried about that, Bill told him he'd never have to leave the ranch. He was anxious to go home.

Thelma spent most of the time in Scottsbluff. The rest of Melvin's family took turns staying at the hospital. He was never alone. When Bryan arrived, Melvin asked him to help him come up with a ramp for the ranch house. They designed a system to help Melvin go from the house to the four-wheeler so he could get around the ranch. He told Annette[550] he might need some help for a while when he got back home. He may have had doubts that he'd get back to full strength, but he never expressed them.

---

[550] Annette had a CNA degree and had worked in both nursing homes and as a geriatric home care nurse.

Melvin appreciated each of his grandchildren for his or her specific characteristics. "Annette," he always said, "is kind."

His family kept a log. They recorded his struggles and his triumphs and the fact that he never quit fighting to get back to the ranch. A steady line of visitors came through his hospital room, old friends like Pat Drinkwalter and Hank Cappen.[551] Joe Nunn spent a whole day visiting and planning the future. When he left, he told Melvin he loved him; Melvin wiped a tear away and said he loved him too. His sisters, Anita, Frances, and Mildred, and his sisters-in-law, Betty, and Lucille, called. He told them about the 100- year celebration he was planning for the home place that summer and told Lucille he'd be there for her birthday party in May.[552]

"I never knew so many people cared. I just didn't think people thought I was that important," Melvin told Moni one morning near the end of February. "Put something in the paper to tell them thank you, will you." Later that afternoon he told Moni, she had to write down his story, but it wasn't to contain any bull-shit.

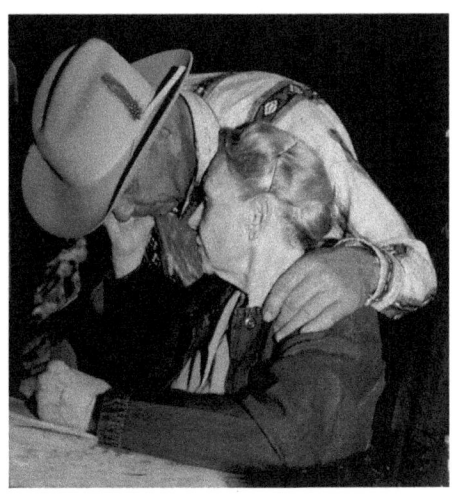

Most of Melvin's family attended a family reunion in Harrison in July 2003. This picture of Melvin and Lucille captured the continued closeness Melvin always shared with his family.

---

[551] Both Pat and Hank rodeoed with Melvin during the Hoover years. Pat who ranched near Crawford and Melvin often spent time together at various events. He didn't see Hank as often, but when he did they carefully discussed all their old times.

[552] Melvin asked Moni Hourt to send a picture of him and Lucille to her for her birthday. She did.

In the early morning hours of February 22, 2009, Melvin suffered another stroke. He never regained consciousness and died on February 25, surrounded by his family including four of his children.

This photograph taken in 2003, features Thelma and Melvin and four of Melvin's five children: Robbin Oldaker, Gary and Bob Pliely, and Moni Hourt. JimBob died in 1985.

Approximately 500 people attended the funeral, including the crew from NETV who prepared a video clip including many interviews from the *Beef State* documentary. He was buried in the red Square Top 3 emblazoned vest that Bill had given him for Christmas one year. A handkerchief was tucked in his back pocket—a white one. And his granddaughter Amy, slipped a can of snus in his shirt pocket. Joe Nunn's poem about "Old Mel" (Appendix 6) was written carefully within the funeral card.

When Olive Bucklin asked Melvin how he'd like to be remembered, he told her as someone who was just who he was, someone who made a lot of mistakes, but tried to learn from every one of them.

"We were put here on earth because we are supposed to contribute a little something in life," he told her. "You're supposed to raise a family and grow that family up to be good men and omen. That's your number one priority in life. When you leave this earth, you want it to be better than when you went into it. I think that's all you can hope for."[553]

---

[553] Interview Melvin Nation by Olive Bucklin, 2007.

*Throughout his lifetime, Melvin strived to make the world a better place.
This picture of Melvin and great-granddaughter Brylee Allred shows that he succeeded.*

"The last three weeks of Grandpa's life were tough for him. I'm not a religious man, but I do believe in a higher power. I couldn't understand why a God would do this to any man, let alone a man as good as Grandpa was. Then I came the conclusion that this was Grandpa's final lesson to us. This was the final thing he was able to teach us. I know he'd have preferred to have died out there in the middle of the pasture. He knew he was screwed, that he'd never get out of there. But he didn't give up. He was kind to all the nurses and the physical therapy staff. He didn't complain. He had always told us the metal of a man is measured in the tough times. He'd say, 'It's easy to be a good guy in the good times, but it's during the tough times that the true man comes out.' Grandpa showed us in his final few days what it meant to truly be a great man."[554]

---

[554] Bryan Hourt, February 28, 2009.

Janet, Amy, Bryan, and Lindsey, Melvin Oldaker's future wife share a joke and unmitigated affection with their grandfather at Melvin's graduation party.

EPILOGUE

Shortly after Melvin suffered from his last stroke, tests revealed that Thelma's cancer had returned. She accepted more chemotherapy. She and Sis continued their more than daily conversations. When Sis's daughters deemed her driving habits "dangerous," they took the keys to her car. Thelma chastised them—severely. She had spent a lifetime fighting for her sister. She wasn't about to stop. However, when Joe quietly told her that Sis had been driving very erratically, that he'd seen her drive an entire block on the wrong side of the road, Thelma told her sister that she really didn't need to drive anyway. Sis had moved into senior living housing in Crawford that spring. Thelma reminded her that she could use the Handi-Bus, plus she'd be down to see her every day, and she was. She truly believed it was her job to protect and guide here sister. She never lost that "fire in her belly" that Melvin had so often mentioned with snapping eyes and a crooked smile of pride.

Velma Rising and Thelma Nation, Sis and Babe, spent their lives reveling in each other's friendship.

Cody and Thelma continued to live at Hat Creek. She watched the daily activities from the dining room table and discussed them when Cody returned from high school. She didn't cook for the men anymore, but made sure Cody was well fed and expressed absolute indignation that he wasn't given more respect than he was by the men.

"That damn Cody, knows more than any of them," She irritably told her daughter. "Hell, they fed the cows the wrong feed the other day. Killed a bunch of cows. Melvin would be so damn disgusted."

In August of 2009, she accepted the AKSARBEN plaque given to the Nation family for 100 years of ranching in Nebraska.

Melvin was looking forward to accepting the 100-Year Ranch commendation for the family's ownership of the Home Place. Thelma did it for him.

That fall she decided to move to Harrison. She didn't attend the sale that disposed of 30 years of her life. She continued her chemotherapy treatments, coddled Cody as much as he would allow and kept a close eye on her sister.

Pic of Sis Mom and Norman. Sis, Norman, and Thelma at a family reunion in 2007.

Sis died in February 2010. Thelma's cancer returned that summer. She didn't give up, but she told her daughter she just wasn't sure she had the heart to battle it anymore. In August, her brother and many other members of the family joined Thelma for a celebration in Harrison. She thoroughly enjoyed her time with a brother, Norman,[555] who she said she hadn't always understood. The next week she taught her granddaughters how to make hollyhock dolls. She made arrangements for Melvin and JimBob's bodies to be moved to a family cemetery on Robbin and Ed's ranch. On August 24, 2010, with her family close by, she quietly slipped away.

Buffy and her two daughters were driving back to Harrison from the Hourt's place at the bottom of Smiley Canyon that afternoon. Five-year-old Mahayla watched the sky at the top of the canyon fill with color and light as sunbeams stretched from the earth toward the sky. "God just sent the angels to come get Grandma Nation," she told her mother.[556] "It's a sad day for us, but a good day for Grandpa, and Grandma Sis. They're waiting for Grandma and her happy, happy, heart."

Thelma was buried beside Melvin and JimBob in the Nation Family Cemetery in northern Sioux County. She outlived her cancer diagnosis by three years.

Shortly before the cancer returned, Thelma told her oldest daughter that she'd been to Melvin's grave[557] at the Crawford cemetery. She said she'd finally decided to forgive him for

---

[555] Norman died in July of 2022, just four months short of his 80th birthday.
[556] Mahayla was right, Thelma died at approximately the same time that they topped the canyon.
[557] Melvin was buried beside JimBob in the Crawford cemetery. At the end of her life, a cemetery was established on Robbin and Ed's ranch. Melvin and JimBob's bodies were exhumed. They were reburied in the cemetery shortly before Thelma's burial.

leaving her. "I do miss him," she added. "He was a pain in the rear sometimes, but I sure do miss him."

In 2013 Melvin was inducted posthumously into the Sandhills Cowboy Hall of Fame. He would have written it in his journal.

Melvin Nation was the persona of the great American Cowboy, a man who loved a horse, respected a "damn cow" and primarily treated those around him the way he wanted to be treated. Thelma would have snorted and said that "he sure the hell wasn't perfect," but then she'd smile. She would agree that he did indeed leave the world a better place because he lived.

In 2009, I promised to write a story. I kept my promise.

BIBLIOGRAPHY

Primary:
Books:

Brewster, Benjamin Brewster. *Benjamin Emmons Brewster, 1951-1935 An Autobiography Covering His Boyhood and Career Raising Cattle.*

    An unpublished memoir written by the second owner of the Warbonnet Ranch area. The manuscript was provided by Sara Coffee Radill.

Carnegie, Dale. *How to Make Friends and Influence People?* October, 1936.

    Melvin, Virginia, and Bill all went to the class in Crawford, NE.

Cook, James H. *50 Years on the Old Frontier.* University of Oklahoma Press, 1925.

    James Cook was one of the early ranchers in Sioux County. This book also provided background.

Harvard University Class of 1861, pamphlet. 1861.

    This booklet printed by Harvard University provided insight into the life of Samuel Franklin Emmons who surveyed, then claimed, the Warbonnet Ranch area in 1877. He turned it over to his nephew, B.V. Brewster, in 1979.

Hourt, Moni Nation. Diary beginning in 1960-2008.

    Entries beginning when Moni was nine, discuss many aspects of the Nation family life.

Morton, J Sterling and Albert Watkins. *History of Nebraska.* Lincoln: Western Publishing and Engraving Company, 1918.

    This book was used as a reference to check facts about early-day Nebraska.

Nation Melvin. Tally books. Many different years from 1970-2009.

    Melvin always carried a pen and a small book, known as a tally book, in the front pocket of his shirt. Although the collection of the tally books is not complete, the information they contained was vitally important to the production of the book.

Nation, Thelma. Diary, 1951-52.

This diary is incomplete but does contain many entries about the couple's life at the Hoover Ranch and during their early years. One entry discusses the Fourth of July Rodeo of 1951. Thelma said Monie slept the whole night and that Melvin did very well.

Schnurr, Clarence. "Warbonnet-John Anderson." *Sioux County Memoirs of Its Pioneers*.

An early story of the Warbonnet Ranch.

Standard Atlas of Sioux County, Nebraska. Chicago: George A Ogle and Company, 1918.

A partial page from the Platt Book was used to show the sections in Sioux County Nebraska that were owned by Earl and Iva Nation. The Nation family did not homestead on the Sioux County land; they purchased a relinquishment, then later added another section. In 2009, the Nation family received the Aksarben award for Nebraska land that remained in a family for 100 years. Those sections remain in the family in 2022. The Platt Book shows just how many people lived in Sioux County in 1918.

Shumway, Grant Lee. *History of Western Nebraska and Its People*. Lincoln, NE: The Western Publishing and Engraving Company, 1921.

Grant Shumway's book was used many times as a reference to check information. Nothing specific is listed in the footnotes.

Wilbur, Charles Dana. "The Great Valleys and Prairies of Nebraska and the Northwest." Omaha: Nebraska Daily Republican Printing Company, 1881.

There is an excerpt in this book from Samuel Aughey who claimed that "Rain Follows the Plow." It was that philosophy that resulted in hundreds of unsuccessful homesteads in the Northern Plains.

Wyoming Stock Growers' Association Brand Book. Cheyenne: *Livestock Journal*. 1885.

The Coffee Brands 010 and Square Top Three are located in this book.

Documents:

Buckley, Joy. Scrapbook, cassette tapes, newspaper articles.

Joy Buckley's material, including taped interviews from many former residents of Glen, Nebraska and the surrounding area, provided an incredible reference source for Melvin's story. One interview, recorded on cassette tape, clarified the story of the man who was killed by a pig.

"Cattle Ranching in the United States." *US Department of Agriculture,* January 1973.

Information about cattle grazing and cattle prices in the 70s.

Catalog: *Chadron Academy, 1907-1908*. Located in Iva Nation scrapbook.

This catalog found in Iva Nation's scrapbook covered the years that she attended the Normal School in Chadron. She was enrolled in teaching classes, but never went back her second year. The catalog included a historical sketch that provided the background of the Academy.

Coffee, Virginia. Scrapbooks, material about the Coffee Ranches.

Virginia allowed Moni Hourt to copy the Coffee family scrapbook and many photographs. Information from that material enhanced Melvin's story.

Dyer, Ailine Hamaker. Scrapbook.

Ailine Dyer, daughter of Paul, granddaughter of RSQ Hamaker, allowed Moni Hourt to copy many pieces of her scrapbook including pictures, letters, and documents. She had copies of her grandparents' wills which she also allowed Moni to copy.

Dyer, Ruth Hamaker." Threshing." Unpublished document.

This document was given to Thelma Nation by Ruth Hamaker Dyer, Dave Hamaker's daughter. It is a great description of threshing on Spud Ridge.

"First Annual Permanent Registered Quarter Horse Colt Sale." October 6, 1956.

According to Melvin, the first Quarter Horse Sale at the Hat Creek Ranch sent all of them in a panic. No one was sure if the horses would sell. He said by the end of the sale, everyone was relaxing and took time to have "a beer or three." The horses, according to Bill's figures on the back cover, averaged $284.12.

Nation, Melvin. "Erosion Study Notebook." 1961-1962.

This small booklet was discovered when the Warbonnet Ranch House was demolished. Herb Fricke recognizing Melvin's name brought the book to Moni Hourt. In it Melvin had recorded data from his trips to the Badlands. After Jerry Parker left in September, Melvin was paid to record the data from the Erosion Study project in the Badlands east of the Warbonnet Ranch.

Nation, Thelma. Genealogy records. Hourt family research library.

Thelma Nation did extensive research into both sides of the family including the Nation family. Her records include emails, birth and death records, census records, and various books and documents. All of her records were given to her daughter, Moni Hourt and now are available at the Hourt Library.

Nunn, Joe. "Ole Mel." Poem written for Melvin Nation.

Shon Whetham said when Joe read this poem in Melvin's presence for the first time, at a branding dinner at the Nunn Ranch, Melvin suddenly left the room. It was included on Melvin's funeral card.

Quarter Horse Association Registration Files. Various Years.

    The lineage of Bill Coffee's horses was registered by the Quarter Horse Association. Registration papers courtesy of Ann Coffee Wachman.

"Remarks of President Roosevelt at Crawford, NE—April 25, 1903." *Theodore Roosevelt collection*. Theodore Roosevelt Center, Dickinson State College, Dickinson, North Dakota.

    Remarks made by Roosevelt when he stopped in Crawford in 1903. Site also included pictures that are included in the Appendix.

"School Rosters *1897, 98, 99, 1900, 1900, 1901.*" *Belmont Memories*. 2018.

    The Belmont school rosters were published in *Belmont Memories*. They included the names of Iva, brothers, and her sister.

Udall, Lyn/Kennett, Karl. "Stay in your own Back Yard," *Dick Hyman and Arthur Pryor Publishing*, 1899.

    This document includes the original lyrics and music of what today is considered a very racist song. Iva Nation often sang the song. Her actions could be considered racist, unless you heard her speak about the sadness of racism. She often told her children that God made everyone equal.

Will of William Beakes. 1711. Thelma Nation genealogy records.

    In this will, William Beakes lists John Nation as a servant boy. Melvin was a direct descendant of John Nation.

Essays:

Hamaker, Alice Berthene Haworth. Ailene Hamaker Dyer scrapbook.

    Essay written in 1934, for her granddaughter.
    This essay was found in Ailene Dyer's scrapbook. It discussed the family's early history.

Hamaker, Alice Berthene Haworth. *Crawford Nebraska, 1886-1961*, pg 78.

    Discussed the trip to Crawford.

Hamaker, Alice Berthene Haworth. *Belmont Memories, 2013*. Pgs 33-34.

    A combined history of the family and the family's trip to Nebraska.

Hourt, Bryan. "What Makes a Real Cowboy?" 1983.

    An essay for an elementary English assignment in which Bryan tells why his grandfather is a real cowboy, not one of those "swaggery guys in a cowboy hat who just pretend."

Hourt, Buffy. "What is a Rancher? —A Granddaughter's Point of View." 1983.

Written for Buffy's eighth grade English class. Discusses what it was like to grow up working with and getting to know "all about Granddad and ranching."

Oldaker, Cody. "Granddad is a Great Guy; Grandma is a Great Girl" 2000.

Essay written for elementary assignment.

Oldaker, Melvin. "Grandpa's Canyon."

An essay written for a college class.

Nation, Ramona. "Our Family Vacation." 1965.

Recorded in a plaid notebook, this essay about the family's trip to the Black Hills, received an "A" in her freshman English class at Sioux County High School.

Images:

Allred, Buffy. Image of fire beginning in Pants Butte Canyon, 2006.

Buffy and her children were driving home from Hat Creek after visiting Melvin and Thelma when she saw a tendril of smoke curling up from the prairie. She stopped and took a picture, not knowing at the time that the fire would destroy thousands of acres. She also took several family shots included in the book.

Avey, Cecil. Image of Pants Butte, 1960.

Cecil was a game warden in the Crawford area. Moni often accompanied him on his early morning tours of the region. He gave her this photograph that he took in 1960 of an "intact" Pants Butte.

Buckley, Joy. Images and scrapbooks and recorded interviews.

Joy Buckley's photographs, and scrapbooks provided knowledge and supporting information about the Glen and Crawford region.

Callaham, Lula. Drawing of sod house.

This drawing was made by Thelma Nation's cousin. It represented the thousands of "soddies" that dotted the Nebraska prairie.

Chlanda, Ridge. Photographs of the Hoover Ranch and 1950s PRCA rodeos.

Ridge gave a collection of photographs to Moni Hourt in 2003.

Coffee, Virginia. Photographs featuring the Coffee Ranch.

The story of the Coffee Ranch is very much a part of Melvin's story. The photographs Virginia provided included a picture of Melvin on a hay wagon.

"Crawford City Park Fountain. *Crawford Historical Society.*

The original fountain at the Crawford Park was built in 1917. This photograph was given to Moni Hourt by Nellie Slider who with her husband, Ralph, managed the park for 13 years.

Dodd, Howard. "Equine show." Fort Robinson State Park.

Howard Dodd worked at Fort Robinson State Park. He took numerous pictures while living there. Photographs shared by Dave Dodd.

Hourt, Moni. Photographs from various years.

In 1963, The *Quarter Horse Journal* sponsored a contest for children up to the age of 18. Moni sold enough subscriptions to win a Kodak Brownie Camera. She has taken pictures her entire life, working as a photo-journalist for The Crawford Clipper/*Harrison Sun* and for various newspapers and magazines across the United States. Her photographs have been featured in *Pro-Rodeo Sports News* as well as in The *Farm and Ranch* magazine.

Kennedy, Deb. Photograph of Hourt place surrounded by water.

Deb Kennedy was working for *The Crawford Clipper* when she took this photograph of the Hourt place surrounded by the flood waters. Nation Family album.

Nation, Iva Hamaker scrapbook.

Iva spent many hours building her scrapbook. Within the scrapbook were obituaries, marriage and baby announcements, a few photos, and stories about World War II. The scrapbook also included a booklet from the Chadron Academy.

Nation family albums. These albums contain dozens of photographs of the Nation family, including Melvin's immediate family and his wife and children. Many of the photographs within the album were taken by Thelma. Others were taken by Verna Callaham, and Sis (Velma) Rising.

Norman, Tom. Drawing of "Toad," stallion owned by Bill Coffee.

Tom Norman drew and painted some incredibly detailed images of horses, primarily Quarter Horses. Permission to use the image from Tom Norman family.

Olbricht, Frances Kreman. Glen region photographs.

Frances Kreman Olbricht and her husband, Bill, were both raised in the Glen community. Her grandparents, John and Ella Newlin operated *The Harrison Sun* newspaper. She shared her collection of newspaper articles and photographs with Moni Hourt.

Packard, Shari. Picture of Nation family in 2008.

Every member of the Nation family, except Shawn Allred, was on hand for a celebration in November 2008. Sis also joined them for the party to commemorate the apparent remission of Thelma's cancer. It was the last family picture ever taken.

Schmidt, Sam. Photographs of Crawford, the Crawford viaduct, and city of Crawford during '49 Blizzard.

Sam Schmidt was married to Paul Hamaker's daughter, Betty. He was an amateur photographer and an electronic genius. After divorcing his wife, he built a home in a dugout beside the walk-through viaduct on Elm Street. The CB he constructed connected him with people all over the world. He had the first television in the city and set it up in his front yard. His daughter, Linda and all her friends, met in the yard to watch the scratchy reception. Many years after Sam's death, Moni Hourt asked Linda if she could copy Sam's photos and negatives. The original photographs were returned to Linda; a copy of them is now available at the Crawford Historical Society Museum.

Sioux County Historical Society Museum. "Hillview District 51 photograph."

Taken in 1943 when Melvin was in seventh grade, this picture shows that a windmill dominated the school yard.

Snook, Frank. Aerial photograph of Fort Robinson and Crawford.

Snook was an early day pilot who shot dozens of photographs from his plane. His photographs belong to his family.

Theodore Roosevelt collection. Theodore Roosevelt Center, Dickinson State College, Dickinson, North Dakota.

Pictures of Theodore Roosevelt in Crawford, NE.

Victory, Janet Oldaker. Drawing of Melvin and Ed Oldaker.

Janet created many excellent pencil drawings. This drawing was based on a photography by Connie Nunn.

Interviews:

Allred, Buffy Hourt. Personal Taped Interview with Moni Hourt.

Buffy spent most Sundays of her childhood at the Home Place. She helped her grandfather move cattle and worked for a short time in the hayfield at Hat Creek. After she married, she spent her summers in Nebraska and made sure her children, Brylee and Mahayla, were well acquainted with her grandparents.

Benson, Becky. Personal interview with Moni Hourt, 1994.

Becky Benson, who worked at the Crawford told Hourt that she remembered how sick she had been when she was hospitalized. She said she brought her vanilla ice cream several times a day. "And no matter how sick you was, you always said 'thank you.' That showed me that your Mama and Daddy had taught you right."

Buckles, Buck. Personal interview with Moni Hourt, 2007, 2010, 2018, 2021.

A longtime friend of Melvin Nation, Buck Buckles was originally interviewed when Moni Hourt photographed his use of horses in his hay fields in 2007. He was also instrumental in inducting Melvin into the Nebraska Sandhill's Cowboy Hall of Fame in 2018. He helped Moni clarify some of the details of using teams of horses to handle hay.

Buckley, Doug. Personal interview with Moni Hourt.

Doug accompanied Moni Hourt and Don Housch when they visited the dugout at the head of White River. Doug also helped Moni verify different piece of information, throughout her years as a local historian and writer.

Buckley, Opel. Personal Interview with Joy Buckley, 1976.

In this audio tape given to Moni Hourt by the Buckley family, Opel Buckley talks about the death of her grandfather. She said her father, William Case and his family went to church early one morning. William's father stopped to feed the family's pigs before joining them at church. When the man did not arrive at church, the family returned to their homestead to find him. They found his shoe, his foot still inside, within the confines of the pig confinement pen. This story spawned the legend that circulated across the rural region of Sioux County, that a "Buckley was killed by a pig."

Callaham, Norman. Personal taped interview with Moni Hourt, 2017.

Thelma's only brother who survived childhood, Norman spent his fifteenth summer working at Warbonnet. He related several stories about his time on the ranch.

Callaham, Verna. Personal interview with Moni Hourt, 2000.

Over the years, Moni Hourt interviewed her grandmother many times. In this interview Verna talked about her relationship with the Nation family who lived southwest of the place Callaham's rented in 1949.

Chlanda, Ridge Hoover. Personal interview with Moni Hourt, 2017.

In 2017, Ridge spoke to Moni Hourt about her association with the Nation family and her life on the Hoover Ranch.

Coffee, Bill. Personal taped interviews with Moni Hourt, 1990-2005.

The story of Melvin Nation must include stories about the Coffee Ranches. Bill spent hours discussing the ranch and its operation.

Coffee, Virginia. Personal taped interviews with Moni Hourt, 1990-2012.

Virginia's interview provided a different viewpoint about the area and the ranching community including that at the Coffee Ranches.

Drinkwalter, Pat. Personal interviews with Moni Hourt.

Pat rodeoed with Melvin when they were young. The men remained friends throughout their lifetimes.

Fernandez, Melody Nation. Personal taped interview by Moni Hourt, 2003. Hourt home.

Melody Nation discussed many different incidents on the "Home Place" where she was raised. Melody worked at the Johnson Space Center in Houston, Texas. She died in 2002.

Gillette, Terry. Personal interview by Moni Hourt.

Terry Gillette's family went to school with Melvin Nation. He was able to add some details about District 51 that enhanced the story.

Glendy, Tim. Personal interview by Moni Hourt.

Tim accompanied Melvin on the elk-hunting excursion.

Gray, Eva Nation. Personal taped interview by Moni Hourt, 1996, 1997.

Eva was Melvin's oldest sister. She and her husband, John, ran the Log Cabin Motel in Chadron, NE. It was across the street from the Branding Iron Motel owned by Eva's younger sister, Frances and her husband Jack.

Grooms, Joyce Nation. Personal telephone interview with Moni Hourt, 2017.

One of Melvin's nieces, Joyce remembered Melvin as a child growing up and discussed his relationship with her father, Merlin.

Hamaker, Bud. Personal telephone interview with Moni Hourt.

Bud is Melvin's first cousin, the son of Paul Hamaker, Iva's brother. He rodeoed with JimBob and spent many hours with Melvin's family.

Hamaker, Chris. Personal telephone interview with Moni Hourt.

The grandson of Dave Hamaker, Chris and his family lived about three miles west of the Home Place. He often helped Melvin with work on the ranch. He also owned a team of horses. Chris and Melvin drove teams on the Christmas tree hunt and during the Christmas wagon rides in Crawford. They also went on the same trail rides.

Hamaker, Fred and Goldie. Self-taped stories, 1950s.

Fred and Goldie were part of a band "Rattlesnake Ramblers," so they owned a sound system that included a reel-to-reel recorder. They used that recorder to recorded Earl and Iva Nation's wedding anniversary and other family events, including dances in which they provided music. One tape included stories ranging from the 49 Blizzard to everyday life. Moni Hourt also interviewed Goldie Hamaker in 1993 when the Glen School was researching the Glen School. At that time, Goldie also talked about living near the Home Place when Elvin and Frances lived there. The interviews provided good background for several stories.

Hamaker, Ray. Personal taped interview by Moni Hourt, Ray Hamaker Home, Glen, NE, 1999.

Ray was interviewed several times over the years: at the Hourt home, the Glen School, and at his home.

Hanley, Opal. Personal Taped Interview with Moni Hourt, 1993.

Opal Hess Hanley and her husband, Octave, visited the Glen School where Moni Hourt was teaching. Hourt's theme for the year was community and many members of the community came to the school to talk to the students about their lives along the Niobrara River.

Hourt, Bryan. Personal Taped Interview with Moni Hourt.

Throughout his childhood, Bryan spent large amounts of time with Melvin and Thelma. He went with his grandfather whenever he could, helping move cattle, hay, work in the wheat fields, and travel in the combine. He continued spending many hours with the Nations after they moved to Hat Creek. Even after he became an engineer for the Honda Corporation in Ohio, he often flew back to Nebraska to help with branding or moving cattle.

Hourt, Joe. Personal interview with Moni Hourt.

It was Joe Hourt, in 2015, who encouraged Moni to begin writing Melvin's story. He was in the room when Melvin asked Moni if she'd write his story and in the ensuing years infrequently reminded his wife she should get started. He often told her stories about his times with Melvin which she dutifully recorded. In the early summer of 2015, he told her that no-one else could write the story but her, and that nothing she'd ever write was more important than Melvin's story. Every night, he'd come into Moni's office to go over the day's work. Joe died in 2016, but Moni said she knew she had to continue the story. She often told people that she never would have accomplished anything without Joe. This book is another example.

Housch, Don. Personal interview with Moni Hourt.

Don approached Moni in 2015 and asked if she knew of the existence of a dugout at the head of White River. Moni said she did. Housch said he had found information that determined the dugout was once a fur traders trading post. Bill Coffee always said the dugout was a "Beaver Man's" place, in other words, a fur trader lived and worked there. In the mid-1880s the dugout was used by several area homesteaders including the Tucker family and reportedly by Alois Studenmaier's family. Alois was the great grandfather of Ed Oldaker. Glen area rancher, Charles Russell was accused of killing Staudenmaier in 1900, but Volume 66 of the Nebraska Supreme Court verified that the case was overturned because of insufficient and erroneous evidence.

Jordan, Bob. Personal video and audio interviews with Moni Hourt.

Bob Jordan's interviews included stories about his life as a horseman in Western Nebraska as well as stories about his friendship with Melvin. Part of the interviews were included in a story written about Bob that was published in The Harrison Sun newspaper.

Jordan, Dan. Personal interview with Moni Hourt.

Dan Jordan or Danny as he was known by his family and friends, was Bob Jordan's oldest son. He spent a great deal of time with Melvin and his family and had great respect for Melvin as a person.

Klug, Victor. Personal interview by Moni Hourt, 2019.

Victor was one of Melvin's last hired men on the Hat Creek Ranch. He said he asked Melvin for a job believing he was too old to land the position. Melvin gave him a chance "to prove I was still worth something."

Leeling, Vera Lantz. Personal interview with Moni Hourt, 1997.

Vera Lantz attended District 51 rural school with the Nation children. She said she and Melvin were "best friends" all through their childhood.

Lemmon, Jim. Personal interview by Moni Hourt, 1997.

Cody Oldaker said Melvin told him, Jim Lemmon was the man who kept him going after JimBob's death. Lemmon was the superintendent at Fort Robinson and gave Melvin a job when bankruptcy loomed on the horizon. Melvin also worked at the Fort after JimBob's death. Jim's interview focused on Melvin as a man who loved to laugh, loved to play a joke, and had the courage to survive.

Lemmon, Joe. Personal interview by Moni Hourt, 2015, 2016, 2020.

Related many "Melvin and me" stories. He had great respect for Melvin.

Marshall, Con. Personal interview by Moni Hourt, many times over the years.

Con clarified information about the Chadron Normal School and about Chadron State College.

Miller, Monica. Telephone interview. Pioneer Village, Minden, NE. December 4, 2020.

Ms Miller verified the June 13, 1979 sale of the Japanese furniture by Ailene Dyer. She said the receipt of the furniture signed by Harold Warp, the Museum's developer, was attached to a handwritten note. The note said RSQ bought the eight piece set in December 1916. It said the furniture had been on display at The Japanese Pavilion at the Panama Pacific International Exposition which was part of the World's Fair of 1915. Although it could be assumed that the Hamakers attended the Exposition, it ended in 1915. So either the date of the sale to the Hamakers is incorrect or the furniture was purchased after the Exposition ended. Paul Hamaker died in 1971; Mabel died in 1980, so the furniture was sold before Mabel's death.

Nation, Betty Curtis. Personal taped interview by Moni Hourt. 1997-2012.

Betty was Melvin's sister-in-law. She and Clark, her husband, lived in Miles City, Montana. She married Clark when Melvin was nine years old. She too offered perspectives on Melvin's growing up years. She was also able to explain the early dynamics of the Nation family.

Nation, David. Personal interview with Moni Hourt.

Dave, Melvin's nephew, worked at the Coffee Ranches in 1962. He related many incidents about his time on the ranch.

Nation, Earl. Personal taped interview by Fred Hamaker, 1957.

In this interview, Earl talked about meeting Iva on the road the day they were married. He also talked about the religion and about the ups and downs of establishing the farm on the plateau.

Nation, Earl. Personal taped interview by Jack Roberts. 1959.

Frances Roberts gave Moni Hourt this interview. It wasn't very long, but it did explain how Earl met Iva and explored his family's dynamics.

Nation, Elvin. Interview with Moni Hourt, 1982, 1988, 2001.

The first taped interview with Elvin was about World War II. Later he was interviewed in his home about his life on the farm in Nebraska and his life in Washington state. The last interview was when Eva Nation Gray's family gathered at the Joe Hourt place after Eva's funeral.

Nation, Iva Hamaker. Personal taped interview by Fred Hamaker, 1957.

This interview was found in Merlin Nation's closet in 1997. It is an incredible mix of interviews of family members and stories of Earl and Iva's life. On the tape, Iva sings, "Stay in Your Own Back Yard," which today is considered very racist, but coming from Iva's mouth it is a song that commiserates with those who face racism. Listening to the voices of Iva and Earl was an incredible experience.

Nation, Lucille, Clure. Personal taped interviews by Moni Hourt. 1998-2001.

Lucille was Melvin's sister-in-law. She married Merlin Nation in 1935 when Melvin was five. She said she loved Melvin like he was her own child. Her perspective on Melvin as a teenager and a young man helped build a more complete picture of Melvin's early years.

Nation, Melvin. Personal taped interviews by Moni Hourt. 1996-2009.

There are over 22 hours of both audio and video taped interviews with Melvin Nation—recorded between 1996 and 2009. The last interview was completed in his hospital room shortly before he died. Melvin always had time to do interviews even when he was tired. At one point he went out to an abandoned slide-stacker and explained its operation to his great-granddaughters. He even allowed Moni Hourt's students to interview him several times over the years.

Nation, Melvin. Personal taped interviews by Olive Bucklin for NETV Beef State documentary. 2006-2007. When Olive Bucklin of Nebraska Public Television first contacted Melvin to be one of her featured individuals in the *Beef State* video, he turned her down. She convinced him that he should do it. In the end, he enjoyed doing the interviews and said the cinematographers "didn't hurt a thing." He told his daughter he liked the finished video, but did not attend the premiere at the Haythorn Ranch near Ogallala, NE. He said he had too much work to do.

Nation, Merlin. Personal taped interview by Moni Hourt. 1996-2001.

Merlin Nation was Melvin's oldest brother. He moved to Washington state when Melvin was 16. He had a copy of the audio tape made by Fred Hamaker in 1957 and shared it with Moni Hourt. Each one of Melvin's siblings brought a different perspective to Melvin's story because they were each born in a different era of the family's history. Merlin grew up in the years when Iva and Earl were really struggling financially while Melvin and Mildred lived in an era when their family had more financial stability.

Nation, Thelma Callaham. Personal interview with Moni Hourt, 1995-2010.

Thelma Nation did extensive research on the Nation family. Her research was invaluable for this story. She was determined that the true story of the Nations was told, even though it tromped on family "stories." Moni Hourt wrote Thelma's story in 1993. It is included in the book, *Beyond the Five Us,* an unpublished compilation of family stories.

Norgard, Donna Rising. Personal interview with Moni Hourt.

Donna, her sisters Dixie and Rhonda, and her brother, Kasey, spent many hours at the Warbonnet Ranch. They often joined the Nation family for Christmas.

Nunn, Joe. Personal interview with Moni Hourt.

Joe was one of Melvin's best friends. He and Bill Coffee were partners for many years. He attended most of the brandings when Melvin returned to Hat Creek. He was one of the "old cowboys" who visited Melvin in the hospital after Melvin's stroke.

Olbricht, Frances Kreman. Personal interviews with Moni Hourt. Various years between 1996-2010.

Frances Olbricht and her husband, Bill spent many hours visiting with students at the Glen School. She shared photographs and research material about the Glen and Crawford areas, with Moni Hourt.

Oldaker, Annette. Personal interview with Moni Hourt. Several times over the years.

As Melvin and Thelma's second oldest granddaughter, Annette was able to remember many incidents that she shared with her grandparents. She is Cody Oldaker's mother.

Oldaker, Cody. Personal taped interview with Moni Hourt.

Since he lived with Melvin and Thelma from the time he was two years old, Cody helped flesh out the last years of Melvin and Thelma's story. His recollections were essential to the final chapters of the book.

Oldaker, Ed. Discussions and visits both in person and by telephone.

Several of Ed's stories are included in the book.

Oldaker, Melvin. Discussions and visits both in person and by telephone.

The youngest of Melvin and Thelma's grandchildren, Melvin was also part of the branding and cattle moving crew, an excerpt of his essay on moving cattle to White River is included in the book.

Oldaker, Robbin Nation. Discussions and visits both in person and by telephone.

Robbin grew up on the Warbonnet Ranch. She and her husband own a ranch about six miles west of Warbonnet. She spent many hours horseback helping her father. She was also a proficient member of the hay crew. Every branding day, she helped her mother prepare the noon meal.

Pelton, Rhonda. Personal interview with Moni Hourt. Many times over the years.

Rhonda spent much of her childhood at Warbonnet. She remembered several stories about life with Melvin and Thelma.

Phipps, Juanita. Personnel telephone interview with Moni Hourt, 1997.

Juanita Phipps was one of three teachers who made a strong impression on Melvin. She told Moni Hourt that Melvin had a sharp mind and unless a teacher kept that mind busy, he got into trouble.

Pliley, Bob (Mike). Discussions and visits with Moni Hourt.

Mike Pliley, Melvin's second son visited the ranch in 1964. It was the first time he recognized Melvin as their father.

Pliley, Gary. Discussions and visits with Moni Hourt.

Gary and his brother, Mike, were not told that Melvin was their father until 1964. At that time, they visited the ranch.

Porter, Alice. Interview with Moni Hourt, 1999, 2000. Porter home, Belmont, NE.

Alice Thornton Porter and her husband, John, owned a small ranch near the Belmont Tunnel. When Moni Hourt's students created a History Day video on the Belmont Tunnel in 1999, they interviewed Mrs. Porter. Moni also interviewed her when she celebrated her 100th birthday. She was a friend of both Iva Hamaker and her sister, Bertha.

Quintard, Jean. Personal interview with Moni Hourt.

Although at seven, Moni Hourt said she was determined to hate Jean because she stole Bruce, whom she certainly had intended to marry, she eventually developed a lifelong friendship and affection for Jean. Jean always encouraged Moni's writing: bringing her notebooks, pencils, and often asking to read her latest story. In several interviews, Jean gave her permission to use the stories about her husband, Bruce.

Reece, John. Personal interview with Moni Hourt.

John was working for Melvin when Melvin had the stroke.

Reece, Sandy. Personal interview.

Sandy's husband, Steve was on the elk hunting trip with Melvin.

Rising, Dale. Personal interview with Moni Hourt.

Dale was able to confirm the story about the climb to the top of the Warbonnet Barn.

Rising, Keal. Personal interview with Moni Hourt, several times over the years.

The first time Moni Hourt interviewed Keal Rising was in 1991, when he was the Glen School's guest for Veteran's Day At that time he discussed his military service during the Korean War. In other interviews he discussed rodeoing, the Hoover Ranch, and living in Glen, Nebraska.

Rising, Marvin. Personal interview with Moni Hourt. Several times over the years.

Marvin worked at Fort Robinson, Nebraska during the horse-remount era. He played polo with Bill Coffee and was a lifelong friend of Melvin and the rodeo crew around Crawford. He was Keal's brother. He and his wife operated Marv's Bar, a cowboy hangout, in Crawford.

Rising, Wilbur. Personal interview with Moni Hourt. Several times over the years.

Wilbur provided additional material about Melvin's rodeoing days as both a contestant and as arena help.

Rising, Velma (Sis). Personal Taped Interview with Moni Hourt. Many times over the years.

Sis was an integral part of the Nation family. Her stories mirrored and complimented Thelma's stories who was her best friend throughout their lifetimes. She and Melvin were always good friends too.

Roberts, Frances Nation. Interview with Moni Hourt, 1999-2000.

Frances Roberts was married to Jack Roberts. They owned the Branding Iron Motel across the street from Eva and John Gray's Log Cabin Motel in Chadron, NE. Frances was the only one of the sisters who did not join the religion. She was interviewed several times over the years.

Robison, Anita Nation. Personal taped interview by Moni Hourt, 1997, 1998, 1999, 2001.

Anita was Melvin's second oldest sister. She lived with her parents for many years. She was one a telephone operator's in Crawford.. She married Dwayne Robison later in life. Every one of Melvin's family members told a different story which helped expand the story.

Sharp, Roy. Personal interview with Moni Hourt.

Roy worked for Melvin at Warbonnet and considered him a good friend.

Sahara, Butch. Personal interview with Moni Hourt, 2016.

Dr. Sahara performed the veterinary duties at Fort Robinson and participated in the annual Buffalo Roundups. He and Melvin became good friends. They were always finding ways to "out-prank" each other.

Smith, Ronald. Personal interview with Moni Hourt. 1997.

Ronald Smith worked for the Red Cloud Refinery in Crawford. He told Moni Hourt that Earl Nation never bought more gasoline or oil than he could pay for.

Swisher, Amy Oldaker. Personal interview with Moni Hourt. Several times over the years.

Amy Oldaker helped Melvin hay most summers during her high school years. She also helped with moving cattle and branding until Melvin's death.

Thomas, Everett. Personal interview with Moni Hourt, 1999.

Everett lived a few miles from the Warbonnet Ranch on the ranch, that in 2022, is owned by Robbin and Ed Oldaker. He was able to provide several stories about Melvin's life in the Warbonnet Valley.

Victory, Janet Oldaker. Personal interview with Moni Hourt.

Janet and her sister, Amy were the backbone of Melvin's hay crew while they were in high school. She also spent many hours in the branding corral and helping Melvin move cattle.

Ward, Bessie. Personal interview with Moni Hourt, 2019.

Bessie's husband, Benny accompanied Melvin on the elk hunt and was with him when he moved his cattle to town in 1982.

Widel, Mildred. Personal taped interview by Moni Hourt. 1996-2021.

Mildred was Melvin's youngest sister and his best friend. She outlived all of her brothers and sisters and throughout the years told many stories about her family.

Whetham, Shon. Personal interview with Moni Hourt. 1997-2019.

Shon and Melvin were great friends, although Shon was considerably younger. Shon read Melvin's book in 2020. He liked it which gave Moni Hourt courage to move forward.

Witt, Gary. Personal interview with Moni Hourt,2012

Gary and Mike Witt lived on the Witt place about two miles east of the Home Place. They spent many hours with JimBob. Melvin also hired them to work on the ranch.

Witt, Mike. Personal interview with Moni Hourt, 2017.

Mike Witt said he spent hours with Melvin and JimBob at the Home Place. He told Moni Hourt several stories about their interactions.

Zimmerman, Keith. Personal interview with Moni Hourt. 2017.

Keith knew the name of the horse killed in the lightning strike at Hat Creek. He also ranched near Hat Creek. He was involved in the organization of the first high school rodeo in Harrison.

Letters:

CF Coffee to Harry Crain. *Letters from Old Friends and Members of the Wyoming Stockgrowers Association.* Wyoming Stockgrower's Association: 1923.

Interesting letter that relates CF Coffee's arrival in Hat Creek Valley in Nebraska.

Hall, Frank. Commercial First Bank. October 28, 1909. Letter of support for RSQ Hamaker.

Says it will honor his check up to $2,000. It says the bank considers him worth about $35,000.

Hamaker, Alice to RSQ Hamaker. Various years, various subjects.

Many of these letters were a wonderful example of a frontier woman's life. Although RSQ was often on the road, she handled whatever problem came along and never complained

Hamaker, Bertha to Nation, Iva. Oct 2, 1939.

In this letter, Bertha tells Iva that she doesn't feel that the "Jap" furniture should leave Paul and Mabel's house. She says she doesn't know how the pieces could be divided evenly and says that Paul is so much like her father that she believes that he will handle the furniture honorably. This letter was in response to a letter from Iva where she says she feels the furniture should be divided between the kids.

Hamaker, RSQ. Various years about various subjects.

RSQ wrote regularly to his wife often from Omaha, or even when he was in Crawford and headed to another sale. All found in Aline Hamaker Dyer scrapbook. Copied by Moni Hourt 1999.

Hamaker, RSQ to Alice Hamaker. Various dates from 1900 to 1910.

Found in Aline Hamaker Dyer scrapbook. Copied by Moni Hourt 1999.
Since RSQ traveled so much, he and Alice constantly communicated through letters.

Hamaker, RSQ to William Cox Haworth. November 31, 1889.

This letter was written to RSQ Hamaker's father-in law by RSQ. He talked about the region and how much he disliked it.

Herren, Dick. Personal interview with Moni Hourt, 1988.

The owner of Herren Brothers in Harrison, Dick discussed his friendship with Melvin over the years. He said he was really proud that Melvin, after being forced to declare bankruptcy in 1985, still paid every creditor..

Minick, CA, cashier First National Bank in support of RSQ. October 28, 1909.

Mr. Minick was one of the many bankers who supported RSQ as a commission man.

Nation, Elvin. Letters to his family during World War II.

Most of these letters were V-Mail letters. They were always upbeat. They were located in both Thelma Nation's collection of data and in Iva Nation's scrapbook.

Nation, Melvin to Eva Nation, not dated.

Melvin wrote several letters to Eva expressing his worry about Elvin. In two of them he said "workers" had shared Bible passages with him that he used while praying for Elvin's safe return.

Nation, Melvin to Thelma Callaham. 1949, 1950, 1951.

This collection of letters was given to Moni Hourt in 1990. They cover a myriad of subjects.

Porter, J.E. to Paul Hamaker, November 10, 1937.

Says that Iva has been at the office several times worrying about the final settlement of her parents' estate. Porter asks Paul stop by as soon as possible to complete the inventory of the estate.

Voorhis, Lee Van. Letter of support for RSQ Hamaker. October 31, 1903. Located in Aline Dyer scrapbook.

In the letter, Mr. Voorhis says the letter is an introduction to Mr. Hamaker who exhibits unquestionable integrity."

Periodicals:

"Bill Coffee and Bill Coy Quarter Horse Sale." Advertisement: *News Letter Journal.* Newcastle, Wyoming, September 27, and October 4, 1956.

An advertisement for a production sale at the Hat Creek Ranch.

"Buzz Hoover Jr. Dies in Car Wreck." *Harrison Sun,* June 4, 1958.

Article reporting the head-on car wreck that killed Buzzy and another couple.

"Car lost." *Crawford Clipper.* May 1, 1931.

This article reported that Earl Nation lost his potato cellar and a car in a fire. The fire destroyed Merlin's new automobile. He always said he knew who started the fire, but wouldn't reveal the name.

"Chappell Moore Breaks Leg." *Chadron Record.* January 23, 1964.

This article confirms the date of Chappell's injury which then confirmed the time period in which the horses were killed by lightning. Moore left the ranch that spring and eventually moved to Chandler, Arizona. He died in April 1995.

Clark, Timothy B. "Borrowing Trouble," *National Journal* 17, no. 36 (September 7, 1985), available: LEXIS, Library: NEWS, File: NTLJNL

Specifically addresses issues high interest.

"Coffee purchases Quarter Horse." *Harrison Sun.* January 25, 1945.

Coffee's first registered Quarter Horse, Buckskin Moccasin, was purchased at the Western Livestock Show in Denver, Colorado.

"Crisis in Agriculture, 1975-1999." nebraskastudies.org.

A summary of the problems facing agriculture during the years that Melvin operated the "Home Place."

C. S. Thompson, "Effects of Farmland Market," 19.

The statistics in this article were derived from the U.S. Department of Agriculture, *Agriculture Statistics* (1983), 517.

C. S. Thompson, "Effects of Farmland Market," 20.

Banking and the Agricultural Problems of the 1980s-FDIC.
Information about the role banking had on the problems that faced ranchers in the 80s.

"Denver Man Arrested." *Crawford Clipper.* October 31, 1985.

When the Nation/Hourt family visited the "hippie cabin" they had no idea that they were walking around on thousands of dollars of gold. This article reports that the cabin's owner, William Munson, hid about $50,000 worth of gold on the property.

Duft, Ken D. "Chapter 12 Bankruptcy in Retrospect; Its Impact on Agribusiness Firms." *Agribusiness Management.* College of Agriculture, Washington State University,1990. Explanation about Chapter 12 Bankruptcy. This helped the author understand Chapter 12 Bankruptcy.

"E.A. Hoover Jr. Killed in Head-on Crash in Wyoming." *Greeley Daily Tribune,* May 31, 1958.

This article was found in Thelma Nation's scrapbook. It explains that the only survivor in the crash was a young boy found trapped under the car's dashboard.

Easterbrook, Greg. "Making Sense of Agriculture." *Atlantic Monthly Archives*, July 1985.

Another article attempting to make sense of what was transpiring in agriculture.

"Erosion Studied in Sioux County Project." *Chadron Record.* November 13, 1961.

This article discusses the Warbonnet Project at the Badlands that was supervised by Jerry Parker.

"Farm Policy," *America*, v151, September 22, 1984-138.

Another article trying to negotiate the troubled waters affecting agriculture.

"Home Happenings." *Crawford Tribune.* August 11, 1911.

This article was simply used to prove the story about Earl and Iva's chokecherry picking adventure at Glen, Nebraska. The article said the couple lost their horses, but were able to save their own lives. The author spent a full day looking for the article and was elated when it was found.

"Inspects Quarter Horses." *Harrison Sun.* July 8, 1948.

Bill Coffee purchased his first Quarter Horse in 1945. Members of the Quarter Horse Association came to Harrison in 1948 to inspect his herd to determine if the animals met the specifications needed for Coffee to be identified as a Quarter Horse breeder. According to this, article they did.

Hourt, Moni. "Football Team Tackles Four-Legged Opponents." *Northwest Nebraska Post*. June, 1994.

Following that first excursion into the branding pen in 1994, football players from Chadron State College always arrived on branding day to help Melvin brand the Hat Creek and Warbonnet cattle.

Hourt, Moni. "Harrison Brangus Cattle Head Home." *Northwest Nebraska Post*. October 1979.

Story about moving cattle from Home Place to the Crawford Livestock Market.

Hourt, Moni. "Jackrabbit Thanksgiving." *Harrison Sun.* November 24, 1966.

Moni Hourt's first published essay. It is a non-fiction story, based on a story her father, Melvin Nation told about a family Thanksgiving. The story is included in the book.

"In Search of a Solution to the Farm Crisis," *ABA Banking Journal* (April 1985), available: LEXIS, Library: BANKING, File: ABABJ.

Discussions about the problems facing agriculture filled numerous journals, but very few solutions were available.

"Jordan Hauls Horses." *Harrison Sun*. July 26, 1956.

A story reporting that Buck Jordan hauled Coffee Quarter horses to shows in South Dakota.

"Last Rites Held for Kasey Keal Rising. *Crawford Tribune*. August 19, 1960.

Obituary for Keal and Sis's son, Kasey. He drowned in 1960 at the age of 18 months. His sister Roxanne died the previous November of 1959.

"Local boy killed at Luzon." *Crawford Clipper*. July, 1945.

Story that Pvt. Paul Hamaker, aged 19 was killed in action on Luzon on June 3, 1945. Elvin Nation was at the site when the accident happened.

Lyn, Jack. "Because They Were So Bred—I had a Horse Called Toad." *Quarter Horse Journal. Eastern/Western*. December 1988.

A story explaining how Bill Coffee started raising Quarter Horses. The story also discusses Bill's foundation stallion, Toad.

"Mountain Lion seen in local area; plaster cast made of tracks." *Harrison Sun,* September 11, 1958.

Article verifies both Moni's and Norman's memories about the mountain lion at Warbonnet Ranch.

"Mrs. Elmer Callaham injured in accident." *Crawford Tribune*. April 15, 1949.

Verna Callaham was injured when the tractor she was driving tipped over the edge of a bridge. Iva Nation visited her several times during her recovering.

Nebraska Farmer. July 1, 1979. Front cover.

Image of Melvin Nation and Bryan Hourt in one of Melvin's wheat fields.

Norman Horse Edges Coffee Horse" *Harrison Sun*. September 1, 1949.

Tom Norman's horse "Shortening Bread" and Coffee's horse, "Rusty Gold," met in three matched races, although this is the only result reported in The Harrison Sun. Norman won all three races "by a nose."

"Narrow Escape from Drowning." *Crawford Tribune*. August 11, 1911.

Mrs. George Zeller and her daughter were nearly drowned in the same Glen, Nebraska flood that killed Iva and Earl's horses.

"Our Country School." *Harrison Sun.* January, 1922; September, 1932; September, 1941; November, 1942; March 1938; May, 1937.

Melvin and his siblings were frequently mentioned in this column that featured the events in Sioux County's rural schools. In later years the column also reported events surrounding Moni Nation Hourt's years at District 76 also in Sioux County.

"Rancher Killed." *Harrison Sun.* April 24, 1930.

Peter Swanson who lived west of Fort Robinson was one of many people in the area who was killed when dragged to death by horses. Earl Nation refused to allow his younger children to use saddles, primarily because of the deaths of many area riders.

"Results Saddle Rock Riding Club Rodeo." *Crawford Tribune.* October 8, 1964.

Moni Hourt still has the buckle she won at the rodeo. Melvin wore his until his death in 2009. It now belongs to Bryan Hourt. The pair are styled identically, but Moni's features a barrel racer and Melvin's a bull-dogger.

"Rudy Hartman purchases Harrison Locker Shop." *Harrison Sun,* November 9, 1950.

This article is important because it proves information included in the story about Hartman's butcher shop and his activities as an area butcher. He always butchered pigs and cattle at the ranch. When Al Hourt arrived in Harrison from his native Luxembourg, in October 1922, he didn't speak English. Rudy was summoned to help translate the new immigrant's request to send a message to his brother, John, who lived north of Harrison. In later years, Al Hourt and both of his sons, Joe and Henry, worked with Rudy at the "Locker Plant."

"School News." *Chadron Record.* November 1907, March 1908, April 1908.

Finding these articles was additional proof that Iva Hamaker did indeed go to the Chadron Academy. It was fun to see what she was doing in her only year of Normal School education.

"Smoky Hills Trail." *Rocky Mountain News.* May 7, 1959.

This newspaper story says that many emigrants who traveled on the route were devastated by the lack of water and food along the trail.

"Snake Balls." *Current Opinion*, Vol. 23, pg 17, 1898.

This article confirmed that either during mating season or during the winter when they sought warmth, snakes, wrapped tightly around each other often created a ball like the one Melvin saw rolling down the hill at White River.

"Spud Items." *Harrison Sun.* February 3, 1928.

In this section of the "gossip column" as the local news was called, the reporter said the Maytag salesman brought a new washing machine to the Earl Nation family.

"Twenty- Five Years Ago." *Northwest Nebraska News*. June 11, 1911 and November 26, 1937, November 20, 1942.

The first story about the viaduct said it was being constructed on Elm and Main Streets. The later story discussed the repair of the viaduct.

"Two Killed in Light Plane Crash Near Here Sunday." *Harrison Sun. January 14, 1954*.

This story reported the deaths of Harry Engebretsen, 35, and Billy Andrews, 21.
Melvin was one of the men who searched for the wreckage.

"Tunnel Finished." *Crawford Tribune*, August 25, 1889.

Story of the Belmont Tunnel being finished at Belmont, NE. Great story that contained several different sections.

"Warbonnet News." *Harrison Sun*. March 28, 1957.

This "gossip section" of the newspaper reported that "Ramona Nation was a patient in the Crawford Hospital." She was hospitalized with the Asian Flu. (Influenza A H2N2)

"Young Woman Recovering." *Crawford Tribune*. November 23, 1935.

A section of the newspaper set aside for neighborhood gossip, reported news of community members. Frances Nations and her battle to recover from appendicitis was the subject of this news section.

Videos:

Bucklin, Olive, producer. *Beef State*. NPPR-PBS. 2008.

Melvin was one of the three ranchers featured in the film which explored ranching and agriculture in Nebraska.

Bixby, Onie. "Ranching in the Sandhills." Video shot in the 40s and 50s.

This video footage, , including haying, working cattle, and even calving, were produced by Bret Bixby's uncle, Onie. Lawrence Bixby, Bret's father, worked for the Spade Ranch and bought it following the death of Bartlett Richards. The Bixby family still owns the ranch.

Coffee, Peg. Videos shot in the 30s, 40s and 50s.

In 1930, Peg Coffee purchased one of the earliest hand held video cameras. Bill Coffee allowed Moni Hourt to copy all of these videos. They are an incredible source of first-person images and actions.

Hammacher family video. Taped by Naomi Galey, great-granddaughter of RSQ Hamaker. Hershey Company land, Hershey, Pennsylvania.

Naomi and her family traveled to Hershey, Pennsylvania to take part in the Hammacher Cemetery dedication. The cemetery was discovered when Hershey Candy workers were constructing a new building. They immediately stopped the construction and excavated the site. Many of the headstones had been broken and scattered. They were reconstructed and attached to a wall that surrounds the cemetery. It can be visited by Hamaker family members if they make arrangements with Hershey Company personnel.

Hourt, Moni. Videos recorded various times between 1990 and 2009.

The video footage records memories, ranch life, and landscape in and around the Hat Creek and Warbonnet Ranches. There are also numerous video-taped interviews in the collection.

Secondary Sources
Books:

Belmont Memories, 2013. "RSQ and Alice Hamaker."

No author is recorded for this story about RSQ and Alice Hamaker. It is a basic story about a very dynamic couple.

Belmont Memories, 2013. "Hamaker family."

No author. Basic information all confirmable.

"Belmont a Brief History." Dickson, Ephriam D III. *Belmont Memories,* 2015.

Story about Belmont, NE including information about the town and the tunnel. This book also included an elementary school roster that listed Iva Hamaker, her sister, Bertha; and her brothers, Carl, Ray, Paul, and Frank.

Buecker, Tom. *Fort Robinson and the American West, 1874-1899*. University of Oklahoma Press. 2003.

This book provided some good solid background about Fort Robinson. There was a story in here that said John Coffee had not returned his stud horses—twice. (Local ranchers were allowed to borrow stallions, breed mares, and sell the colts back to the Fort.

Burroughs, John Rolfe. *Guardian of the Grasslands. The First Hundred Years of the Wyoming Stock Growers Association.* Cheyenne: Pioneer Printing and Stationery Company, 1971.

Important information about ranching in Wyoming and western Nebraska. It was vital to understand agriculture so that the industry was presented correctly.

Crawford Nebraska 1886-1961. Nation, Frances Locker. "Henry Thomas." Crawford, NE: Jubilee Committee Press, 1961.

There were several errors in this story because it was written from family history stories. In later years, Thelma Nation was able to find more information that enabled her to record the true story of Henry Thomas and his family.

Crawford Nebraska 1886-1961. Crawford, NE: Jubilee Committee Press, 1961.

Alice Hamaker's story of coming to Crawford is included in both this history book and the history book, *Belmont Memories*. Many different excerpts from this book were used in Melvin's story.

Hammacher Cemetery Booklet. Hershey Pennsylvania. Available at http://www.hersheyhistory.org/hammaker.html

This booklet was given to Thelma Nation by Naomi Galey after her family attended the dedication of the Hammacher Cemetery uncovered during construction at the Hershey, Pennsylvania.

Lee, Wayne C. *Trails of the Smoky Hill*. Lincoln, University of Nebraska Press, 1980.

This is the story of the Smoky Hill Trail in Kansas. In her story about coming to Crawford, Alice Hamaker described coming across a trail in Kansas.

Marshall, Con. *The Story of Chadron State College, 1911-1986*. South Dakota: Pine Hill Press, 1986.

This story explains the history of Chadron State College. It was a useful book because it showed that the Normal College closed in 1910. Family history said Iva attended Chadron State College. She didn't. She attended the Chadron Normal School.

Nebraska Blue Book. Nebraska Legislative Reference Bureau. Nebraska Legislative Council, 2008.

This was used to check facts about many different aspects of the book.

Van Ackerman, Ruth, ed. *Sioux County Memoirs of Its Pioneers*. Harrison: *Harrison Sun*. 1976.

"Dave W and Belle Hamaker." This article was written by the couple's children. It was an important source because it provided information about Dave Hamaker and his wife, two very important people in the Nation's early world.

Van Ackerman, Ruth, ed. *Sioux County Memoirs of Its Pioneers*. Harrison: *Harrison Sun*. 1976.

"Henry T Nation" written by Thelma Nation. This information also helped expand the author's knowledge of the Nation family.

Websites:

"Average Yearly Cattle Prices." *United States Department of Agriculture.* Washington D.C. www.nass.usda.gov

Information and comparisons about cattle prices.

Carter, John. "Birth of the South Omaha Stockyards." *History Nebraska blog.* https://history.nebraska.gov/blog/rare-pictures-omaha-stockyards

History of the Omaha Stockyards where RSQ and later Bill Coffee delivered cattle.

Center of Disease Control and Prevention, 13th edition, April 2015. https://www.cdc.gov

Information about polio cases in Nebraska and the United States.

"Farm Collector." The Versatility of Early Farm Wagons. http://www.farmcollector.com/equipment/versatility-of-early-farm-wagons.

Information explaining a "reach" on a wagon.

"Union Stockyards of Nebraska." *Nebraska History.* https://history.nebraska.gov/blog/rare-pictures-omaha-stockyards.

Background information about the Union Stockyards in Omaha.

"The Gospel Comes to Nebraska, 1907." *First Missions—America.* Telling the Truth.info. February 26, 2011.

Little is known about the religion embraced by Earl and Iva Nation. It does not have a name. Four of the family children joined the religion. This article does present the basic story of the religion.

Gower, Calvin W. "The Pikes Peak Gold Rush and the Smoky Hill Route."

Available at: www.kshs.org

A website that discusses the dangers and desolation many emigrants found on the Smoky Hill Route.

History of the Eighties—FDIC. https://www.fdic.gov/bank/...259_290.

During the Eighties, the facts about agriculture were difficult to find and understand because they were so illogical. This article dissects the time period's effect on agriculture.

Homestead Act. *National Documents.* https://www.archives.gov/milestone-documents/homestead-act

The copy of the Homestead Act is present on the site as well as information about the Act.

"Livestock Patterns. Farming in the 1950s and 1960s." *Wessels, Living History-Nebraska.* https://livinghistoryfarm.org/farminginthe30s/crops-3/livestock/
During the 50s and 60s agriculture across the Great Plains was a lucrative business.

"Townships, Ranges, and Acres." *Nebraska Geography.* http://geography.about.com/library
Information about geographical designation on America's prairie lands.

APPENDIX 1

Poems written by Sally Harris for her daughter, Alice upon her wedding. The poem represented a women's commitment to marriage.

> Oh, take her and be faithful still,
> And may the marriage vow
> Be sacred kept and warmly breathed
> In after years as now.
>
> Remember it is no idle toy
> That binds her heart to thine,
> 'Tis one that faith alone should keep
> And naught but death resign.
>
> The joys of childhood days are past,
> The hope of riper years,
> The treasure streams of early youth
> In sunshine and in tears.
>
> The dearest joys her bosom knew
> When her young heart was free,
> All, and more she now resigns
> To brave the world with thee.
>
> Her fate is bound with thine through life,
> Its good and ills to share;
> And well I know 'twill be her pride
> To lighten every care.
> So take her and be faithful still
> And may the marriage vow

Be sacred kept and warmly breathed
In after years as now.
When life's labors all are passed,
And both are faded away,
You may unite on yonder shore
In realms of endless day.[558]

---

[558] No one knows for sure that these were parts of the same poem or if they were meant to be two separate poems. They were found on individual pieces of paper each labeled with the notation, "Composed by Sally Harris for her daughter Alma Harris and husband, Daniel Hamaker on their wedding day in Vermillion, Ohio."

APPENDIX 2

Campaigning Theodore Roosevelt came into Crawford on a train in July 1900. He was met by the 10th Cavalry from Fort Robinson with whom he had fought during the Spanish American War in 1898.

APPENDIX 3

RSQ purchased the large ornate pieces of mahogany furniture at The Japanese Pavilion, a large exhibit located at the Panama-Pacific International Exposition which was part of the World's Fair of 1915. He paid $1,560 for the eight pieces.

APPENDIX 4

I went to the animal fair,
The birds and the beasts were there;
The little raccoon by the light of the moon
Was combing his auburn hair.
The monkey he got drunk
And sat on the elephant's trunk,
The elephant sneezed and went down on his knees
And what become of the monk?

APPENDIX 5

Montgomery Ward Mail Order House | The Princeton | Daily Bungalow | Flickr

APPENDIX 6

Written by Joe Nunn 2004

Ol Mel

If you're looking for cow hands,
And you want the best
Just go out to Hat Creek
'Cause that is his nest.
You will have to be early
To catch him at home,
After the sun rises
He will already be gone
He is a real cowpuncher
And his name is Mel
But don't tell him who sent you
Or he'll say, "Go to hell."
He is as tough as a pine knot,
But as gentle as a pup,
With one built in feature.
He NEVER gives up.
If it came up for lease
And there was grass on the moon,
Turn the herd over to Mel
He'll say, "We'll be there by noon."
Mel is one of a rare breed
Who thinks like a cow,
He is usually one step ahead,

If he isn't, he gets there—somehow.
The horses he rides are tops,
The best they can be
The way they work
together
Is a sight to see.
His chores and the gathers
Are challenges met,
He has never failed
To conquer one yet.
Mel regrets in his youth, not hiring on
a big outfit in the Texas red sand.
He has been on the Square Top Three,
ni on fifty years.
But he could ride for most any brand
To ride with Mel you learn of the man,
He is strong, he is kind,
He is serious, and a joker.
If you try to read his blue eyes,
You're glad you aren't playing poker.
He is true to his convictions,
his family, and friends.
Every morning is the start
of a "beautiful day."
I am proud to call
Mel Nation—friend,
That's all.
What more can I say!

ABOUT THE AUTHOR

Moni Hourt

At 15, Moni Hourt published her first story about her father, Melvin Nation, but long before then, dozens of non-fiction stories about life on the Coffee ranches were handwritten in notebooks and often shared as school essays. Many times those stories were accompanied by photographs shot with a Kodak Brownie, earned by selling magazine subscriptions.

In 1979, she joined the staff of the newly established newspaper, The *Crawford Clipper* published in Crawford, Nebraska, where she and her husband, Joe, and their two children, Buffy and Bryan lived. She covered sports and local events with a trusty Vivitar 35 mm camera Joe gave her for her 19th birthday. She edited all the film in the newspaper darkroom and wrote both "hard news" and feature stories based on local resident interviews. She loved the feature stories, believing that recording lives with a camera and a story meant those people never disappeared.

By 1980, other newspapers and magazines across the nation, *Pro-Rodeo Sports News, Farm and Ranch Living, The Denver Post, Omaha World-Herald, Quarter Horse Journal, Nebraska Farmer,* and many others. were publishing her stories and images. In 1984, Pro-Rodeo Sports News named her their "Contributor of the Year" and presented her with a Gist belt buckle. Since 1975, she has photographed and cataloged every Old West Trail Rodeo in Crawford, Nebraska, a milestone recognized by the OWTR committee in 2015.

Although she continues to work as a photojournalist at *The Crawford Clipper* on a part-time basis, Moni earned a teaching degree from Chadron State College in 1991 and served as a western Nebraska teacher for 25 years. Many of those years were spent in "country schools" where she incorporated her love of history and non-fiction writing into her student curriculum. The students recorded their families' histories, hosted community events, interviewed residents, and sponsored Veterans Day programs featuring local Veterans. The activities filled the pages of student-produced yearbooks and newspapers. The National History Day competition was added to the curriculum in 1993. Again, most of the projects centered around western Nebraska and its people. Between 1998 and 2022 western Nebraska students under Moni's direction, including her great niece and nephew, Bailey and Bryce Oetken have qualified for consecutive National History Day competitions in Washington D.C.

Several awards decorate her office wall. They include the first "James Olson Memorial Award," "Rural Teacher of the Year," "Peter Kiewit Distinguished Teacher Award," "History Educator Award" presented by the History Channel, "Chadron State College Distinguished Alumni Award," and in 2022, "the Nebraska History Advocacy Award." In addition, she has conducted numerous history workshops and presentations. For seven years, in coordination with the Coffee Gallery at the Mari Sandoz Center at Chadron State College she organized "Ranch Day" to educate students and teachers about the unique history found in the prairie lands of Nebraska. Moni's two grandchildren, Brylee and Mahayla Allred are following her lead and have already written dozens of non-fiction stories.

"My great-nephew says I just like to take people on adventures," Moni said. "I think he's right."

www.ingramcontent.com/pod-product-compliance
Lightning Source LLC
Chambersburg PA
CBHW041236240426
43673CB00011B/352